Luminos is the Open Access monograph publishing program
from UC Press. Luminos provides a framework for preserving and
reinvigorating monograph publishing for the future and increases
the reach and visibility of important scholarly work. Titles published
in the UC Press Luminos model are published with the same high
standards for selection, peer review, production, and marketing as
those in our traditional program. www.luminosoa.org

The publisher and the University of California Press Foundation
gratefully acknowledge the generous support of the
Joan Palevsky Imprint in Classical Literature.

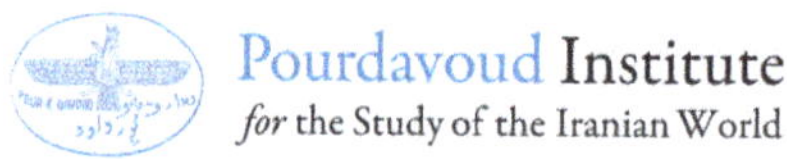

IRAN AND THE ANCIENT WORLD

Iran and the Ancient World supports original studies in the history, literary traditions, material culture, and religions of ancient Iran, while seeking to relate these to the broader historiographic mainstream account of the ancient worlds. The series aims to foreground the interconnection of the Iranian world to other contiguous cultural expanses, fostering comparative and interdisciplinary perspectives on questions of broad import to the humanities and social sciences. The publisher and the University of California Press Foundation gratefully acknowledge the generous support for this series by the UCLA Pourdavoud Institute for the Study of the Iranian World.

Series Editor: M. Rahim Shayegan, University of California, Los Angeles

1. *Aspects of Kinship in Ancient Iran*, by D. T. Potts

2. *The Arsacids of Rome: Misunderstanding in Roman-Parthian Relations*, by Jake Nabel

The Arsacids of Rome

The Arsacids of Rome

Misunderstanding in Roman-Parthian Relations

Jake Nabel

UNIVERSITY OF CALIFORNIA PRESS

University of California Press
Oakland, California

Suggested citation: Nabel, J. *The Arsacids of Rome: Misunderstanding in Roman-Parthian Relations*. Oakland: University of California Press, 2025. DOI: https://doi.org/10.1525/luminos.227

Cataloging-in-Publication Data is on file at the Library of Congress.

ISBN 978-0-520-41306-1 (pbk.)
ISBN 978-0-520-41307-8 (ebook)

33 32 31 30 29 28 27 26 25
10 9 8 7 6 5 4 3 2 1

For my mother, Susan Nabel,
my kin

CONTENTS

ILLUSTRATIONS

FIGURES

TABLES

Jake Nabel's *The Arsacids of Rome: Misunderstanding in Roman-Parthian Relations* is the second volume in the series Iran and the Ancient World, which supports original research foregrounding the interconnection of ancient Iran with other cultural expanses in antiquity.

The present study, which in ways more than one is groundbreaking, benefitted from time spent by the author at the University of California, Los Angeles as a Pourdavoud Research Associate, Lecturer in the Department of Near Eastern Languages and Cultures, and Scholar in Residence in the Department of Classics in the academic year 2018/2019. Moreover, a Postdoctoral Fellowship at the Getty Research Institute in the academic year 2017/2018, in conjunction with the Getty Villa theme "The Classical World in Context: Persia," afforded the author a stimulating environment in which to pursue his work and this study.

The Series Editor would like to acknowledge and thank the above institutions for their support.

M. Rahim Shayegan

Translations from Parthian, Middle Persian, Armenian, Greek, Latin, and New Persian are my own except where otherwise noted. Translations from other ancient languages are specified in the references.

For some Iranian names, I use the form that commonly appears in the scholarly literature in English (e.g., "Shapur" rather than "Šābuhr"). Parthian names are provided in the Parthian language rather than Greek or Latin, however, unless the Parthian form of the name is unattested (as is the case for Vonones, Seraspadanes, and Rhodaspes).

The transliteration and transcription scheme for Iranian languages follows Stausberg and Vevaina 2015. Armenian transliteration follows the Library of Congress system.

Frequently used abbreviations are collected in the list below. Other abbreviations for Greek and Roman texts follow the *Oxford Classical Dictionary*, 4th ed. Abbreviations for Zoroastrian texts adhere to Stausberg and Vevaina 2015.

AD 3	Astronomical Diaries from Babylon, vol. 3 (Sachs and Hunger 1996)
AE	Année Epigraphique
BD	Bactrian Documents from Northern Afghanistan, vols. 1 (Sims-Williams 2000) and 2 (Sims-Williams 2007)
Cass. Dio	Cassius Dio, *Roman History*
CIL	*Corpus Inscriptionum Latinarum*
EA	Letters from El-Amarna (Moran 1992; Rainey 2015)
Egh.	Eghishē, *History of Vardan and the Armenian War* (trans. Thomson 1982)

FRHist   Fragments of the Roman Historians (Cornell 2013)
Joseph. *AJ*   Josephus, *Antiquitates Judaicae*
GhP   Ghazar Pʿarpetsʿi, *History of the Armenians* (trans. Bedrosian 2021)
Mon. Anc.   *Monumentum Ancyranum* = The *Res Gestae* of Augustus
              (Cooley 2009)
MKh   Movses Khorenatsʿi (trans. Thomson 1978)
NPi   The inscription of Narseh at Paikuli (Skjærvø 1983 with Cereti
              and Terribili 2014)
PAT   Palmyrene Aramaic Texts (Hillers and Cussini 1996)
PB   Pʿawstos Buzand, *Epic Histories* (trans. Garsoïan 1989)
RIC   Roman Imperial Coinage (Sutherland and Carson 1984)
RINAP   Royal Inscriptions of the Neo-Assyrian Period
SAA   State Archives of Assyria
SCPP   Senatus Consultum de Cn. Pisone Patre (Potter and Damon 1999)
ŠKZ   The inscription of Shapur I at the Kaʿba-ye Zardošt (text and trans.
              Huyse 1999)
Strab.   Strabo, *Geography*
Tac. *Ann.*   Tacitus, *Annales*
Vell. Pat.   Velleius Paterculus

Introduction

A medieval chronicler tells of a rivalry between two kings. One was Harald Fairhair of Norway, the other Aethelstan of England. The pair competed for prestige and rank, each seeking supremacy over the other. One day, Harald devised a ruse to gain the upper hand. He gave his young son Hakon to his ambassador, Hauk, and sent them on an embassy to Aethelstan. When they came into the king's presence,[1]

> Hauk seized the boy and placed him on Aethelstan's knee. The king looked at the boy and asked Hauk why he did this. Hauk answered, "King Harald bade you foster for him the son of his maidservant." The king flew into a rage and seized the sword at his side and drew it as though he would kill the boy. "You have set him upon your knee," said Hauk, "and you may murder him if you so wish, but in doing so you will not do away with all sons of King Harald." Then Hauk and all his men left the hall and made their way to their ship. They sailed out to sea as soon as they could make ready and returned to Norway and King Harald, and he was well pleased with the outcome, for people say that he is a lesser man who fosters a child for someone.

Harald's trick turned on a Norwegian custom unknown to the Englander Aethelstan: to set a child on one's knee was to commit to raising it. Aethelstan was furious once the meaning of the choreography was explained to him, but when he forbore to kill Hakon, he accepted, if grudgingly, the logic of the maneuver. His acquiescence was a victory for Harald. Why? The last sentence of the passage explains: "he is a lesser man who fosters a child for someone."

Medieval Scandinavia may seem an unlikely point of departure for a study of Parthia and Rome, two empires of the ancient Near East and Mediterranean. But at

1. Snorri Sturluson, *Saga of Harald Fairhair* 39, trans. Hollander 1964: 93.

the heart of this book is the idea that something similar to Harald's and Aethelstan's exchange took place in Roman-Parthian relations at the dawn of the current era. The topic of the study, as with the vignette above, is the circulation of royal children between cultures that did not understand each other, and the implications for power and prestige that their misunderstanding produced. Here, too, the themes are interstate rivalry, ruling families, the pursuit of rank and reputation, divergent cultural practices, and the dynastic heirs who were caught in the web of these forces. The children I examine lived in ancient Rome, not medieval England. But the story of how they came to reside there is not far off from Hakon's.

That story began in the final decades B.C.E., when the family that ruled Parthia sent its children to the one that ruled Rome. Parthia belonged to the Arsacids, a dynasty that had held the kingship since the days of the empire's inception in central Asia over two centuries prior. Rome was a newcomer to monarchy, but its emperors soon adopted hereditary principles of succession like their Arsacid counterparts, producing an inaugural dynasty known today as the Julio-Claudians. The heads of this family received Arsacid children not once but several times over the course of nearly a century. They never reciprocated: no Julio-Claudian scion ever went to Parthia. Rome hosted these princes and princesses for years, decades, or even for their entire lives. Some returned to Parthia to become kings, while others died in Italy.[2] I call these children the Arsacids of Rome, and they are the subject of this book.

Why did the Arsacid kings send their children to the emperors? Scholars who have dealt with this question have done so on the basis of Roman literary sources. Since the Roman authors call the Arsacids of their empire "hostages" (*obsides* in Latin, or *homēroi* in Greek), this classification has been central to all discussion of who they were and why they went to Rome. At face value, the term implies that Rome was stronger than Parthia and received its royal children as guarantees for its good behavior. Was this so? Some say yes and endorse the use of the label;[3] others highlight the misleading aspects of "hostage" as a translation for the Greek and Latin terms;[4] and still others qualify, reject, or avoid the designation altogether.[5] Many studies, however, simply use the word by force of Romano-centric scholarly habit. Because the Roman sources constitute the bulk of the direct evidence for the Arsacids of Rome, they have always been allowed to set the terms of the inquiry. The Roman perspective dominates. Modern scholars may accept, problematize, or reject it, but they have offered nothing to take its place.

The present book rectifies that imbalance through a different approach to the question. My argument is this. Non-Roman sources from the ancient Near

2. See table 1 for transfers from Parthia to Rome, and table 2 for transfers from Rome to Parthia.

3. Walker 1980: 128; Nedergaard 1988: 111; Lee 1991: 367.

4. Braund 1984: 12–13; Campbell 1993: 224 n.2; Jussen 2022: 148; Álvarez-Pedrosa 2022: 107–8; Goldsworthy 2023: 45.

5. Dąbrowa 1987: 63; Wiesehöfer 2010; Gregoratti 2015: 732; Wheeler 2016: 193.

East suggest that the Parthians would have viewed the Arsacids of Rome not as hostages, but as foster-children. Like the Norwegian prince Hakon, they were sent abroad to implicate a foreign ruler in a pro-parental relationship. For the Parthians, moreover, fosterage was a social institution with distinct connotations for prestige and rank. The maxim that caps Hakon's story above applies to the world of the Arsacids, as well: "he is a lesser man who fosters a child for someone." Anthropologists call this paradigm "cliental fosterage," which means that a subordinate raises the child of their superior.[6] The evidence for Parthian fosterage is diverse, but most of it supports this model. The Parthians would have interpreted the social status and function of the Arsacids of Rome within this framework.

Where hierarchy and reputation were concerned, then, the Parthian view of the Arsacids of Rome was diametrically opposed to the Roman one. Throughout this study, I refer to this divergence as *pragmatic misunderstanding*, a term for a situation in which two parties hold discordant views of an exchange that nevertheless satisfies each side. In the case of Harald and Aethelstan, conflicting cultural paradigms played a limited role. Aethelstan did not know that he had committed to Hakon's fosterage when he allowed the boy to be placed on his knee, but once Hauk explained the Norwegian custom to him, he grasped the insult, since both Norway and England practiced cliental fosterage. In Roman-Parthian relations, by contrast, misunderstanding ran far deeper. The two sides interpreted the submission of children through institutional frameworks that led them to contrary assessments of their relative power. The Parthians understood the emperor's reception of Arsacids as an acceptance of foster-fatherhood—and of cliental status along with it. The Romans, for their part, saw the emperor taking Arsacid "hostages" and drew the opposite conclusion that Parthia had accepted Rome's superiority. Through expedient incomprehension of their counterpart's view, each party could walk away from the transfer of children convinced of its supremacy over the other.

With the phrase *pragmatic misunderstanding*, I mean to encompass two types of pragmatism along with varying degrees of intercultural awareness. For most Romans and Parthians, outright ignorance of the other party's view supported a pragmatic arrangement that benefited the two empires not by design but by accident: both sides could win because, unbeknownst to the other, they kept score in opposite ways. Yet ignorance need not have been total. There were versions of hostageship in Parthia and fosterage in Rome, and one can posit (though not prove) limited breakthroughs of intelligibility among the actors who dealt most frequently with the interlocutor. But here too, I suggest, pragmatism may have discouraged comprehension in order to ensure that mutual awareness did not spoil an arrangement of mutual benefit. Misunderstanding along these lines would have been no accident, but a choice, a preference, a strategy. *Pragmatic misunderstanding* covers pragmatism in both these senses.

---

6. See esp. Parkes 2003: 743; discussion and bibliography in chapter 1.

My ideas about Parthian fosterage and pragmatic misunderstanding depend on a method of investigation that departs from previous studies: I reconstruct the Parthian view from ancient Near Eastern sources rather than Roman ones. Prior treatments have based their conclusions about the Arsacids of Rome on evidence from the territories of the Roman empire, and on historiographical texts in Greek and Latin above all. To be sure, there are reasons to approach the topic in this way. Almost all the texts that report directly and in detail on Arsacid children are Roman, and with the exception of a few coins, there are no contemporaneous, internal Parthian sources that immediately pertain to the topic. Yet reliance on the Roman sources has drawbacks, too. One is that Roman categories, namely hostageship, have remained the touchstone of scholarly debate over the Arsacids of Rome. Another is that the Romans knew little about Parthian society and culture, and their literary depictions of the Parthians often resorted to stereotypes, clichés, and free invention, as many scholars stress.[7] How can historians hope to understand Parthia if they rely on Roman sources that did not? These intractable challenges warrant a new approach.

My effort to counter the hegemony of the Roman perspective depends on two types of Near Eastern sources. The first comprises evidence of immediate relevance to the Parthian empire on the basis of chronological proximity and geographic provenance. For the most part this evidence does not directly pertain to the Arsacids of Rome, though one passage from an Armenian historian does, and is connected to their lives for the first time in this study.[8] Rather, such sources establish the social context in which the Arsacids of Rome should be situated. They show the enduring importance of fosterage and created kinship to high politics in the ancient Near East, especially in the Seleucid, Arsacid, and Sasanian periods. Pride of place goes to inscriptions from the original era and territory of the Parthian empire (c. 248 B.C.E.–224 C.E.).[9] These are few in number, but they constitute precious testimony for the operative social institutions in the lands the Arsacids ruled. Even after the dynasty lost its original empire, it reigned for another two centuries in Armenia (63–428 C.E.), and late antique historiography in the Armenian language sheds further light on its fosterage practices there. Additional evidence comes from the Sasanian empire (224–651 C.E.), Parthia's successor and the heir of its fosterage practices. Late antique sources like Sasanian epigraphy, Middle Persian romances, Bactrian documentary texts, and Zoroastrian literature can be used to delimit the institutional parameters of Iranian fosterage and hostageship and to gauge the applicability of these categories to the Arsacids of Rome. Finally, the period after the Arab conquest of Iran offers useful material. This background is essential in any

---

7. See Lerouge 2007; Wiesehöfer and Müller 2017: vii; Alidoust 2020; Overtoom 2020: 9–10; Schlude 2020: 9; Babnis 2022: 11.

8. The passage in question is MKh 2.27.2–3; discussion in chapter 1.

9. For Parthian primary sources and German translations, see Hackl et al. 2010.

event, since many Sasanian compositions took written form only under Muslim rule. But there are also postconquest texts that reflect and rework pre-Islamic material, even if they were authored by strong literary personalities in the late language of New or Classical Persian. Together these sources compose an eclectic corpus, but one that is sufficient to establish fosterage's centrality as a child circulation mechanism among the elites of the Parthian era. Though valuable in their own right, they also afford fresh perspectives on the Roman evidence, defamiliarizing the usual testimonies and highlighting new elements in well-worn passages.

In employing late antique evidence to fill in the lacunae of Parthian history, I do not intend to elide the distinction between Arsacid and Sasanian history, or still less to reify "pre-Islamic Iran" as a construct that stands outside of historical critique. There are major debates in Iranian studies (the nomenclature of the field itself, of course, stakes a position) about the utility of *Iranian* and, relatedly, *Zoroastrian* as labels for pre-Sasanian people and practices.[10] The early Sasanians were the first kings to apply the toponym *Ērān* to the heartland of their territorial empire, and while variants of the word appear in older Avestan and Greek texts, there is no evidence that the Arsacids ever used it.[11] Nor was this the only Sasanian innovation. In areas like administration, urbanism, and the union of political and religious power, the Sasanians built a state that diverged from the Parthian one. Recent research, however, highlights elements of continuity as well as change: Parthian noble families persisted in the Sasanian aristocracy, the Parthian language remained in use, and royal Zoroastrianism was not inaugurated but developed from Arsacid precedents, even if the faith's relationship to the state was reconfigured.[12] Other Sasanian elite practices have clear antecedents in the Parthian period, including next-of-kin marriage, heterographic writing, hunting, and indeed, fosterage itself. The late antique evidence is useful, then, not because *Iranian* is a timeless and immutable category, but because demonstrable continuities between Arsacid and Sasanian culture recommend the later material for informed reconstruction of the earlier period.

The second body of Near Eastern evidence that I employ comes from cuneiform texts that long predate the emergence of imperial powers on the Iranian plateau, especially epistolary correspondence in Akkadian among various Near Eastern rulers during the Bronze and Iron Ages. Such evidence is useful not because pharaonic Egyptians, Anatolian Hittites, or Kassite Babylonians had an immediate or straightforward influence on the Arsacids, though it is true enough that, as ancient Near Eastern predecessors, their empires are upstream from the Parthian

---

10. "Iranian": de Jong 2017a; Payne 2017: 179; Potts 2023: 5–6; Strootman 2023. "Zoroastrian": Rose 2011: 31–32; de Jong 2015: 86, 89–93; Kellens 2021: 1212–13.

11. Gnoli 1989: 129–74; Payne 2013: 6–10.

12. On Parthian families, see Pourshariati 2008; Shayegan 2022; and chapter 4. On the Parthian language, see Gyselen 2016; on Arsacid Zoroastrianism, see de Jong 2022.

one, if by some distance. Instead, the cuneiform sources illustrate how kings and queens in an adjacent period of antiquity actually talked to their royal peers across political and cultural lines. That correspondence, in turn, can help reconstruct the potential dynamics of Arsacid communication with the Julio-Claudians. The epistolary materials, scribal practices, and archival traditions of the pre-Achaemenid Near East mean that royal letters from these earlier periods survive for study. No such documentary evidence exists for Roman-Parthian or even Roman-Sasanian relations. The only accounts of direct address between Iranian kings and Roman emperors appear in problematic literary sources whose authors were no literal transmitters of archival texts. The cuneiform evidence cannot prove anything about the Arsacids of Rome, but it can aid in modeling the interdynastic dialogue that would have attended their exchange.

The final aspect of my method is the use of comparative history. The issue at the heart of this book is how two ruling families made sense of one another and conducted business across the political and cultural gulf that divided them. Additional perspective on this question can be gleaned from the many other geographic and temporal settings where power was concentrated within family groups. Dynasties were widespread in pre- and early-modern world history, and so were their efforts to engage with other ruling families on the basis of kinship. Like the cuneiform evidence, comparative history cannot demonstrate that Roman-Parthian relations must have played out in any given way. But it can help delineate the realms of the plausible and the likely, adding intercultural context to the meager evidence for antiquity.[13] Comparison is especially incumbent on students of Parthia. Even by the standards of ancient Iranian history, the empire's lack of internal sources is pronounced, and in their absence, scholars have resorted to a Greco-Roman tradition that is hostile, uncomprehending, or both. Countering this evidentiary imbalance calls for the creative use of comparative material to consider Parthian views other than those posited by their western neighbors. Such reconstructions will never be definitive, but they can be generative.

Together, these lines of inquiry allow for a new perspective on the Arsacids of Rome that can better reconstruct the Parthian view and account for its divergence from the Roman one. All approaches to the study of the past have limitations, and the one I have adopted is not, in an absolute sense, *better* than traditional reliance on Greco-Roman texts. Compared to Armenian historiography, Iranian epic, or Akkadian letters, the Roman literary sources have the advantage of chronological proximity to the Arsacids of Rome, and they remain indispensable for the political circumstances that attended the transfer of Arsacid children. In certain respects, an account of Parthian motives that is external but contemporary may be preferable to one that looks for the internal in a range of noncontemporary sources. But as long as Roman texts remain the baseline for the discussion, they will set the

---

13. Cf. Scheidel 2019: 21–22 with n.29 for earlier literature.

agenda, dictate the relevant social categories, and circumscribe the range of views that can be reconstructed on the Parthian side. Greco-Roman historiography has been allowed to set the line of scrimmage in scholarly debates for long enough. A fresh set of sources deserves its chance to do the same.

The moment is ripe for a revisionist treatment of the Arsacids of Rome, since the topic channels the momentum of recent trends in premodern history on several fronts, including burgeoning interest in pre-Islamic Iran, ongoing efforts to counter the predominance of Rome in ancient studies, and a turn toward global antiquity. I situate my thesis in a growing body of recent work that affirms the world-historical significance of ancient Iran and insists on its study from an internal vantage point, not simply as an adjunct to the classical Mediterranean.[14] This book also contributes to growing literatures that decenter Rome through connected and comparative histories of premodern empires, and that grapple with the problem of excavating non-Roman points of view from the "cognitive aftershocks" of Roman hegemony.[15] Such research does not imply that the Roman case is unimportant, and indeed, my concern with it is equal to the Parthian one. But Rome can be better understood when it is set in a larger global context, which will bring out both the particularities and the common features of its history.

The Arsacids of Rome present an optimal case for the investigation of these themes, unconfined as these figures were by the boundaries of any single ancient empire. To explore their lives is to venture beyond circumscribed imperial histories for a more holistic view. For Roman historians, attention to the Iranian side will aid in the distinction between Roman ideological claims and the complexity of actual power arrangements. That prospect is sometimes dismissed out of hand. Harry Sidebottom, for instance, writes that "it must be uncertain whether barbarian hostages interpreted their role in the same way Romans did."[16] Such fatalism is unjustified. In the Parthian case, there is enough evidence to reconstruct the cultural logic of the givers; or, at the very least, one should resort to agnosticism only *after* assessing the Near Eastern sources, not before. At stake is not just the Parthian viewpoint, but a better contextualization of the Roman one. On the Near Eastern side, fosterage has long been recognized as a vital social institution in ancient Iran, and Iranists will easily observe my debt to Geo Widengren's seminal treatment of the practice. Widengren did not include the Arsacids of Rome in that discussion, however.[17] Meret Strothmann and Everett Wheeler cite Widengren and

14. Daryaee 2009; Shayegan 2011; Payne 2015; Khatchadourian 2016; Canepa 2018; Overtoom 2020; Jacobs and Rollinger 2021; Gross 2024.

15. Connected histories: Canepa 2009; Smith 2016; Andrade 2018; Schlude 2020; Chen 2021; Rollinger 2023. Comparative studies: Bang and Kołodziejczyk 2012; Scheidel 2015; Ando and Richardson 2017. "Cognitive aftershocks": Padilla Peralta 2020: 169.

16. Sidebottom 2007: 23.

17. Widengren 1969: 64–95; cf. Widengren 1976: 251–52, 268–69. Widengren 1969: 109 mentions Vonones, but only in a section on Arsacid succession procedures, not fosterage.

do connect Rome's Arsacid children to Iranian fosterage, but in footnotes, and without examining the Near Eastern evidence or the divergence between the hostageship and fosterage paradigms.[18] The exposition is worth the effort, as the direct comparison of Iranian and Roman practices will help integrate Parthia into the broader research landscape of global antiquity.

Moreover, a fuller account of the Parthian viewpoint affords the opportunity to reframe not just the exchange of Arsacid children, but the study of Roman-Parthian relations and ancient interstate affairs more generally. Despite the profusion of recent contributions to the literature, this corner of ancient history remains undertheorized and hamstrung by presentist assumptions about interstate politics. In the absence of clearly articulated theoretical frameworks, many studies map the conceptual apparatus of the modern state onto the ancient world. The Parthian and Roman empires are treated as states, both in their own right and in their engagements with the other. They interacted through state-formulated "foreign policy." Most attention is devoted to military conflict, especially the great battle of Carrhae and the episodic jockeying over the "buffer state" of Armenia. Nonviolent interaction is relegated to the sphere of "diplomacy"—a modern term with no counterpart in any language known to the Parthians and Romans, since they had no conception of it as a distinct sphere of activity. Treaties are the most studied feature of Roman-Parthian relations in this area, and the Arsacids of Rome are sometimes annexed to this topic.[19] Elsewhere they are regarded as features of "diplomacy" inasmuch as they regulated the relationship between the Parthian and Roman states.[20] In every case, the particulars of Roman-Parthian interaction are made to conform to the conceptual analytics of the modern nation.

Whereas studies that lack an explicit theoretical orientation tend to smuggle modern assumptions into the analysis of ancient interstate politics, Arthur Eckstein and Nikolaus Overtoom have recently done the field a great service by integrating political science frameworks into their treatments of Roman and Parthian imperialism.[21] Their discussions apply a theory of international politics variously called neo-, offensive, or structural realism as formulated by the political scientists Kenneth Waltz and John Mearsheimer.[22] The theory consists of a few key propositions. First, the state is the basic unit of world politics.[23] Second, states interact against a backdrop of anarchy. This condition imposes uniformly aggressive behavior on states to survive, since no domestic mechanism like law, kinship, or

---

18. Strothmann 2012: 91–92 n.36; Wheeler 2016: 193 n.157.

19. Ziegler 1964; Elbern 1990: 99. On treaties, see further Keaveney 1981; Keaveney 1982.

20. Lee 1991; Campbell 1993: 224; Campbell 2001: 17.

21. Eckstein 2006; Eckstein 2008; Overtoom 2020.

22. On the distinction between neorealism and conventional or classical Realism, see recently Kirshner 2022: 43–80.

23. Waltz 1979: 93–97; Mearsheimer 2001: 17.

morality can alleviate the inherent violence of the interstate environment.[24] Third, the structure of the interstate system as determined by the relative power of state units is the key to understanding world politics.[25] A multipolar world with several great powers tends to see much violent conflict, for instance, whereas two great powers will tend to balance in a bipolar system. Eckstein has used this framework to explain Rome's conquest of the eastern Mediterranean as a function of weakening Hellenistic empires that prompted the intervention of a strengthening Roman state.[26] Overtoom makes a similar argument for the other end of the Hellenistic world: the Parthian empire's rise came amid "power-transition crises" precipitated by Seleucid and Bactrian decline.[27] These pioneering studies have put ancient history and international relations scholarship in dialogue, and they usefully provide an explicit theoretical basis for the comparative study of ancient imperialism. Eckstein's work has been especially influential among Romanists, and his theoretical perspective has since been taken up by Michael Fronda, Steve Mason, Craige Champion, Pierre-Luc Brisson, and others.[28]

If such studies have demonstrated the analytical purchase of neorealism in ancient history, however, the Arsacids of Rome can show the theory's blind spots and problematize its core assumptions. Eckstein and Overtoom themselves limited their applications of neorealism, because the perspective neglects a variable that each scholar deemed decisive in their respective cases: domestic political culture. Both historians point to unique internal features—Eckstein to Roman assimilationism, and Overtoom to a Parthian trifecta of societal versatility, military innovation, and dynastic stability—to explain why Rome and Parthia succeeded where neighboring states failed.[29] Reference to political culture on the unit level is necessary, they continue, because interstate politics are complex and multivariate, and multicausal explanations are needed to understand historical change in this arena.[30] Neorealism can engender a fuller appreciation of structural, system-level factors, but domestic politics and culture matter, too.

I agree that a multiplicity of perspectives is necessary for a full exposition of ancient foreign relations, and I see additional problems with neorealism as an analytical frame for Roman-Parthian relations in the first century C.E. (a period, it should be said, with which neither Eckstein nor Overtoom was expressly concerned). One issue is neorealism's conception of the state as a transhistorical, universal, and immutable political unit. On this logic, ancient empires become the

---

24. Waltz 1979: 88; Mearsheimer 2001: 30.

25. Waltz 1979: 99–101; Mearsheimer 2001: 3, 21, 53.

26. Eckstein 2008.

27. Overtoom 2020: 22–23, 68, 75, 132, 149; see also Overtoom 2016; Overtoom 2019.

28. Fronda 2010: 16–21, 281–87; Mason 2014: 195–204; Champion 2017: 79–121; Brisson 2023: 7; see also Morley 2015: 6–10; Bradley and Hall 2018: 197, 206–7; Scopacasa 2019: 53–55.

29. Eckstein 2006: 33–35, 244–316, esp. 245–57, 312–13; Overtoom 2020: 7, 27–64.

30. Eckstein 2006: 8–9, 33, 67–69; Overtoom 2020: 4, 23–24.

analytic equivalents of Greek *poleis*, tribal confederations, and modern nations. This is not to deny that Rome and Parthia can be meaningfully spoken of as states, though some have advanced serious objections to the use of that term in antiquity.[31] But even modern empires (to say nothing of ancient ones) have operated with different models of sovereignty and territoriality than those of nations, and elision on this score may occlude more than it clarifies.[32] Moreover, even if one accepts that the ancient world was a collection of formally equivalent state units, historians are in a poor position to analyze the structure of ancient interstate systems in the way the neorealists intended. For Waltz and Mearsheimer, "structure" refers to the distribution among state units of *material* capabilities, by which they mean population size, territorial extent, financial wealth, natural resource endowment, technology, economic productivity, and especially military personnel and armaments.[33] Such demographic and economic metrics are very difficult to establish from antiquity's paltry and fragmentary datasets. Difficulty need not entail radical skepticism, and on the Roman side, recent work has made great progress toward meaningful quantification in the face of uncertainty by assigning probabilities to numerical estimates.[34] But the challenges are even more acute in Parthian studies, where the secondary literature on demography and economy lags far behind the treatments available for Rome.[35] Neorealist analysis of Roman-Parthian relations based on material capabilities is possible, but it will require extensive quantitative groundwork that accommodates a high degree of uncertainty. Finally, neorealism's exclusive focus on states overlooks the transimperial forces that operated across the Roman-Parthian frontier—a major blind spot for an era where state institutions were minimal compared to modern ones.[36] Several such entities were implicated in high politics on both sides of the Euphrates: the Jewish community and, later, the Christian one; the Janus-faced client kingdoms in Armenia and Mesopotamia; Palmyra and its sprawling commercial networks; and, indeed, the Arsacid family itself.

The concept of pragmatic misunderstanding can further unsettle the assumptions of these state-centric and neorealist literatures and highlight three different dynamics at play in Roman-Parthian relations. First, the Arsacids of Rome call for the dynasty instead of the state to be centered as the key unit of analysis.

---

31. See the recent discussions of this issue in Hall 2021; Strootman 2021: 333.

32. Burbank and Cooper 2010: 16–17.

33. Waltz 1979: 131; Mearsheimer 2001: 55–56.

34. Lavan 2016; Rubio-Campillo et al. 2017; Lavan 2019.

35. Compare, for instance, the divergent estimates for the size of the Parthian army in Potter 2006: 157; Olbrycht 2016b: 326–29; Overtoom 2020: 230. McEvedy and Jones 1978: 126, 152 seem to put the population of the Parthian empire at five million people. That may be too low, as their estimate for Rome probably was (Scheidel 2019: 533; Lavan 2019: 94), but further research on the topic is badly needed.

36. Cf. the critique of Waltz in Nexon 2009: 33–34, discussing early modern Europe.

Dynasties are ruling families that claim political authority on the basis of kinship and descent.[37] They often supply a state with its king, but their power over the state is not absolute, and their members need not be confined within its territorial borders. Moreover, dynasties tend to interface with others of their kind through institutions that unite the two families in kinship. Cross-culturally, marriage is the best attested of such practices, but fosterage plays a part as well. From this vantage point, the Arsacids of Rome can be numbered among the scions of world history who went abroad to network with foreign rulers—in their case, with the inchoate Julio-Claudian dynasty. By means of fosterage, the ruling families of Parthia and Rome were entangled through kinship even as they maintained divergent views on the exchange of Arsacid children. The story, then, is not one of antipodal states arrayed on either shore of the Euphrates, but of an interdynastic family of Arsacids and Caesars who parsed their underlying relationship in different ways.

Second, the Arsacids of Rome foreground the importance of culture and ideas to Roman-Parthian relations instead of the material factors that are central to neo-realism. An exposition of pragmatic misunderstanding must attend to the conflicting social frameworks through which Parthians and Romans made sense of their interactions. Such an approach takes its cues from the political science tradition of constructivism, which holds that the interstate environment is shaped by the culturally contingent beliefs, norms, and practices of its participants.[38] Most historians will find that proposition unobjectionable, but the field of ancient interstate relations has largely escaped the type of anthropological critique that proximate domains of antiquity have received.[39] An analysis in this vein underscores that power relations are not simply a function of material conditions, as neorealist theory would have it. Rather, the interpretation of power is part of its constitution: the cultural criteria by which prestige, rank, and hierarchy are judged shape how power manifests in the world. To be sure, historians need not make a binary choice between ideas and materials; both can be accorded significance. Eckstein and Overtoom contend that the structure of the interstate system has considerable explanatory power. They do not claim that their subjects are reducible to this single variable.[40] The same qualification applies for culture and ideas. These variables are privileged in this study not because they were the only ones that mattered in Roman-Parthian relations, but because they produced a consequential arrangement—pragmatic misunderstanding—that has thus far been overlooked.

37. Duindam 2016: 4.

38. Classic articulations of the constructivist position in political science are Wendt 1992; Finnemore 1996; Katzenstein 1996; Adler 1997.

39. Burton 2011 is an express application of constructivism to early Roman imperialism. Several studies of ancient interstate politics adopt the perspective without using the term: Gagé 1959; Badian 1967; Lendon 2002; Lendon 2010; Payne 2013. See also Low 2007: 27 n.85.

40. See esp. Eckstein 2006: 185–87; Overtoom 2020: 23–24.

Third and finally, pragmatic misunderstanding challenges the realist contention that anarchy is the universal condition of interstate politics. The exchange of Arsacid children produced a regime of misunderstanding, an order that emerged from disharmony and conflicting inputs. The Parthians and Romans held divergent views about the distribution of power between them, but the divergence created an equipoise, a symmetry, a balanced antithesis. Order prevailed even in the absence of an orderer. Eckstein identifies only two means by which states may escape from anarchy: international law, backed by a robust enforcement mechanism, or hierarchy, a system in which a recognized hegemon achieves supremacy.[41] But pragmatic misunderstanding forged an order that was maintained neither by law nor by hegemony. Instead, order arose from harmonizing incomprehension. The two empires achieved equilibrium through interpretations of the Arsacids of Rome that were both mutually unintelligible and mutually satisfying. Equilibrium did not always mean peace, for wars continued in this period. Yet even war was subsumed by a script that operated above the immediate understanding of the actors. Competition could be violent, but it took place within an arena that order had circumscribed.[42] While a relationship built on the unstable foundations of misunderstanding was necessarily complex and chaotic, chaotic systems can nevertheless produce moments of emergent order, even if that order succumbs to entropy in the end.[43] It need not be the case, of course, that all moments in interstate relations are governed by forces like these. Pragmatic misunderstanding is no general theory, and even in Roman-Parthian relations, it prevailed only between c. 30 B.C.E. and 66 C.E. Neorealism *does* claim universal applicability, though, on the grounds that anarchy is a transhistorical and ubiquitous feature of foreign relations.[44] Pragmatic misunderstanding may be only a single exception to the universality of anarchy, but that is enough to mount a challenge to the putative rule.

To assess the impact of the Arsacids of Rome on the Roman-Parthian relationship, the following chapters compose an abstract model of their circulation, each dealing with different phases of their lives. My focus is not chronological or narrative political history, especially since many such treatments of the first centuries B.C.E. and C.E. are available elsewhere.[45] Rather, I am interested in the patterns that governed the lives of these Arsacid dynasts: their journey to Rome; their residence in Rome; their return to Parthia; and their subsequent careers in Parthia. Not every Arsacid of Rome followed this trajectory. Many or most died in Rome, and some were *born* in Rome. But the prospect of their remission to Parthia, whether

---

41. Eckstein 2008: 8, 342–43.

42. On war within the framework of pragmatic misunderstanding, see chapter 2 and the conclusion.

43. An insight of chaos theory in mathematics and the natural sciences; see Gleick 1987: 8; Kellert 1993: 81–82, 110–14; Strogatz 2003: 287. For the concept in political science, see Kissane 2014.

44. Eckstein 2006: 9–10 with n.16 for literature.

45. See recently van Kooten 2015: 508–85; Harl 2016; Canepa 2020: 291–94; Curtis and Magub 2020; Fabian 2020: 209–17; Schlude 2020; Ellerbrock 2021: 22–70.

realized or not, was part of the logic of their exchange, and the bidirectional travel of Parthian royalty was central to the transimperial history of this period. The structure of this book traces that journey from beginning to end.

The first two chapters cover the submission of Arsacids to the Roman emperor from the Parthian perspective. They ask why, and under what circumstances, the Arsacid kings of Parthia chose to send their children to Italy. My main answer is that they were sent to be foster-children. Chapter 1 supports this argument by laying out the evidence for interdynastic kinship as a channel of foreign relations in the ancient Near East, and for fosterage as a channel of kinship in pre-Islamic Iran. Within this framework, I then revisit the question of Arsacid motives in chapter 2, exploring the contingent Arsacid objectives that could be subsumed under the general heading of cliental fosterage. At two chapters rather than one, the submission phase receives more attention than others in the book. But the lengthier treatment is warranted. This is where the Roman sources and thus the Roman perspective have weighed heaviest, and where the application of creative force is most required to dislodge them.

Chapter 3 proceeds to Rome and surveys the Roman side of pragmatic misunderstanding. Hostageship was the main paradigm through which the Romans interpreted the arrival of Arsacid children in their city, and triumphal exhibitions of these "hostages" used them to broadcast a message of Roman supremacy over Parthia to the widest possible audience. But fosterage had purchase on the Roman side as well, since the young age of the hostages often invited their captor to play a quasi-parental role. Yet misunderstanding would have reigned here, too, for fosterage as it emerges from Roman sources was a patronal institution, not a cliental one. Even where the Julio-Claudians may have fulfilled Arsacid expectations for the establishment of kinship, the two sides would have maintained antithetical assessments of the underlying power relationship between them.

Where chapters 1–3 deal with the movement of Arsacids from Parthia to Rome, chapters 4–5 look at their return in the opposite direction. With the emperors' blessing, several Arsacids of Rome were remitted to Parthia, where they mounted bids to claim their ancestral throne. In every case, these episodes were triggered by petitions from the Parthian nobility, a group of nonroyal elites who held a variety of positions within the Parthian empire. As the wider evidence for pre-Islamic Iran can establish, it was this group that routinely served as fosterers for the royal children of the ruling dynasty. Accordingly, in chapter 4, I analyze the petitions of the Parthian nobility to the Roman emperor as a dialogue among cliental fosterers, a perspective that unsettles the usual interpretation of these events as Roman "interference" in the hermetically separate realm of Parthian domestic politics.

Chapter 5 returns to Parthian territory with the Arsacids of Rome who managed to become king, but never with much success or for very long. The Roman literary sources attribute their failure to Parthian recognition of Roman hostageship, which was perceived as a degrading background for an Arsacid king. The Parthian enemies of the Arsacids of Rome thus reviled them as the emperor's slaves and as the acculturated creatures of their Roman captors. I find major grounds to mistrust this tradition, which is based on internal Roman discourses and literary tropes far more than authentic Parthian rhetoric. But comparative history and internal Parthian sources also lend the tradition credence. The return of interdynastic children from foreign lands often triggers anxieties in their home country as locals grapple with the prospect of foreign influence over a scion of their ruling family. In this sense, the Roman sources on Arsacid return may be both underinformed and correct. The Parthian counterreaction that they describe may indeed have been instrumental in ending the circulation of Arsacid children.

The book's conclusion examines the end of pragmatic misunderstanding, weighing several factors that could have led to the collapse of the arrangement. I close by contextualizing the kinship between the Arsacids and Julio-Claudians with interdynastic relationships from other historical settings, including Roman-Sasanian late antiquity. The Arsacids of Rome were not at the center of a robust, well-integrated, or cosmopolitan interdynastic family like those that emerged in the late Bronze Age or early modern Europe. But their history shows a spark from a fire that elsewhere grew with a roaring flame. The Romans and Parthians may have maintained divergent interpretations of the Arsacids of Rome, but these ambulant children connected, in their way, the circles of two ruling families, constructing an order of incomprehension through their mutual exchange.

Submission I

The Fosterage Background

Over the course of roughly a century, from 30 B.C.E.–66 C.E., the Arsacid kings of Parthia sent members of their own family to live at the court of the Julio-Claudian emperor. Most of the direct evidence for these figures comes from literary histories composed by inhabitants of the Roman empire, who called them "hostages" (*obsides* in Latin, *homēroi* in Greek). Modern scholars have variously affirmed or rejected that label, but the literature on the Arsacids of Rome has never escaped from the framework of Greco-Roman hostageship. In this chapter, I strike a new course and argue that, from the Parthian point of view, the Arsacids of Rome are better understood not as hostages, but as foster-children.

My argument relies on a methodological intervention that supports a different perspective on these figures: to reconstruct the Parthian vantage point, I will give precedence to sources from the ancient Near East rather than Greco-Roman literature from the Mediterranean. Scholars have traditionally investigated Arsacid motives on the basis of Roman historiography. That approach is defensible and to a degree necessary, since there are few surviving documentary or literary sources from the Parthian empire, and virtually none that bear directly upon the Arsacids of Rome. But a broader set of Near Eastern texts can support a different way of understanding the circulation of royal children between two imperial dynasties. Much of the evidence I will bring to bear was neither produced by the Arsacids nor created during their reign. All the same, these sources offer insight into the role of fosterage in Parthian culture that Greco-Roman literature cannot supply.

Attention to fosterage can show how the Arsacid understanding of "hostage submission" stood in stark contrast to the Roman one. To Parthian eyes, the Roman emperor's custody of Arsacid dynasts could indicate his subjection to Parthia, not his dominance over it. Anthropological studies of political fosterage distinguish between *patronal* and *cliental* arrangements; in the former, superiors raise the children of subordinates, but in the latter, it is the other way around.[1] An application of this heuristic to pre-Islamic Iran shows that, on balance, cliental fosterage was the dominant paradigm, and there is ample evidence that subordinates of the king of kings could raise his children. In this framework, the transfer of Arsacids from Parthia to Rome can be seen as the product of a pragmatic misunderstanding: the Arsacids could maintain that they had found a new cliental fosterer, while the Romans could insist that they had obtained high-status hostages. Because of their divergent cultural interpretations of these exchanges, both sides could walk away convinced of their supremacy over the other.

Moreover, the reinterpretation of the Arsacids of Rome as foster-children supports a new conceptualization of Roman-Parthian relations centered on interdynastic kinship instead of interstate rivalry. Studies of foreign affairs between Rome and Parthia tend to privilege the interactions that modern observers associate with foreign politics, especially war, diplomacy, and treaty making. The categorization of the Arsacids of Rome as hostages has subsumed their histories under this heading. Since the Romans associated hostageship with the conclusion of treaties, most discussions connect the Arsacids to formal agreements between the Roman and Parthian empires or, more generally, to the feuds over territory that led to military and diplomatic engagements. On these readings, Rome's Arsacid inhabitants were human collateral for agreements between states or tools for managing the balance of power between the imperial giants of the ancient Mediterranean and Near East.

A shift of focus from hostageship to fosterage offers a corrective. It puts not the state but the dynasty at the center of analysis, and it shows how ruling families transcended, and were not coterminous with, the political borders of the empires they ruled. War and diplomacy mattered to Roman-Parthian relations, to be sure. Just as important, however, was the formation of an interdynastic family linked by the bonds of kinship—bonds that were forged by the Julio-Claudian emperor's fosterage of Arsacid royalty. Instead of the structural pressures of a clash between two great powers, fosterage highlights how the Parthians constructed and understood their relationship with Rome, and how kinship was a central feature of this construction.

ARSACID "HOSTAGESHIP"

The general outlook of the Roman sources is clear: the Arsacids of Rome were hostages. Only one author, Tacitus, draws on the vocabulary of fosterage to describe them, and even he uses the designation of "hostage" more often.[2] The term is applied to the earliest Arsacid to take up residence in Rome in c. 30 B.C.E., and

---

1. For literature, see below, nn.56–58.
2. For a discussion of fosterage language in Tacitus, see chapter 3.

TABLE 1 Arsacids Sent from Parthia to Rome

Name(s)	Date	Sources
Son of Frahād IV	c. 30 B.C.E.	Cass. Dio 51.18.2–3, 53.33.1–2; Just. 42.5.6–9; cf. *Mon. Anc.* 32.1
Vonones, Frahād, Seraspadanes, Rhodaspes, two wives, four sons	19–9 B.C.E.	*Mon. Anc.* 32.2; Vell. Pat. 2.94.4; Strab. 6.4.2, 16.1.28; Joseph. *AJ* 18.42; Tac. *Ann.* 2.1.2; Suet. *Aug.* 21.3; Just. 42.5.11–12; Fest. *Brev.* 19.4; [Aurel. Vict.] *Epit.* 1.8; Oros. 6.21.29; Eutrop. *Brev.* 7.9; *CIL* 6.1799; cf. Ausonius *Epist.* 23.6; Suda s.v. *epaggelei*
Dārāw; other Arsacids	c. 36/7 C.E.	Joseph. *AJ* 18.96, 101–5; Suet. *Calig.* 14.3; *Vit.* 2.4; Cass. Dio 59.27.2–3
Several Arsacids	55 C.E.	Tac. *Ann.* 13.9.1
Daughter of Tirdād; other Arsacids	63 C.E.	Tac. *Ann.* 15.30.2; Cass. Dio 62.23.4
Several Arsacids*	66 C.E.	Cass. Dio 63.1.2; cf. Plin *HN* 6.23; Joseph. *BJ* 2.379
Daughter of Husraw; other Arsacids*	c. 114 C.E.	SHA *Had.* 13.8; Aurel. Vict. *Lib. Caes.* 13.3
Zalaces*	c. 117 C.E.	Juv. 2.164

to the participants of the last major transfer in c. 66 C.E.[3] It is also used consistently by Roman authors across a range of periods, from the early empire through late antiquity. The testimonies, predominantly literary, are collected here (table 1). Cases of uncertain historicity are indicated with an asterisk. The main exchanges of the Julio-Claudian period are clear enough, but the evidence for the continuation of the practice after the reign of Nero is thin.

For most of these authors, the residence of Arsacid royalty at the Julio-Claudian court was a sign that Rome had subordinated the Parthian kingdom to its imperial order, because hostage submission was an obligation imposed upon subjugated peoples. The long history of hostageship as a corollary of republican imperial expansion had taught them as much, and the expectation persisted under the principate. As many scholars stress, the English word "hostage" is in one respect a misleading translation of Latin *obses* and Greek *homēros*. English speakers expect a hostage to suffer bodily harm if the hostage's surrenderers fail to comply with the captors, but out of dozens of Roman cases, only a few fulfill this expectation, and even these are of doubtful historicity.[4] However, English speakers also imagine hostage takers to be in a position of strength over hostage givers, and that connotation suits Roman hostageship well. When for instance the early imperial author Velleius Paterculus writes that "the king of the Parthians even sent his sons

3. The precise date of the transfer of Vonones and his brothers is debated. See Dąbrowa 1987: 64; Wheeler 2002: 289 n.5; and esp. Rose 2005: 36–37.

4. Cases of Republican hostage taking are tabulated in Walker 1980: 214–59. On the connection between conquest and hostageship, see esp. Allen 2006: 95–125, and 52–57 for rare bodily punishment. The shortcomings of "hostage" as a translation are stressed by Braund 1984: 12–13; Campbell 1993: 224 n.2; Jussen 2022: 148.

as hostages to [Augustus] Caesar in fear of the reputation of such a great name," he reflects a widespread attitude that the acquisition of hostages from foreign lands showed the emperor's power and the enemy's weakness.[5] The act conferred even greater prestige if the hostages were royalty, and in the early principate there was no greater game to bag than the Arsacids, the rulers of the only remaining empire whose power rivaled Rome's own.

Even the authors who questioned the jingoistic interpretations of their peers did so within the framework of hostageship. Strabo's explanation of one Arsacid king's motives in sending his family members to Rome highlights factors within Parthian politics. The king feared that domestic opponents might find a more compliant monarch in one of his sons, Strabo says, so he sent some of his children to Rome to ensure that they could not be used to dethrone him.[6] Yet Strabo still calls these children hostages, and despite his discussion of internal motives, he elsewhere describes the transfer as a sign that the Parthians were "very close to surrendering all their authority to the Romans."[7] The same holds for the testimony of Tacitus, who suggests that a later king sent Arsacids to Nero "to remove those suspected of rivalry through a nominal hostage submission."[8] That final phrase styles the exchange as a hostage transfer in appearance only; in reality, it was a purge of opponents. Yet Tacitus routinely applies the designation of hostage to Rome's Arsacid residents. Even if he saw ulterior motives at play that had nothing to do with Roman preeminence, hostageship remained central to his narratives.

Scholarly studies of the Arsacids of Rome have inherited these limitations from the Greco-Roman authors on whose testimony they exclusively rely. Some historians echo ancient Roman views of Parthian hostage submission as a concession to Julio-Claudian supremacy. After a nuanced discussion of the motives of Frahād IV, Elisabeth Nedergaard concludes that "it is difficult to believe that he would have wanted to hand over the legitimate heirs to the Parthian throne to Augustus of his own free will."[9] For the events of 37 and 55 C.E., A. D. Lee finds that the reigning king gave hostages "either in response to Roman demands or in circumstances which clearly indicated his acknowledgment of Roman ascendancy."[10] Irene Huber and Udo Hartmann likewise see Tirdād's submission of his daughter as a hostage (63 C.E.) as an act of deference to Roman superiority, since in their view Rome did not reciprocate.[11] These assessments accord well with more general studies

---

5. Vell. Pat. 2.94.4. The fear inspired by a ruler's name is a common motif in Latin literature: see Maguinness 1932: 56; Woodman 1977: 102, with references.

6. Strab. 16.1.28; cf. Joseph. *AJ* 18.42–44.

7. Strab. 6.4.2.

8. Tac. *Ann.* 13.9.1; cf. *Ann.* 2.1.2. On the phrase, see further Thijs 2019: 10 n.30.

9. Nedergaard 1988: 111.

10. Lee 1991: 367.

11. Huber and Hartmann 2006: 505. But cf. Tac. *Ann.* 15.28.3, where two high-ranking Romans (including Corbulo's son-in-law) enter Tirdād's camp as a "pledge" (*pignus*).

of Roman-Parthian relations that highlight Roman belligerence, aggression, and expansionism in the face of Parthian weakness.[12]

Other scholars have rehabilitated Parthia and made space for explanations rooted in Arsacid agency, but without moving beyond the concept of hostageship. Edward Dąbrowa, Emma Strugnell, Josef Wiesehöfer, Marek Olbrycht, and Juan Antonio Álvarez-Pedrosa interpret Frahād IV's use of hostage submission as a way to manage Parthian dynastic rivalries—always a concern in the large, polygamous ruling families of the ancient Near East.[13] Karl-Heinz Ziegler also foregrounds this dynamic while insisting that the king's submission of his children would not have diminished his sovereignty or rank.[14] A similar reading is favored by Jason Schlude, who takes the transaction as a sign that "Phraates [= Frahād] trusted Augustus" and did not dispatch his children under compulsion.[15] Erich Gruen holds that the arrival of Frahād's children in Rome "did not signify deference or subordination, as sometimes portrayed; rather, it provided a means whereby the Parthian king could defuse opposition at home and stabilize his hold on the throne."[16] But while such treatments offer a valuable corrective to a long tradition of Eurocentric scholarship on Parthia, their conclusions still rest on Roman literary evidence, and they are accordingly circumscribed by Roman social categories. These scholars push back against the hegemonic narratives of Roman history, but they still allow Greco-Roman historiography to set the terms of a discussion that revolves around hostageship.

An approach that privileges non-Roman evidence and the institution of political fosterage can advance the debate beyond its customary poles of Roman superiority or Parthian resistance. No scholarly discussion of the Arsacids of Rome has used Near Eastern sources to recover the Parthian vantage point. The landmark study of pre-Islamic Iranian fosterage remains that of Geo Widengren, whose pioneering discussion greatly informs the following pages. The Arsacids of the first century C.E. do not appear in his treatment of the topic, however.[17] Meret Strothmann and Everett Wheeler have alluded in footnotes to Widengren's work in their discussions of the Arsacids of Rome, but they did not use the evidence he employed to reconstruct matters on the Parthian side.[18] I rectify this gap in

---

12. Isaac 1992: 28–33; Cornell 1993: 143.

13. Dąbrowa 1987: 64–65; Strugnell 2008: 283; Wiesehöfer 2010: 187, following the explanation in Joseph. *AJ* 18.41–42; Olbrycht 2018: 391; Álvarez-Pedrosa 2022: 109–10. See also Cameron 2019: 313; Thijs 2019: 52 and n.294. On royal polygamy in the ancient Near East, see further below, and chapter 2.

14. Ziegler 1964: 52.

15. Schlude 2020: 100.

16. Gruen 1996: 160, citing Braund 1984: 12–13. Cf. Gregoratti 2015: 732, where Vonones et al. are "not hostages in the true sense, but guest princes who had voluntarily come to Rome on their own initiative."

17. Widengren 1969: 64–95; cf. Widengren 1976: 251–52, 268–69.

18. Strothmann 2012: 91 n.36; Wheeler 2016: 193 n.157.

the literature here. In the absence of a robust corpus of first-century texts from Parthia itself, recourse will be made to histories that both pre- and postdate the Arsacid empire—a method that is not, in an absolute sense, *better* than a reliance on Greco-Roman historiography, since some of the sources I will consider are far removed in time from the Parthian period. But the Near Eastern evidence supports a new perspective on these figures that is irrecoverable from Greco-Roman authors. The story that emerges is not about hostages caught between empires, but rather the interconnection of dynasties through pro-parentage and kinship.

THE NEAR EASTERN BACKGROUND

Interdynastic kinship was foundational to interstate relations in the ancient Near East. From the earliest attestations of the Bronze Age to the final days of the Sasanian empire, the connections among ruling families were a key factor in how foreign relations were conceptualized, formulated, and conducted. These kinships could take several forms, including brotherhood, intermarriage, and fosterage. While the mechanisms varied in prevalence across historical periods and regions, the articulation of politics in the idiom of family relations was more than a rhetorical device; it structured and controlled the realm of ancient Near Eastern interstate affairs.

Expressions of interdynastic brotherhood appear at the very beginning of the epistolary record among the rulers and administrators of different Near Eastern polities. Early testimony survives in a clay tablet from the archives of Ebla, a kingdom in present-day Syria.[19] Dating to c. 2350 B.C.E., the cuneiform tablet bears the Elbaite text of a letter from one Ibubu, steward of the Eblan king Yirkab-Damu, to an unnamed messenger in the service of Zizi, king of the north Iranian polity of Hamazi. The document preserves two invocations of brotherhood. First, a request from Ibubu to the messenger is bracketed with the sentence "you are (my) brother and I am (your) brother." The repetition of the claim places a strong emphasis on fraternal connection. Second, the passage closes by affirming the relationship not of the correspondents, but of the rulers they serve: "Yirkab-Damu, the king of Ebla is the brother of Zizi, the king of Hamazi; Zizi, the king of Hamazi, is the brother of Yirkab-Damu, king of Ebla."[20] The reverse of the tablet confirms that the letter was in fact sent, or at least given to Zizi's messenger.

The letter reflects an ancient Near Eastern tendency to map the structures of the family onto larger units of social and political organization. At the highest level, the entire state could be viewed as an extended household over which the king presided in the capacity of father.[21] When kings of more or less peer status

---

19. Podany 2010: 22; see also Archi 2015: 77–120; Ristvet 2017: 44–47.

20. Translations from Michalowski 1993: 13–14 (no. 2); see also Bonechi 2016 for a recent study of the letter.

21. Liverani 2000: 18; Westbrook 2003: 83; Podany 2010: 29; Giorgieri and Mora 2010: 147.

communicated with one another, the language of brotherhood offered a way to both articulate equality and establish a foundation for reciprocal claims. A key sentence in Ibubu's letter references kinship as a basis for the mutual fulfillment of wishes: "[this is] what is (appropriate) to brother(s): whatever desire you express, I shall grant and you, (whatever) desire (I express), shall grant."[22] On this logic, the behavior of kings toward one another was to be modeled on fraternal relations. Such kinship had no biological basis, but it was no less concrete or meaningful for that reason.

The tradition of interdynastic brotherhood that began under the Ebla system would long outlast it. For the early second millennium B.C.E., evidence for brotherhood survives in various Mesopotamian letters, some of which attest the extension of kinship language to the kings of Elam on the Iranian plateau.[23] It was not until the fourteenth century B.C.E., however, that the phenomenon reached its high-water mark. The efflorescence is captured in the Amarna letters, a cache of around four hundred documents mostly in Akkadian found at Tell el-Amarna in Egypt.[24] Around thirty-six of these letters preserve correspondence among the great kings of the Hittite, Egyptian, Mittani, and Assyrian kingdoms, among others.[25] In the Amarna system, the standard salutation in letters between rulers is "brother" (Akkadian *ahum*). The relation was transferrable: if a king died and was replaced by his son, foreign counterparts could hail the new king as "brother" just as they had the old.[26] This kinship appellation was no mere metaphor or diplomatic nicety. As Raymond Cohen puts it, "when Great Kings called each other 'brother,' appealed to past and present family ties, and negotiated dynastic marriages, this was literally the way they understood the working of the international system."[27] The kings belonged to an interdynastic kin group that transcended their respective polities, and membership in this group shaped the interactions among them.

22. Translation: Michalowski 1993: 14.

23. Examples: first, in 2425 B.C.E., an inscription from the Mesopotamian city of Lagash records that "Enmetena, ruler of Lagash, and Lugalkiginedudu, ruler of Uruk, established brotherhood"; translation from Cooper 1986: 58. For the Sumerian text see also Barton 1931; Frayne 2008: 200–202; for discussion, see Cooper 2003: 244; Podany 2010: 33. Second, for "brother" in eighteenth century B.C.E. correspondence between Mesopotamian kings and Elam, see Charpin and Durand 1991: 64; Potts 1999: 169. Third, for brotherhood in the letters from Tell Shamshāra, see Eidem and Læssøe 2001: 140–41 (no. 67).

24. On the site, see Stevens 2016.

25. Number of documents preserving correspondence among the Great Kings: Mayes 2016: 152. Assyria was a new arrival on the interstate scene in the fourteenth century; see EA 15 = Moran 1992: 37–38. Mycenean Greece may have been included in this system as well, though the evidence is not clear: see Cline 1995: 146; Cline 2014: 43–53.

26. See e.g. EA 29, in which the Mitannian king Tushratta refers to both the (recently deceased) Egyptian pharaoh Amenhotep and Amenhotep's son Akhenaten as "brother."

27. Cohen 1996: 21; cf. Liverani 2001: 135–38; Podany 2010: 28–36.

Brotherhood coexisted with and complemented another method of forging kinship bonds that was in equally frequent use throughout the Bronze Age: interdynastic marriage. Early evidence for such unions survives in the Ebla archives, where scribes recorded the dowries that accompanied princesses on their journeys to foreign courts.[28] Eblaite royal women married the kings of neighboring cities and those of more distant powers like Tell Brak and Kiš.[29] Further examples are evident throughout Mesopotamia and its neighboring regions: at Ur, Akkad, Babylon, Mari, and Elam, among others.[30] By the time of the late Bronze Age, the Amarna letters along with other documentary evidence reveal a dense network of marital connections among the ruling families of the eastern Mediterranean.[31]

Intermarriage outlived brotherhood after the late Bronze Age collapse, though its prevalence was somewhat diminished in an interstate environment that was less interconnected than the Amarna period. Neo-Assyrian kings in the first millennium B.C.E. would sometimes marry their daughters to foreign rulers, and onomastics may suggest that they took foreign wives as well. The evidence, however, is less extensive than it is for the late Bronze Age.[32] Achaemenid kings, for their part, intermarried with the Persian nobility, and perhaps with foreigners as well.[33] Intermarriage also played a role in Achaemenid relations with the polities on the empire's western frontier. Herodotus discusses two cases of Persian intermarriage with the Argead monarchy of Macedon and the Philaidae of Athens, though no Achaemenid royalty were involved.[34] Perhaps the best-known case is that of Pausanias, an Agiad of Sparta, though his alleged efforts to marry an Achaemenid princess may have been slander cooked up by his Greek detractors.[35] Finally, marriage was a key mode of interaction among the dynasties of the Hellenistic period, when royal women circulated among the Seleucid, Ptolemaic, and Antigonid courts.[36] If the political consequences of these interdynastic unions were far from

28. Biga 2003: 349; Ristvet 2017: 45.

29. Catagnoti 2003: 232–33; Archi 2015: 257–58, 437. On the marriage of the Eblaite princess Kešdut with a prince of Kiš, see further Archi and Biga 2003: 26–29; Podany 2010: 34–35.

30. Ur: Potts 1999: 136–39; Sallaberger and Westenholz 1999: 159–61. Akkad: Potts 1999: 108; Buccellati and Kelly-Buccellati 2002: 13–18. Babylon: Van De Mieroop 2005: 49; Richardson 2010: 63; Jakob 2017: 118. Mari: Lafont 1987; Lafont 2001: 313–14; Sasson 1973. Elam: van Dijk 1986; Roaf 2017: 182–95.

31. Röllig 1974: 17; Melville 2005: 225; Cline and Cline 2015: 20; Miller 2017: 98–100. See also Schulman 1979, with a focus on New Kingdom Egypt.

32. On Assyrian royal marriage, see Melville 2004; Radner 2013; for other levels of Assyrian society, see Fales 2017: 412–14; Michel 2017: 84–87.

33. Brosius 1996: 35–82; see also Hyland 2018; Brosius 2021: 150–51; Potts 2023: 56–64.

34. See Hdt. 5.21.2, 6.41, 8.136.1; Just. 7.3.9 with Müller 2021: 299.

35. Hdt. 5.32; Thuc. 1.128.7; Diod. Sic. 11.44.2–4; Just. 2.15.14; variously assessed in Wolski 1954; Lippold 1965; Fornara 1966; Lang 1967; Vogt 1969; Blamire 1970; Westlake 1977; Andrewes 1978: 92–93; Hornblower 1991: 214.

36. The evidence is collected in Seibert 1967: 129–34; see also Cohen 1974. For dedicated treatments of individual Hellenistic courts, see D'Agostini 2021; Strootman 2021: 337–40.

straightforward, the system within which they took place was clear: marriage forged bonds of kinship across the Hellenistic world's political boundaries.[37] Even when Hellenistic kings clashed, as they often did, the dense interconnections among their dynasties meant that these conflicts were feuds within a family, not just wars between distinct empires.

WHY MARRIAGE FAILED

When Roman-Parthian interaction began in the first century B.C.E., then, the ancient Mediterranean and Near East had seen over two millennia of ruling families creating kinship through brotherhood and interdynastic marriage. Yet the Julio-Claudians and the Arsacids did not intermarry, and their rulers did not call one another "brother." Why not? The eclipse of brotherhood and intermarriage requires an explanation, as does the rise of fosterage as the mechanism that took their place.

Intermarriage failed as a mode of Arsacid-Caesarian engagement because Roman marital customs were, by ancient dynastic standards, anomalous. This was the case in two respects. First, the Julio-Claudian emperors practiced monogamy, as did the Greek and Roman populations they ruled. In this they differed from the royalty of nearly every other premodern imperial power, not only in the Near East, but in China, India, Southeast Asia, and pre-Columbian America as well.[38] Monogamy did not mean that emperors were limited to sexual relations with a single partner. Prostitution, slavery, and other extramarital avenues offered Roman men (especially the wealthy and powerful) various ways to practice what Walter Scheidel calls "polygynous monogamy."[39] No more than one marriage was legal or socially sanctioned, however, and this norm limited the scope of possible interdynastic connections.

The second anomalous feature of Roman elite marital politics was their narrowness and insularity, a cultural proclivity that further discouraged intermarriage as a mode of interaction with foreign powers. Like many ancient societies, the Romans could use marriage alliances as a way to play the game of power politics. But this game was played only among a relatively small (if slowly expanding) group of Roman and Italian families with strong endogamous tendencies, and foreigners were not allowed a seat at the table.[40] In the republic and early principate, highborn Roman men did not bring foreign wives into their households in

---

37. On the political consequences of interdynastic marriage in the Hellenistic period, see Ogden 1999; Carney 2000: 18–23; Miron 2000; Ma 2013: 129; Strootman 2014: 107–10. Ager 2017 discusses the symbolism of royal weddings. Macurdy 1932 remains foundational on Hellenistic queenship.

38. Scheidel 2009a: 283; Scheidel 2011: 108–9; Duindam 2016: 108–27.

39. Scheidel 2011: 109.

40. Wiseman 1971: 53–64; Hopkins and Burton in Hopkins 1983: 48–49, 86–89; Dixon 1985; Severy 2003: 63. Not every marriage need have been political, however, and for many attested marriages there is no evident political motive: see Shackleton Bailey 1960: 267.

the city, and highborn women did not go abroad to become the wives of eastern kings. As a rule, Roman law and custom restricted marriages between citizens and noncitizens.[41] The prohibition was not always the reality for members of the lower classes, to be sure, and it eroded even for elites in later antiquity, when numerous Romano-"barbarian" marriages were contracted at the highest levels of power.[42] But in the age of Augustus—a ruler whose marriage legislation mandated purity, chastity, and resistance to foreign encroachment, especially for members of the senatorial order—elite Roman men and women could marry only each other.[43]

Responsibility for the failure of intermarriage should thus be imputed to the Roman side, because Parthian sources suggest that the Arsacids were no less open to the practice than their Hellenistic and Near Eastern predecessors. Internal documentary evidence and Greco-Roman historiography amply attest Arsacid polygamy and intermarriage with foreign dynasties. Key internal references come from the Avroman documents, which name the king and his wives by way of a dating formula in their opening lines. One of the three wives mentioned in Avroman 1 is Aryazate, "daughter of the great king Tigranes"—almost certainly Tigran II (r. 95–55 B.C.E.), the Artaxiad king of Armenia—while "Cleopatra," one of the four wives mentioned in Avroman 2, may have been a Hellenistic princess.[44] A Commagenian wife of Urūd II is also attested.[45] Greco-Roman literary sources record further Arsacid marriage connections with the Seleucids, Armenia, Media, and the Parthian nobility.[46] The Roman imagination could run wild when it came to Parthian sexual customs, but there is no reason to doubt Roman reports of Arsacid polygamy, next-of-kin unions, and dynastic intermarriage, all of which are sufficiently confirmed by internal sources.[47] Going abroad to marry was, after all, business as usual in ancient Near Eastern interstate politics.

41. The legal sources are collected in Grubbs 2002: 154–56. For discussion, see Cherry 1990; Roselaar 2014.

42. On Roman elite intermarriage with those considered barbarians (mostly Germans, but some Iranians as well), see the cases collected in Soraci 1974: 183–205; Blockley 1984: 66–71; Mathisen 2009: 145–48, discussing the law against Romano-barbarian intermarriage in *Cod. Theod.* 3.14.1.

43. See esp. the speech of Augustus in Cass. Dio 56.7.5. For the effects of the Augustan marriage legislation on the upper classes, see Frank 1975; McGinn 2002; Wallace-Hadrill 2014.

44. Aryazate: Avroman 1, version A, lines 3–4 = Minns 1915: 28; Hackl et al. 2010: 2.467–72. Cleopatra: Avroman 2, version A, line 2 = Minns 1915: 30; Hackl et al. 2010: 2.472–76 with Madreiter and Hartmann 2021: 236–38.

45. *SEG* 33.1215; cf. Cass. Dio 49.23.4; discussion in Brijder 2014: 60–62.

46. The relevant passages are collected and discussed in Huber and Hartmann 2006: 499–505; see also Kaim 2016: 92; Dąbrowa 2018.

47. For Roman views of Parthian sexuality, see Lerouge 2007: 339–49. On next-of-kin marriage (*xwēdōdah*) in pre-Islamic Iran, see Scheidel 1996: 324–27; de Jong 1997: 424–32; Skjærvø 2013; Vevaina 2018; Potts 2023: 64–71. Condemnations of the practice in Indian Buddhist texts parallel Roman disapproval; see Silk 2008.

It was Roman rather than Parthian customs, then, that obstructed intermarriage between elites of the two empires. For Irene Huber and Udo Hartmann, the refusal of Ardawān IV to wed his daughter to Caracalla points to a Parthian distaste for Roman spouses, but the historicity of the entire episode has been contested.[48] The story was richly elaborated by Herodian, who has Ardawān intone that "marriage with a barbarian is not suitable for a Roman."[49] This is a Roman sentiment expressed through the mouthpiece of a foreign king, an admonition against intermarriage characteristic of Roman customs, not Parthian ones. The final word on the matter should rest with Lucan's Lentulus, who, imagining Pompey's wife Cornelia in the power of the Arsacid king, exclaims in horror, "the offspring of Metellus, a woman so illustrious, will stand by a barbarian's bed, one among a thousand wives!"[50] The prejudice, disgust, and fear behind his words explain, as well as any piece of evidence, why marriages among highborn Romans and Parthians never caught on.

FOSTERAGE

With the failure of intermarriage to effect robust and meaningful kinship bonds between the ruling dynasties of Parthia and Rome, another mechanism came to the fore: fosterage, defined here as the rearing of a child by nonnatal parents. Like intermarriage, this institution had a long history in the ancient Mediterranean and Near East, though its role in interstate politics was less visible until the Hellenistic period.

Fosterage was long marginalized in anthropological and historical studies of kinship, but work in recent decades has clarified its ability to forge kinship in past and present cultures across the globe. Early theorists of kinship privileged biological connections and assumed the primacy of ties derived from sexual procreation.[51] In this framework, kinships unrelated to birth or marriage were dubbed "fictive" and relegated to second-order status beneath natal affiliations.[52] But subsequent scholarship has shown that these ideas about kinship reflected Euro-American preoccupations rather than universal truths, and the shortcomings of such biocentrism for the study of other world cultures have received extensive discussion since the 1960s.[53] The decentering of biology has increased interest in fosterage (along with adoption, a related and overlapping practice) as a mode

48. Huber and Hartmann 2006: 504; cf. Madreiter and Hartmann 2021: 240. Skeptical of the episode are Timpe 1967; Zimmermann 1999: 210.

49. Herodian 4.10.5.

50. Luc. 8.410–11.

51. See David Schneider's critique (1984: esp. 53–56) of the focus on biology in, e.g., Fortes 1949; Radcliffe-Brown 1952; Lévi-Strauss 1969.

52. See Howell 2009: 154–55, with references.

53. Key discussions include Needham 1971; Schneider 1984; Strathern 1992; Carsten 2000. For antiquity, see Potts 2023: 2–11. Useful overviews of the bibliography are offered by Wilhite 2007: 76–80; Johnson and Paul 2016: 75–83.

of kinship creation.[54] No longer regarded as a second-rate adjunct to biological parent-child relations, fosterage's vital role as a kinship mechanism has been identified and traced across a range of historical and contemporary cultures.[55]

Anthropological studies of fosterage among political elites distinguish between cliental and patronal varieties, a useful conceptual framework for thinking through the valences of the practice in the context of Roman-Parthian relations.[56] In a patronal fosterage arrangement, a child's biological parents send their son or daughter to a political *superior* to be raised; in cliental fosterage, the child goes to a political *subordinate*.[57] Historians have identified examples of both types in pre- and early modern cultures.[58] The patronal/cliental heuristic has limitations, of course, especially if it is conceived as a rigid binary. The fostered and fostering parties may be equals in power, for instance, or the two paradigms may be in simultaneous operation.[59] More importantly, however, the scheme assumes that the distribution of power is straightforward, agreed upon, and legible to both the fosterers and the fostered: clients understand and affirm their own clientage and the superiority of their patron, and vice versa. But political groups can disagree about matters of hierarchy and status, especially when they belong to different polities or societies and act on different cultural assumptions. Moreover, the scholarly categorization of a fosterage arrangement as patronal or cliental assumes the scholar's ability to correctly assess the underlying power dynamics—a simple proposition in some cases, perhaps, but not in others.

With these considerations in mind, the following discussion of the evidence for ancient Near Eastern fosterage practices will advance two ideas about the case of the Arsacids of Rome: first, that cliental fosterage is likely to have been the dominant paradigm on the Parthian side; and second, that this frame of reference produced a pragmatic misunderstanding with Rome about what it meant for Arsacid

54. On the relationship between fosterage and adoption, see Leinaweaver 2018.

55. For contemporary cultures, see Goody 1969; Goody 1982; Weismantel 1995; Carsten 2004: 137–46; Leinaweaver 2008; Howell 2009; Leinaweaver 2014. For past cultures, see Bühler 1964; Parkes 2003; Parkes 2004a; Parkes 2004b; Parkes 2006: 359–61. See further below.

56. Esther Goody distinguishes between *kinship fosterage*, where a child is raised by relatives or close kin, and *alliance fosterage*, where "a patron-client bond expressed in terms of quasi-kinship . . . [is] used to establish reciprocal claims on loyalty and support": Goody 1982: 114; cf. Lallemand 1988: 31. The latter applies especially to families among a society's political elite.

57. Parkes 2003: 743. Parkes prefers the term *allegiance fosterage* to *alliance fosterage*; cf. Parkes 2004a: 588.

58. For cliental fosterage arrangements, see Anderson 2004; Charles-Edwards 2013: 298 on medieval Wales; Conlan 2005: 160–61 on tenth–fourteenth century C.E. Japan; Cathcart 2006: 80–85 on late medieval/early modern Scotland; Hansen 2008: 44 on early Icelandic society. For patronal fosterage arrangements, see Adams 2008: 104 on late medieval/early modern France; Thornbury 2014: 144–47 on Anglo-Saxon England. Preston-Matto 2011; Preston-Matto 2018 describes both patronal and cliental arrangements in medieval Ireland; cf. Booker 2018: 170–77; O'Donnell 2020: 100.

59. See Parkes 2003: 764 on "reciprocal" fosterage arrangements.

children to circulate. Patronal fosterage arrangements did exist in the ancient Near East, but cliental fosterage is better represented in the sources most relevant to the Arsacid case, namely contemporaneous inscriptions from Arsacid territories, Sasanian texts, late antique historiography from Arsacid Armenia, and postconquest literature in Middle and New Persian. Yet the cliental nature of Parthian fosterage is significant not because it allows the modern analyst to pass new judgment on the structure of Roman-Parthian power relations, but because it shows how both sides could draw on different cultural frameworks to construe interstate politics in a way that flattered their own position. The equation of fosterers with inferiors would have given the Arsacids a basis for claiming, maintaining, and believing that the Roman emperor had become a Parthian dependent—a notion just as viable in Parthia's culture as Arsacid "hostageship" was in Rome's. What the fosterage paradigm uncovers, then, is a Parthian view of Arsacid supremacy, underpinned by interdynastic kinship, that could coexist, in convenient incomprehension, with the opposite idea on the Roman side.

The earliest ancient Near Eastern evidence for fosterage supports the patronal model. In New Kingdom Egypt (c. 1600–1070 B.C.E.), the pharaoh's court hosted many young princes from lands like Syria-Palestine, Nubia, and Libya that were subject to his rule, if to varying degrees. The children "would be raised from childhood in the Egyptian palace, exposed to Egyptian culture, religion, and loyalty to the pharaoh," an upbringing meant to mold them into reliable clients.[60] Nor were their parents always opposed to the practice, which helped them ensure access to the pharaoh and maintain the stability of their local rule.[61] Scholars generally take the view that the institution benefited the Egyptian state, though in some cases a repatriated prince might be rejected by a local population.[62] Egyptian sources sometimes call these young elites "children of the nursery," a designation that used the language of paternalism to describe the pharaoh's relationship to them and to the lands they would rule.[63] The pharaoh was the overseer and sometimes the captor of his young wards, but in another sense he was a father figure as well.

The patronal model is also well supported by the evidence from the Neo-Assyrian empire (c. 911–609 B.C.E.), where young foreign royalty were integrated into the king's household and familial structures by various means. One was hostageship. It was common practice for the Assyrians to take as hostages the sons and daughters of local kings whom they had recently conquered or reconquered in the wake of a rebellion.[64] Unlike mere prisoners of war, these dynasts were treated

---

60. Quotation from Darnell and Manassa 2007: 145; cf. Ahlström 1993: 232; Van De Mieroop 2007: 117–19.

61. Morkot 2013: 946.

62. Wilson 1956: 183; Darnell and Manassa 2007: 109–10, 145.

63. Darnell and Manassa 2007: 109–10; Van De Mieroop 2007: 117–19.

64. See the survey of inscriptional evidence in Zawadski 1995.

with honor and enjoyed personal contact with the king.[65] Karen Radner has argued that the maintenance of these hostages at court aimed at "pro-Assyrian indoctrination"—that is, at the cultivation of royal clients who, once released, would serve as reliable agents of the Assyrian empire at the local level.[66]

But some texts preserve mention of foreign fosterlings who were not described with the Akkadian word for hostage (*līṭu*).[67] A letter of Esarhaddon (r. 681–669 B.C.E.) to the Elamite king Urtaku is especially important, since it reveals a mode of dynastic engagement between Assyria and the major power on the Iranian plateau at this time. The extant portion of the tablet offers greetings "to Urtaku, king of Elam, [my] br[other]. I a[m] well, your sons and daughters are well, my country and magnates are well. May Urtaku, king of Elam, my brother, be well, may my sons and daughters be well, may your magnates and your country be well!"[68] The exchange of children had established brotherhood between the two kings, as well as a relationship between their states that was "surprisingly cordial," at least till the end of Esarhaddon's reign.[69] Other references stress the king's role as child rearer. Sennacherib (r. 705–681 B.C.E.) boasted of his installation of Bēl-ibni, "a scion of Šuanna (Babylon), who had grown up like a young puppy in my palace," as one of his inscriptions relates.[70] Esarhaddon uses similar language to record his imposition of "the lady Tabūa, who was raised in the palace of my father," as ruler over the Arabs.[71] Bēl-ibni and Tabūa are relatively clear cases of patronal fosterage, since Babylon and Arabia were Assyrian subjects. The Esarhaddon-Urtaku exchange is not obviously cliental or patronal, as Assyria and Elam were more or less equals in this period.

It would seem reasonable to assume that the Achaemenid Persians (c. 550–330 B.C.E.) were influenced by these antecedents, but the evidence for the continuity of Near Eastern fosterage traditions under their empire is limited. To be sure, there is reason to believe that the Persians were exposed to the Assyrian model. Another Assyrian inscription records that one "Kuraš, king of the land of Parsumaš," sent his oldest son, Arukku, to Aššurbanipal in c. 646 B.C.E. after the Assyrian sack of

65. Zawadski 1995: 456.

66. Radner 2012: 473–74; cf. Richardson 2016: 53.

67. For the term, see Zawadski 1995: 449–50.

68. SAA 16 001 = ABL 918; translation from Luukko and van Buylaere 2002: 4 (no. 1).

69. Carter and Stolper 1984: 49–50, quotation on 49; see also Waters 2000: 42–47.

70. RINAP 3/1, text 1, line 54; text and translation in Grayson and Novotny 2012: 36.

71. RINAP 4, text 1, column iv, lines 15–16; text and translation from Leichty 2011: 19. The phrase reoccurs several times in Esarhaddon's inscriptions, with one major variation: in two places, Tabūa is said to have been raised in the palace of Esarhaddon's father, Sennacherib (one is the text quoted above; the other is RINAP 4, text 6, column iii, lines 9–10 = Leichty 2011: 49). In two others, however, Esarhaddon states that she was raised in his own palace (RINAP 4, text 2, column ii, lines 60–62 = Leichty 2011: 30; RINAP 4, text 3, column iii, lines 3–5 = Leichty 2011: 38). A fifth inscription appears to repeat the phrase, but a lacuna conceals in whose palace Tabūa was raised (RINAP 4, text 97, lines 12–13 = Leichty 2011: 180). See also Eph'al 1982: 127–28.

Susa.[72] The identification of this Kuraš with Cyrus I, the grandfather of the Cyrus who founded the Persian empire, has proven to be contentious.[73] Even if the Kuraš of Aššurbanipal's inscription was not the direct ancestor of Cyrus the Great, however, the text clearly attests the circulation of royalty between Assyria and Persia in the run up to the Achaemenid empire's emergence.[74] Early Persian dynasts could therefore have been familiar with royal fosterage as a mode of interdynastic relations, and the Assyrians may have taught them to see pro-parentage as the prerogative of an overlord. Evidence that the Achaemenids actually exercised this prerogative, however, is thin.[75]

The more plentiful sources of the Hellenistic period (323–31 B.C.E.) herald a shift to cliental fosterage as the role of child rearer was delegated to a royal subordinate. Like the rulers of the Bronze Age, Hellenistic monarchs could refer to their royal peers as "brother" without biological basis, and other familial designations were employed as well.[76] For Macedonian royal families and the nobility who kept them in power, the primary mechanism for the creation of kinship bonds was the institution of the royal children (*paides basilikoi*, usually translated "royal pages").[77] Housed at the king's court, this group comprised the sons of the realm's nobility, who grew up alongside the king's offspring. The children were supervised by a foster-father (*tropheus*), a dignitary of high but not royal rank. Philip II seems to have inaugurated the institution, and it is attested for all of the major Successor kingdoms.[78] Some scholars have tried to locate an earlier origin for the royal children in the Achaemenid empire or pre-Hellenistic Macedon, but ultimately the protohistory remains obscure.[79]

---

72. RINAP 5, text 12, column vi, lines 7–13; cf. RINAP 5, text 23, lines 114–17. Arukku is not mentioned in the second passage, on which see Waters 2011: 292–93. The text does not explicitly call Arukku a hostage (*līṭu* and *līṭūtu* in Akkadian), though several scholars identify him as such (Zawadski 1995: 458; Waters 2014: 35–36; Stronach 2019: 53–54). He appears nowhere else in the historical record.

73. On the problems with the identification, see Young 1988: 26–27; Briant 2002: 17–18, 878.

74. See Fuchs 2017: 267.

75. Xenophon writes that children of the nobility were educated at the Achaemenid king's court: Xen. *Anab.* 1.9.3; *Cyr.* 8.8.13; see further Briant 2002: 327–30; Klinkott 2005: 286 with n.29. But he also gives the impression that the Persian nobles themselves were usually in attendance, as well, so this is no indication that children would have been separated from their natal parents: see Xen. *Cyr.* 8.1.6, 16, 20. Akkadian and Aramaic texts do preserve the title "Son of the House," which apparently extended the language of kinship to dignitaries who were not directly related to the Achaemenid family: Benveniste 1966: 22–26; Briant 2002: 310; Tuplin 2020: 31–38.

76. See esp. *OGIS* 257, line 2 (a letter from the Seleucid king Antiochus VIII (or IX) to Ptolemy X, in which the addressee is called *adelphos*). For further references, see Coloru 2012: 87–88.

77. For overviews of the institution, see Hammond 1989: 56–57; Strootman 2014: 136–44; Carney 2015: 207–16.

78. Strootman 2014: 136–37 with n.3.

79. Kienast 1973: 255 posits an Achaemenid origin, which Carney 2015: 208 finds "not so much wrong as simplistic." Hammond 1990: 261–64 argues for the existence of the page service before Philip II; Lane Fox 2011: 215 disagrees.

Where sources are available, however, they reveal an institution that forged kinship between royalty and nobility, despite the constant possibility of dissension between kings and aristocrats. The Hellenistic monarch's need to keep the nobility in line has led some scholars to see the royal children as "quasi-hostages" on whom punishment might fall if their family failed to keep faith with the throne.[80] But while an implicit threat may indeed have existed, the institution's ability to create kinship ties was no less potent. Hellenistic inscriptions show that the designations "fosterer" (*tropheus*) and "foster-sibling" (*syntrophos*) were part of the titulature of high-ranking political figures.[81] Literary references also attest to the close bonds, both personal and political, that fosterage could create.[82] When the Seleucid dynast Demetrius I entered Roman hostageship, for instance, his *syntrophos* Apollonius apparently went with him.[83] Years later, when Demetrius contrived his escape, Apollonius and his two brothers were his closest confidants, and Demetrius's *tropheus* Diodorus paved the way for his return to the throne in Syria.[84] Even if the families of pages were compelled to send them to the king's court, such coercion was no impediment to the formation of kinships that shaped Hellenistic high politics.

While internal sources for the Parthian empire (c. 248 B.C.E.–224 C.E.) are scarce, the earliest relevant epigraphic evidence with a direct connection to the Arsacid family shows an Iranian cliental fosterage tradition emerging from Hellenistic precedents. The key testimony consists of two Greek inscriptions brought to light in 1996 during excavations at the site of Armaztsikhe/Bagineti in Georgia.[85] These show that political subordinates fostered Arsacid children. David Braund's edition of the texts runs as follows:[86]

80. Quotation from Grainger 1990: 6; cf. Golden 2009: 49; King 2018: 114.

81. Examples include Heliodorus, called *syntrophos* of Seleucus IV in several inscriptions (*IG* XI 4.1112, 1113, 1114; Savalli-Lestrade 1998: 44); Kraterus, foster-father of Antiochus IX (*OGIS* 256; Savalli-Lestrade 1998: 83); Apollodorus and Helenus, foster-fathers of Ptolemy X Alexander (Fayoum 1.5; *OGIS* 148; discussion in Van't Dack 1989/90; Savalli-Lestrade 1998: 383–84; Savalli-Lestrade 2017: 107); and Theophilus, foster-brother of Attalus (*SEG* 14.127; Savalli-Lestrade 1998: 153).

82. In addition to the foster-relations of the Seleucid Demetrius I (below), see Plut. *Alex.* 5 (Alexander the Great's relationship with his *tropheus* Leonidas); 2 Macc. 9.29 (Antiochus IV's body cared for by his *syntrophos* Philip).

83. Apollonius first appears at Polyb. 31.11.6, and seems to have been with Demetrius in Rome for some time. At 31.13.2, he is called *syntrophos*. Gera 1998: 261–62 and Savalli-Lestrade 2017: 104 assume a long co-captivity with Demetrius.

84. Polyb. 31.12.3, 13.1–3.

85. On the archeological context, see Nikolaishvili 2015: 178–80. On the place of the Greek language in Iberia, see Braund 1994: 212–13.

86. Text from Braund 2002: 23–27. Braund's text differs in some places from the original publication of Qaukhchishvili 1996 (in Georgian, which I do not read); cf. Traina 2004: 256. See further Labas 2014: 110; Nikolaishvili 2015: 179; de Jong 2017b: 87–88; Preud'homme 2019: 609–18.

. . . | Ἀρμενίας Οὐολο- | γαίσου, γυναικὶ δὲ | βασιλέως Ἰβήρων | μεγάλου Ἀμαζάσ- | που Ἀναγράνης ὁ | τροφεὺς καὶ ἐπίτρ- | <ο>πος ἰδίᾳ δυνάμ<ε>ι | τὸ βαλανῖον ἀφιέρω- | σεν

[To the daughter(?) of] Walgaš, [king] of Armenia, (and to) the wife of Amazasp the Great, king of the Iberians, Anagranes the foster-father and guardian dedicated the bath building from his own resources.

. . . [βασι-] | λέως Ἀναγράνης [τρο]φεὺ[ς καὶ ἐπί-] | τροπο[ς ἰδια δυ]νάμ[<ε>ι ? τὸ βαλ]ανῖον ἄρτισας | ἰδίᾳ τροφίμῃ | Δρακόντιδι βασ- | ιλίσ(σ)ῃ ἀφιέρωσεν

. . . of. . . [ki]ng, [Anag]ranes the fost[er-father and guar]dian dedicated the ba[th building(?)] having outfitted it [from his own resou]rces to his own foster-child, queen Dracontis.

The fragmentary state of both texts precludes certainty, but since the inscriptions come from the same archeological context and indeed from the same structure, Braund concludes that the dedicator and the dedicatee of the two inscriptions are the same. That the dedicator was in both cases Anagranes seems almost certain, since the restoration of his name on the second stone is well supported by the names and titles on the first. Also reasonable, though less secure, is the argument that the dedicatee of both inscriptions was Dracontis. The name of the female dedicatee is absent from the first stone. But the dedicator, his titles, and perhaps the dedication (i.e., the bath building) are the same in both texts, and it stands to reason that Dracontis is the royal wife of the first inscription as well.[87]

If that identification is sound, the fosterage relationship attested by the texts can be situated with some confidence in a historical context. Dracontis was the daughter of Walgaš/Vologaeses, the Arsacid king of Armenia, and she was the wife of the Iberian king Amazasp/Amazpus. Neither the nomenclature nor the paleography supports a firm date, but the probable range can be narrowed down to the second or third century C.E. Two Arsacid kings of Armenia by the name of Walgaš are known for the second century.[88] There are many candidates for an Iberian king named Amazasp, including one mentioned in an inscription of the Sasanian king Shapur I (c. 262 C.E.).[89] There is not enough resolution in current chronologies of Armenian and Iberian kings to securely identify the figures, but considering the information at hand, it seems most likely that they lived in the late second or early third century C.E., and that the inscription dates to the same period.

87. For these arguments, see Braund 2002: 27. As he notes, it is unclear whether the second inscription refers to the bath-building as a whole, or merely a part of it. If the latter, the two texts may attest two distinct dedications.

88. For the Arsacid Armenian king list, see Toumanoff 1986: table 13. Specific dates are disputed; see Braund 2002: 30–31; Preud'homme 2019: 138–42.

89. ŠKZ 44 = Huyse 1999: 56–57; cf. Phiphia and Kobakhidze 2021: 928–31. On the Anagranes inscriptions in the context of marital politics in the ancient Caucasus, see Fabian 2021: 230.

The reconstructed inscriptions supply enough information to identify this fosterage arrangement as cliental. Anagranes was evidently a dignitary of high status, but he was not a king like Dracontis's father or husband. All the same, it is evident that "foster-father" was a position of honor, since Anagranes identifies himself as such in at least two (and possibly three) inscriptions.[90] He also takes care to identify Dracontis as "his own foster-daughter," a description that again underlines their fosterage relationship and the prestige that Anagranes derived from it. Unfortunately, the absence of an ethnonym obscures the details of Anagranes's role in relations between Arsacid Armenia and Iberia—a murky enough realm to begin with, to be sure.[91] The situation would have a different valence if he were an Armenian rather than an Iberian subject, for example, but the surviving text cannot be pressed for answers on this point. In any event, the inscription provides clear evidence that the Arsacid family sent its young dynasts to be fostered by cliental retainers, and moreover that fosterage bonds were recognized beyond the territory that their family directly ruled.[92]

Elsewhere in the Parthian west, inscriptions in Semitic languages shed further light on fosterage during the Arsacid period.[93] From Birecik Kalesi in southeastern Turkey, the Syriac epitaph of one Zarbiyan (6 C.E.) tells the reader that he was the *mrbyn'* of one 'Awidallat.[94] The word *mrbyn'* literally means "one who rears (a child)," and could be translated as tutor, fosterer, or guardian.[95] The title is again found within Parthian territory at Hatra in an Aramaic statue inscription for "Abdšalmā, *mrabbyānā* of Sanatruq, king of 'Arab."[96] The fostered child's designation as king of a nearby region points to the cliental nature of the arrangement, and while educational instruction may well have been part of the relationship, it would appear that (like the Greek *tropheus*) the *mrbyn'* was a pro-parental role, not merely an academic one.[97] A final piece of Semitic evidence that may reflect a Parthian milieu is the *Hymn of the Pearl*, a Syriac text of uncertain date whose connections to Parthian society have been convincingly demonstrated by Markus

90. Anagranes' name may appear in one other Greek inscription from Georgia along with the title *tropheus*, but the text is too poorly preserved to draw any firm conclusions. See Qaukhchishvili 2009: 228–29; Labas 2014: 110; Preud'homme 2019: 610.

91. On Armenian-Iberian relations in this period, see Braund 1994: 224–45; Lenski 2002: 157.

92. Traina 2004: 260; Preud'homme 2019: 387–89. Both scholars situate Anagranes and Dracontis' relationship within the Armenian institution of *dayeakut'iwn*, on which see further below.

93. On Aramaic in the Parthian empire, see generally Gzella 2008.

94. Text and translation from Drijvers and Healey 1999: 140.

95. Drijvers and Healey 1999: 142 translate "tutor," as do Hoftijzer and Jongeling 1995: 313 and Healey 2018: 60.

96. H 203 = Beyer 1998: 68–69 (on whose German translation I base my own translation above). On the name Abdšalmā, see Marcato 2018: 97. On H 203, see also Caquot 1964: 271; Retsö 2003: 445; Yon 2013: 168 n.31.

97. On the relationship between Hatra and 'Arab, cf. Drijvers and Healey 1999: 105; Palermo 2019: 242.

Zehnder and others.[98] At the outset of the poem, the narrator speaks of his early life spent in enjoyment of "the wealth and abundance of my *mrbyny*."[99] The evident power and wealth of the narrator's fosterer firmly situate the text in the realm of elite social relations, where children could apparently expect both emotional care and financial support from their fosterers.

The Semitic-language evidence from Parthia can be complemented by other documents from Roman territory, especially Palmyra. Eleonora Cussini has identified six Palmyrene epitaphs that commemorate fosterers, five of whom were foster mothers.[100] An additional funerary text commemorates a fosterage relation without an explicit title: "Maliku son of Ḥ[. . .] whom Makkibel brought up (*rby*). Alas!"[101] The derivation of *mrbyh* and *mrbyn* (the masculine form of the noun) from the verb *rby* ("to raise") seems to outline the basic function of such figures, who assumed "a legal role as to upbringing and guardianship of children" that was evidently close enough to warrant inclusion in funerary inscriptions and even portraits.[102] South of Palmyra but still within Roman territory, a Nabataean inscription from Umm al-Djimal (present day northern Jordan) in Greek and Aramaic records that one "Fihr, son of Sullay" was the "foster-father of Gadhīmat, king of Tanūkh."[103] Grammatical problems with both the Greek and the Aramaic pose problems of interpretation and the use of Aramaic *rbw* to mean "fosterer" is unattested elsewhere, but the translation is supported by the word *tropheus* in the Greek text.[104] Though Michael Macdonald has challenged the conventional view, most scholars date the inscription to the mid-third century C.E. and identify Gadhīmat with Djadhīma al-Abrash, ruler of the southern Mesopotamian city of al-Hira (near present day Najaf in southern Iraq).[105] Nothing further is known of Fihr, but if he was indeed an inhabitant of Nabataea, then the inscription is provocative evidence for political fosterage across the Roman-Sasanian frontier.[106] These Semitic texts from Roman territory further attest to the prevalence of

---

98. Zehnder 2010: 237–48, esp. 239, with references. For the text's connections to Parthian society, see also Russell 2004; de Jong 2017b: 87; Andrade 2018: 191–95.

99. *Hymn of the Pearl*, line 2; text and translation from Zehnder 2010: 248.

100. Cussini 2016: 51–52, citing PAT 2695, 0840, 1767, 1220, 2813, and 0839. The glossary in Hillers and Cussini 1996: 386 translates *mrbyh*/*mrbyn* as "foster-mother" and "foster-father," respectively.

101. Translation of PAT 1769 from Cussini 2016: 52.

102. Cussini 2016: 52.

103. Petrantoni 2021: 67–70 (no. 16). The word here translated as "foster-father" is *tropheus* in the Greek and *rbw* in the Aramaic, on which see below.

104. Compare Mascitelli 2006: 233–35 with Hackl et al. 2003: 197, who translate *rbw* as "Erzieher" and note "[w]örtlich: 'Grosser/Chef'; in der Bedeutung 'Erzieher' nur hier."

105. Macdonald et al. 2015: 28–30. For the conventional view, see Hackl et al. 2003: 197–98; Shahîd 2012. On Djadhīma's place of residence, contrast Powers 2011: 139–41 and Bowersock 1983: 132–33. See further Beeston and Shahîd 2012; Morley 2017: 274–75.

106. Hackl et al. 2003: 198 n.610 note that the name Sullay (Fihr's father) is well attested among the Nabataeans.

fosterage arrangements among elites in the Near East, and they suggest that such arrangements could cut across imperial boundaries.

Parthian fosterage is even observable in a Latin inscription from Rome, though this piece of evidence has never been connected to the social history of the practice in pre-Islamic Iran. The text records the renovation of a building by one Narcissus, who identifies himself as "a Parthian by birth," a freedman of the emperor Antoninus Pius (r. 138–61 C.E.), and a pedagogue of (probably, though a lacuna precludes certainty) the emperor's children. Most importantly, though, Narcissus calls himself the *papas* of Lysistrate, a freedwoman of the empress Faustina and a concubine of Pius.[107] Together with the related terms of *tata* and *mamma, papas* is a marker of kinship that can be a familiar or child's word for a biological mother/father (like "mommy" or "daddy" in modern English), but it was also used for pro-parental figures without natal affiliation to the child.[108] Discussions of this inscription have situated it within its Roman context, foregrounding Narcissus's pedagogical duties or the royal concubinage of his foster-daughter.[109] But the significance of the freedman's Parthian heritage has been missed, and his origin can cast a different light on his self-description as *papas*: this freedman was proudly commemorating his cliental fosterage of the ruler's consort, just as Anagranes had done in Iberia. *Papas* was Narcissus's Latin translation of the role that his imperial homeland called *tropheus* in Greek, *mrabbyānā* in Aramaic, or, as discussed below, *dāyag* in Parthian. Despite the substantial wealth that Narcissus had amassed in Italy—the inscription commemorates his renovation of a building, after all—the virtual membership of Lysistrate in the imperial family must have made her analogous, in the eyes of her *papas* at least, to the fostered royalty of the Parthian empire like Dracontis or Sanatruq. After his manumission, then, Narcissus articulated and advertised his status not just in Roman terms, but in Parthian ones, too.

Parthian fosterage is also attested in Roman literary sources unrelated to the Arsacids of Rome, though the cases in question are ambiguous on the patronal/cliental issue. According to Josephus, the Parthian client king Monobazus of Adiabene sent his favorite son Izates to grow up with Abinerglos, the ruler of Spasinou Charax.[110] Josephus is a good authority for the life of Izates, whose conversion to Judaism forged a strong bond between Adiabene and Judaea, so the passage is reliable evidence for horizontal fosterage links among the client kings of the Parthian empire.[111] The case is not clearly cliental or patronal, however, since there is no obvious way to hierarchize Adiabene and Mesene. Even more obscure is

---

107. *CIL* 6.8972 = *ILS* 1836, trans. Gardner and Wiedemann 1991: 62; cf. Demandt 1997: 94; Boatwright 2021: 114.

108. Bradley 1991: 76–102; Stawoska-Jundziłł 2002 (in Polish, which I do not read).

109. Mohler 1940: 266–68; Edmondson 2014: 573; Wheeler 2016: 194–95; Boatwright 2021: 114.

110. Joseph. *AJ* 20.22–23, 20.34. On Abinerglos/Abinergaos I, see Schuol 2000: 226–27, 320–26.

111. On Izates' conversion and Judaism in Adiabene, see Neusner 1964; Marciak 2014: 16–19, with references.

another scene in Josephus from the reign of Ardawān II. The Parthians temporarily deposed Ardawān and replaced him with an otherwise unknown figure named Cinnamus, but Cinnamus subsequently abdicated and returned the kingship. He did so, Josephus writes, because "he had been raised by [Ardawān]."[112] If Ardawān had raised Cinnamus while he was king and was not his natal father, then the story might refer to a patronal fosterage arrangement. However, Cinnamus is nowhere else attested in either Parthian sources or Roman literature, and the historicity of this passage has been questioned.[113] Finally, Tacitus describes the same Ardawān as "having grown up among the Dahae" and "brought up among the Scythians."[114] The phrases need not mean that Ardawān was fostered among the Dahae away from his natal parents and/or the Arsacid court, but it is possible to understand them in this way, as Marek Olbrycht suggests.[115] The latter two cases are problematic, and even the collective three do not, in and of themselves, point to a wider Parthian institution. When read alongside the attestations of *tropheus* and *mrbyn*ʾ in Parthian epigraphy, however, the passages suggest that instances of Parthian fosterage came to the attention of Roman authors, even if those observers lacked the social context to understand such exchanges.

Sources from ancient China for a potential Arsacid at the Han court adumbrate a tantalizing parallel to classical historiography on the Arsacids of Rome, though the case is ultimately too dubious to admit for consideration. A diverse set of late antique Chinese sources refers to a figure named An Shigao, who was, in the words of one biographical text, an "attending son (*shizi*) of the king of Anxi" at the court of the Han dynasty.[116] Another An Shigao of the Han period features in Buddhist sources, which remember him as a translator of Buddhist texts into Chinese. Some authors in this tradition also call him a prince of Anxi.[117] Since it is generally accepted that Anxi is a Chinese transcription of Aršak/Arsaces, some scholars have assumed that An Shigao was an Arsacid prince from the Parthian empire.[118] This identification is doubtful, however, because the geographic referent of "Anxi" is disputed, and other historians put An Shigao's homeland in Indo-Parthia, Bactria, or Margiana.[119] If he were indeed a dynast from Parthia's ruling family, the Arsacids of Rome might have had counterparts at the other end

---

112. Joseph. *AJ* 20.63–65.

113. Chaumont 1991.

114. Tac. *Ann.* 2.3.1, 6.41.2. The ethnonyms are not incompatible, since Roman authors used the label "Scythian" as an umbrella term for diverse peoples of the Eurasian steppe; see e.g. Strab. 11.8.2.

115. Olbrycht 1998c: 142. On the Dahae, see Potts 2014: 89–94; Olbrycht 2021a: 21–25, 32–34, 123–25.

116. *Wei shu* 30.712, trans. Forte 1995: 14–15. The "secular" sources are collected and discussed in Forte 1995: 13–63. On the term *shizi*, cf. Yang 1952: 509.

117. Forte 1995: 65–90; Zacchetti 2019.

118. E.g., Golze and Storm in Hackl et al. 2010: 3.510; additional references in Zacchetti 2019.

119. de la Vaissère 2005: 77–78 (Indo-Parthia); Tremblay 2007: 80, 92–93 (Bactria or Bukhara); Utz 2012: 180–82 (Margiana); Kotyk 2024: 18–21. Cf. Forte 1995: 80; Zacchetti 2019 (noncommittal).

of Eurasia whom the Chinese, much like the Romans, described as hostages surrendered to the seat of their universal empire.[120] On balance, though, An Shigao was probably not an Arsacid.

Arsacid history is on much firmer ground in late antique Armenia (63–428 C.E.), where historiographical sources supply strong evidence for cliental fosterage. Armenian authors make oblique but frequent reference to the institution of *dayeakut'iwn*, a form of fosterage whereby a child of noble birth was reared by foster-parents outside of his or her clan. The fosterer was called a *dayeak*, a word of Iranian origin whose root meaning is "wet nurse" or "nurturer."[121] Whereas in modern Persian *dāyeh* has come to mean "wet nurse," in antiquity the term applied not only to women but also to male fosterers. The late antique Armenian histories reveal that youths of the Arsacid clan were routinely raised by noble Armenian families who were subordinate to the Arsacid king.[122] *Dayeakut'iwn* was also related to, and overlapped with, a Georgian form of the practice, known from late antique and early medieval Georgian texts, in which the fosterer was called the *mamamdzudze*.[123] In the Armenian context, *dayeakut'iwn* arrangements were predominantly cliental, because the Arsacid dynasty that held the kingship sent its children to powerful but still subordinate families among the Armenian nobility.

This background is critical, for one Armenian historian supplies the sole explicit reference to the Arsacids of Rome that does not belong to the Greek and Latin sources of the Roman tradition. Despite the manifest importance of such evidence, the scholarly literature has never connected the passage in question to the Arsacids of the Julio-Claudian period. The report comes from the *History* of Movses Khorenats'i, a text that purports to belong to the fifth century C.E., though most scholars now put its composition in the eighth.[124] The Arsacids of Rome are mentioned in the portion of the narrative that deals with Abgar, a composite figure based on the historical Abgar V of Edessa but subsumed by Movses into the ranks of Armenian kings. In Movses's telling, Abgar had a complex relationship with the Roman empire, becoming tributary to the Romans during the reign of Augustus, but subsequently fighting a war against the Judaean king Herod alongside "Arshavir, king of Persia"—a Parthian king who is himself a composite figure and does

---

120. On this Sinocentrism, see Golze and Storm in Hackl et al. 2010: 3.484; Rawski 2012: 234–35.

121. Bremmer 1976: 66–67 adduces no Iranian or Armenian evidence for his view that *dayeak* means "mother's brother," and his contention that "among the [ancient] Persians fosterage found place at the home of the MoBr" is untenable. On the avunculate, see Potts 2023: 37–45.

122. Bedrosian 1984 (esp. 23 for the use of *dayeak* to indicate male fosterers); Bedrosian 1994; Garsoïan 1989: 521; Thomson and Howard-Johnston 1999: 48 n.297, 331; Meyer 2017: 308; Read 2023: 15–16. On the word in Iranian languages, see Omidsalar and Omidsalar 1996.

123. Rapp 2003: 271; Rapp 2009: 673; Phiphia and Kobakhidze 2021: 928.

124. Thomson 1978: 60; Russell 1986: 254–55; Darling Young 2018: 82. Contrast Traina 2007: 158, favoring an earlier date.

not map neatly onto any historical Arsacid. Movses writes the following about that war's resolution:[125]

> Զկնի ոչ բազում աւուրց վախճանի Աւգոստոս, եւ փոխանակ նորա թագաւորէ Հռովմայեցւոց Տիբեր. եւ Գերմանիկոս կեսար եղեալ՝ ծաղէ զառաքեալքն ի Հռովմ զիշխանսն Արշաւրի եւ Աբգարու, յաղագս պատերազմին նոցա, յորում սպանին զեղբաւրորդին Հերովդի: Ընդ որ խստացեալ Աբգարու, խորհի ապստամբութիւն եւ պատրաստութիւն պատերազմի:

> Not many days afterward, Augustus died, and in his place, Tiberius became king of the Romans. Germanicus became Caesar and used in his triumph the princes whom Abgar and Arshavir had sent to Rome on account of the war in which they killed the nephew of Herod. Abgar bristled at this. He contemplated rebellion, and prepared for war.

To be clear, the passage is evidence for the Armenian reception of the events in question, not the events themselves. Movses conflates different personages, transposes various events, and is disingenuous as to his source material; for what actually happened, he is not the place to turn. For the Armenian *memory* of the Arsacids of Rome, however, he is useful and revealing. Movses does not use the language of fosterage or hostageship in describing these children, but he does give a sense of the power dynamics behind their exchange. Both Abgar and the Arsacid king Arshavir sent royal sons to Rome after their war against Herod. The boys were then put on display by the "Caesar" Germanicus when he led them in a triumph. Is this corroboration of Arsacid hostageship in a non-Roman source? Does Movses describe Roman domination of the east through the forcible extraction of royal children?

In fact, the opposite is the case: the section assumes the superiority of the givers of children. To be sure, the princes of Abgar and Arshavir were sent to Rome in the wake of a war with Herod, a Roman subject. But this was a war that they *won*, killing Herod's nephew and putting his army of "Thracians and Germans" to flight.[126] The children of the Armenian and Arsacid kings thus went off to Rome in the wake of their fathers' victory, not their defeat. Moreover, Movses writes that Abgar became angry when he learned of Germanicus's insulting use of his children. This reaction indicates the subversion of his expectations for how they would be treated. The degrading ordeal of triumphal exhibition is well captured in Movses's use of the word *dzaghem* to describe what Germanicus did to the princes. The verb can mean "to lead in triumph" but also "to deride, mock, jeer at."[127] Such humiliation did not accord with Abgar's understanding of the exchange, and the discrepancy

---

125. MKh 2.27.2–3.

126. MKh 2.26.

127. Petrosian 1879: 425; Martirosyan 2010: 336. Thomson 1978: 165 n.2 points to Movses's use of the Armenian translation of Eusebius's *Chronicle* here, but that text says that "Germanicus triumphed over the *Parthians*" (Aucher 1818: 2.262). Movses must have learned of the princes elsewhere.

was sufficient grounds for him to abandon his earlier accommodation with Rome and plan for war. Movses says nothing of Arshavir's reaction, but since the Armenian and Parthian kingdoms act in lockstep in this section, there is every reason to attribute the same sentiments to him. In Armenian tradition, then, the memory of the Arsacids of Rome diverges from their portrayal in the Greek and Latin sources of the Roman empire. Those who submitted them did so not from weakness but from strength—a move fully in keeping with the cliental *dayeakut'iwn* system as it emerges from other Armenian historians of the Arsacid period.

Moreover, the Armenian sources attest that cliental fosterage arrangements were not confined to Arsacid Armenia; they also were to be found at the highest levels of the Sasanian empire (224–651 C.E.). To take one example from the fifth century C.E., the brothers Hormozd III and Peroz fought for the Sasanian throne in a bout of internecine strife that the latter would eventually win. Reports of the war survive in two Armenian authors, Ghazar and Eghishē, contemporaries who were much concerned with resurgent Sasanian influence in Armenia during this period.[128] Both historians hold that Peroz's foster-father was the decisive element in his victory. Eghishē's more extensive report says:[129]

Իսկ կրտսեր որդւոյն Յազկերտի դայեակն, Ռահամ անուն ի Միհրան տոհմէն, թէպէտ եւ ետես զգունդն Արեաց ընդ երկուս բաժանեալ, սակայն կիսովն զազանապար յարձակեցաւ ի վերայ երէց որդւոյ թագաւորին. հար, սատակեաց զգունդն, եւ ձերբակալ արարեալ զորդի թագաւորին՝ անդէն ի տեղւոջն հրամայէր սպանանել: Եւ զմնացեալ զաւրսն ածէր հաւանեցուցանէր, եւ առնէր միաբանութիւն ամենայն Արեաց զգնդին. եւ թագաւորեցուցանէր զիւր սանն, որում անուն էր Պերոզ:

The fosterer (*dayeak*) of Yazdgird's [= Yazdgird II] younger son [= Peroz], Ṙaham by name from the Mihran family, though he saw that the army of the Iranians was divided in two, nevertheless with one half he fiercely attacked the king's elder son [= Hormozd]. He defeated and massacred his [= Hormozd's] army, and having captured the king's son ordered him to be put to death on the spot. He took control of the remaining forces and won them over, and he effected the unity of the entire army of the Iranians. Then he crowned his own foster-child (*san*), who was named Peroz.

The relevant passage in Ghazar is briefer, but it too mentions Peroz's connection to the Mihrān.[130] This family numbered among the great noble houses of Sasanian Iran. While it was a powerful force in its own right, it operated under the

128. For the history of this succession struggle, see Shahbazi 2004a; Pourshariati 2008: 71, 300 n.1725, both of whom privilege the Armenian sources.

129. Egh. 197 = Ter-Minasyan 1957: 197; cf. Thomson 1982: 242 for complete English translation.

130. GhP 60, 64; translation in Thomson 1991: 159, 166; Bedrosian 1985: 204, 217 (where the translation makes clear that Peroz has been raised by a *dayeak*). Ghazar's text specifies that Peroz's foster-brother was Yezatvšnasp, son of Aštat from the house of Mihrān.

suzerainty of the Sasanian dynasty.[131] Thus, Ṙaham of the Mihrān was a figure like Anagranes or the Armenian *dayeak*s of late antiquity—a member of the political elite who fostered a young dynast from a royal family superior to his own.

Nor is it necessary to rely solely on Armenian texts for cliental fosterage under the Sasanians, because the institution is also evident in Iranian sources. Valuable testimony comes from the inscription of Shapur I at the Kaʿba-ye Zardošt (šKZ), a trilingual inscription in Middle Persian, Parthian, and Greek at Naqsh-e Rustam in Iran (c. 262 C.E.).[132] The end of the text includes a list of dignitaries who lived during Shapur's reign and administered the empire as his subordinates. Among them are two fostered children. The Parthian version of the inscription reads:[133]

s'sn BRBYTA ME pty prdkn HHSNt AHRN s'sn BRBYTA ME pty ktwkn HHSNt
Sāsān wispuhr, čē pad Farragān derd, any Sāsān wispuhr čē pad Kadugān derd

. . . Sasan, the prince who was brought up in (the house of) Farragān; another Sasan, the prince who was brought up in (the house of) Kadugān.

The operative word here is the Arameogram *HHSNt* for the Parthian verb *derdan*, "to have," or (as here) "to raise."[134] The Greek text likewise describes the two Sasans as, respectively, "reared in the house of Farragān" and "brought up in the house of Kadugān."[135] In other words, the inscription specifies that these two noble youths were raised by pro-parents who were not, it would appear, their natal kin.

The rank of the two figures indicates that their fosterage was cliental rather than patronal—in other words, that their upbringing was delegated to a subordinate. Both foster-sons are called *wispuhr* in the Parthian and Middle Persian texts and *tou eg basileōn* ("those near the kings") in the Greek—that is, as princes. The designation allows for a closer look at their political status. Based on the inscriptional evidence from the šKZ and elsewhere, scholars have found that the Sasanian nobility was organized into four tiers. At the top were the kings (*šahrdārān*), below them the princes (*wispuhrān*), and in the third and fourth ranks the greater and lesser nobles (*wuzurgān* and *āzādān*, respectively).[136] The two Sasans of šKZ 45 both belonged to the second tier, that of the princes. As for their foster parents, the Kadugān are

---

131. On the Mihrān in the Sasanian empire, see Pourshariati 2008: 70–75, 103–4; Maksymiuk 2015.

132. On the date, see Huyse 1999: 10–14.

133. ŠKZ 45; transliteration and transcription from Huyse 1999: 57. The Parthian is privileged here not because it may have been the primary version of the text from which the Middle Persian and Greek versions were produced (on which question see Rubin 2002: 270–77, with references), but because it is better preserved.

134. Gignoux 1972: 52.

135. The Greek verbs are *trephō* and *anatrephō*, both of which were used for child-rearing in ancient Greek. See Griffith 2010: 301.

136. Lukonin 1983: 698–99; Wiesehöfer 1993: 228–29; Hauser 2005: 193–94. The terms here are provided in Middle Persian.

mentioned nowhere else in the inscription, but members of the Farragān are found in two other passages, which reveal that the family had played a prominent role in the Sasanian empire since its inception.[137] They are not, however, identified as members of the first two tiers, and it therefore seems that they belong to the third or fourth—a great noble family, but not at the apex of Sasanian society.[138]

This passage from the Shapur inscription thus shows the use of cliental fosterage among the Sasanian ruling classes—another indication that ancient Iranian royalty could be raised by families who were politically subordinate to their own. Judging by their identification as "princes," the two Sasans were members of the royal family or closely related to it (though not direct descendants of Shapur himself).[139] Their foster-parents, meanwhile, were prominent members of the nobility, but not royalty. The situation is similar to the one recounted in Ghazar and Eghishē above: the status of the Kadugān and Farragān closely matches the Mihrān, the family that both the Armenian authors name as the raisers of royal children. In Arsacid Armenia and Sasanian Iran, then, fosterage helped build and strengthen the relationships between monarchs and nobles.

Additional evidence for cliental fosterage in the Sasanian period comes from Syriac literature on the engagement between Iranians and Christians in late antiquity. Richard Payne discusses a case from a Syriac martyr act in which an Iranian named Mihryar entrusts his son Yazdin to a Christian foster-father. The text is clear on the distribution of power between the two parties: Mihryar was a preeminent figure in the region, "distinguished more than all the other Magians before the king," whereas the Christians were recently resettled captives.[140] Cliental fosterage, the text shows, was a key mechanism for the integration of this community into the political structures of the Sasanian empire. The institution also emerges as a problematic in the writings of Mar Aba, a patriarch of the sixth century C.E. who sought to police the fractious East Syrian Christian community and its relationship to Sasanian and Zoroastrian authorities. One of his reforms interdicted the fosterage of East Syrian elite children by members of the clergy, forbidding the latter to "be foster fathers (*mrabyana*) or guardians for the worldly," as Mar Aba set down in the synod of 544 C.E.[141] In his efforts to promote solidarity among ecclesiastical leaders and strengthen the institutional coherence of the Church of the East, the patriarch felt it necessary to dissolve the bonds of kinship that could link clerical

---

137. ŠKZ 40, 43. The former passage attests that one Farrag was already an important figure under King Pabag, father of the dynasty's founder Ardashir.

138. Lukonin 1983: 705.

139. Cf. Lukonin 1983: 703.

140. Translation from Payne 2015: 67, after the text of Bedjan 1891: 560. See also Widengren 1969: 75. The highly fragmentary Sogdian version of the act preserves mention of the child's foster-parents (*zynbrt*), but not their religion: Sims-Williams 1985: 32.

141. Translation from Payne 2015: 103, after the text of Chabot 2010 [1902]: 82 (French translation on 335).

fosterers to the children of secular East Syrian elites. "For Mar Aba," Payne writes, "[fosterage] generated precisely the personal loyalties and sectional interests that prevented bishops and lesser clergy from acting in concert with their superiors as representatives of an empire-wide universal church."[142] Thus Mar Aba's prohibition reveals not only the adoption of Iranian fosterage by non-Iranian subjects of the Sasanian empire, but the ability of the institution to create consequential political relationships that could require regulation.

It must also be entered into evidence, however, that one key Sasanian source supports the patronal fosterage model, not the cliental one. The text in question is the *Kārnāmag ī Ardaxšēr ī Pābagān* (The Book of the Deeds of Ardashir, Son of Pabag), a literary composition in Middle Persian that tells the story of the Sasanian dynasty's founder. It was committed to writing during the late Sasanian or early Islamic period, and as a source for the historical setting of the tale in the third century C.E., it is of little value.[143] The *Kārnāmag*'s account of Ardashir's life is steeped in myth, legend, and heroic archetypes, and few scholars put much stock in its narrative of his birth and early career.[144] All the same, the text reflects the late Sasanian and early Islamic milieu in which it was composed and redacted, and as such it can shed light on prevailing social attitudes and institutions during the formative centuries of Middle Persian literature.[145]

One passage from the *Kārnāmag* speaks to the conditions under which an Iranian ruler might send his children to the court of the king of kings who ruled over him. At the beginning of the story, Ardashir is born and raised at the house of Pabag, a provincial governor of Pars under Ardawān IV, the last Arsacid king. When Ardawān hears of Pabag's distinguished adopted son, he insists that the boy be sent to his court:[146]

> Ka Ardaxšēr ō dād ī pānzdāh sālag rasīd, āgāhīh ō Ardawān mad, kū Pābag rāy pus-ēw ast ī pad frahang [ud] aswārīh frahixtag [ud] abāyišnīg. U-š nāmag ō Pābag kard, kū amā ēdōn ašnūd kū ašmā rāy pus-ēw ast ī abāyišnīg, pad frahang [ud] aswārīh abēr frahixtag, u-mān kāmag, kū ōy dar [ī] amā frēstē ud nazdīk *ī amā āyēd, tā abāg frazandān [ud] wāspuhragān bawēd, u-š pad frahang ī-š ast bar [ī] pādašn framāyēm. Pābag, az ān čiyōn Ardawān mas kāmgārtar būd, juddar kardan ud ān

---

142. Payne 2015: 103.

143. On the dating, see Cereti 2011, discussing the conclusions of Grenet 2003: 26, 116–17, 125.

144. For discussions of the literary and historical nature of the *Kārnāmag*, see Grenet 2003; Yarshater 1983: 365; Cereti 2001: 192–200; Cereti 2011; Stoneman 2012: 12–14; Macuch 2013: 290; Askari 2016: 87–88; Daryaee 2016: 138. For historically oriented treatments of Ardashir's heritage and career, see Huff 2008; Macuch 2014.

145. On the dating of the compositions that are now analyzed under the label of Middle Persian or Pahlavi literature, see Macuch 2009: 116–21; Daryaee 2018: 104.

146. *Kārnāmag ī Ardaxšēr ī Pābagān* 2.5–9; transcription from Grenet 2003: 58–60. Ardashir is also fostered out in Tabari's *History*, though in that work his foster-father is a eunuch named Tīrā who subsequently adopts him. See Tabari 1.815 = Bosworth 1999: 6.

framān bē spōxtan nē šāyist. U-š, andar zamān, Ardaxšēr ārāstag, abāg dah bandag ud was čiš [ī] abd wēšist [ud] sazāgwār ō pēš Ardawān frestīd.

When Ardashir reached the age of fifteen years, Ardawān learned that Pabag had a son who was skilled and accomplished in matters of learning and horsemanship. He wrote a letter to Pabag, which said: "We have heard that you have a son who is accomplished and very skilled in matters of learning and horsemanship, and it is our will that you send him to our court and that he be near us, so that he may associate with our children and princes, and I may order profit and reward for him in accordance with his learning." As Ardawān was very great and powerful, Pabag was not able to do otherwise or reject this command, and he immediately sent Ardashir well-equipped with ten servants and many wonderful and marvelous things for the acceptance of Ardawān.

There is no single word in the text to describe what Ardashir's role will be once he reaches the court of Ardawān, so it is difficult to label the social institution that the passage describes. The power dynamics, however, are clearly articulated. Ardawān is the superior, a "very great and powerful" king whose commands Pabag cannot disobey. The ruler who sends his son—or, in this case, his adopted son—is subordinate to the ruler who will serve as the child's pro-parent.

The patronal direction of the transfer mirrors the Egyptian and Assyrian practices of the pre-Hellenistic period. Ardawān wants Ardashir at his court so that the boy can "be near" him, associate with his children, and receive favors commensurate with his abilities. In other words, Ardawān wants to control Ardashir's advancement within the ranks of the Parthian empire's administration. The child's road to power and prestige must run through the Arsacid court. Meanwhile, through his association with Ardawān's sons, Ardashir will bond with the dynasts who will be his peers in running the Arsacid empire—and, in the case of Ardawān's eldest son, with the boy who will one day reign as king of kings. The parallels with the pharaonic nursery and the Assyrian court are clear, and the case suggests that the traditions of patronal fosterage may have been observed even at the end of pre-Islamic Iranian antiquity.

Further Middle Persian evidence comes from Zoroastrian texts, which like the *Kārnāmag* were mostly composed under the Sasanians but redacted after the Arab conquests. The religious orientation of these works makes them obscure sources for political and social history, and they shed little light on the patronal/cliental question. In one dialogue between Ahura Mazda and Zoroaster, for instance, the god tells his prophet that "each one of us [the Immortal Amahraspands, an order of divinities] has given to the material world a *dāyag* of our own, through whom they accomplish in the material world the activity that is uniquely theirs in the spiritual world."[147] That is, each god has a representative in the material world of

---

147. *Šāyest nē šāyest* 15.4 = Kotwal 1969: 57–58.

human beings that fosters the activity unique to the god. Ahura Mazda's fosterer is the just man, for example, because such an individual nourishes in the material world the justice that Ahura Mazda dispenses in the spiritual one.[148] It is difficult to draw conclusions about political fosterage arrangements on the basis of these passages, though they do show that the word *dāyag* and its derivatives were evocative of care and nourishment.[149] However, a more useful passage comes from the *Pahlavi Rivāyat*. As the hero Kersasp speaks with Ahura Mazda and Zoroaster about his battle with the dragon Gandarw, he mourns that his enemy "dragged away my wife, and he dragged away my father and my *dāyag*."[150] The fosterer is included among the speaker's closest family relations, and is mentioned in the same breath as his father. The Zoroastrian texts therefore show that a *dāyag* numbered among one's most intimate kin.

New Persian literature composed after the Arab conquests offers mixed testimony on patronal and cliental fosterage in pre-Islamic Iran, but the cliental model remains better represented on balance. Like the Middle Persian *Kārnāmag*, the *Shahnameh* (Book of Kings) of the tenth/eleventh century C.E. author Ferdowsi describes the patronal fosterage of Ardashir at the court of Ardawān IV.[151] However, later episodes in the Sasanian section of the *Shahnameh* show the cliental model in operation. Clientage is prominent in the story of Bahram Gur (= Bahram V, r. 420–38 C.E.), a Sasanian prince raised among the Arabs by the Nasrid king Monzer.[152] The episode begins with the following speech delivered by the advisers of Yazdgird I, Bahram's father. The Yazdgird of the *Shahnameh* is a tyrannical king, so his advisers make the case that his son should be raised elsewhere:[153]

بگفتند کین کودک برمنش   ز پیغاره دورست و از سرزنش،

جهان سربسر زیر فرمان تست   به هر کشوری باژ و پیمان تست،

نگه کن به جایی که دانش بود   ز داننده کشور به رامش بود،

ز پرمایگان دایگانی گزین   که باشد ز کشور بر او آفرین،

هنر گیرد این شاخ خرم نهان   ز فرمان او شاد گردد جهان!

---

148. *Šāyest nē šāyest* 15.5–8 = Kotwal 1969: 58–59.

149. Also of unclear import for political fosterage are two appearances of *dāyag* in the Parthian Manichaean text *The Sermon of the Soul*: see Sundermann 1997: 64, 68, 121 (sections 60, 83) with Sundermann 1991: 14.

150. *Pahlavi Rivāyat Accompanying the Dādestān ī Dēnīg* 18f12, transcription from Williams 1990: 105. Cf. Widengren 1969: 78–79.

151. For the verses from this section that pertain to fosterage, see Khaleghi-Motlagh and Omidsalar 2005: 143 line 150; 145 line 175; 146 lines 190–93; 147 line 204.

152. On the other sources for the fosterage of Bahram Gur, see Toral-Niehoff 2014: 64 n.31, 69 n.54, 81; Munt et al. 2015: 458–59, 499–500; Hanaway 1988. On al-Hira, the residence of Monzer, see Toral-Niehoff 2013; Fisher 2020: 97–99. Bahram's cliental fosterage is paralleled in a passage from the mythical section of the *Shahnameh* where the hero Rustam serves as *dāyeh* to Siyavash, the son of the Iranian king Kay Kavus; see Khaleghi-Motlagh 1990: 207, line 74.

153. Ferdowsi, *Shahnameh* = Khaleghi-Motlagh and Omidsalar 2005: 364–65, lines 52–56.

"This child," they said, "is blameless and beyond reproach. The world is entirely under your command. From every land you extract tribute or promises of allegiance. Look for a place where knowledge exists, and the country thrives thanks to the presence of the wise. From the nobility there, pick someone to serve as a fosterer (*dāyagān*) so that he may earn the country's praise. There this tender-hearted sprout can learn his craft, and the world can be made joyful under his reign."

The operative word is *dāyagān*, technically a plural noun but used here as a singular with the meaning "fosterer."[154] Elsewhere in the poem, Middle Persian *dāyag* yields to classical / New Persian *dāyeh*, which like its predecessor can mean either "nurse" or "foster-parent." The abstract noun *dāyagānī* for its part can signify not just an activity but an office—it is the act of nursing and especially breastfeeding, but also the institutional position of the fosterer.[155]

Along with the other sources for Bahram's life, Ferdowsi's account underlines the cliental nature of this fosterage arrangement as well as the politically consequential kinship that it created. All of the delegates whom Yazdgird considers as potential fosterers—including, tellingly, a set of representatives from Rome—declare their submission before the Sasanian king, calling themselves his "servants." Monzer applies this label to himself, as well.[156] Once Bahram is in Monzer's custody, Ferdowsi illustrates the kinship force of fosterage in his description of Bahram's dual lineage, which becomes both Arab and Persian. Monzer's first act is to find wet nurses for the Sasanian prince; he chooses "two Arabs and two Persians" for his breastfeeding (*dāyagānī*).[157] The combination is meaningful: breast milk was (and is) a kinship-forging substance in a variety of Near Eastern traditions, so Bahram's nurses connect him with his Persian origin while creating a kinship bond with the Arabs, as well.[158] That bond will turn out to be a close one. After reaching manhood, Bahram initially returns to his father, but then despairs at his poor treatment at Yazdgird's hands. In a letter to a Roman envoy about

---

154. For the plural form but singular meaning of *dāyagān* in this passage and elsewhere, see Dehkhoda's Lexicon (Dehkhoda and Muʿin 1947) *s.v. dāyagān*.

155. See the lexical entries on *dāyeh* and *dāyagānī* in Wolff 1933: 364; see also Khaleghi-Motlagh 2012: 86.

156. Ferdowsi, *Shahnameh* = Khaleghi-Motlagh and Omidsalar 2005: 365–67, lines 57–81 (trans. Davis 2006: 601–2). Monzer identifies himself as the "servant" (*bandeh*) of Yazdgerd and Bahram on lines 74 and 79, respectively; the rest of the delegates do the same on line 67. Romans are referred to in lines 58 and 70. The inclusion of Rome among Bahram's potential foster-homes is also mentioned by Tabari (1.854 = Bosworth 1999: 82).

157. Ferdowsi, *Shahnameh* = Khaleghi-Motlagh and Omidsalar 2005: 367, line 91. Tabari reports the same story (though with one Persian nurse rather than two) at 1.855 = Bosworth 1999: 82–83; cf. Munt et al. 2015: 458–59.

158. On breastmilk as a substance that creates kinship in Near Eastern traditions, see Chapman 2012 on biblical literature; Altorki 1980; Parkes 2005; Schine 2019: 170; Rahbari 2020 on Islamic literature and jurisprudence. On the role of substances in different cultural ideas about kinship, see Carsten 1991: 425–26 on food; Carsten 2011 on blood.

his plight, he laments, "[Yazdgird] might as well send me to my *dāyagān*, since I prefer Monzer to my mother and father!"[159] He soon returns to Monzer in Yemen and, following Yazdgird's death, a war for the throne begins. Monzer's financial and military support is a decisive factor in this conflict, and with the help of his foster-father, Bahram eventually wins the succession struggle.

In addition to the *Shahnameh*, another work of New/Classical Persian poetry provides additional evidence for cliental fosterage in pre-Islamic Iran. This is *Vis and Ramin*, a romance composed under Seljuk rule by Fakhraddin Gorgani. As with the *Shahnameh*, the dating of *Vis and Ramin* is a complex matter. On the one hand, the poem is a composition of an exceptional literary talent who wrote in the eleventh century c.e., but on the other, the story it relates is certainly older, and perhaps much older.[160] In fact, Vladimir Minorsky and Mary Boyce specifically thought the origins of the tale dated to the Parthian period—a plausible (though not provable) idea that has found broad (though not universal) support.[161] At the very least, the notion of a Parthian provenance accounts for some features of the work that are otherwise difficult to explain. Early in the story, for instance, the protagonist Vis marries her brother Viru.[162] Such a union would be forbidden under Islamic law and custom, but it was acceptable and indeed encouraged in pre-Islamic Iran, when such arrangements were not only tolerated but promoted under the Zoroastrian tradition of next-of-kin marriage (*xwēdōdah*).[163] Such glimpses into the poem's social world strongly suggest a pre-Islamic substrate, even if this layer is intertwined with later accretions.

One such facet of *Vis and Ramin*'s cultural milieu is fosterage among elites, the social class to which all of the poem's main characters belong. The practice is central to the poem's plot, because its title characters first meet as children in foster care. "The moment [Vis] was born from her mother [Shahru], her mother gave her to a *dāyagān* who took her to Khuzan, where she lived and had house and home," the poet writes.[164] Ramin is also reared by this woman, who throughout the

---

159. Ferdowsi, *Shahnameh* = Khaleghi-Motlagh and Omidsalar 2005: 384, line 298.

160. See Cross 2015: 32 on a reference to the story in the work of the Abbasid poet Abu Nuwās, who died in the early ninth century c.e.; Nuwās names the story of Vis and Ramin among other relics of pre-Islamic Iran like the Avesta.

161. Minorsky 1964: 151–99; Boyce 1957: 10, 18, 36–37; Boyce 1983: 1158–59; Boyce 2002. Other scholars have accepted the idea that *Vis and Ramin* is Parthian in origin, though to varying degrees: see Meisami 1987: 22 n.44; Davis 2005; Pourshariati 2010: 373; Shayegan 2016: 34; de Jong 2017b: 88; Cross 2018: xxviii; Silverstein 2018: 119 n.90; Sadeghi 2018: 41; Gregoratti 2023: 400–1; Cross 2023: 5 n.3.

162. Gorgani, *Vis u Ramin* = Todua and Gwakharia 1970: 48–50. For English translations of the poem, see Morrison 1972; Davis 2008.

163. For this argument as applied to *Vis and Ramin*, see Southgate 1985: 20 (who details the poem's other divergences from Islamic mores, as well); Davis 2008: xii–xiv. On *xwēdōdah* in pre-Islamic Iran generally, see above, n.47.

164. Gorgani, *Vis u Ramin* = Todua and Gwakharia 1970: 43, lines 17–18. On the geographical referent of Khuzan, see Cross 2015: 187–88 n.112; Silverstein 2018: 119 n.91.

poem is called the *dāyagān* or (more often) the *dāyeh*.[165] Her role as fosterer is a cliental one, for although she is a woman of great wealth and means, she nonetheless "inhabits a decidedly inferior social rank in comparison to the other actors in the story," as Cameron Cross puts it.[166] Moreover, the nurse's facilitation of the love between her two foster-children is a matter of not only romance, but also political sedition. Her loyalties and allegiances vacillate throughout the poem, but in the end she urges Vis and Ramin to overthrow the reigning king and claim his throne, which they do.[167] However powerful and rich she may have been at the beginning of the work, by its conclusion she has maneuvered her foster-son onto the throne of the king of kings, with her foster-daughter by his side. The nurse does not command armies like Ṙaham or Monzer, but she resembles these aristocrats in her use of cliental fosterage to secure political advancement.

HOSTAGESHIP AND FOSTERAGE:
A PRAGMATIC MISUNDERSTANDING

The evidence for political fosterage in the ancient Near East is necessarily diverse and multifaceted, reflecting as it does the course of many centuries and the tenure of various imperial powers in Anatolia, Egypt, Mesopotamia, and the Iranian plateau. The sources suggest that pro-parentage could have different valences among different populations at different points in time—and all the more so in the high-stakes realm of interstate relations, where transfers of royal children cut across political and cultural boundaries. Does the diversity of the evidence preclude a schematic reconstruction, or is there a recognizable pattern to how fosterage worked?

The general trend appears to be a shift from patronal to cliental models over time, even if the former never disappeared. When the pharaohs of Egypt and the kings of Assyria emphasized their pro-paternal roles in the upbringing of foreign dynasts, it was to highlight their suzerainty over the lands from which these children came. When the pharaoh wanted to mount a claim to a non-Egyptian territory, he brought up its royalty in his nursery. The same was true in Assyria, where Babylonian and Arab dynasts might grow up at the king's court. The rulers did the raising. The boasts of the kings about the extent of their power could be ideological statements rather than accurate descriptions of political reality, of course. All the same, they reflect the dominant paradigm of elite fosterage within Egyptian and Mesopotamian societies.

---

165. Todua and Gwakharia 1970: 44, lines 49–51.

166. Quotation: Cross 2015: 208; cf. Cross 2023: 91 n.54. For the Nurse's wealth, see Todua and Gwakharia 1970: 43, lines 19–23; 46, lines 11–13; 100, line 17. In the Georgian translation of *Vis and Ramin*, the Nurse is explicitly called "a nurse of good birth" (trans. Wardrop 1914: 9).

167. Todua and Gwakharia 1970: 498–99, lines 26–58.

Beginning in the Hellenistic period, however, a shift to cliental fosterage begins to emerge in the evidence. The courts of the Argead, Seleucid, Antigonid, and Ptolemaic dynasties hosted a range of noble, foreign, and otherwise elite children, but the fosterer of these youths was usually not the king himself. The sources show that this role more often went to dignitaries of various stripes who, while politically influential, were not royalty. A similar pattern is evident in the epigraphic record from the Parthian empire itself, thin though it may be. Anagranes's fosterage of Dracontis seems to have shaped relations between Iberia and Arsacid Armenia, but Anagranes was not a king. From Parthian Hatra and its adjacent territories, inscriptions commemorate people who fostered kings, but not kings who fostered.

The late antique and early Islamic evidence for cliental fosterage from Arsacid Armenia and Sasanian Persia is more ample, even if there are indications that patronal fosterage was in operation as well. Late antique Armenian historiography, Sasanian epigraphy, and New Persian literature show a fosterage landscape where royalty from the Arsacid and Sasanian dynasties were sent to noble families to be raised. These families were influential in their own right, to be sure, and the ruling house needed their support to maintain its grip on power. But they were still notional subordinates, and fosterage offered them a chance to cultivate a close relationship with a dynast who might one day become king or queen. The picture is complicated somewhat by the testimony of the *Kārnāmag*, which despite its composition date might reflect a late Sasanian practice that saw noble children leave their parents to grow up at the court of the king of kings. In that case, however, it is striking that such patronal fosterage is unattested in Sasanian royal inscriptions, whereas cliental fosterage is.

Since fosterage was the lens through which the Arsacid kings and their Parthian subjects would have seen the Arsacids of Rome, how can this view be squared with hostageship, the concept at the center of virtually all Roman discussions of these figures? If the dominant fosterage paradigm in Arsacid Iran was indeed the cliental one, then the entire enterprise would have run on a fortuitous and mutually profitable misunderstanding. The Romans considered hostage submission to be the obligation of a subordinate, so when they saw Arsacid "hostages" arriving in their city, the power of Rome over its eastern rival seemed to be confirmed. The Parthians, for their part, viewed the fosterage of royal children as the obligation of a subordinate. In their eyes, the Arsacid king's dispatch of his family members to Rome would have been a sign not of weakness, but of strength. Despite or perhaps even *because of* their divergent interpretations of what these exchanges meant, the Parthians and Romans enjoyed a fruitful miscommunication that left each side convinced of its dominance over the other.

The privileging of Near Eastern evidence for the study of these exchanges, at any rate, shows that Parthian historians have neglected fosterage by allowing

Roman authors to prefigure modern scholarly discussions as debates around hostageship. The sources closest to the world of the Arsacids suggest that kinship and pro-parentage were at the center of the Parthian frame of reference. From this vantage point, the emperor's court was not a place of confinement for the Arsacids of Rome, but rather their nursery. The emperor himself was not a captor. He was kin.

2

Submission II

Parthian Pragmatism

The last chapter used Near Eastern sources to argue for a Parthian view of the Arsacids of Rome as foster-children rather than hostages. Evidence from the greater pre-Islamic Iranian world reveals a long tradition of political fosterage and casts a new light on the transimperial circulation of Iranian royal children. When Roman sources are not the basis for narration, the story of the Arsacids of Rome can be told in a different way. Their trajectories can be explained as the product of a pragmatic misunderstanding, an accidentally harmonious arrangement where the Romans received them as hostages, but the Parthians sent them for cliental fosterage. The framework of fosterage meant that the Arsacid viewpoint not only circumvented the logic of Roman hegemony, but inverted it.

But to express the antithesis so neatly risks oversimplifying the complexity behind Arsacid exchange, and this chapter expands on what pragmatic misunderstanding might have looked like among diverse Parthian actors with varying levels of intercultural awareness. A shortcoming of my thesis as stated thus far is that it assumes total Parthian and Roman ignorance of the other's views. This need not have been the case. One reason to doubt the proposition is that post-Hellenistic Iran had a word for hostage and historical experience with hostageship. Couldn't the Parthians have had this institution in mind as they sent Arsacid children off to Rome? While Iranianate sources suggest an affirmative answer to this question, I respond here that pragmatic misunderstanding may have meant choosing to misunderstand. Where both fosterage and hostageship supported reasonable interpretations of what the Arsacids of Rome were, the Parthians could have exploited intercultural ambiguity to apply a label that was politically expedient rather than mutually intelligible. Though there was common ground between Parthian and Roman conceptions of hostageship, considerations of prestige may have militated against meeting on this terrain. A range of possibilities between mutual comprehension and total misunderstanding must be accounted for, along with the motivated reasoning that could have discouraged Parthian accommodation of the Roman view.

The concept of pragmatic misunderstanding must encompass another type of pragmatism, as well, because the thesis as formulated thus far cannot completely explain the Parthian decision to dispatch Arsacids to Rome. Reigning kings may have thought that they were sending their sons and daughters as foster-children, but why did they want their children fostered? In fact diverse Parthian motives were at play. Kinship creation was a desirable end in its own right, but other objectives had nothing to do with kinship, and indeed not much to do with Rome at all. Reigning kings could use cliental fosterage to purge Arsacid rivals by nonlethal means; to protect vulnerable Arsacids from internal enemies; or to protect the entire Arsacid dynasty from an extinction-level event. Nor were kings the only actors whose agency mattered: the women of the Arsacid court, and their agendas, made an impact on these decisions as well. So while fosterage was an important tool in the Parthian kit, tools can be utilized for different jobs and in different situations. Rome did not determine everything that Parthia did, and one feature of Parthian pragmatism was the empire's exploitation of foreign relations to address its own domestic issues.

To flesh out these two aspects of pragmatic misunderstanding, the evidentiary basis for the following discussion will include both Roman texts and Near Eastern evidence. Here the Roman sources are useful not because they offer direct insight into Arsacid motives, which is more than can be expected of them. Rather, although they are framed by hostageship rather than fosterage, they contain plausible accounts of dynastic management strategies that can be supported by comparative evidence from a range of premodern historical and regional contexts. Direct sources for interstate royal correspondence are absent from the textual record of Roman-Parthian relations (except for problematic summaries in historiography), but they are extant for the Bronze Age, and the epistolary dialogue among earlier Near Eastern rulers can be used to explore the potential dynamics of Arsacid-Caesarian exchange. By the same token, sources from late antique Iran, Central Asia, and Armenia bear witness to dynastic politics in an age shaped by the legacy of the Parthian empire, due not least to the survival of the Arsacid dynasty itself. These disparate forms of evidence allow no direct access to the innermost thoughts of Parthian elites. No surviving sources permit that. But it is possible on this basis to assess the diversity of objectives that the Arsacids may have pursued within—or even outside of—the institutional framework of cliental fosterage and interdynastic kinship.

HOSTAGESHIP

Could Parthia *really* have misunderstood its interlocutor's view, so fundamentally and so dramatically, on the matter of the Arsacids of Rome? As empire builders no less practiced than the Romans in techniques of coercion and control, surely the Parthian ruling classes had their own experience of hostageship and the power relations that the institution entailed. Moreover, nearly a century separated the first and final cases of Arsacid departure for Roman residence. Could confusion have persisted that whole time on an issue with such massive implications for imperial prestige and rank?

The case for mutual comprehension must begin with the internal evidence for hostageship, which offers ambiguous testimony on the prevalence of this institution in pre-Islamic Iran. Enough survives to establish that Arsacid kings saw the value in keeping foreign dynasts at their court under compulsion—what M. Rahim Shayegan calls the Arsacid "hostage policy."[1] Ancient evidence preserves one case of Arsacid hostage taking, though as with the Arsacids of Rome the word hostage is found only in Greco-Roman literary sources. Both Strabo and Justin say that the Artaxiad Armenian dynast Tigran II was given to the Parthians as a hostage during his youth.[2] Tigran also appears in internal Parthian sources, namely the Babylonian astronomical diaries, but the relevant passages are too fragmentary to draw any conclusions independent of the classical texts. On the basis of Strabo and Justin, the diaries can be understood to refer to Tigran's return to Armenia to occupy its vacant throne at the Arsacids' behest. However, none of these passages contain the Akkadian word for hostage (*līṭu*). They refer to Tigran simply as the "son of the king of Armenia," and they do not otherwise specify how Tigran's residence in Parthian custody was to be understood.[3] To the case of Tigran, Shayegan adds others that collectively establish "the Parthian practice of cultivating foreign princes in exile with the intent of restoring them."[4] The Arsacid captivity of the Seleucid king Demetrius II certainly illustrates this tendency, though Demetrius

1. Shayegan 2011: xv, 144.

2. Strab. 11.14.15 (using the verbal form of Greek *homēros*); Just. 38.3.1 (*obses*). On the political backstory to this event, see now Patterson 2020.

3. AD 3, nos. −95 A, −95C, −95D (with "son of the king of Armenia" on line 11); compare the divergent editions, restorations, translations, and chronologies in Sachs and Hunger 1996: 416–23 with Shayegan 2011: 92; Böck 2010: 109–10; Geller and Traina 2013: 447–48.

4. Shayegan 2011: 92.

was a prisoner at the Arsacid court, not a hostage or an exile.[5] Shayegan also adduces Kammaškiri the Younger of Elam and Artabazus of Characene.[6] These dynasts too can be shown to have taken control in their respective territories with Arsacid help and under Parthian suzerainty, but no ancient sources identify them as hostages. Though their cases are suggestive, the Parthian conception of hostage-ship remains unclear.

Indeed, not until the late third century C.E. is a word for hostage preserved in a Middle Iranian language, and even then, the reference comes from a Sasanian text, not an Arsacid one. At the site of Paikuli in modern day Iraqi Kurdistan, the Sasa-nian king Narseh (r. 293–303 C.E.) erected a bilingual inscription in Middle Persian and Parthian to commemorate his successful overthrow of his grand-nephew as king of kings.[7] The closing lines of the inscription are fragmentary and difficult to reconstruct, but they preserve the word for hostage in both languages. P. Oktor Skjærvø's edition and translation of the relevant passage in Middle Persian are as follows:[8]

> W MNW BNPŠE OL BBA ZY LNE YATWN ʾynyʾ plys[tky] W dʾšny W npyky W npʾ(k) [Parthian version: nypʾk] p[t]st[w](kʾn ? OL BBA ZY [LNE ŠDRWN- OLE ? hws?]lwbyhy W CBW ZY AHRN gwnky YHSNNt

> And whoever came to Our Court himself or [sent ?] an envoy and presents and let-ters [and] hostages (as) promises (of loyalty) (?) to [Our] Court, he would have fame (?) and other things (?).

Despite the poor state of the text, some conclusions can be drawn. Narseh lists here several different tokens that one could send to acknowledge his kingship in lieu of a personal visit: a messenger (*plystky*), a gift (*dʾšny*), a letter (*npyky*), or a hostage or pledge (*npʾk*; Parthian *nypʾk*, or *nēpāk* in transcription). Grammati-cally, *nēpāk* seems to be in apposition to a word that Skjærvø restores as *ptstwkʾn*, which means "promises" or "guarantees." The passage therefore suggests that the submission of a *nēpāk* was a way to recognize Narseh's kingship and to assure him that the sender would remain steadfast in that recognition. However, it is not certain that the *nēpākān* in question were human hostages rather than financial pledges or securities, since the word can have both meanings in Middle Iranian

----

5. For discussion, see Dąbrowa 1992: 46–50; Shayegan 2003b; Nabel 2017b: 27, 31–34 with table 2.1 for additional Seleucid prisoners at the Arsacid court.

6. Shayegan 2011: 89–94.

7. For the political background, see Daryaee 2009: 10–13.

8. NPi 94 = Skjærvø 1983: 1.73 (text and translation), 2.130 (commentary). The Middle Persian text is reproduced here, since the Parthian version of the pertinent section (as for the whole text) is highly fragmentary. As indicated, however, the reading of the Parthian *nypʾk* is clear. Unfortunately, the new blocks and readings of the Paikuli inscription published by Cereti and Terribili 2014 do not apply to this section of the text.

languages.[9] Moreover, even if the text does refer to human hostages, it does not specify who their senders were. The immediately preceding sections rehearse a long list of dignitaries who "stayed by [Narseh's] advice and counsel." This obscure phrase seems to amalgamate Sasanian subjects and independent foreign powers, and in any event there is no reason to identify the figures named there with the presumptive hostage givers in the next section.[10] Narseh's inscription could attest an operational concept of hostageship among Persians and Parthians in the late third century C.E., but the contours and scale of the institution remain unclear.

Less ambiguous, and vitally important, is the late antique evidence from Armenian historiography, where hostageship mediates the Arsacid dynasty's relationship with the (eastern) Roman empire. Whereas the classical Armenian word for "foster-father," *dayeak*, directly reflects Middle Iranian *dāyag*, the language uses a different word for hostage: *patand*.[11] Crucially, the sources use this word in reference to Arsacid dynasts who serve as hostages at the Roman court. P'awstos Buzand and Movses Khorenats'i attest various Arshakuni ("Arsacid" in Armenian) children sent to Rome in this capacity during the fourth century C.E., including several family members of king Tiran; two nephews of Arshak II; and later, a son of Arshak II.[12] The Sasanian king Shapur II is said to have taken hostages from Armenia's nobility, as well, though not from the Arsacids.[13] In a few places, P'awstos and Movses also speak of Arsacid hostage *taking* from Armenian populations and from neighboring lands. In one of these passages, Movses describes a case of hostage taking as "in accordance with ancestral custom," which suggests a major role for the practice during the reign of the Arshakuni.[14] All this background makes the Armenian sources highly pertinent to the case of the Arsacids of Rome. If the Arshakuni of the fourth century C.E. were giving "hostages" to Rome as they understood it, then perhaps the same can be said of their Arsacid predecessors in the first century.

Additional evidence for hostageship in the greater Iranianate world can be found in documentary evidence from central Asia, which shows the institution

9. Sims-Williams 2000: 206; Durkin-Meisterernst 2004: 239; Cheung 2007: 288; see further below.

10. NPi 92–93 = Skjærvø 1983: 1.70–73. The phrase in Middle Persian is *PWN pndy W p'dysy ZY LNE YKOYMWNd*. The words are badly damaged in section 93, but Skjærvø restored them on the basis of their appearance in section 21, where the Parthian survives as well; see Skjærvø 1983: 1.36; Weber 2012: 204. This restoration has now been partly confirmed by the new blocks published by Cereti and Terribili 2014: 382. On the relationship of these dignitaries to the Sasanian empire, see Skjærvø 1983: 2.120; Weber and Wiesehöfer 2010: 119–21.

11. Alternately *pandand, pantand,* or *padand*. On the etymology of the word, see Olsen 1999: 303.

12. Tiran's family members: MKh 3.13. Arshak II's nephews: PB 4.5, 4.11; MKh 3.21. Son of Arshak II: PB 4.15; MKh 3.29–30. On these passages, see further Garsoïan 1969; Lenski 2002: 155–56.

13. MKh 3.18.

14. In P'awstos: PB 5.8–19. These sections all pertain to the activities of Mushegh Mamikonean. Garsoïan 1989: 314 n.6, 593 notes that the phrase "[he] took hostages" appears as a formulaic repetition here, but nowhere else in P'awstos' text. In Movses Khorenats'i: MKh 2.65, 2.85.

operating in social strata below the level of royal families. Variations on the Parthian word *nēpāk* are found in several corpora, including the Bactrian documents from the Sasanian east in late antique Afghanistan.[15] In Bactrian, the *nēpāk* of the Paikuli inscription is *nabago* or *nibago*, which can have two meanings. The first is "hostage," as is attested in two letters from the mid- to late fifth century C.E. In one, the local ruler of Rob, Kirdir-Warahran, writes to the leader of the Afghan clan concerning a case of horse theft for which the Afghans are suspected; the relevant part of the letter is lacunary, but Kirdir seems to demand a hostage from the Afghans while he investigates the matter.[16] In another letter from the fourth century C.E., a scribe writes to a fortress commander that he has been unable to procure a hostage from a local family because its members "do not have anyone in the house" who can serve in this position—other than "servants and staff," that is, and it is assumed that the fortress commander will be unwilling to accept these.[17] A different letter from the same period is from an elderly man to a lord who holds the elderly man's son as one among many hostages from different families. The man pleads with the lord, "do not beat them, nor arrest (them), nor cause loss (to them)." Though the elderly man calls his son a *pidistobarago* ("surety") rather than a *nabago*, his role is clearly comparable to those called hostages in the preceding documents.[18] The second meaning of *nabago* in this corpus is "security" or "pawn," and several documents apply the word to parcels of land as economic assets.[19] In a purchase contract for a slave, however, it is applied to the person who has been sold, and in a receipt for a loan, the borrower applies the word to his son, who serves as security for the transaction.[20]

The word *np 'k* also evinces these two meanings in the Middle Iranian language of Sogdian. A Sogdian purchase contract for a female slave dating to 639 C.E. attests that the woman's new owners may pledge/pawn her (*np 'kw*), among many other prerogatives.[21] In a set of two marital contracts from the early eighth century C.E., the first document contains a clause that dissolves the marriage in case either party is taken as a hostage; in the second, the husband promises the bride's father

---

15. For overviews of this corpus, see Sims-Williams 2020; Sheikh 2023.

16. BD 2, Document cm, line 19 = Sims-Williams 2007: 90–91. For discussion of this document, including the composer of the letter and its chronology, see Sims-Williams 2008: 93–94; Jackson Bonner 2020: 124.

17. BD 2, Document cp, lines 11–15 = Sims-Williams 2007: 94–95, whose translation is quoted. For the date of the document along with Document ce (cited below), see Sims-Williams 2020: 241; on the preference for family members as hostages rather than servants and staff, see King 2020: 261.

18. BD 2, Document ce = Sims-Williams 2007: 76–77 (translation quoted).

19. BD 1, Document Ll, line 21; Document V, line 24; Document W, line 20 = Sims-Williams 2000: 68–69, 118–19, 130–31.

20. Purchase contract for a slave: BD 1, Document P, line 8 = Sims-Williams 2000: 84–85. Loan receipt: BD 1, Document ac, line 4 = Sims-Williams 2000: 152–53.

21. Yutaka (trans.) in Hansen 2003: 160; Sheikh 2023: 129.

that he will not use his new wife as a pawn (or surety, or security).[22] The carceral dimension of hostageship is again on full display in a Sogdian Manichaean text about the five elements, which in this passage are captured by the forces of darkness, specifically by the demon Greed. As the text narrates, Greed "took [the five elements] prisoner, stole them, and corrupted them. It bound them in this tower of darkness, imprisoned them, and took them hostage (*np ʾq*)."[23] The meaning of *np ʾq* here is close to "prisoner," which accords well with the unfree status of hostages in the Bactrian documents.[24] Finally, a possible occurrence of *np ʾk* on a sixth or seventh century C.E. Middle Persian ostracon from southern Turkmenistan might attest the manumission of a hostage, but the reading of the text is questionable.[25] Other attestations are in obscure contexts that elucidate the practice no further.[26]

How do these diverse forms of evidence bear upon the interpretation of the Arsacids of Rome? In the crucial case of Tigran, caution is necessary, since it is once again the Roman authors who apply the vocabulary of hostageship, while the Akkadian texts refer to Tigran only as an Armenian prince. By contrast, the Paikuli inscription firmly attests a word for hostage in the Parthian language, and perhaps a tradition of hostageship that had its roots in the Arsacid period. If the documentary sources from the Iranian east are any indication, that tradition had significant points of contact with Greco-Roman hostageship: the vocabulary for hostages and financial securities blurred together, and hostages were routinely taken from families to gain leverage over the kinship group. Yet the documentary texts also pertain to a social context that was some distance below the realm of high politics in which the Arsacids of Rome circulated. They reveal hostages who were taken as part of the investigation of crimes, who were in real danger of physical harm, who were human collateral for financial lending, and who were tantamount to prisoners. If this was the type of *nēpāk* that Narseh had in mind, the relationship between the Paikuli inscription and the Arsacids of Rome would be a tenuous one.

As for the Armenian sources, one of their features suggests a major discrepancy between the Arsacids of Rome and Arshakuni hostageship, and that is the divergence in terminology between the Parthian and Armenian languages. On

22. Yakubovich 2006: 307, 310–15 (Nov. 3 text lines 11, 14; Nov. 4 text line 11). See also Gershevitch 1962: 91–92; Henning 1965: 248 n.37 (on the double meaning of "hostage" and "pawn").

23. M 133, lines 10–16; I translate the German of Sundermann 1992: 128.

24. Cf. also Martin Schwartz's restoration of *np ʾq* in a Sogdian Christian text on the basis of a Syriac parallel text; he translates the word "captive" (Schwartz 1967: 4, 14).

25. Nikitin 1992: 109 (document 5), 129 (sixth/seventh century C.E. date); also catalogued in Livshits and Nikitin 1995: 320 (no. 5).

26. A Sogdian graffito at the site of Shatial may read *np ʾ ʾk*, but the word is doubtful: Sims-Williams 1992: 16 (no. 481), 61. An appearance of *nb ʾg* in a Middle Persian Manichaean text with the apparent meaning of "relative" is unparalleled but may be connected to the word for "grandson" (Avestan and Parthian *napāt*, Middle Persian *nab*), which would make sense in the context of the passage; see Sundermann 1973: 16 (line 76), 128; Durkin-Meistererrnst 2004: 239; cf. MacKenzie 1971: 57; Diakonoff and Livshits 2001: 198.

the face of it, the submission of Arshakuni children to the Roman emperors in the fourth century C.E. looks like an extension of the earlier history of the Arsacids of Rome. But there is a problem with this conclusion: the Armenian word for hostage, *patand*, does not come from the Parthian or Middle Persian words for hostage, which are *nēpāk* and *napāk/nipāk*, respectively. If Arsacid hostage submission to Rome represented one continuous phenomenon from the late first century B.C.E. through the fourth C.E., then classical Armenian would presumably have inherited its terminology for the institution from Parthian, the language to which it is otherwise profoundly indebted not only for fosterage vocabulary, as discussed in the last chapter, but for political vocabulary in general. That is, if the Arsacid kings of the first century thought that they were sending *nēpākān* (hostages) to Rome, one would expect their Armenian descendants in the fourth century to have inherited the word and to have used a derivative of it to describe their own hostage transactions. Instead, late antique Armenian speakers used a different term for hostage, one they did not share with Middle Iranian speakers.[27] This lexical divergence cannot prove that first-century Parthians did not call the Arsacids of Rome *nēpākān*, but it does suggest that the submission of Arshakuni children to Rome in late antiquity relied on a different conceptual category than the exchanges of the first century C.E.

All told, on the question of whether the Parthians would have called the Arsacids of Rome hostages as the Romans did, the evidence from the Iranianate world is inconclusive. The Parthians had a word for hostage in their own language, and they used the institution of hostageship to build and maintain their empire. Yet there are reasons to doubt the relevance of this framework to the Arsacids of Rome, especially in light of the preponderant evidence for fosterage. The Roman and Parthian conceptions of hostageship exhibit real and meaningful overlap, but to judge by Iranianate sources, one cannot assume the Parthian application of this label to the Arsacid dynasts who were sent to reside at the emperor's court. The potential for mutual comprehension existed, but it need not have been realized.

Since overlap between Parthian and Roman views was possible but is not demonstrable, it may be best to assess misunderstanding not as a binary but on a continuum, with total incomprehension on one end and reciprocal accommodation on the other. After all, the Parthian empire was a composite of various stakeholders. Arsacid kings, Parthian aristocrats, royal concubines, provincial administrators, client kings, city councils, rural villagers—different views of the Arsacids of Rome were probably to be found among these groups and within them, too. Likewise, familiarity with Parthian practices of fosterage and hostageship, and with Roman hostageship, will have varied, as will the readiness and

---

27. On the strong influence of the Parthian language on classical Armenian, see Schmitt 2005; Meyer 2017: 255–339. Armenian *patand* may have an Iranian origin, as suggested by Olsen 1999: 303, but it is not cognate with *nēpāk*.

inclination of different individuals to apply these categories to the Arsacids of Rome. The internal evidence from pre-Islamic Iran cannot illustrate this variety with any meaningful resolution, but a diversity of perspectives can be reasonably posited given the size and complexity of the empire and the range of experiences its inhabitants would have had with Rome.

Given the diversity of forms that incomprehension could have taken, the pragmatic dimension of misunderstanding should be interpreted not only as a fortuitous accident, but also as a considered decision. Even if some or all Parthians were familiar with Roman hostageship and could see the Arsacids of Rome in this capacity, why would they have been motivated to do so? In this scenario, pragmatism of a second type would have been in operation. The first type has been covered: accidental misunderstanding was *useful* to Parthia and Rome because it flattered the self-conception of both sides. The Romans were happy to have hostages, which they understood as a sign of their own superiority, while the Parthians saw Arsacid foster-children as a sign of theirs. Mutual ignorance was mutually beneficial, but not by design. However, *pragmatic* can have a second meaning in this context, namely that certain actors were aware, to whatever degree, of the other's view of the transaction, but they sidestepped their own knowledge and cultivated the interpretation most satisfactory to their self-image. This is not to say that either party engaged in self-deception or denial. Rather, despite their awareness of an alternate viewpoint, they maintained their culturally conditioned exegesis even in the face of incompatible input from the other side. They perceived divergence, and let it be. In this sense, pragmatic misunderstanding was not an accident, but an intentional strategy. The givers and receivers of the Arsacids of Rome could have chosen to misunderstand, and to encourage misunderstanding among their compatriots, because it was advantageous for them to do so.

One comparative illustration of this type of misunderstanding in intercultural relations comes from Richard White's study of the "middle ground" between Native American and white settler populations in the Great Lakes region. For White, the middle ground was not only the physical terrain where interaction took place but also a process by which "diverse peoples adjust their differences through what amounts to a process of creative, and often expedient, misunderstandings."[28] In the period he considered, the middle ground formed because neither whites nor Native Americans were predominant in strength, but each needed the other for the pursuit and achievement of certain goals. Persuasion was required, and in order to achieve it, both parties searched for points of contact with the other, or what White calls "congruences, either perceived or actual, between the two cultures."[29] One such congruence centered on kinship and specifically on the

---

28. White 2011 [1991]: xxvi. For recent applications of White's concept to ancient history, see Sears 2013: 180–81; Heffron 2017; Candelora 2019.

29. White 2011 [1991]: 52.

cultural framing of father-son relations. In 1706 C.E., a bout of violence threatened to break the fragile alliance between the Ottawa and the French. White explains the subsequent diplomatic talks as follows:[30]

> The [Ottawa-French] alliance was centered on Quebec, the home of Onontio, and it was formulated in the language of kinship to which both the French and the Algonquians attached great significance. Leaders of both the French and the Algonquians negotiated according to ritual forms which placed the French governor, Onontio, in the position of father to the Indians, of whom the Ottawas were his eldest sons. The French were quite at home with such patriarchal formulations and attached quite specific meanings to them. For them all authority was patriarchal, from God the Father, to the king (the father of his people), to the father in his home. Fathers commanded; sons obeyed. The Ottawas understood the relationship somewhat differently. A father was kind, generous, and protecting. A child owed a father respect, but a father could not compel obedience. In establishing a middle ground, one took such congruences as one could find and sorted out their meanings later.

Father-son kinship offered both parties a framework within which questions of alliance, hegemony, and obedience could be negotiated—even as each side maintained different cultural views about the parameters and implications of such a relationship. Misunderstanding ensued, but it was productive and generative misunderstanding, for it allowed the Ottawa and the French to develop a mode of engagement through which accommodation could be reached. By leveraging congruences that were the products of incomprehension, each side could use the other to pursue its own objectives, even though they were not on the same page.

Where was the "congruence" between Parthian and Roman political culture that would have underpinned the exchange of the Arsacids of Rome? It is conceivable that it lay in hostageship, an institution known to both empires. Yet for the Parthians that framing would have had the disadvantage of connoting political inferiority, since inferiors gave hostages to superiors. Instead, they may have sought and found a congruence elsewhere. The Romans were accustomed to receiving royal children, the Arsacids to sending them out—but for cliental fosterage, not hostageship. Considerations of prestige could therefore have enjoined the fosterage interpretation upon Parthian actors who were concerned about the relative status of their empire as compared to Rome's. Here, unlike White's Ottawa and French, the Parthians would have had no reason to further cultivate the conceptual middle ground with Rome or to "sort out the meanings later." The pragmatism of the arrangement depended on the maintenance of misunderstanding. Mutual comprehension, where it existed, would have been undesirable, a problem to paper over rather than a promising lead to pursue.

---

30. White 2011 [1991]: 84.

If White's selective congruences suggest one potential model of Roman-Parthian accommodation on the matter of the Arsacids of Rome, a letter from the Bronze Age suggests another. In this paradigm, rulers understand one another, but they conceal their comprehension in order to exploit the ignorance of their subjects. The text in question comes from the Amarna letters of the fourteenth century B.C.E., and perhaps belongs to the correspondence between the Kassite king Kadašman-Enlil and the Egyptian pharaoh Amenhotep III.[31] The Kassite author of the letter is upset with the pharaoh, who has not sent him an Egyptian woman to marry. His text describes the impasse and broaches a possible workaround:[32]

> You, my brother, when I wrote [to you] about marrying your daughter, in accordance with your practice of not gi[ving] (a daughter), [wrote to me], saying, "From time immemorial no daughter of the king of Egy[pt] is given to anyone." Why n[ot]? You are a king; you d[o] as you please. Were you to give (a daughter), who would s[ay] anything? Since I was told of this message, I wrote as follows t[o my brother], saying, "[*Someone's*] grown daughters, beautiful women, must be available. Send me a beautiful woman as if she were y[our] daughter. Who is going to say, 'She is no daughter of the king!'?"

Egypt, it emerges, is unique among Bronze Age kingdoms in its refusal to play the game of marital politics by the rules that its contemporaries follow. Whereas royal women from the Kassite or Hittite dynasties are sent abroad to marry foreign kings, Egyptian royal women are not. The writer of this letter is frustrated with the custom and is dissatisfied with the pharaoh's excuse. All the same, he proposes a compromise, of a sort: the pharaoh can send *any* beautiful woman to Babylonia under the pretense that she is his daughter. The final line of the excerpt leaves room for interpretation, but the Kassite king either means that no one will suspect that the woman is anything short of royal or, if they do suspect as much, they will not dare to publicly express their doubts.

The letter shows that ancient kings could collude to enact fictions for domestic political gain. The Kassite king intends to create the mistaken impression among his subjects that he has an Egyptian royal wife, and the successful staging of the charade requires the complicity of the pharaoh—any Egyptian woman will do, but she has at least to be Egyptian, and such a person only the pharaoh can provide. The text highlights the power gap between kings and those they rule, but also the knowledge gap: the Kassite king has a firm conviction that kings may act with impunity even to propagate a falsehood, while his proposed ruse assumes that the correspondents can keep the truth between them as a lie is foisted on the broader public. Indeed, the king regards the successful execution of the plot as eminently achievable. There is no hint that the scribes who composed and read the letter,

---

31. On the precise identities of the correspondents, see Rainey 2015: 1328 contra Kühne 1973: 56.
32. EA 4, lines 4–13, trans. Moran 1992: 8.

or the messengers who carried the letter, or the attendants who heard the letter's recitation will reveal the secret of the kings they serve. In a word, this piece of royal correspondence suggests a type of interstate politics where understanding is the prerogative of kings, a resource they monopolize as they foist a politically convenient but fictitious vision of intercultural relations upon their domestic subjects.

Despite the intimation that true intercultural understanding is the exclusive preserve of a ruling cabal, however, the letter also evinces a serious misunderstanding between its author and recipient. As Trevor Bryce notes, the author fails to realize that the pharaohs keep their daughters at home because, in their eyes, it would be a blow to Egyptian prestige to marry them to foreign kings. The pharaohs viewed themselves as first among peers in the interstate brotherhood, and for them, the givers of brides were the subordinates of those who received them. From this perspective, the proposed solution misses the point. If the pharaoh had agreed to the ruse and sent a fake royal woman, Egypt's dignity would have suffered just as if he had sent a real one; public belief in the princess's royal status, even if mistaken, would create the same perception as actual royal status.[33] Even as the letter floats the prospect of a conspiracy between the two rulers that will join them as partners in the concealment of the truth, it reveals that the sender and recipient have divergent understandings of the marital transactions about which they are corresponding. The prospect of interdynastic collusion *and* cross-cultural misunderstanding are both present in the same ancient text. Kings can conspire to conceal the truth between them even as they maintain different interpretations of what the truth is.

Indeed, it is even possible that Kassite-Egyptian marital interactions represent the same type of pragmatic misunderstanding that underpinned fosterage/hostageship transactions in Roman-Parthian relations. So much is argued by Samuel Meier in his treatment of interdynastic marriage during the Amarna period. Outside of Egypt, Meier contends, the most prevalent type of political marriage was the lord's bestowal of his daughter upon a vassal; that is, the receiver of the bride was subordinate to her giver. Case studies from the Hittite empire and from the Mesopotamian kingdom of Mari support this model. Thus, while the pharaohs of Egypt thought themselves superior in their refusal to send their daughters abroad, kings elsewhere in the Near East may have made the opposite assumption.[34] Moreover, a certain level of intercultural understanding did not cause this fortuitous arrangement to unravel. As Meier explains:[35]

> The various ethnic and linguistic entities knew that their neighbors had different customs and saw the world from a different (inferior!) point of view. The lingua

---

33. Bryce 2003: 101–2. But cf. the different reading of Westbrook 2000: 381, for whom the Kassite king's proposed ruse was a rhetorical strategy to expose the pharaoh to a charge of hypocrisy.

34. Meier 2000: 171; but cf. Kitchen 1998: 254–55 on Near Eastern expectations of reciprocal marriage arrangements.

35. Meier 2000: 173.

franca and international marriages allowed sufficient ambiguity and imprecision so that those who participated as equals could actually appear so on the international stage. But the ambiguity and cultural games allowed each of the Great Kings to rest satisfied that the others did not really measure up to the stature that each envisioned for himself.

As Meier sees the situation, a modicum of mutual understanding did not spoil the harmonious accident that the Near Eastern givers and Egyptian receivers of royal brides both felt themselves the superior partner in the exchange. Awareness of the other party's view did not entail acceptance or endorsement of it, because it could be written off as "inferior" or papered over by means of "ambiguity and cultural games." Meier's thesis might not account for all the evidence—if non-Egyptian kings saw marrying a foreign princess as a sign of domination by her royal father, why is the Kassite king so keen to secure an Egyptian bride in the letter quoted above?[36] As a general explanation, however, the idea helps account for the one-sided nature of Egyptian marital relations with the other powers of the Mediterranean and Near East during the late Bronze Age. Successful marital politics may have rested on the divergent expectations that each party brought to the negotiating table—and on the conscious allowance of such divergence in order to exploit the ambiguity and misunderstanding that it produced.

If one applies these comparative models to the case of the Arsacids of Rome, the result is a pragmatic misunderstanding that could have accommodated various levels of mutual comprehension and leveraged different types of pragmatism to deal with it. At one end of the spectrum, the Parthian view could have been rooted in fosterage, and the Roman one in hostageship, in complete and total ignorance of the alternate framework on the other side. In this scenario, no accommodation would have been necessary or indeed possible, since the discrepancy of interpretations would have gone unnoticed. Alternately, à la White, the Romans and Parthians may have noticed a "congruence" between their cultures: the Roman emperors were used to receiving royal children, the Arsacid kings to sending theirs out. The dispatch of Arsacids to Rome could have taken advantage of this congruence while the other party's divergent interpretation—if noticed—could be downplayed, glossed over, or ignored, so long as the arrangement remained mutually beneficial. By contrast, the Amarna letter quoted above suggests still another possibility: the Arsacid king and Roman emperor understood the divergence between their two cultures because of direct and intimate contact, and intrigued together to exploit it. "Send me a foster-child whom I may present as a hostage to my people," an emperor might have written along these lines. Rulers could have cultivated the misunderstanding of their subjects through deception even if they themselves knew how the other side thought.

36. Cf. the critique of Meier in Wang 2023: 428–29.

Pragmatic misunderstanding encompasses all these possibilities, which can only be enumerated, and none of them proven. As discussed in the last chapter, the sources for Parthian fosterage are mostly indirect, and no surviving evidence grants access to the inner thoughts of Arsacid kings or, still less, their Parthian subjects. A range of perspectives can be posited, but no single view can be attributed with confidence to a specific historical figure. The submission of royal children to Rome happened on several occasions under three different kings, each operating in different circumstances. The various cases may all have been prompted by similar motives, or by different ones; the evidence admits of no definitive answers. Moreover, since Parthia was a vast and populous empire, it is reasonable to imagine a diversity of interpretations by various actors—kings, nobles, royal women, and so on—at any given point in time. The prominence of political fosterage in ancient Iranian cultures means that this institution is likely to have provided the overarching framework of interpretation, and to have bracketed the views of those who participated in, or observed, the trafficking of Arsacid children. But frameworks are only guidelines, and their power to circumscribe is not absolute.

There is one additional aspect of White's study that has important implications for the case of the Arsacids of Rome, namely his view that two parties will search for congruences between their cultures and seek creative accommodation only if they are approximate equals in power and cannot achieve their goals through force. This supposed precondition should be addressed, because it might occasion a neorealist dismissal of pragmatic misunderstanding as a pivotal feature of Roman-Parthian relations. An analyst in the vein of Waltz or Mearsheimer might contend that the fosterage/hostageship discrepancy was epiphenomenal to a rough balance of power between Rome and Parthia, a footnote to the body text of systemic equilibrium between two hegemonic neighbors. What really mattered was the underlying structural power relationship. Pragmatic misunderstanding might indeed have existed, but its existence is inconsequential to a proper appraisal of Roman-Parthian relations, which should proceed, in the final analysis, only from the distribution of material power between the two empires.

What that neorealist objection would miss, however, is that calculations of power are ideological constructions, and not just reflections of material reality. Human beings judge power, and culture conditions human judgment. The conceptual confusion behind the Arsacids of Rome was not an incidental outgrowth of a pregiven equilibrium; it was an integral factor in that equilibrium's emergence. Put differently, pragmatic misunderstanding was not a byproduct of power, but part of its constitution. Neorealism cannot account for this element, since the proponents of that theoretical orientation calculate power by "size of population and territory, resource endowment, economic capability, military strength, political stability and competence"—in other words, overwhelmingly by material metrics.[37]

37. Quotation from Waltz 1979: 131; cf. Mearsheimer 2001: 55–56.

These variables matter, to be sure, but they have to be interpreted by human beings, and they are applied toward objectives that humans formulate within the cultural parameters of their societies. Since those cultural conditions shape interstate politics no less than material factors, pragmatic and mutually profitable misunderstanding between Rome and Parthia could not only reflect but also *create* balance by simultaneously assuring each side of its own supremacy in rank.

MOTIVES IN DEPTH

While the concept of pragmatic misunderstanding must encompass a spectrum of possibilities between total incomprehension and selective congruence, it likewise needs to account for a diverse set of Parthian motives for the dispatch of royal children. The argument as stated covers how the Parthians understood the conduit that brought Arsacid children to Rome, but it does not explain, at least not exhaustively, why they chose to make use of that conduit. The factors behind those decisions need to be investigated, as do the key actors involved. Neglect of this issue would produce an impoverished Parthian history, where the subject is in view only inasmuch as it intersects with Roman affairs. The submission of Arsacids was of course a facet of Roman-Parthian relations. Yet the decision to send royal children also took its cues from factors that were internal to the Parthian empire, and had little or nothing to do with Rome. It was characteristic of Parthian pragmatism that an interstate mechanism could be used to address a range of issues of domestic origin.

Accordingly, a set of Parthian motives is explored in greater detail here. The installation of Arsacids at Rome could be used to purge Arsacid rivals to the reigning king; to protect Arsacids otherwise vulnerable in the brutal competition of dynastic politics; to fulfill the aspirations of Parthian royal women; and to protect the dynasty as a whole from extermination. To these internal incentives, another should be added that was interdynastic in scope: the Arsacid desire to establish kinship with the Caesars. Kinship formation could be a valuable end in its own right as a form of networking that connected Parthia's reigning family to its peers and colleagues in world rule. The cumulative weight of these motives shows that the exchange of royal children was much more than a mechanism of interaction between the Roman and Parthian states. It was a way to manage a dynasty, at home and abroad, in a way that transcended the borders of the state that the dynasty ruled.

FOSTERAGE AS POLITICAL PURGE

For a fosterage arrangement to be established, at least one child must leave the house of his or her parents to be raised elsewhere. But the Arsacid kings had many more than one child in their households at any given time. How did they choose which children were sent to Rome for fosterage and which remained in Parthia?

On this question, the Roman literary sources offer an answer that is worthy of serious consideration: Arsacid children were selected for fosterage because the king saw them as direct threats to his reign. In such situations, relocation to Rome allowed the king to neutralize a rival without resorting to open violence or assassination, which came with their own costs. The earliest author to explain the submission of Arsacids to Rome in this way was Strabo, who in two places discusses the motives of Frahād/Phraates IV in sending his family members to Rome. In the first locus, Strabo views the move as an effort to solicit the friendship of the Romans. In the second, however, the king is said to have acted "out of fear of civil strife and those who plotted against him. For he knew that no one could get the better of him unless they had someone of Arsacid stock, since the Parthians were exceedingly devoted to the Arsacids. So he got his children out of the way, seeking to remove this hope from evildoers."[38] Tacitus saw a similar motive behind the same submission, which took place "not so much because [Frahād] was afraid of us, but because he mistrusted the loyalty of his compatriots." The idea reoccurs later in the *Annals* as Tacitus writes of the 54 C.E. exchange between Walgaš and Nero. On this occasion, the king initiated a transfer of Arsacids "in order to prepare war from an advantageous position—or to remove those suspected of rivalry through a nominal hostage submission."[39] Thus, the explanation is applied to two different Arsacid kings by a contemporary of Augustus (Strabo) and a second-century C.E. historian of the Julio-Claudian period (Tacitus). With potential rivals in Roman custody, the logic runs, seditious Arsacids would be unable to maneuver for the throne, and conspiratorial Parthians would be deprived of a royal replacement for the reigning king.

The explanation should not be accepted at face value or uncritically. A cautionary note is sounded by Joel Allen, who detects in Strabo and Tacitus a common historical trope underpinned by rhetorical concerns rather than historical reality. The political purge motif offered Roman writers an out-of-the-box interpretation of Arsacid motives that they could deploy for their own literary purposes. Tacitus, for instance, could use it to indict the early emperors for their smug belief in their own omnipotence even as they misconstrued apparent acts of Parthian submission.[40] Allen has a point. The political purge explanation contributes to Tacitus's general indictment of Roman imperial vanity, a critical endeavor that informs much of his writing and his digressions on Parthian affairs not least.[41] Moreover,

38. Strab. 6.4.2; quotation from 16.1.28. On the relationship between these two passages, see also above, chapter 1. On the necessity of the Parthian king's being an Arsacid, cf. Joseph. *AJ* 18.44.

39. Tac. *Ann.* 2.1.2 (Frahād); *Ann.* 13.9.1 (Walgaš).

40. Allen 2006: 145–47.

41. On Tacitus's criticism of the Principate in his passages on Parthia, see Ehrhardt 1998: 304; Wiesehöfer 2010: 190; Heil 2017: 266–68.

Tacitus's attribution of the motive to two different Arsacid kings in two different episodes arouses suspicion. Did the historian really have separate and distinct sources of information about the intentions of Frahād IV and Walgaš I, or did he simply reapply a trope to two cases that seemed analogous? The question must remain open, but the latter is a distinct possibility. What appear to be separate analyses may be more accurately described as the strategic reuse of a stock motif. Such concerns underline the limitations of the Roman sources for reconstructing Arsacid motives. They suggest the substitution of rhetorical and literary commonplaces for meaningful knowledge of Parthian politics—substitutions that may have stemmed from authorial ignorance, disinterest, or both.

Yet the "political purge" explanation should not be dismissed, either, for it is buttressed by comparative evidence from other pre- and early modern historical contexts. The idea that interstate fosterage could serve as a conduit for Arsacid purges is not true, or exclusive of other interpretations, simply by virtue of its appearance in Roman sources. But a comparative perspective can demonstrate its inherent plausibility. The tension between king and prince is a common theme in theoretical and didactic literature on dynastic politics. In third century B.C.E. China, the philosopher and Han dynast Han Fei Tzu intoned that "if the ruler puts too much trust in his son, then evil ministers will find ways to utilize the son for the accomplishment of their private schemes," and added as a coda, "if someone as close to the ruler as his own consort, and as dear to him as his own son, still cannot be trusted, then obviously no one else is to be trusted either."[42] The author of the *Nitisara*, a political handbook from late antique India, warns readers that "princes taking advantage of the slightest lapse (on the part of the king) invariably kill the sire like the lion cubs mauling the keeper unawares."[43] In his eleventh-century C.E. work on governmental administration, the Persian statesman Nizam al-Mulk quotes an anonymous poet on the treachery of princes: "One obedient slave is better than three hundred sons; for the latter desire their father's death, the former his master's glory."[44] These references establish that a broad range of premodern cultures were attuned to the fraught relationship between rulers and their potential dynastic successors. In ruling families across Eurasia, brutal competition among kin was a normal and expected state of affairs.

The statements of Strabo and Tacitus on the Arsacids of Rome may be further compared with testimony from the *Arthaśāstra*, a Sanskrit treatise on political philosophy and statecraft. The work is attributed to the Mauryan imperial official

---

42. Han Fei Tzu, *Precautions within the Palace*, trans. Watson 1964: 84–85. On Han Fei's biography, see Goldin 2013.

43. *Nitisara* 7.10.4, trans. Mitra 1982: 133. On the date and authorship of this work, see Roy 2014: 517; Singh 2017: 196.

44. Nizam al-Mulk, *The Book of Government or Rules for Kings* 27.22, trans. Darke 2002: 117.

Kautilya (fl. late fourth / early third century B.C.E.), though the text is more likely the product of diverse authorship and various composition and redaction phases down to c. 300 C.E.[45] Within a work that is generally, as Upinder Singh puts it, "obsessed with the danger of assassination," one section is devoted to the tactical use of hostage giving to circumvent threats to the king's person.[46] The author advises that shrewd rulers can turn foreign demands for hostages to their own advantage: "The taking of a kinsman or a chief constitutes a hostage. In this event, the one who gives a traitorous minister or a traitorous offspring is the one who outwits. One who does the opposite is outwitted; for the enemy strikes without remorse at the vulnerable points of someone who is full of confidence because of receiving a hostage."[47] Wise rulers, the author explains, can fool their enemies into taking an undesirable as a hostage. Kings are expected to give hostages from the ranks of their own family or from their ministers. In either event, the king can select "a kinsman or a chief" of known or suspected disloyalty for hostageship. The hostage giver thereby removes a source of domestic conspiracy, and the hostage taker is rendered vulnerable by the mistaken impression that they now have leverage. This is precisely the line of reasoning that Strabo and Tacitus attribute to Frahād and Walgaš.

The *Arthaśāstra* thus contains valuable comparative evidence that buttresses the testimony of Strabo and Tacitus on Arsacid motives. The source cannot of course confirm the Roman authors or offer direct insight into the minds of Frahād IV or Walgaš I. While Mauryan India did share points of contact with Parthian Iran, there is no reason to believe that the text of the *Arthaśāstra* directly shaped, or was shaped by, the ruling strategies of the Arsacid kings.[48] Rather, the work is independent testimony that the succession anxieties attested by Strabo and Tacitus did in fact figure in the calculations of ancient rulers, and that the dispatch of princes to the courts of foreign kings was one potential method for the alleviation of such concerns. Regarding Allen's warning, moreover, the appearance of the "political purge" strategy in this Sanskrit text cannot be attributed to the tropes and rhetorical conventions of Roman literature—a textual milieu of which the *Arthaśāstra* is entirely independent. Even if the Arsacid motives attested by Strabo and Tacitus are purely productions of this literary tradition, then, they cannot be dismissed for that reason. In comparative and intercultural context, the political-purge explanation is inherently plausible given the usual dynamics of dynastic politics, and it is explicitly attested in a source from

45. On the composition, redaction, and dating of the *Arthaśāstra*, see Olivelle 2013: 6–31 with the literature cited at nn.15, 49; Bisht 2020: 12–16.

46. Singh 2021: 15.

47. *Arthaśāstra* 7.17.11–14, trans. Olivelle 2013: 323–24; cf. Rangarajan 1992: 562.

48. Like the Arsacids, the Mauryans interacted with the Seleucid dynasty, for instance; see Thapar 2002: 176–78, 182; Ray 2021: 199.

ancient India. It should be numbered among the potential motives of Frahād IV or Walgaš I in sending their children to Rome.

ARSACID FOSTERAGE AND PARTHIAN ROYAL WOMEN

The Jewish author Josephus offers an alternate explanation for the dispatch of Frahād IV's children. For Josephus, the entire episode is part of the story of Thea Musa, one of the most prominent royal women in Arsacid history. As Josephus relates, Musa was given by Augustus to Frahād IV at an uncertain date.[49] She began her life at the Arsacid court as a concubine, but so charmed Frahād that he soon elevated her to the status of wife.[50] The couple had a son, Frahātak.[51] Musa wanted her child to succeed his father as the Arsacid king of kings, but an obstacle stood in the way: Frahād had other sons who apparently outranked Frahātak in the line of succession. Here Rome entered the picture. Musa asked Frahād to send his other children to Rome "as hostages." The king complied, slavishly devoted as he was to Musa's commands. His other sons went to Rome, and Frahātak became the heir apparent. All this appears in Josephus, and nowhere else.[52]

How seriously can this story be taken as an explanation for the dispatch of Arsacids to Rome? Some scholars are prepared to accept Josephus's explanation more or less at face value. Emma Strugnell, for instance, argues that "Phraates [Frahād] IV's decision to send his legitimate heirs to Rome should be conceived not as a sign of deference to Rome, but as the will of Musa. This view is supported by Josephus."[53] Josef Wiesehöfer and Edward Dąbrowa favor a similar interpretation, but with an important variation: in their view, Frahād's dispatch of his children to Rome was no heartless purge, but an act of kindness to spare them the fate of assassination (or worse) after Musa's ascent to power.[54] For J. M. Bigwood, however, Josephus's account contains "something of the truth" but also "much that is unsatisfactory." She compares the account to a folk-tale and prefers to follow Strabo and Tacitus on the matter of Frahād's children.[55] Erich Gruen writes

---

49. Josephus names Musa's giver as "Julius Caesar." But Caesar was assassinated long before Frahād IV's enthronement in 38 B.C.E., so most scholars assume that Augustus must be meant. See Bigwood 2004: 38–39 for discussion.

50. Joseph. *AJ* 18.40. The terms in Greek are *pallakis* (concubine) and *gametēs* (wife).

51. Called Phraataces by Josephus and Cassius Dio (55.10.20, 10a.4). The name *prhtk* / Frahātak is attested in the Nisa ostraca: Diakonoff and Livshits 2001: 179 (no. 2692 line 7); Schmitt 2016: 161 (no. 358). Many scholars refer to Phraataces as Frahād/Phraates V (thus, e.g., Karras-Klapproth 1988: 145; Edwell 2021: 33–34; Olbrycht 2021b; Olbrycht 2021c), but he is never unambiguously referred to by that name in an ancient source. The one possible exception is *Mon. Anc.* 32.1, on which see Nabel 2015: 311–12.

52. Joseph. *AJ* 18.39–44; "as hostages" at 18.42.

53. Strugnell 2008: 283; cf. Schottky 1991: 61–62; Edwell 2021: 33.

54. Wiesehöfer 2010: 187; Dąbrowa 2017: 173; cf. Bivar 1983: 67–68; Gregoratti 2015: 732.

55. Bigwood 2004: 42 (quotation), 46 (folktale).

along similar lines that "[Josephus] here seems less interested in history than in a moralistic pronouncement on the actors of this drama, one that is unrecorded by our other sources."[56] To what extent, then, can Josephus be considered a reliable guide to the issue of Arsacid motives?

On the one hand, there are good reasons to doubt the historical value of the passage. Leonardo Gregoratti, for instance, suggests that Josephus has drawn on a standard set of Greek literary tropes for the representation of Persian royal women in historiography. Like the Atossa of Herodotus or the Parysatis of Ctesias, Josephus's Musa is a scheming, immoral, and ruthless operative who manipulates her husband to brazenly intervene in the otherwise male world of politics.[57] Her portrayal may thus adhere to the classical penchant for recycling Greek historiography on the Achaemenids into Roman historiography on the Arsacids, and it may derive from stock topoi rather than information specific to her case. Also suspicious is Josephus's description of Frahād's would-be successors as "legitimate" children (*gnēsioi* in the Greek)—in contrast, it would seem, to the "illegitimate" Frahātak. The word implies a formal Arsacid hierarchy in which maternity could qualify or disqualify royal children for the kingship. But there is no corroborating evidence for such a system. A key passage from Justin attests primogeniture as the general Arsacid succession rule, but also the considerable latitude that kings enjoyed in determining their successors.[58] Other Greco-Roman authors record that the children of concubines could become Arsacid kings without apparent issue, and Josephus's distinction between legitimate and illegitimate heirs finds no support in internal Parthian sources.[59] These features of the passage raise serious doubts about its value as evidence for Musa's career.

Yet another problematic element is Josephus's reference to the alleged sexual relationship (not a marriage, though this may be implied) between Musa and Frahātak.[60] The existence of such a relationship cannot be otherwise confirmed, but it is plausible enough in a pre-Islamic Zoroastrian milieu where *xwēdōdah* (next-of-kin marriage) was consistently practiced from the Achaemenid through the Sasanian periods. To be sure, mother-son marriages are otherwise unknown from contemporaneous Arsacid sources, which only attest *xwēdōdah* of the

---

56. Gruen 2017: 231. Cf. Allen 2006: 147 ("Josephus's account is a clear polemic against [Musa]").

57. Gregoratti 2013: 184–87. See also Bigwood 2004: 45–47 on parallels to the story of Semiramis.

58. Just. 41.5.9–10. The contention of Harl 2016: 107 that the Arsacid kings followed a "lateral succession principle" is not supported by the evidence.

59. The Arsacid king Walgaš I was the son of a Greek concubine and ruled with the acquiescence of his brothers: Tac. *Ann.* 12.44.2. Internal Parthian evidence has little to say about Arsacid children, but the royal polygamy attested in e.g. the Avroman documents suggests a large pool of royal heirs and an ad hoc, contingent approach to succession. See Madreiter and Hartmann 2021: 237–38 for discussion.

60. Josephus's avoidance of marital terminology is stressed by Schottky 1991: 62; Bigwood 2004: 44; contrast, e.g., Schlude and Rubin 2017: 73. See also Olbrycht 2021c.

brother-sister variety.[61] But the preponderance of evidence from both classical authors and late antique Zoroastrian literature makes it abundantly clear that such unions not only existed, but were judged superior to marriages with nonkin.[62] The relative clarity on this point makes one of Josephus's claims difficult to accept: he writes that the Parthians were scandalized by the sexual relationship between Musa and Frahātak, and that this outrage fueled their eventual rebellion and deposition of the pair. The same evidence that establishes the inherent plausibility of this mother-son union enjoins a rejection of Josephus's testimony on this point. *Xwēdōdah* was unremarkable in pre-Islamic Iran, and it could not have furnished the grounds for a coup d'état, even on the level of rhetoric. The disgust with "incest" belongs to Josephus and his readership, not to the Parthians to whom the emotion is imputed. Such editorializing is typical of the reports on *xwēdōdah* by Greco-Roman authors, who often get the basic parameters of the practice right even as they express their shock and horror at its operation. In sum, Josephus's handling of Arsacid sexuality and marital customs reveals an author who is underinformed about Parthian society and culture. Here, too, his testimony on Musa is suspect.

But there are also reasons to accept the general proposition that Josephus asks the reader to consider, even if the author cannot be trusted on the details of the case itself: the dispatch of certain Arsacids to Rome was influenced by Parthian royal women and their interventions in the politics of succession. In the case of Musa, it is hard to gainsay Josephus's portrayal of this enslaved woman-turned-queen as a canny political operator who reached exceptional heights of power and influence, because Arsacid evidence, namely coinage, produces the same impression. As Bigwood has noted, Musa is the only queen to be both depicted and named on Arsacid numismatic issues (see figure 1), where she appears opposite her son Frahātak with the title of *basilissa*, or queen.[63] The coins cannot be used to confirm specific details from Josephus's account like the supposed sexual relationship between Musa and Frahātak or, still less, the notion that Musa persuaded Frahād to send his other children to Rome. But they do reveal a queen who featured on a key medium of Arsacid political communication in a conspicuous departure from centuries of numismatic precedent. It is easy to imagine such a woman exerting influence in debates over the Arsacid succession, Josephus's use of orientalist and misogynistic tropes notwithstanding.

The particular case of Musa aside, comparative studies of court politics support the idea that Parthian queens could influence fosterage transactions in order

61. See Avroman 1 and 2.

62. From Greco-Roman literature, see esp. Philo, *De specialibus legibus* 3.13 on mother-son marriages. From Zoroastrian literature, see esp. the *Pahlavi Rivāyat* 8c1, 8d1 = Williams 1990: 1.50–53, 2.11–12. On the prevalence and high valuation of *xwēdōdah* marriages in pre-Islamic Iran, see de Jong 1997: 424–32; Vevaina 2018: 121–24.

63. Bigwood 2004: 47. See also Schlude and Rubin 2017: 72–78; Madreiter and Hartmann 2021: 239–40.

FIGURE 1. Tetradrachm of Frahātak (obverse) and Musa (reverse), 2 B.C.E.–4 C.E. Sellwood 1980: 190 (type 58.9). Photo credit: American Numismatic Society (ANS 1944.100.82979).

to pursue their own designs. Josephus's use of Greek literary models to describe the influence of royal women in an eastern court is grounds for caution, but it is not necessarily a reason to discount his testimony. As Lloyd Llewellyn-Jones argues in a recent study of female violence at the Achaemenid court, "what is recorded of Persian royal women are not orientalist fantasies on the part of Greek writers, as might easily be supposed, but accurate reflections of the politicking practices within the royal harem."[64] Influential and politically savvy Persian queens were not merely figments of the Greek imagination. Instead, they were the products of competitive court environments where royal women exercised real power. This dynamic of court life is amply attested in other historical settings. Michael Flower and John Marincola reached much the same conclusion as Llewellyn-Jones about Achaemenid women by way of comparative study with the city of Kano in early modern Nigeria.[65] Leslie Peirce's work on the Ottoman harem explored a period of over a hundred years when the women of the sultan's household were, in her analysis, instrumental "in creating and manipulating domestic political factions, in negotiating with foreign powers, and in acting as regents for their sons."[66] In his comparative studies of pre- and early modern dynasties Jeroen Duindam finds few female rulers or queens regnant, but numerous cases where royal women played pivotal roles in the determination of a king's successor.[67] The sensationalist tendencies of Greco-Roman historiography

---

64. Llewellyn-Jones 2020: 361.

65. Flower and Marincola 2002: 292, citing Mack 1991.

66. Peirce 1993: vii.

67. Duindam 2016: 147–48. On the rarity of ruling queens, see Duindam 2016: 89–95; Duindam 2021: 153–55.

on pre-Islamic Iranian empires should not be ignored, of course. But as Walter Scheidel writes in a discussion of Persian polygamy, "significant structural properties of the putative oriental counterworld constructed by Mediterranean authors coincide far too closely with information transmitted from within these and comparable societies to have been 'constructed' from scratch or distorted beyond recognition."[68] Josephus's tendentious deployment of Musa as a cautionary tale of female royal power is no basis for concluding that her possession of power must be unhistorical.

As for whether an Arsacid royal woman would have chosen to use her court influence to advance the interests of her son, comparative history can once again establish the inherent plausibility of the proposition. In a study of Hellenistic history, Daniel Ogden described dynastic politics as "amphimetric," that is, characterized by factional strife between groups of royal children who had different mothers but the same father.[69] Ogden saw such conflict as a consequence of royal polygyny without formal rules of succession, since Hellenistic kings produced numerous children with numerous mothers but had no clear procedures for establishing a hierarchy among them. Mothers and sons made for natural allies in such an environment, and other maternally defined groups were often their rivals. Hellenistic history does not entirely conform to this paradigm, and Arsacid history does not either—in one case, for instance, an Arsacid succession dispute turned on one dynast's membership in the royal family through his matriline rather than patriline.[70] But the structural features of the Arsacid and Hellenistic royal families match so closely that amphimetric conflict must have figured in the Arsacid case as well.

Nor were the Hellenistic dynasties alone in sharing polygyny, concubinage, and multitudinous royal heirs with the Arsacids. In the late sixteenth century C.E., the Ottoman empire saw fierce competition among numerous royal concubines who vigorously prosecuted their sons' claims to power.[71] Munis Faruqi's survey of princedom in the Mughal empire likewise finds that mothers were central to the lives and political fortunes of their royal sons.[72] Debby Chih-Yen Huang and Paul Goldin discuss polygynous households in early imperial China, where "the emotional bond between a mother and her natural son would often be enhanced because they faced the same rivalries and crises."[73] On balance, then, Musa's effort

68. Scheidel 2009b: 279.

69. Ogden 1999: x.

70. Tac. *Ann.* 6.42.3 has the inhabitants of Seleucia on the Tigris berate Ardawān II for inheriting his Arsacid status only from his mother; on this passage, see further chapter 4. Judicious criticisms of Ogden's view are mounted in Strootman 2014: 94, 103–10; Penrose 2018; Llewellyn-Jones and McAuley 2023: 13–14.

71. Peirce 1993: 23–24; cf. Imber 2002: 91–92.

72. Faruqui 2012: 72.

73. Huang and Goldin 2018: 27; cf. McMahon 2013: 929–32.

to enable her son's accession by purging the Arsacid court of other princes looks eminently plausible in intercultural context.

Ultimately, Josephus's text is a reasonable basis for concluding that the agency of Parthian royal women was one factor behind the submission of Arsacids to Rome. It is probable that the women of the Arsacid court could influence the reigning king's decision to initiate this transaction in the first place, and also that they played a part in determining which Arsacids would go and which would stay once the decision to send children had been made. These propositions are not acceptable simply by virtue of their appearance in Josephus, as some scholars contend, but they can be maintained in light of comparative evidence for dynastic women in other polygynous court environments. It must remain an open question whether a wife or concubine was ever *entirely* responsible for the initiation of a transfer, as Josephus would have it in the case of Musa. Josephus's account is too problematic to serve as conclusive evidence on this point, and no other sources offer a window into this aspect of dynastic politics. One need not accept Josephus's description of Frahād and Musa's agencies as a zero-sum game that reduced Frahād to a mere puppet of his wife's will, and it is better to imagine a dynamic process in which kings and queens negotiated. But Josephus's Musa excursus is a salutary reminder that Arsacid women would have been key players in debates over the future of Arsacid children. Josephus may not be reliable on the details of Musa's case, but he is surely right about this.

A related but distinct interpretation of Musa's story in modern scholarship reveals yet another potential Arsacid motive: against the backdrop of competitive and violent dynastic politics at court, familial compassion may have been just as important as ruthless politicking in determining the fate of the Arsacids of Rome. Wiesehöfer, Dąbrowa, and others understand Frahād IV's decision as an effort to *spare* his children from the brutal measures that attended succession struggles, assassination perhaps above all.[74] Once the king had accepted Frahātak as his heir, the argument goes, he sent his other offspring to Rome to save them from the mass purges that often accompanied the accession of a new king. This question of sentiment cannot be proven on the basis of the direct evidence for this episode. But Josephus twice adduces parental benevolence as an explanation in comparable scenes set at Adiabene. In one passage, the Adiabenian king Monobazus fears that his favorite son, Izates, will be murdered by his jealous brothers, so he sends Izates to grow up at the court of Abinerglos, the king of Spasinou Charax. In a later episode, the same Izates (now king of Adiabene) uses "hostage" submission to both Parthia and Rome as a way to avoid assassinating his brothers and other relatives suspected of coveting his throne.[75] The anthropologist Peter Parkes notes the

---

74. See above, n.54.

75. Joseph. *AJ* 20.22–23, 20.34 (Izates to Abinerglos); 20.29–37 (Izates' brothers and relatives sent to Parthia and Rome); cf. 20.71 (Izates' young children sent to Judaea to study).

frequent appearance of this alleged motive in other historical contexts: "Fears of family violence being done to children—by jealous brothers and agnatic cousins or uncles, as by step-mothers promoting their own offspring—were commonly supposed to explain the out-fostering of heirs in Ireland and Celtic Britain, as in mountain kingdoms of Central Asia." Parkes himself favored the idea that foster-age in these settings aimed "simply to use children as pawns for the construction of familial clientage," but these explanations are not mutually exclusive; indeed, they may even be synergistic and complementary.[76] Clemency and familial affection have no explicit basis in the sources for Musa's reign, then, but comparison suggests that they merit consideration among the diverse set of motives that could have spurred Arsacid kings and queens to send their children to the court of a distant ruler.

A final word on Musa and Frahātak is needed to situate the pair in the development and maintenance of pragmatic misunderstanding between Rome and Parthia. For a few years, the Arsacid empire had an Italian queen and a half-Italian king, and one might well ask: couldn't such rulers have bridged the gap between Roman and Parthian views of Arsacid child circulation? That potential must indeed have existed, but the history of Musa's and Frahātak's reign suggests that it was not fulfilled. In the first place, it should not be an automatic assumption that Musa accepted the cultural valuations of the empire that had reduced her to sexual slavery instead of the one that put her on the throne. Musa surely understood Roman hostageship, but she had as much reason as any Parthian to reject its logics. More importantly, though, Musa was ousted along with her son after only a few years, and the first Parthian queen from the Roman empire was also the last. Where the potential spark of mutual intelligibility and the exchange of cultural views was kindled, it was quickly snuffed out. If Musa was indeed transmitting the Roman view of the Arsacids of Rome, the Parthians shut down the signal before too long. In White's terms, Musa's queenship could have been a step toward meeting on a middle ground. By all indications, however, the Parthians were not interested in scouting this terrain.

EXTINCTION

Another objective that fosterage could serve encompassed the protection of the entire Arsacid dynasty rather than individual members. The installation of Arsacid children at Rome was extermination insurance. Dynasties can go extinct, and the prospect of total annihilation can be a powerful inducement to distribute dynastic eggs among several different baskets on the grounds that geographically dispersed ruling families are harder to eradicate.[77] Dispersal could turn an Arsacid

76. Parkes 2006: 382 (both quotations).
77. van der Steen 2022: 97.

weakness—namely an overabundance of royal children whose competition made succession violent and destabilizing—into a strength. Reigning kings may thus have viewed a fosterage arrangement with the Roman emperor as a guarantee not so much against Roman behavior as against dynastic catastrophe within Parthian territory itself.

One scholar has advanced this thesis about political fosterage, but in the context of late antique Armenian history rather than Roman-Parthian relations in the first century C.E. In his study of *dayeakut'iwn* ("noble fosterage"), Robert Bedrosian located the origins of this institution in the "concern for clan survival" that was widespread among the Armenian noble families living under the Arsacid/ Arshakuni kings.[78] The Armenian clans of *nakharar* status had a tempestuous relationship with the Arshakunis. They acknowledged the dynasty's royal status, but they could also take issue with the royal prerogatives that it claimed for itself. Nor were the *nakharar* families a monolithic group; they could fight each other in addition to the crown. When violence broke out among these ruling clans, its scope could be genocidal. Assassination was employed not only against the adult men and women of the offending family, but against its children too. The aim was the complete elimination of the clan as a political and legal entity. Bedrosian catalogs several episodes along these lines in late antique Armenian historiography.

The Arsacids of Rome offer an early glimpse of the family's late antique profile as both an employer of dynastic annihilation and a survivor of it. By securing the Roman emperor as a foster-father, the dynasty could spread itself out and establish an alternate base of power in case a calamitous event befell it in Parthian territory. This strategy operated in tandem with a second survival mechanism, which was the installation of Arsacid family members on the thrones of Parthian client kingdoms to create "cadet branches" of the dynasty.[79] The most consequential and effective of these initiatives was the one that secured Armenia as an Arsacid territory, an event that is traditionally dated to 63 C.E. It was above all its possession of this kingdom that allowed the dynasty to live on for an additional two centuries when it lost its Iranian empire to the Sasanians in 224 C.E. The Arsacids would hang on in Armenia until 428 C.E., and their base in the Caucasus would grow to encompass nearby Albania as well.[80] These were the collective efforts of a dynasty that knew and understood the dangers of extinction, and that took careful steps to avoid the overconcentration of its family representatives in a single place. In a world where kings and their families were in constant peril from domestic enemies, fosterage could represent a form of contingency planning to guard against total

---

78. Bedrosian 1984: 26.

79. For the term *cadet branch* in general, see Hey 1996: 63; for its use in Parthian history, see Neusner 1966: 6; Gregoratti 2018: 25. On the installation of Arsacids as kings over client territories, see Hauser 2016: 438–39.

80. On the Arsacids of Albania, see recently Gadjiev 2020.

eradication. The Arsacids certainly availed themselves of this strategy in late antique Armenia, and the Arsacids of Rome can be viewed as an earlier instantiation.

KINSHIP AS ITS OWN MOTIVE

While many Arsacid motives stemmed from domestic politics, one incentive to initiate a fosterage arrangement with Rome was interdynastic in scope: the inherent desirability of a kinship bond with the Julio-Claudians. As the preceding discussion has shown, the establishment of kinship could be a means to various ends, but it could also be an end in itself. In diverse historical and regional contexts, geographically disparate dynasties may interliaise because it is only in foreign ruling families that a king or queen can find a partner commensurate with their own royal dignity. Domestic subjects, by contrast, are no more than that—subjects—and thus unsuitable for this purpose. In this respect, rulers may have more in common with each other than with the people whom they rule, regardless of the distance between their dynastic centers. Indeed, geographical separation between members may make interdynastic kinship more valuable rather than less, conferring as it does an "aura of prestige and awe" on the people with knowledge of what is territorially remote.[81] Where such dynamics prevail, a kinship connection with a colleague in world rule can be its own reward.

The reputational stakes of interdynastic kinship are well illustrated in an exchange of letters between two sovereigns from the late Bronze Age. In c. 1327 B.C.E., the Hittite king Šuppiluliuma received a message from an Egyptian queen.[82] According to a later Hittite reproduction, the text read, "My husband died. I have no son. If you would give me one of your sons, he would become my husband. Never shall I pick out a servant of mine and make him my husband!"[83] Šuppiluliuma was wary at first, but an exchange of diplomatic agents verified the story: Egypt had no reigning pharaoh, and the invitation to supply one was genuine. In a second letter, the Egyptian queen reiterated her refusal to take an Egyptian husband. Moreover, she had approached no other foreign ruler with her request. Only a Hittite prince would do.[84] In the end, Šuppiluliuma overcame his suspicion and dispatched his son Zannanza to wed the queen. The young man was assassinated en route to Egypt for reasons that are unclear, for at this point the evidence that supports detailed reconstruction of the episode trails off.

---

81. Helms 1988: 5.

82. Which queen is debated, but inconsequential here. On her identity, see Bryce 1990; Parker 2002: 36–37; Bryce 2003: 179–81 and n.3–4; Miller 2007; Theis 2011; Stavi 2015: 178–82. The date of the letter given above follows Bryce 2003: 181 on the year of the pharaoh's death. But other interpretations are possible; cf. Schneider 2010: 399, 402–3.

83. *The Deeds of Šuppiluliuma* A iii, lines 10–15 = Güterbock 1956: 94 (translation lightly adapted); see also Hoffner in Hallo and Younger 2003: 1.185–92.

84. *The Deeds of Suppiluliuma* A iv, lines 6–13 = Güterbock 1956: 96–97.

The primary source for this interdynastic proposal is *The Manly Deeds of Šuppiluliuma* by the king's son Muršili II, a work that has been pieced together from fragments excavated at the Hittite capital of Hattuša. Shorter references also appear in two "plague prayers" by the same author.[85] Muršili's *Deeds* is a sophisticated work of historiography by a strong literary talent. The author treats the episode from the Hittite side, but in a measured, circumspect fashion free of obvious jingoism.[86] The words of the widowed Egyptian queen quoted above come from Muršili's text, and how faithfully he reproduced her message is an open question. A copy of one of the queen's letters to Šuppiluliuma has also been found at Hattuša, but the text is too fragmentary to shed much light on Muršili's treatment of it. At the very least, Muršili translated the queen's words from Akkadian, the usual language of interstate correspondence in the late Bronze Age, to Hittite, the language in which he wrote the *Deeds* and other works. A more extensive reworking is possible, but not provable on the basis of the extant text.[87] Be that as it may, no scholar questions the basic outlines of the episode as presented by Muršili, and the historicity of the Egyptian queen's request is secure enough.

The queen's proposal shows how the appeal of interdynastic kinship could override and transcend domestic political pressures and state interests. As many discussions of this episode stress, the Hittite kingdom and Egypt were often enemies in the late Bronze Age, when their armies repeatedly clashed over sites in Syria and the Levant.[88] But great power competition did not prevent the Egyptian queen from seeking a Hittite husband. If anything, close rivalry *encouraged* that decision, since only royal coequals could supply a husband commensurate with the queen's rank and prestige. Only the "great king brotherhood," an interdynastic and interstate network of royal kin, would allow the Egyptian queen to escape the undignified fate of marriage to one of her own "servants."[89] This imperative overrode the routine business of foreign relations, armed conflict, and hegemonic competition in peripheral territories. State business operated on one register, interdynastic kinship and its logics on another.

Kinship networking among dynasties can write its own rules, then, and the dynamics of this Bronze Age episode clarify one potential Arsacid motive in seeking Caesarian fosterage. The dictates of royal prestige could have incentivized the Arsacids to secure the most distinguished possible partner in kinship

---

85. Beckman in Hallo and Younger 2003: 1.158; Singer 2002: 67–68.

86. van den Hout 2021: 146. More critical remarks are offered by Miller 2007: 262.

87. Edel 1994: 1.14–15 (text and German translation), 2.22–26 (commentary). Bryce 2003: 184 writes, "In fact we have fragments of the queen's original letter, enough to demonstrate how faithfully Mursili's quotation reflects her actual words." But this assessment is unsupportable without Edel's extensive restorations, which are on based on Muršili's renditions of the queen's letters. Cf. Stavi 2015: 165.

88. Liverani 2001: 192; Bryce 2005: 177–78; Theis 2011: 302; Cline 2014: 67; Wang 2023: 405.

89. Podany 2010: 285–86.

creation—even or perhaps *especially* if that partner presided over a distant imperial competitor. The military and diplomatic clashes of the first centuries B.C.E. and C.E. gave Rome an impression of Parthia as a political formation of comparable size and strength to its own, and it is a reasonable assumption—though not verifiable on current evidence—that Parthia reached a similar conclusion.[90] The rulers of these empires thus had peers in each other that were not to be found within the territories that they ruled. Like Šuppiluliuma's Egyptian interlocutor, the Arsacids may have seen in their imperial rivals the potential for a kinship connection that would befit their high status, even if they cultivated other kinship relations with domestic dependents at the same time. And since intermarriage between the ruling families of Parthia and Rome was a nonstarter, fosterage offered a workaround—an all the more attractive one if cliental fosterage was the dominant institutional framework.

The ability of interdynastic kinship to transcend the squabbles of great power rivalry has been missed by some scholars of ancient interstate relations, especially those who are explicitly or implicitly realist in theoretical orientation. Writing of the Amarna period, for instance, Steven David finds interdynastic kinship (or Podany's "brotherhood of kings") superficial and incapable of explaining the dynamics of late Bronze Age interstate affairs: "That leaders of countries would refer to one another as 'brother' did not prevent them from fearing one another, subverting the power of potential rivals, and occasionally going to war with one another. Precisely because the discourse of brotherhood and family did not cause the leaders to behave in ways inconsistent with Realism, the Constructivist view is found wanting."[91] From the literature on Roman-Iranian relations, a similar assessment is on offer in Beate Dignas and Engelbert Winter's treatment of the Sasanian period: "As a concept, the notion of a 'family of kings' existed throughout the history of Roman–Sasanian relations. West and East agreed on this notion, which contributed to a mutual acknowledgement of the other's sovereignty and compliance with an emerging international law. However, this did not reduce concrete political conflicts between the two."[92] In David's view, interdynastic kinship was entirely inconsequential in ancient interstate politics. Dignas and Winter concede some effect, but ultimately conclude that kinship "did not reduce concrete political conflicts." These discussions are underpinned by similar logic: if interdynastic kinship had been a serious force in foreign relations, then rulers and their empires would have been more benevolent and peaceful toward one another. Since antagonism, brinksmanship, and military conflict persisted even after the establishment of the brotherhood of kings, one must conclude that anarchy, not family, was the

90. For expressions of coequality with Parthia in Roman sources, see Vell. Pat. 2.101.2; Strab. 11.9.2; Plin. *HN* 5.88; Joseph. *AJ* 18.46; Tac. *Ann.* 2.56.1, 2.60.4, 12.10.2, 15.13.2; Cass. Dio 40.14.3; Herodian 4.10.2.

91. David 2000: 64.

92. Dignas and Winter 2007: 233.

ultimate constitutive principle of interstate politics. When the modern analyst strips away the rhetorical cloak of kinship, they expose the timeless realities of foreign affairs: rivalry, competition, and violence unchecked by law or convention.

Such dismissal of kinship goes astray on a number of counts, however. First, both these discussions are premised on the mistaken notion that kin do not fight. Relations among kin are assumed to entail harmony, accord, and peace; the absence of these things means the absence of kinship. These assumptions do not hold up. Many theorists reject the idea that positive emotions like love and affection are essential features of kinship relations. As Cecilia Busby puts it: "However much one loves one's mother's brother, for example, and however much he acts like a father, he remains *categorically* different. The kinship system is categorical, while emotion and affect are individual and haphazard, and one cannot be explained in terms of the other. Not all brothers love their sisters (or even *like* them), yet all brothers *are* related to all sisters in a particular way."[93] In this formulation, affect is incidental to kinship, not a necessary condition for it. Siblings, parents, and children may compete with one another. They may dislike one another, or even hate one another. But these negative emotions do not nullify their kinship, just as positive emotions do not constitute it. Kinship is a system of relatedness that may correlate with certain kinds of sentiments, but it is not premised upon them. It is an error, then, to assume that the creation of a kinship group must necessarily entail harmonious accord among its members.

This conclusion is all the more problematic when the kinship unit under consideration is the dynasty—a type of social group that routinely witnesses violent competition for power within its own ranks. As discussed above, conspiracy, coups, and assassination are rife in the histories of pre- and early modern dynasties across a range of temporal and regional contexts.[94] Such rivalries were often exacerbated by royal polygyny and by the numerous dynastic offspring this practice could produce, though monogamy and limited reproduction (as in Rome) did not guarantee familial harmony either.[95] In the case of the Arsacids, several episodes of intradynastic mass murder are attested, as are polygamy and polygyny.[96] Greco-Roman literature treated these practices in sensationalist fashion, but their main lines are confirmed by internal sources, and in any event, they are unremarkable in comparative perspective. As a typical dynasty, the Arsacid family was subject to typical dynastic infighting, which has lethal consequences for members of the kin group as a matter of course. If in nonruling families kinship often correlates with feelings of love and devotion, in dynasties, it often doesn't.

---

93. Busby 1997: 29 (emphases in the original); quoted in Sahlins 2013: 10.

94. Burling 1974: 256–57; Peirce 1993: 21; Duindam 2016: 87–88, 127–53.

95. Duindam 2016: 121–25. On ancient Mediterranean and Near Eastern marital practices in comparative perspective, see Betzig 1986: 70–78; Scheidel 2009b: 268–99.

96. For mass murder, see the references collected in Nabel 2017a: 81 n.8; cf. Ellerbrock 2021: 40, table 3.2. On polygamy and polygyny, see Madreiter and Hartmann 2021.

Given the regular, violent competition for power in intradynastic contexts, why should interdynastic kin have behaved otherwise? Transimperial kinship groups like those of the late Bronze Age or Roman-Iranian relations pursued the usual rivalries of the dynastic arena, but on an interstate stage. When once disparate ruling families become intertwined through marriage, fosterage, adoption, or other mechanisms, dynastic competition is internationalized. Assassination or factional strife at the domestic level becomes large-scale war in the interstate environment, as rulers prosecute feuds against their interdynastic kin with the state resources at their disposal. For commentators like David, Winter, and Dignas, war puts the lie to interdynastic kinship, on the grounds that family connections must necessarily curb violence. But kinship is premised on no such behavioral imperatives, and in the case of dynasties, comparative evidence shows that kinship is often attended by lethal forms of violence directed against other family members. If the family in question includes the kings of foreign states, war may result. Realism has no monopoly on explaining violence. Whether in the late Bronze Age or in Roman-Iranian relations, war can be explained as dynastic feuding within an interstate brotherhood of kings, waged with the imperial armies that were at the disposal of the brotherhood's various members.

From a realist perspective, interdynastic kinship might seem to entail contradictory propositions: the construction of an interstate ruling family ran the risk of internationalizing the brutal dynastic politics of the domestic court—and yet such family bonds could be treasured, since they connected rulers across great distances to their few peers in power on the entire earth. But the establishment of interdynastic kinship was valued not because it brought peace, but because it reflected the ruling family's prestige and underlined its transcendence of the polity that it governed. By joining an interdynastic "brotherhood of kings," rulers signposted their membership in a rarified political community, an elite family without borders in which kings had more in common with their foreign counterparts than with the subjects they ruled. Antagonistic relations with those same counterparts did not undercut the arrangement and might even *support* it, on the grounds that only a rival in strength was a true peer and thus suitable for kinship networking. When the Arsacids obtained the Roman emperors as foster-fathers for their children, they did not gain peace, but they did gain a relative whose integration into their family structures redounded to their own glory.

By the same token, understanding interdynastic kinship as a systematized political arrangement can account for many practical questions about how the Parthians cemented the Roman emperor as a long-term Arsacid fosterer across generations. Several Arsacid kings died with their children still in Rome, so there were inevitably cases where the newly installed ruler was not the father of his fellow dynasts at the emperor's court. Moreover, emperors like Caligula and Nero may well have been younger than some of their foster-sons, and from the case of Vonones and his brothers, it is clear that certain Arsacids of Rome were already fathers themselves when they entered Roman custody. Comparative evidence can establish that such obstacles would have been perfectly superable, however. As discussed in chapter 1, interdynastic brotherhood was a conveyable relation in the late Bronze Age. If a king died and a son took his place, foreign rulers who had called the elder king "brother" could swiftly transfer that appellation to his child. Such flexibility may well have applied to the Arsacid-Caesarian case, with the positions of father, foster-father, and foster-son readily re-assignable as needed.[97] Cross-culturally, anthropologists have noted methods for the creation of kinship through symbolic acts that circumvent inconvenient realities like age. For instance, grown men may gesturally suckle from the breast of an older woman to obtain milk kinship, as attested in early Islamic Arabia as well as early modern Abkhazia and northern Pakistan.[98] In such situations, neither age nor personal sentiments are significant. What matters is the system of kinship that needs to be created to achieve a social goal. The ancient evidence cannot illustrate in detail how the Parthians would have squared a long-term fosterage arrangement with the ages of its participants, which must sometimes have mismatched the desired parent-child relationship. Comparison suggests, however, that they would have had an array of tactical methods at their disposal to maintain their kinship arrangement of choice.

CONCLUSION

On the Parthian side, then, misunderstanding was pragmatic in multiple senses. Incomprehension of the Roman view was useful, since it allowed stakeholders in Arsacid power to imagine the family atop an interdynastic hierarchy. The utility of this perspective could have meant that, even where commonalities with the Roman understanding appeared, the Parthians looked for ways to avoid mutual intelligibility, not achieve it. Evidence from the Iranianate world is sufficient to show an operative institution of hostageship similar to the Roman one. The parallel was no doubt available to Parthian observers of interstate politics in the first century C.E., and those who were adversarial to the reigning king may well have invoked it to challenge the triumphalist framing of cliental fosterage. But the expediency of the fosterage view for Parthian prestige and self-conception would have been a powerful inducement for its broad adoption. As Upton Sinclair's oft-quoted maxim intones, "it is difficult to get a man to understand something when his salary depends on his not understanding it."[99] At stake for the Arsacids and the

97. See chapter 1 on EA 29. For a corollary in Roman-Parthian relations, see chapter 3 on the *altor Caesaris* of Tac. *Ann.* 6.37.4.

98. Giladi 1999: 28; Parkes 2001: 10; Parkes 2004a: 591. For a potential Assyrian parallel, see Chapman 2012: 6 n.29.

99. Sinclair 1994 [1935]: 109.

agents of their empire was not just wealth, but honor and reputation—a potent disincentive to cultivate shared meanings with Rome.

Pragmatism also allowed the actors of Parthian domestic politics to use the submission of Arsacid children to pursue internal objectives that had little to do with the empire's relationship with Rome. The reigning Arsacid king had a motive and, thanks to the emperor, an outlet for purging rebellious princes who might seek to supplant him, whether on their own initiative or as the pawns of a rebellious aristocrat. But the practice also benefited the dynasty as a whole. It integrated a powerful foreign ruler into the ranks of Arsacid kin, which conferred prestige in and of itself, and it offered a form of insurance against dynastic extinction by dispersing the family's scions across a wider territory. The interests of royal women mattered, too. Arsacid sons were numerous, and their mothers had scope to exercise agency through their efforts to determine which children, precisely, would be sent to Rome to effect a fosterage relationship. The Arsacids of Rome and the cultural miscommunication behind them were useful not merely as instruments of interdynastic relations, but as a form of internal regulation. Parthia got maximal mileage out of misunderstanding.

3

Reception

The Arsacids at Rome

What did the Romans make of the Arsacids who arrived in their city? How did they understand who these figures were, and how could their residence in Italy be explained? In this chapter, I argue that two paradigms shaped Rome's view of its Arsacid residents. The dominant one was a tradition of hostageship that construed the Arsacids of Rome as tokens of Roman supremacy over the Parthian empire. The second, less prevalent one—abstruse but still detectable in the evidence—was patronal fosterage. Previous scholarship has sketched the outlines of these paradigms, but the relationship between them has yet to be clarified, and no treatment has comprehensively integrated the sources for the Arsacids of Rome. I survey the full range of Roman views here to describe the Roman side of pragmatic misunderstanding with Parthia: the Arsacids buttressed Roman pretensions to world rule first and foremost as hostages, but also as foster-children.

The imperialist dimension of hostage taking in Roman political culture is well established, and several scholars have demonstrated that Romans of the early principate saw Arsacid "hostages" as proof of Parthian inferiority. Josef Wiesehöfer has shown how the reception of Arsacid dynasts was collocated with Parthia's return of the standards in 19 B.C.E. to establish "the irreversible division of roles between Roman masters and Parthian servants."[1] In a similar vein, Elisabeth Nedergaard writes that "Augustus presented the [Arsacid] princes as proof of what he called a relation of '*amicitia*' between Rome and Parthia. It is evident from his words that this relation was not an equal one."[2] Such interpretations have made valuable

1. Wiesehöfer 2010: 189: "die unumkehrbare Rollenverteilung zwischen römischen Herren und parthischen Dienern."
2. Nedergaard 1988: 111.

contributions to the historiographical rehabilitation of the Parthian empire, since they show that Arsacid inferiority was a construction of the Roman sources rather than an objective political fact.[3]

As far as hostageship is concerned, however, no single treatment has traced the entire Julio-Claudian arc of what I will here call "Arsacid exhibition," by which I mean the repeated, quasi-triumphal practice of displaying Arsacid dynasts to Italian audiences as symbols of Rome's ascendance over Parthia. Three such events under Augustus, Caligula, and Nero shaped the place of Parthia in the Roman worldview and impressed upon the emperor's subjects how the Arsacids were to be regarded. The enormous public profile of these exhibitions explains why hostageship, not fosterage, was the primary classification assigned to the Arsacids of Rome. It was through spectacle that most Romans were introduced to their city's Arsacid residents, and the jingoistic nature of such displays helped cement the designation of the Arsacids in the extant Roman literary sources as *obsides* in Latin or *homēroi* in Greek.

In addition to the dominant discourse of hostageship, some sources also adumbrate an understanding of the Arsacids of Rome as Julio-Claudian kin, and a few commentators have touched on this dimension as well. Taking their cues from a surge of research on the Roman family and especially on the *domus* or *familia Augusta*, these scholars argue that the subordination of Roman imperial machinery to the structures of the Julio-Claudian family extended to the Arsacids, who were placed under the "parentage" of the Roman emperor—a form of "personal international relations," in Beth Severy's words.[4] Meret Strothmann is explicit: "with their reception, the sons of the Parthians became members of the *familia Caesaris*."[5] Ann Kuttner reaches the important conclusion that fosterage and kinship could coexist with the more belligerent dimensions of hostageship. As she puts it, the Arsacids could be "welcomed into the imperial *domus*" and at the same time "displayed as emblems of Roman triumph and superiority"—a reception that could even be accompanied by a simultaneous effort to give them "open honor."[6] Other historians have discussed the Arsacids alongside dynasts from Rome's provincial or "client" kingdoms who also had a familial relationship with the emperor.[7]

But while the literature on the early Principate as an imperial household has brought the familial aspect of Julio-Claudian politics into clearer focus, the patronal nature of Roman fosterage has yet to be fully reconstructed, and perhaps more importantly, it has never been contrasted with the cliental form of the practice

---

3. On these lines see also Ziegler 1964: 52; Dąbrowa 1987: 63; Strothmann 2012: 91; Gregoratti 2015: 732; Gregoratti 2020: 82.

4. Severy 2003: 150.

5. Strothmann 2012: 96: "Mit ihrer Aufnahme werden die Söhne der Parther Mitglieder der *familia Caesaris*."

6. Kuttner 1995: 112–13.

7. See Allen 2006: 135–36; Kleiner and Buxton 2008: 59–60.

on the Parthian side. Key pieces of Roman evidence have more to say on Arsacid-Caesarian kinship than previous discussions have made clear, and passages from the *Res Gestae*, Ovid, and Tacitus will be examined here with this issue in mind. The chief shortcoming of previous discussions, however, is the failure to put Roman ideas in dialogue with a Parthian view that has been independently reconstructed on the basis of Near Eastern sources. Where the last chapters concluded that cliental fosterage was the primary framework in Arsacid Iran, this one shows that—to the limited degree that the fosterage paradigm gained purchase in Rome—the operative Roman model was patronal. Whether through hostageship or fosterage, then, misunderstanding reigned, and the Romans, like the Parthians, could see the Arsacids of Rome as a sign of their own supremacy.

ARSACID EXHIBITION

The majority of the Roman sources for the Arsacids in Italy are the productions of emperors and lettered elites, and they equate Arsacid residence in Rome with Parthian submission. While Augustus's reference to his possession of Arsacid "pledges" (*pignora*) is a more complex statement than is usually acknowledged, Nedergaard and others have rightly shown how the passage claims the higher ground in an unequal Roman-Parthian relationship.[8] Moreover, the literary sources that constitute the bulk of the direct evidence for the Arsacids of Rome suggest that Roman elites may have been even more triumphalist than the emperors themselves. Velleius's contention that Frahād IV sent his children to Rome "in fear of the reputation of such a great name [i.e. Caesar]" is one case where an Augustan author goes even farther than Augustus himself in the chest-thumping ascription of supremacy to an Arsacid hostage taker.[9] Suetonius offers a similar assessment, for he mentions the sons of Frahād as one of several signs that the Parthians "yielded" to the emperor.[10] Moreover, the widespread adoption of this view by later Roman authors like Festus, Justin, and Orosius shows that it predominated in Roman historical memories of the Arsacids.[11]

As previously discussed, a different set of authors did not attribute Arsacid "hostage" submission to fear, or not solely to fear, but their testimony does not overturn the proposition that the Arsacids were, in the eyes of most Romans, Caesarian trophies from a Parthian victory. Strabo's discussion of Parthian internal politics as the impetus for hostage submission coexists with a different passage in his work where the geographer speaks of Parthian obsequiousness and Roman

---

8. *Mon. Anc.* 32.2; but on a possible invocation of kinship in this passage, see below. Statement of unequal relations: Nedergaard 1988: 111; cf. Drijvers 1998: 290; Master 2016: 96; Olbrycht 2018: 391; Gregoratti 2020: 82; Álvarez-Pedrosa 2022: 109.

9. Vell. Pat. 2.94.4.

10. Suet. *Aug.* 21.3.

11. Just. 42.5.11–12; Fest. *Brev.* 19.4; [Aurel. Vict.] *Epit.* 1.8; Oros. 6.21.29; Eutrop. *Brev.* 7.9.

preeminence.[12] Modern scholars may see a contradiction, but Strabo evidently did not. To his mind, domestic motives must have been compatible with a readiness to appease Rome.[13] The same can be said of Josephus. In his account, hostage submission is purely a result of conditions at the Arsacid court, and interstate relations with Rome do not factor into his explanation at all.[14] Yet he, too, imagines the Parthians furious at the degrading nature of the practice, since the transaction relegated their empire to an inferior position.[15] Consideration of Parthian motives did not deter Roman authors from interpreting Arsacid hostageship as a sign of Rome's superiority.

The exception is Tacitus, but his divergence on this point should be read as pushback against the mainstream imperial chauvinism of his peers. Frahād IV, Tacitus says, was motived "not so much by fear of us [the Romans] as by mistrust of his countrymen," and later Walgaš I sent Arsacids "in order to prepare war from an advantageous position—or to remove those suspected of rivalry through a nominal hostage submission."[16] Both statements trade on a prevailing Roman belief that the surrender of *obsides* is tantamount to political subjection. Tacitus anticipates that the reader will automatically supply fear of Rome as the Parthian motive, and his sentence undercuts the assumption. As scholars have shown, Tacitean historiography routinely challenges such blithe overconfidence in Roman imperialism, and while it may go too far to call this a programmatic objective, it is at least a recurring theme in his work.[17] Tacitus does indeed push back against the notion that the Arsacids of Rome were trophies, then, but his stance is that of a contrarian attacking what is otherwise a widespread presumption.

If emperors and lettered elites held Rome's Arsacids to be tokens of eastern victory, at least for the most part, what about the rest of Roman society? The evidence furnishes only a tenuous basis for the investigation of this topic, but one approach is to look at the spectacles where the Arsacids were marketed to mass audiences. These exhibitions have been studied individually, but they represent a consistent practice that ran from Augustus through Nero. For as long as Arsacids arrived in Rome, they were displayed to the public in elaborate, choreographed ceremonies. Individual responses are irrecoverable, but it is possible to speak about the precedents of such events, their place in the public fashioning of Roman imperialism, and the spirit in which they were celebrated.

What emerges is a tradition of Arsacid exhibition that evolved from the Republican triumphal display of foreign dignitaries to assert and celebrate Roman suzerainty over distant regions. This is not to say that the events themselves were

12. Strab. 16.1.28 (Parthian domestic politics); 6.4.2 (Roman dominance).
13. E.g. Drijvers 1998: 289; Olbrycht 2018: 392–94.
14. Joseph. *AJ* 18.41–42.
15. Joseph. *AJ* 18.47.
16. Tac. *Ann.* 2.1.2, 13.9.1.
17. Syme 1958: 529–30; Allen 2006: 224–26; Adler 2011: 136–39.

formal triumphs by the criteria of the late republic. They were not, especially given the ritual's shifting boundaries during the transition from republic to empire.[18] But Arsacid exhibition took its cues from the assertion of conquest that the triumph represented, and the carefully stage-managed presentation of "barbarian" royalty was a practice whose historical antecedents lay in the parades of the late republic. So while the Julio-Claudian emperors never sent an army into Parthia, to say nothing of actually conquering it, they did not need to, in a sense. The Arsacids of Rome gave them the tools to achieve emblematic domination of their eastern neighbors, which, in view of the risks and costs of military expeditions and direct administration, might even have been preferable to the genuine article.[19]

In their efforts to stage the subjugation of Parthia, the Julio-Claudians could draw on republican precedents, but with the creative license that came from the confinement of the triumph to members of their family alone. The employment of hostages and prisoners has been well treated by a profusion of recent studies on the triumph, which have clarified the role of captive bodies in heightening the theatrical impact of the procession.[20] In two republican cases, the sources designate certain participants as hostages.[21] But these figures are mentioned in the same breath as other captive royalty, and the distinction between hostage and prisoner seems to have been subject to elision, both for spectators who attended the events and the authors who wrote about them later.[22] What mattered was the social rank of the coerced foreign dignitary, and the higher, the better. That principle remained in effect even as the ritual was otherwise transformed in the late republic and early empire. Augustus and his successors exploited their opportunities to exhibit high-status foreigners in triumphs and related public spectacles—and the Arsacids of Rome were among their most prominent showpieces. Three episodes show the Julio-Claudian emperors drawing on republican triumphal precedents with their Arsacids as the main attractions.

The first Roman exhibition of Arsacid dynasts was organized by Augustus. The date is not specified, but it was probably not long after the first coordinated transfer

18. On changes to the triumph during the late republic, see Lange 2016b: 71–94. On the changes under Augustus and the later Julio-Claudians, see Itgenshorst 2008; Itgenshorst 2016; Goldbeck 2016.

19. When territory across the Euphrates was later annexed under Septimius Severus, for instance, Cassius Dio (75.3.3) complained that it brought nothing except "continuous wars and enormous expenditures."

20. See esp. Allen 2006: 97–101; Beard 2007: 107–42; Östenberg 2009: 128–67. Additional recent works on the triumph include Itgenshorst 2005; Krasser et al. 2008; Pittenger 2009; Goldbeck and Wienand 2016. Versnel 1970 remains foundational.

21. Hostages in the triumph of Quinctius Flamininus in 193 B.C.E.: Liv. 34.52.9; Eutrop. 4.2.3; Oros. 4.20.2. Pompey's in 61 B.C.E.: Plut. *Pomp.* 45.4; App. *Mith.* 117. The Iberian hostages who marched in Pompey's triumph were likely the children of the Iberian king Art(h)oces: Flor. 1.40.28; Cass. Dio 37.2.7.

22. Östenberg 2009: 166–67.

under Frahād IV in 19–9 B.C.E.[23] The occasion is described only by Suetonius, who includes it in a section on Augustan spectacles that took various forms and featured diverse participants:[24]

> Ad scaenicas quoque et gladiatorias operas et equitibus Romanis aliquando usus est, verum prius quam senatus consulto interdiceretur. Postea nihil sane praeterquam adulescentulum Lycium honeste natum exhibuit, tantum ut ostenderet, quod erat bipedali minor, librarum septemdecim ac vocis immensae. Quodam autem muneris die Parthorum obsides tunc primum missos per mediam harenam ad spectaculum induxit superque se subsellio secundo collocavit. Solebat etiam citra spectaculorum dies, si quando quid invisitatum dignumque cognitu advectum esset, id extra ordinem quolibet loco publicare, ut rhinocerotem apud Saepta, tigrim in scaena, anguem quinquaginta cubitorum pro Comitio.

> [Augustus] used to sometimes employ even Roman knights at theatrical or gladiatorial games, but before this was forbidden by a decree of the Senate. After that he exhibited no one of respectable parentage except for a certain young man named Lycius, and him only as a curiosity, because he was less than two feet tall, weighed seventeen pounds, and had a stentorian voice. But on the day of one of his festivals he led the first Parthian hostages to have been sent [to Rome] through the middle of the arena and sat them above him in the second row. Moreover, scheduled performances aside, it was his habit to put on special exhibitions in any convenient place if something novel and worth knowing about had been brought in—for instance a rhinoceros in the Saepta, a tiger on stage, and a snake of 50 cubits in front of the Comitium.

What is most striking about the inclusion of the Arsacids in this passage is that they were ostensibly on hand to watch a spectacle, not to be the subject of one. They joined the emperor in the audience, after all, and in formal terms the show would have begun only after that point. But Suetonius does not describe the content of this spectacle, and the omission suggests that the Parthians themselves became the main attractions. Public interest was no doubt stimulated by the manner of their introduction: Augustus marched them through the middle of the display ground in what could only have been the most ostentatious possible path to their seats. While the Arsacids of Rome were not performers in the same way that actors or gladiators were, then, their function at this spectacle was nevertheless to be viewed rather than to view.

Suetonius's testimony also illustrates how, like many royal hostages of the republican period, the Arsacids were treated both as dignitaries and as exotic curiosities.

23. Sonnabend 1986: 256 and Wiesehöfer 2010: 188 and n.10 connect the Suetonius passage with the Arsacid child that came into Augustus's custody during the Tirdād episode (see table 1 for sources) rather than the 19–9 B.C.E. transfer under Frahād IV. But Suetonius speaks of a group in the plural, which cannot be a reference to the young prince who accompanied Tirdād; cf. Louis 2010: 349–50; Wardle 2014: 328–29; Schlude 2020: 98.

24. Suet. *Aug.* 43.3–4.

The *autem* that begins the operative sentence in Suetonius acknowledges the royal heritage of the hostages. As with Lycius, the text presents the Arsacids as exceptions to the rule that elites should not participate in spectacles.[25] But the author concludes the passage with a list of fantastical creatures that Augustus produced for the entertainment of the Roman people: a rhinoceros, a tiger, and a giant snake. Such creatures were still novelties, but Roman audiences had long been accustomed to the exhibition of animals that represented newly conquered territories.[26] The proximity of the Arsacids to these exotic curiosities in Suetonius's text is no accident. Just as the display of a tiger on a Roman stage showed the long reach of the emperor's arm into the remote east, so too the parading of Parthian royalty furnished a potent symbol of control over a land freshly reconfigured as the *alter orbis*, the "other world."[27]

The employment of spectacles to articulate Parthia's relationship to Rome would later continue with perhaps the most grandiose public display of Augustus's reign: the Salaminian *naumachia* ("sea battle") of 2 B.C.E. Held in the heart of the city near the Tiber island, the massive display involved the excavation of a pit some 500 by 350 meters in area, with thirty ships and over three thousand men (not counting the rowers) participating as combatants—at least according to Augustus, who thought the event important enough to include in his *Res Gestae*.[28] Dio is the only historian to mention the assigned identities of the competing sides, whom he calls "Persians and Athenians."[29] Those designations are supported by Ovid, a contemporary who probably attended the event himself. He describes a spectacle of "Persian and Cecropian ships"; the latter term is a reference to Cecrops, the mythical king of Athens.[30] The "Athenians" won.[31] The details sufficiently establish that Augustus had reenacted the battle of Salamis, originally fought in 480 B.C.E. between an Athenian-led Greek fleet and the Persian armada of the Achaemenid king Xerxes. In front of one of the largest crowds ever assembled for a Roman spectacle, the emperor chose to present a bygone triumph of Greece over Persia from an era when Rome had yet to arrive as an imperial power.

25. On late republican / early imperial interdictions against senatorial and equestrian participation in public spectacles, see Louis 2010: 348–49; Wardle 2014: 324–29, with consideration of Lycius's status and origin at 328.

26. Östenberg 2009: 168–84; cf. Beard 2007: 321; Östenberg 2014.

27. On the connection between tigers and Indian embassies, see Cass. Dio 54.9.8; Strab. 15.1.73; Flor. *Epit.* 2.34.62–63. On Parthia as *alter orbis*, see Sonnabend 1986; Shayegan 2011: 334–35; Nabel 2019b: 336.

28. *Mon. Anc.* 23. The other ancient sources include Vell. Pat. 2.100.2; Suet. *Aug.* 43; Tac. *Ann.* 12.56.1, 14.15.2; Cass. Dio 55.10.7–8, 66.25.3; Front. *Aq.* 1.22.

29. Cass. Dio 55.10.7–8.

30. Ov. *Ars Am.* 1.171–72; discussion in Hollis 1977: 64; Bowersock 1984: 175.

31. On whether the outcome was incidental or planned, see Coleman 1990: 71; Coleman 1993: 69; Wardle 2014: 324.

To what end? While the east-west opposition of the *naumachia* might have evoked Augustus's defeat of Antony and Cleopatra at Actium, the outcome of Salamis was also pressed into service as a frame for Roman-Parthian relations.[32] Three features linked the display to contemporary eastern affairs. First, the show was staged in connection with the dedication of the temple of Mars Ultor, a structure that Augustus explicitly associated with the restoration of Rome's standards and prisoners by Frahād IV.[33] Second, the emperor's adopted son Gaius Caesar was about to depart for Parthia in order to settle the dispute that had arisen over Frahātak's activity in Armenia.[34] Third and most importantly, the Arsacids had been conflated with the Achaemenids in Roman thinking about the Parthian east. The "Persians" who went down in defeat at this reenactment could therefore be understood as the direct predecessors of the Parthian empire. By extension, the Roman audience was invited to identify with the Athenians and their Greek allies.[35] The effect of the *naumachia*, then, was to graft Roman-Parthian relations onto a deeply rooted civilizational struggle between the Mediterranean and Persia.

Spectacles, then, were one place where Rome's relationship to Parthia was presented for public consumption, stage-managed for proper effect, and infused with world-historical meaning, and the appearance of the Arsacids in the arena was no exception. Augustus's exhibition of these recent Parthian arrivals—ostensibly as audience members, but in fact as showpieces—was proof in the flesh that the east had been tamed. Like rhinoceroses and tigers brought from afar, the appearance of the Arsacids within a Roman spectacular framework furnished a potent demonstration of the emperor's power to superintend the kingdom that their family ruled. Parallels to earlier displays of "hostages" in Roman triumphs would have been easy to draw, and just as in the republican period, the bodies of those from the fringes of Roman power would have been among the most useful props in the performance of empire without end.

The arrival of the Arsacids at Rome coincided with the proliferation of visual media that represented Parthians, and the submissive overtones of hostageship neatly dovetailed with the iconography of subjugation that some—though not all—of these works employed. As a ruler who harnessed "the power of images," Augustus was quick to promote his management of the Parthian east in art.[36] Perhaps the most widely disseminated image of a Parthian circulated on the emperor's coins heralding the return of the standards in 19 B.C.E.—an event in political history that featured on more coin types than any other Augustan campaign.[37]

---

32. Swan 2004: 100–1 mentions the echo of Actium that the event might have provided.

33. For the connection with the *naumachia*, see Vell. Pat. 2.100.2; Cass. Dio 55.10.6–9.

34. On this campaign, see Luther 2010; Schlude 2020: 102–4.

35. Syme 1984: 922; Bowersock 1984: 175; Spawforth 1994: 238–42; Sumi 2005: 267–68; Lerouge 2007: 125; Hardie 2007: 129–30; Shayegan 2011: 338–40.

36. Quotation from Zanker 1988.

37. Rose 2005: 23. On the numismatic evidence generally, see Van der Vin 1981.

FIGURE 2. Denarius of Augustus, 19 B.C.E.–4 B.C.E. The obverse shows the deity Feronia. On the reverse, a kneeling Parthian proffers a Roman standard. *RIC* 1 no. 288. Photo credit: American Numismatic Society (ANS 1944.100.24299).

These issues depicted a kneeling Parthian submissively handing over a Roman standard, drawing on the posture of subjugated barbarians from the visual language of the late republic (figure 2).[38] Moreover, a triumphal arch in the Forum showed Augustus riding a quadriga and flanked by Parthians, who stood on a level below his own.[39] One of them—this time standing in "heroic diagonal" rather than kneeling—proffered a standard to the emperor.[40] The image of the Parthian subordinate was taken up in other works of art from the Augustan period. Fragments of three statues of a visually similar type (the so-called "kneeling barbarians/Orientals") have been dated to the late first century B.C.E. (figure 3). They may have originally been part of a single monument, supporting a bronze tripod dedicated by Augustus to commemorate his "defeat" of the Arsacid kingdom.[41] The image is found in other visual media, as well. Glass gems dating to the Augustan period and produced on a large scale show two kneeling Parthians offering up standards to the goddess Victory, who advances Roman claims to world rule by standing atop a globe.[42] The Homeric scene on one of the Hoby cups showing

38. E.g. *RIC* 1 no. 287–88 (Sutherland and Carson 1984: 62).

39. The arch does not survive, but can be reconstructed on the basis of literary, numismatic, and archaeological evidence; see Rose 2005: 28 n.41 for literature. For the literary evidence, see Cass. Dio 54.8.3; Schol. Veron. in Verg. *Aen.* 7.605 with Rich 1998: 98. Depictions on coins: *RIC* 1 no. 508 (Sutherland and Carson 1984: 82, from Pergamon, 19/18 B.C.E.); *RIC* 1 no. 131 (Sutherland and Carson 1984: 50, from Spain, 18/17 B.C.E.); *RIC* 1 no. 359 (Sutherland and Carson 1984: 68, from Rome, 16 B.C.E.).

40. On the posture of the Parthians on the arch, contrast Rose 2005: 33 with Osgood 2018: 209.

41. Schneider 1986: 18–97; Schneider 2007: 71–72. But cf. the skepticism of Rose 2005: 24 n.22 on this point.

42. Maderna-Lauter 1988: 459, 470–71 (no. 264); Schneider 2007: 61.

FIGURE 3. Colossal statue of a kneeling Parthian from Rome, first century B.C.E.with later reconstructions (Copenhagen Glyptotek). The platform held up by his right arm originally supported a larger structure. This image is a derivative of *Kneeling Barbarian* by Wikimedia Commons user Richard Mortel, used under CC BY 2.0 DEED. This work is licensed under CC BY-SA 4.0 by the author.

Priam's supplication of Achilles probably evoked Parthian affairs, as well; given his Parthian dress, Priam might have been seen as an Arsacid submitting to his counterpart Augustus/Achilles (figure 4).[43] These works were not all commissioned or created by the Augustan regime, of course. Collectively, however, they reflect the triumphalism over Parthia that the emperor espoused and promoted. These abject figures in trousers, tunics, and Phrygian caps would have sent a clear

43. Vermeule 1968: 125; Dowling 2006: 144–45 and n.45.

FIGURE 4. Roman silver cup showing Priam and Achilles. Made and signed by Cheirisophos and found in Hoby, Denmark (c. 30 B.C.E.–40 C.E.). Photo credit: National Museum of Denmark.

message: Parthia might be a world apart from the Mediterranean, but it had been humbled by Roman power all the same.

Roman viewers may or may not have immediately associated such figures with royal hostages, but the exhibition of the Arsacids of Rome would have worked in tandem with these visual media to create the impression of Arsacid subordination. Attempts to identify Parthians in Augustan art with specific historical figures have proven contentious. The Parthian figure on the breastplate of the Primaporta Augustus, for instance, has variously been interpreted as Frahād IV, one of his children, a Zoroastrian deity, or simply a generalized Parthian (figure 5).[44] Definitive identifications exclusive of other possibilities are hard to maintain, and it is best to assume a range of understandings among contemporary viewers. Even so, the Arsacids of the imperial court are likely to have been the only Parthians that most Romans ever saw in person. Arsacid "hostages" provided flesh and blood referents for the beaten, cowering easterners that featured so prominently in the visual media of the age. As the emperor crafted an image of Roman ascendancy over the Parthian kingdom, he put the Arsacids of Rome at the center of the frame.

What did Frahād's offspring make of their own display? The available evidence affords minimal insight, but one inscription presents a contrast with the Roman

---

44. See the various identifications in Kähler 1959: 16; Bastet 1966: 80; Jucker 1977; Van der Vin 1981: 120–21; Zanker 1988: 188–92; Simon 1991: 207–16; Schneider 1998: 97–99; Schäfer 1998: 84–92; Kuttner 1999: 117–18; Rose 2005: 24–28; Pollini 2012: 187. The identifications in older studies are tabulated in Jucker 1977: 37.

FIGURE 5. Parthian and Roman figures on the breastplate of the Primaporta Augustus. This image is a derivative of *Augusto di Prima Porta* by Wikimedia Commons user Sailko, used under CC BY-SA 3.0 DEED. This work is licensed under CC BY-SA 4.0 by the author.

ideology crafted through Arsacid exhibition. It is an epitaph in Latin found on the Via Flaminia at Rome that marked the tomb, now lost, of Seraspadanes and Rhodaspes. Presumably composed by the remaining Arsacids of Rome, the short text describes each brother as a "son of Frahād [IV] Arsaces, king of kings; a Parthian."[45] Neither hostageship nor fosterage figures in the epitaph. What matters instead is the royal titulature of the Arsacid kingship. As Parthian coinage and other internal sources show, "king of kings" was a traditional expression of world rule in Arsacid ideology, articulating a political vision in which various far-flung kingdoms were united under the Arsacid banner.[46] If Augustus's display of Arsacid "hostages" was a sign of his supremacy over Parthia, then, the invocation of Frahād IV in the epitaph of Seraspadanes and Rhodaspes told a different story. The Arsacids who composed this text described their ancestral king with a title that expressly proclaimed him to be a ruler without peer.

The absence of the word hostage from the stone is also significant, because other foreigners did include that label on their funerary monuments. A Parthian example survives in the Latin epitaph of a woman named Ulpia Axse, identified in the text as a "hostage of the Parthians." Axse is otherwise unknown, but onomastics suggest Iranian heritage and the acquisition of a husband during her life at Rome.[47] Most scholars date the inscription to the second century c.e., when Rome launched several invasions of Parthian territory, and Axse's hostageship may have begun during one of those campaigns.[48] She and her family saw fit to include her hostage status on her funerary monument; they must have considered it central to her identity. The same can be said for Sitalces, a Thracian who lived during the reign of Augustus. His epitaph, shared with his sister Julia Phyllis, specifies that he was a hostage.[49] Self-designation as a hostage is rare on funerary texts, to be sure. But the option was available, and at least two hostages took it. Seraspadanes and Rhodaspes did not, despite the premium that the Augustan regime placed on their supposed hostageship. Instead, they chose to memorialize the supreme status of their father.

Of course, even an Arsacid expression of supremacy could be coopted in a Roman imperial landscape. The convex surface of Seraspadanes and Rhodaspes's epitaph suggests that it belonged to a circular tomb, a form employed by many Romans during the late republic and early empire, including Augustus himself. The monument may have been located in a section of the Via Flaminia that hosted

---

45. *CIL* 6.1799 = *ILS* 842 = Hackl et al. 2010: 2.436; cf. Strab. 16.1.28.

46. On "king of kings" as an Arsacid title, see Shayegan 2011: 41–247.

47. *AE* 1979: 78: *opses* [an alternate orthography for *obses*] *Parthorum*. On the onomastics, see Chaumont 2002.

48. Likely second century c.e. date: Priuli 1977: 332–33; Ricci 1996: 576–78; Chaumont 2002; Álvarez Pérez-Sostoa 2010: 173.

49. *CIL* 6.26608 = *ILS* 846.

the tombs of several foreign kings.[50] The structure could thus be interpreted as proof of the cosmopolitan character of Rome's empire: if even the princes of Parthia were living and dying in the city, adopting Latin, and erecting tombs in local fashion, was there any corner of the world that could escape the centripetal force of Roman power? The dynasts of a fearsome and remote foreign empire whose ruler styled himself a king of kings now reposed along a Roman road, perhaps gathered in assemblage with other deceased foreign potentates, a testament to the center of gravity in world politics. There is no evidence that Augustus or his successors explicitly instrumentalized the tombs of the Arsacids of Rome in this manner. But the framing of Arsacid exhibition may have meant that they did not need to, since the emperor had taught his subjects to regard the Arsacid presence in the city as a token of Parthia's submission. The funerary monuments of the Arsacids of Rome would have continued to underline this point even after their deaths.

The second major display of Arsacids was mounted by Caligula as part of his infamous bridge procession on the Bay of Naples in 39 C.E.[51] Over the course of two days, the emperor paraded with great fanfare across a three-mile-long pontoon that ran from Baiae to Puteoli.[52] The elusive meaning of the Baiae spectacle has fueled debate. What did Caligula mean to do, and how did his contemporaries understand the proceedings? The ancient sources offer various explanations for Caligula's construction of the bridge.[53] For their part, modern commentators have connected the affair to several aspects of Caligula's principate, including the abortive British and German campaigns, the relationship between the emperor and the senatorial aristocracy, and, of course, the emperor's personal psychology and alleged madness.[54]

But while divergent scholarly assessments have clarified many features of this abstruse display, there are good reasons to understand the Baiae procession as a reassertion of Julio-Claudian mastery over the Parthian east through the exhibition of an Arsacid "hostage." The Parthian dimension of the spectacle has not escaped notice, and Donna Hurley has made the case that the show constituted a "surrogate triumph over the East."[55] But the importance of Rome's newest Arsacid arrival to the episode has not been sufficiently acknowledged or contextualized.

50. Ricci 1996: 569; Álvarez-Pedrosa 2022: 111. On circular tombs, see Davies 2000: 13–19; Davies 2010: 227–28.

51. For the date, see Wardle 2007.

52. On the geographical termini of the pontoon, see Wardle 1994: 189.

53. Sen. *De Brev. Vit.* 18.5; Joseph. *AJ* 19.6; Suet. *Cal.* 19.3; Cass. Dio 59.17.1; [Aurel. Vict.] *Epit.* 3.9.

54. Scholarly discussions of Baiae with respect to the army and Caligula's British and German campaigns: Kleijwegt 1994: 664; Winterling 2011: 129–30. Slight to senatorial aristocracy: Winterling 2011: 131. Demonstration of manhood: Barrett 1989: 212. The literature on the question of Caligula's madness is large; see Winterling 2009: 103–19, with references.

55. Hurley 1993: 73–74. Balsdon 1934: 53 made much of Dārāw's participation, but held that Caligula's intention was to impress the Parthian visitor, not his Italian audience; cf. Maurer 1949: 100.

Caligula's exhibition of this dynast followed closely on the example that Augustus had set, and the episode shows the development of a tradition as much as it does the emperor's eccentricities.

The newest Arsacid to join the group in Rome was Dārāw (Darius in Latin), the son of Ardawān II, and like the children of Frahād IV, he was trotted out as a prize of conquest. Although the chronology is disputed, Dārāw had been handed over to Lucius Vitellius in c. 36 C.E. and would have recently arrived in Italy at the time of the Baiae procession.[56] His participation in the spectacle is described by Suetonius and Cassius Dio, and while the latter may have used the former as a source, that prospect is ultimately conjecture.[57] Dārāw did not appear on the first day of the show, when Caligula traversed the pontoon from Baiae to Puteoli, marching from west to east. Instead, he accompanied the emperor only on the second day, during the subsequent return in the opposite direction. Dio relates that Dārāw was displayed as a prize of war:[58]

> κἀνταῦθα τῆς ὑστεραίας ἀναπαυσάμενος ὥσπερ ἐκ μάχης, ἀνεκομίσθη διὰ τῆς αὐτῆς γεφύρας ἐφ᾽ ἅρματος, χιτῶνα χρυσόπαστον ἐνδύς· ἦγον δὲ αὐτὸν οἱ ἀθληταὶ ἵπποι οἱ ἀξιονικότατοι. καὶ ἄλλα τε αὐτῷ πολλὰ ὡς καὶ λάφυρα συνηκολούθησε, καὶ Δαρεῖος ἀνὴρ Ἀρσακίδης, ἐν τοῖς ὁμηρεύουσι τότε τῶν Πάρθων ὤν.

> And resting there on the following day as though from battle, [Caligula] was borne back over the same bridge on a chariot, clad in a gold-embroidered tunic; and two champion horses accustomed to winning the most victories drew him. A great many things followed after him as though they were spoils, including Dārāw, an Arsacid man who was among the Parthians serving as hostages at that time.

The operative phrase has Dārāw trail the emperor's chariot "as though [he were] spoils." This is one of several remarks in the passage that signal Dio's sarcasm and contempt for the procession, which he saw as a triumphal parade occasioned by no real victory.[59] That sentiment might very well be justifiable, of course. All the same, the logic of the passage shows that Dārāw's status as human plunder was supposed to be taken seriously, even if some commentators refused to do so.

Two scholars hold that Suetonius offers a divergent account of Dārāw's participation, but the biographer's testimony is in fact compatible with Dio's. Along with the emperor's clothing and mode of transportation, Dārāw is once again high-lighted as a special feature of the return journey:[60]

---

56. On the chronology of Dārāw's journey to Italy, see Balsdon 1934: 52. The name Dārāw (Greek Dareios and Latin Darius) is attested in Manichaean Parthian: Sundermann 1981: 158; Colditz 2018: 279–80.

57. On Dio's potential use of Suetonius, see Millar 1964: 85–86.

58. Cass. Dio 59.17.5.

59. See also Cass. Dio 59.17.1, 59.17.6; discussion in Lange 2016a: 106–9.

60. Suet. *Calig.* 19.2. [Aurel. Vict.] *Epit.* 3.9 describes the emperor's garment as an *aureum paludamentum*.

Per hunc pontem ultro citro commeavit biduo continenti, primo die phalerato equo insignisque quercea corona et caetra et gladio aureaque chlamyde, postridie quadrigario habitu curriculoque biiugi famosorum equorum, prae se ferens Dareum puerum ex Parthorum obsidibus.

Over this bridge [Caligula] passed to and fro for two successive days. On the first day he went on a decorated horse, distinguished by a crown of oak leaves, a small shield, a sword, and a golden chlamys. On the next day he wore the costume of a charioteer on a chariot drawn by a pair of renowned horses, making a prominent display of Dārāw, a boy from among the Parthian hostages.

Along with the remark about the emperor's charioteer outfit, Ann Kuttner and Joel Allen take the phrase *prae se ferens Dareum* to mean that Caligula served as Dārāw's charioteer in a playful inversion of ceremonial norms.[61] But this misunderstands the Latin idiom *prae se ferre*, which means "to make a conspicuous display," as in fact a proximate passage in the life of Caligula demonstrates.[62] Caligula is accused of self-debasement elsewhere in Suetonius's life, to be sure, and it is true that Nero is supposed to have appeared in public as a charioteer. But Suetonius allocates the emperor's shameful behavior—unlike his account of the Baiae procession—to his account of Caligula the monster, not Caligula the emperor.[63] Nero, for his part, is not supposed to have served as a charioteer *for* another individual, foreign royalty least of all, and Tacitus even has him espouse the view that charioteering is a regal activity.[64] In short, there is nothing in Suetonius that contradicts the impression that Dio creates: the audience was meant to conclude that Dārāw was a captive, and Caligula his captor.

It was not only Dārāw's participation that gave the Baiae spectacle its Parthian dimension, however; the geography and timing of the affair also reinforced the connection to recent events in the east. Baiae featured a pontoon bridge that the emperor traversed from west to east on the first day, and back again with his new Arsacid acquisition on the second. Those details matter, because it was by a different bridge of boats over the Euphrates that Dārāw had entered Roman territory three years earlier. "Once the river had been yoked," as Josephus reports, "[Lucius Vitellius and Ardawān II] met one another in the very middle of the bridge, each with a guard around him. . . . And Ardawān sent to Tiberius his son

61. Kuttner 1995: 113; Allen 2006: 122. On Caligula's appearance as a charioteer, cf. Suet. *Calig.* 54.1.

62. Suet. Cal. 14.3: *namque Artabanus Parthorum rex, odium semper contemptumque Tiberi prae se ferens*; cf. Hurley 1993: 77.

63. The transition is made at Suet. *Calig.* 22.1. Wardle 1994: 202 underlines that the division is moral in nature, not chronological. If Suetonius saw anything reprehensible about Caligula's treatment of Dārāw, he could have included it at 32.1, where he does place one instance of the emperor's deeds at Baiae (his throwing of spectators into the sea) in the *monstrum* section.

64. Tac. *Ann.* 14.14.1; cf. *Ann.* 15.44.5. The view is presented as idiosyncratic. Seneca and Burrus clearly found the activity shameful, as did Tacitus and Dio; see Tac. *Ann.* 14.14.2–3; Cass. Dio 63.1.1.

Dārāw as a hostage along with many other gifts."[65] The Baiae spectacle can thus be read as a restaging of the events along the Euphrates that led to the "hostage-ship" of Dārāw, an interpretation supported above all by the east-west orientation of Caligula's bridge. On the first day of the procession the emperor marched from Baiae into Puteoli—that is, from west to east—crossing the "Euphrates" from Roman territory into Parthia. On the next day, he returned with Dārāw from east to west, re-creating the Arsacid prince's departure from Parthia and his entrance into Roman custody. An echo of the diplomatic proceedings at the midpoint of the Euphrates may also be detected in Caligula's decision to deliver a harangue on a makeshift platform near the center of his bridge, as Dio specifies.[66] The Baiae spectacle was thus a repeat performance of the conference on the Euphrates, one in which Dārāw reprised his role as a signifier of Roman supremacy.

Some scholars are skeptical that Caligula's parade was triumphal in nature, but a denial of this aspect is only possible by insisting on republican technicalities for the imperial period. An important objection comes from David Wardle, who maintains that "the details of the episode do not suggest that Caligula mimics a triumph." Wardle adduces the emperor's clothing (a charioteer's outfit, rather than the triumphal *tunica palmata*) as well as the vehicle on which he rode (a *curriculum* pulled by two horses, rather than a full-size chariot pulled by four).[67] Other such objections could be added: the parade was not at Rome; it had not been awarded by the Senate; Caligula wore a crown of oak and not laurel.[68] But it is hard to know how significant such regulations would have been some fifty years after the last republican triumph. Both Dio and the author of the *Epitome de Caesaribus* held that Caligula created the *appearance* of a triumph, even in the absence of a genuine victory to celebrate.[69] As Mary Beard has put it, the crux of the matter is "just how triumph*like* a ceremony has to be before it counts as a triumph."[70] Caligula did not have to stage a triumph by the book to crow over his acquisition of Dārāw, and the scornful judgments of later authors do not mean that his event failed to send its message: the arrival of a "hostage" showed that Rome had beaten the Arsacids in the east again.

Caligula's display of Dārāw at Baiae built on the Greco-Persian wars tradition as a conceptual frame for Roman-Parthian relations, though the ideological

---

65. Joseph. *AJ* 18.102–3.

66. Cass. Dio 59.17.6.

67. Wardle 1994: 192. On Caligula's clothing, see Cass. Dio 59.17.5; Suet. *Calig.* 19.2; cf. [Aurel. Vict.] *Epit.* 3.9. On the triumphal costume, see Versnel 1970: 56–57; Beard 2007: 225–33, esp. 228; Meister 2016: 85–87.

68. On the laurel crown as triumphal dress, see Beard 2007: 246.

69. Cass. Dio 59.17.1 intimates that he considered the event a *pompē*, if on sea rather than land; see also on this point Icks 2016: 324. [Aurel. Vict.] *Epit.* 3.9 describes Caligula with the phrase *quasi triumphans* ("as though he were triumphing"). Cf. Suet. *Calig.* 52.

70. Beard 2007: 271; emphasis in the original.

coherence of the event seems to have been minimal. The construction of a massive pontoon that turned sea into land in defiance of nature did not fail to evoke the crossings of the Bosporus and the Hellespont by the Achaemenid kings Darius and Xerxes. Seneca suggests that Caligula wanted to *imitate* these examples, while Suetonius and Dio say that he wanted to *outdo* them.[71] The exhibition of an eastern prince named Dārāw/Darius as a trophy certainly supports the idea that the ancient Persians were rivals, not exemplars, and the emperor's self-costuming in a supposed breastplate of Alexander the Great makes much the same point.[72] The resurrection of this historical paradigm may have been obscured, even at the time, by Caligula's unpopularity and his resultant association with eastern despotism. But the continuity with Augustan precedent is clear enough: the emperor's putative triumph over the Parthian world furnished the Greco-Roman Mediterranean with another victory over the Persian east. The Arsacid who trailed the emperor's chariot could simultaneously represent three figures whom the Romans called Darius: the Arsacid son of Ardawān II, the foe of Alexander the Great, and the bridger of the Bosporus. The subjection of one "hostage" encapsulated a world-historical narrative.

A few pieces of evidence enable comment on Dārāw's self-conception during his stay in Italy, though they cannot speak to his experience of the Baiae procession. Key testimony comes from fragments of five lead *fistulae* (water pipes) found at Nemi during the excavation of a nymphaeum. The pipes constitute the sole epigraphic attestation of an Arsacid of Rome that includes a status marker, but the title they bear is not "hostage," or "foster-child," or even "prince." They bear the Latin inscription "of Dārāw the *king*," claiming kingship for the man who supplied the nymphaeum with water.[73] Scholars have puzzled over the basis of Dārāw's supposed kingship because it does not seem to correspond to an office he actually exercised. It is difficult to see how he was, in point of fact, king of anything.[74] The difficulty can be alleviated if the title is understood as a polemical claim to the Arsacid kingship rather than as a straightforward description of political reality. By styling himself as "king" on the *fistulae* inscriptions, Dārāw stressed his Arsacid heritage and the political power that he deserved by dint of it. Whether he was adversarial to Rome is unclear, since epigraphic self-description

71. Sen. *De Brev. Vit.* 18.5. Most commentators assume that the "king" in this passage refers to Xerxes; see Barrett 1989: 212; Edmondson 1992: 166; Wardle 1994: 193; Evans 2008: 105; Bridges 2015: 171. Malloch 2001: 208–9 argues on the basis of other passages in Seneca that it refers to Alexander the Great. Suet. *Calig.* 19.3 and Cass. Dio 59.17.11 speak of rivalry with Darius and Xerxes.

72. On Alexander's breastplate, which Dio says Caligula wore on the first day of the spectacle, see Cass. Dio 59.17.3; cf. Suet. *Calig.* 52. On Alexander as a paradigm for Roman conquests in the Parthian and Sasanian east, see Nabel 2018: 205–16.

73. Initial publication in Morpurgo 1931: 252, 280.

74. See the discussions in Morpurgo 1931: 298–99; Chaumont 1992: 59; Leone 2000; Green 2007: 58 n.8; Álvarez-Pedrosa 2022: 113.

as royalty was common within the empire and need not have implied rejection of Roman overlordship.[75] In fact, Dārāw's use of the title could have been aimed at his fellow Arsacids of Rome rather than the emperor. His self-styling may have stressed his superior claims to kingship over those of Frahād IV's children, who represented the established branch of the dynasty in Italy. The precise date of the *fistulae* is unknowable but would add further context; perhaps Dārāw began to call himself *rex* after the death of his father Ardawān II, or after the embassy of 49 C.E. that repatriated his relative Mihrdād to Parthia in preference to him.[76] In any event, Dārāw's *fistulae* present an instructive contrast with his participation in the Baiae spectacle. Despite the degrading choreography of Baiae, the Arsacid dynast's self-conception was robust enough to sustain pretensions to kingship.

Of course, at least in the case of the *fistulae*, those pretensions had to remain, literally, underground. Lead water pipes were buried as a matter of course, leaving Dārāw's claims to kingship out of view. One other inscription from Nemi suggests further public advertisement, but not conclusively. The text in question is a fragmentary inscription of Hadrian datable to 122 C.E. It appears to commemorate the emperor's rededication of a structure originally erected by a figure whose full name does not survive, but who calls himself a "son [of the king of king]s of the Parthians, an Arsacid."[77] As the Arsacid gentilic is fully preserved on the stone, the original dedicator must have been an Arsacid of Rome. Filippo Coarelli identifies this original dedicator as Dārāw, and the original structure as the one Dārāw supplied with water through the *fistulae* inscribed with his name.[78] The lacunary evidence precludes certainty, but these identifications are convincing, and they improve on earlier editions of the text, which had associated it with the children of Frahād IV. It is possible, then, that Dārāw engaged in broader self-advertisement at Nemi, whether as a resident or, more likely, as a benefactor.[79] Yet the extant text of the Hadrianic inscription does not transmit the titulature Dārāw might have used above ground. Dārāw's *fistulae* suggest a figure who was self-assured in his royal power, but it remains an open question whether he claimed the Arsacid kingship in a public text.

The third major display of Arsacids to the Roman public took place in 66 C.E. during the opulent affair that Dio calls the "Golden Day."[80] The main attraction of this event was Nero's coronation of Tirdād I in the Roman forum, though this ceremony was preceded and followed by others. Tirdād was the brother of the Arsacid king of kings Walgaš / Vologaeses I. His investiture by Nero marked

75. See the inscriptions collected in Ricci 1996.

76. On Mihrdād's homegoing, see chapters 4 and 5.

77. *CIL* 14.2216 = *ILS* 843 = Hackl et al. 2010: 2.439–40.

78. Coarelli 1987: 180–81; for other possibilities, see Ricci 1996: 571–73.

79. On this question, see Bruun 1995: 52–57.

80. Cass. Dio 63.6.1. Dio's account of the Golden Day survives mostly in the epitome of Ioannes Xiphilinus, on which see Millar 1964: 2; Mallan 2013.

the end of the longest Roman-Parthian war of the first century C.E., a desultory conflict over Armenia that lasted from 54 to 63 C.E. It was precisely Walgaš's installation of Tirdād on the Armenian throne that had triggered hostilities in the first place, but the end of the war saw Nero ready to sanction this appointment provided that Tirdād visited Rome to receive his crown from the emperor in person.

The geopolitics of the war and its settlement on the Golden Day have been extensively discussed, but their connections to Arsacid "hostageship" have not. A common interpretation holds that Nero's event was an act of face-saving diplomacy: the public "submission" of Tirdād allowed Nero to cede Armenia to the Arsacid family while preserving Rome's reputation.[81] Yet the salvaging of honor depended, in part, on the Roman classification of visiting Parthians as hostages, and the Golden Day's triumphalism was underpinned by the Julio-Claudian practice of Arsacid exhibition. Nero's forum display should be connected to the earlier spectacles of Augustus and Caligula because the evidence suggests that Tirdād brought a new group of Arsacid "hostages" to Nero's court, as argued below. Even if he did not, the earlier pageants of Nero's predecessors had created a framework from which the Golden Day drew meaning, and Roman audiences would have interpreted the apparent "supplication" of Tirdād and his retinue through the lens of Arsacid hostageship. Inasmuch as Nero's regime could present the settlement of 63 C.E. as a Roman victory, the triumphal exhibition of Arsacids held the key.

Did Tirdād bring a group of Arsacid dynasts to Rome who were meant to stay there? Earlier discussions have overlooked this possibility, but it is strongly suggested by an inferential reading of the available sources. The relevant testimony begins with Dio, who notes that Tirdād was not the only Arsacid to journey to Italy in 66 C.E.:[82]

καὶ ὁ Τιριδάτης ἐς τὴν Ῥώμην, οὐχ ὅτι τοὺς ἑαυτοῦ παῖδας ἀλλὰ καὶ τοὺς τοῦ Οὐολογαίσου τοῦ τε Πακόρου καὶ τοῦ Μονοβάζου ἄγων, ἀνήχθη.

Tirdād was brought up to Rome, bringing with him not just his own children, but also those of Walgaš, Pakōr, and Monobazus.

Tirdād came to Rome with the children of the three highest ranking Arsacids: his own; those of his brother Pakōr, the king of Media; and those of the Arsacid king of kings Walgaš.[83] Monobazus was the king of Adiabene, but evidently not a member of the Arsacid family. The text offers no further names or numbers. A group

81. Chaumont 1976: 123; Brunt 1990: 457; Heil 1997: 130–31, 196–97; Campbell 1993: 232–33; Wheeler 2002: 289; Griffin 1984: 227, 232; Lerouge 2007: 131; Mratschek 2013: 52. For a different view, see Frézouls 1995: 494–98, who sees the Neronian settlement as the only lasting accommodation between Rome and Parthia in the first century C.E..

82. Cass. Dio 63.1.2. This was presumably a different group than those mentioned at Tac. *Ann.* 15.30.2 and Cass. Dio 62.23.4; for a discussion of those passages, see Heil 1997: 127–28.

83. On Walgaš, Tirdād, and Pakōr as the three most powerful Arsacids, cf. Tac. *Ann.* 15.2.1.

of children from all these rulers would have amounted to a large retinue, which accords well with Dio's description of Tirdād's bombastic procession "as though in a triumph" from Parthian territory to Italy.[84]

Were these dynasts sent to Rome to serve as "hostages," in Roman eyes at least? Dio does not use the word *homēroi* in this section, so perhaps not. He uses the designation elsewhere in reference to Arsacids, and the simplest explanation for why he did not use it here is that he did not think the children were to serve in that capacity.[85] It may be that the imperfect preservation of his text (for this section, only by the Byzantine excerptor Xiphilinus) has confounded some of the details. An earlier passage describing the conference at Rhandeia in 63 C.E. relates that, after the negotiations had concluded, "both Monobazus and Walgaš came to Corbulo and gave him hostages."[86] That report is problematic, because Tacitus—a far more reliable source for Nero's Parthian war—puts Walgaš at Ecbatana during Tirdād's negotiations with Corbulo. Tacitus attests no such meeting between the Parthian king and the Roman general, and still less another submission of hostages. Perhaps Dio (or his excerptor) has conflated or transposed some of the events of 63 and 66 C.E., but this is mere conjecture.[87]

Yet the testimony of Pliny the Elder further supports the possibility that Tirdād arrived with "hostages" in 66 C.E. The relevant passage is part of Pliny's *Natural History*, an encyclopedic treatment of medicine, botany, and geography published in 77 C.E.[88] An experienced soldier and administrator no less than a scholar, Pliny's sources for the *Natural History* included earlier literary works but also interviews with both Romans and foreigners. The author underlines his recourse to such informants as his account turns to the geography of "the interior of Asia," a region that includes Cappadocia, the Caucasus, and—most importantly for the present discussion—Armenia.[89] He introduces the section with the following words:[90]

> Nunc reddatur ingens in mediterraneo situs, in quo multa aliter ac veteres proditurum me non eo infitias, anxia perquisitis cura rebus nuper in eo situ gestis a Domitio Corbulone regibusque inde missis supplicibus aut regum liberis obsidibus.

> Now let an account be given of the vast area of the interior [of Asia]. I do not deny that I will relate much that differs from the accounts of previous authors, as I took

84. Cass. Dio 63.1.2.

85. See table 1.

86. Cass. Dio 62.23.4.

87. Tac. *Ann.* 15.31. Cf. Griffin 1984: 300–1 n.64: "As the passage closes this excerpter's treatment of the subject of Armenia, it is possible that he is summing up the whole Armenian episode, noting all the salutations Nero took for successes there, including that for Tiridates' visit in 66." See also Heil 1997: 127–28.

88. On the composition and publication dates of the *Natural History*, see Baldwin 1995: 80; Murphy 2004: 3–4; Beagon 2005: 2.

89. Plin. *HN* 6.23–33.

90. Plin. *HN* 6.23.

solicitous care in ascertaining recent events in this area from Domitius Corbulo and from the kings sent from these places as suppliants or the children of kings who were sent as hostages.

Pliny names three sources that have provided him with a more reliable geography of the Asian interior than the version available in earlier authors: Corbulo, suppliant kings, and young royal hostages. Corbulo's testimony probably came from his memoirs rather than oral communication; Nero compelled the general to commit suicide shortly after his return from Armenia, so it is unlikely that Pliny had the chance to reunite with his former commander.[91] But the kings and their children must have been in-person informants. Pliny was often in Rome between c. 59 and 77 C.E. and perhaps even present for the Golden Day itself.[92] He would have been well positioned to interview the foreign royalty attached to the emperor's court, whether under Nero or Vespasian.

Even if certainty is out of reach, Pliny's statement suggests that a new group of Arsacids was installed at Nero's court during Tirdād's visit or shortly thereafter. While the regions discussed in the "interior of Asia" section include Cappadocia as well, the contrastive *autem* in the sentence that follows the quotation above makes it clear that the kings and hostages in question do not come from that land.[93] Moreover, Tirdād is an obvious referent for at least one of the "suppliant kings" of whom Pliny writes: whatever the realities of power behind the Golden Day, Tirdād could easily have merited the designation "suppliant" in the eyes of Romans who saw him bow before Nero.[94] As for the hostage children, Pliny's *liberi* matches well with the *paides* of Dio. Questions and uncertainties remain, since Pliny's statement attests the recent arrival of young hostages from Armenia, but not Parthia or Adiabene, while Dio's would seem to indicate all three. Still, the concordance between the two passages is suggestive. The visit of Tirdād in 66 C.E. may well have included another transfer of young Arsacid dynasts from Parthia to Rome.

Like the displays of Augustus and Caligula, then, the Golden Day can be understood as a public demonstration of Roman superiority to Parthia that involved the display of people whom the Romans called hostages. This dynamic once again lent the affair a triumphal dimension, as evidenced in Nero's costume: as he took his

91. Corbulo was forced to commit suicide in Greece in late 66 or early 67 C.E.; for the date, see Griffin 1992: 462–63; Levick 2013c: 541. On Corbulo's fallout with Nero, see Griffin 1984: 178; Vervaet 2002: 168–81; Drinkwater 2019: 225–27. Pliny the Elder himself had served under Corbulo during the Roman war against the Chauci in 47 C.E.; see Plin. *HN* 16.2; Plin. *Epist.* 3.5.3; Tac. *Ann.* 11.18–19; discussion in Beagon 2005: 3; Dunn 2019: 20–24.

92. For Pliny's whereabouts during the 60s and 70s C.E., see Levick 2013a: 527–28.

93. Plin. *HN* 6.24: "we will begin, however (*autem*), from the people of Cappadocia."

94. On the prostration, see below. The label of *supplex* is further justified by lines 627–28 of the *Octavia*, which must be a reference to Tirdād's coronation. For discussion, see Nabel 2019a: 618.

seat on the rostra at dawn, the emperor wore the garb of a triumphant general.[95] Suetonius speaks only of Tirdād's participation in the spectacle from this point, but Dio notes that a larger group of Parthians was involved:[96]

> καὶ μετὰ τοῦτο ὅ τε Τιριδάτης καὶ οἱ μετ᾿ αὐτοῦ διά τε στοίχων ὁπλιτῶν ἑκατέρωθεν παρατεταγμένων διῆλθον καὶ πρὸς τῷ βήματι προσστάντες προσεκύνησαν αὐτόν, ὥσπερ καὶ πρότερον.

> Next, Tirdād and those with him passed between the rows of heavily armed soldiers, stood before the rostra, and prostrated themselves before [Nero], just as they had done before.

Tirdād's companions would have included his sons and nephews, previously mentioned by Dio as his traveling companions. It was at this point—as a group of Arsacids bent the knee to the emperor in public view—that the crowd is supposed to have roared its approval for the first time.[97] The sources are unanimous that the populace had turned out in droves for the spectacle, covering even the roofs of adjacent buildings with onlookers.[98] As in the days of Augustus and Caligula, the mirage of Roman dominance over Parthia depended on the exhibition of Arsacid bodies to massive crowds and with maximum fanfare. While no Julio-Claudian emperor had ever crowned an Arsacid king of Armenia before, others *had* hosted Arsacid "hostages" and displayed them to the public as symbols of Roman supremacy. The Golden Day continued the tradition.

Nero followed Augustan precedents in other respects as well, since the Julio-Claudian founder was the ultimate reference point for declarations of victory over Parthia. In 54 C.E., the Senate voted Nero a number of honors for his management of the situation in Armenia—prematurely, as it happened, since the crisis turned into a war that dragged on for nearly a decade. Among these honors were the right to wear the triumphal costume, an ovation, and—most significantly—a statue of Nero "of equal size to that of Mars Ultor and [erected in] the same temple."[99] The choice of this deity was anchored in tradition, because Augustus had built the temple of Mars Ultor to commemorate his own "victory" over the Parthians, as discussed above. More recently, the Senate had voted to erect statues of Germanicus and Drusus in the temple after Germanicus imposed a king on Armenia in 19 C.E.[100] Nero's statue and its installation in the temple of Mars Ultor thus connected his

---

95. Suet. *Ner.* 13.1; Cass. Dio 63.4.3. The triumphal element is fully explored by Clark 2021: 8–12; on triumphal clothing, cf. Alföldi 1935: 25–38.

96. Cass. Dio 63.4.3.

97. Cass. Dio 63.5.1.

98. On the large crowds that assembled on the Golden Day, see Tac. *Ann.* 16.24.1; Cass. Dio 63.4.2; Suet. *Ner.* 13.

99. Tac. *Ann.* 13.8.1.

100. Tac. *Ann.* 2.64.1. For Germanicus's installation of Artaxias in Armenia, see Tac. *Ann.* 2.56.3.

initial declarations of success with earlier Julio-Claudian pretensions to mastery in the east.

Nero also followed Augustus and Caligula in connecting Roman-Parthian relations with the Greco-Persian wars tradition by dint of grand spectacle. In 57 C.E., he staged a *naumachia* on the Campus Martius that re-created the battle of Salamis as the combatants assumed Athenian and Persian identities. The show hearkened back to Augustus's *naumachia* of 2 B.C.E., which had reenacted the same battle.[101] Another evocation of this memorable spectacle came two years later, when Nero feasted the people on boats at the very spot along the Tiber where Augustus's *naumachia* had taken place.[102] These choices showed the continued vitality of the Persian wars tradition as a frame for Roman-Parthian relations: hostility to the Arsacids prompted Romans to reprise their roles as Greeks mounting a civilizational struggle against the Persian east. Nero's personal philhellenism may have lent the analogy additional weight, even if scholars debate the extent of his affection for the Greek past.[103] An Athenian inscription in honor of Nero from 61/62 C.E. even suggests that the emperor's Greek subjects could join in the project; its letters were mounted on the Parthenon, a structure that for the Athenians was inextricably connected with the Persian Wars of the fifth century B.C.E.[104] These precedents meant that the Golden Day's spectators could see in Tirdād's prostration not just a recent victory over a troublesome eastern kingdom, but instead the culmination of a historical grand narrative.

Monumental architecture offered another way to build on Augustus's legacy. Like his Julio-Claudian forebear, Nero commemorated his "victories" over the Arsacids with an arch, though in his case the structure stood on the Capitoline Hill.[105] Tacitus wryly notes its ongoing construction in 62 C.E. despite Paetus's recent humiliation at Rhandeia.[106] It was apparently voted by the Senate in 58 C.E. after Corbulo's destruction of Artaxata, though Tacitus is not entirely clear on this point.[107] The arch is not extant, and it is likely that it did not long outlast Nero's reign.[108] But an ancient visual representation survives, because Nero—like Augustus—minted coins to disseminate the monument's image. The series was

101. Cass. Dio 61.9.5; Suet. *Ner.* 12.1; cf. Tac. *Ann.* 13.31.1; discussion in Champlin 2003: 68. On Augustus's *naumachia*, see above.

102. Cass. Dio 61.20.5.

103. On Nero's philhellenism, see Griffin 1984: 208; Mratschek 2013; Drinkwater 2019: 373. But cf. Champlin 2003: 54, who views the emperor's love for Greece as "sharply limited."

104. *IG* ii².3277; but see now the text in Carroll 1982: 16. For the inscription's place in the Persian Wars tradition see Carroll 1982: 67–73; Spawforth 1994: 234–37.

105. Clark 2021: 15–17 discusses the interplay with Augustus's arch. On the topography of Nero's arch see further La Rocca 1992: 408–11.

106. Tac. *Ann.* 15.18.1.

107. Tac. *Ann.* 13.41.4; cf. Furneaux 1907: 339; Koestermann 1963–68: 4.194; Kleiner 1985: 70.

108. Kleiner 1985: 94–95; La Rocca 1992: 404.

minted at Rome and Lugdunum from 64–67 C.E.[109] Unlike Augustus's arch, the top of Nero's apparently featured Roman soldiers rather than Parthians. But both Nero and Augustus topped their arches riding *quadrigae*. Moreover, a statue of Mars in the lower niche could have directed the viewer's mind to the temple of Mars Ultor—another building that represented Roman victory over Parthia, and that also featured a statue of Nero.[110] A relief fragment found at Rome may have originally belonged to Nero's arch: it features a bare-headed Parthian with a full beard and the V-shaped tunic that was characteristic of Parthian dress. Interpretations have varied, but the fragment may date to the reign of Nero, and if so, his Parthian arch is one plausible context.[111] The Parthian's beard and V-shaped tunic might have reminded a Roman viewer of the Parthian on the breastplate of Augustus's Primaporta statue, a visually similar representation.[112]

In a final nod to Augustan precedent, Nero closed the doors of the Temple of Janus to proclaim universal peace after his war with the Parthians was over. Suetonius has Nero shutting the doors after Tirdād's visit in 66 C.E., but coins that date as early as 64 show the closed doors of the temple.[113] The legend on these issues reads "with peace for the Roman people having been obtained on land and sea, he closed (the Temple of) Janus by decree of the Senate."[114] The first phrase ("peace obtained on land and sea") was unmistakably an Augustan slogan. While it was used in reference to several of Augustus's accomplishments, it was most closely connected with his three closures of the doors of Janus.[115] It is not entirely clear whether any of these closures were related to Parthian affairs, but a number of ancient sources both Augustan and later seem to have drawn this conclusion.[116] For Nero as for Augustus, then, the shut doors on the Temple of Janus proclaimed the reassertion of Roman supremacy in the east and the humbling of the Parthian empire.

Inaccurate though it may be, Suetonius's connection of the temple's closure to the coronation of Tirdād shows the immense impact of the king's coronation and the public obeisance of his Arsacid retinue—whether these young dynasts

---

109. Kleiner 1985: 72, 99–153; Champlin 2003: 216–17.

110. Kleiner 1985: 80–81.

111. Neronian date: Hölscher 1988: 537–41, with references to earlier literature. Originally part of Nero's Parthian arch: La Rocca 1992: 411–14.

112. Cf. Hölscher 1988: 538; Schneider 1998: 100–2.

113. Suet. *Ner.* 13.2. See further Townend 1980; Griffin 1984: 122; Syme 1989: 118.

114. For this legend (sometimes with minor variations) see the types cited in Champlin 2003: 307–8 n.92.

115. The connection to Janus is clear in *Mon. Anc.* 13; Suet. *Aug.* 22. But the phrase was also used in reference to the victory at Actium (see the dedication from Octavian's campsite memorial in Murray and Petsas 1989: 76; cf. Liv. 1.19.3) and possibly after the defeat of Sextus Pompeius in 36 B.C.E. (App. *B Civ.* 5.130; cf. Lange 2009: 35). For discussion, see Lange 2009: 111–23, 146–48; Wardle 2014: 181–82.

116. See the sources and discussion in Syme 1984: 1192, who concludes: " . . . at an early stage two of the closures, and even all three, amalgamate to a single transaction which tends to be associated with Parthia."

subsequently became hostages or not. In geopolitical terms, Tirdād's visit meant nothing; it merely ratified the conclusions of the Rhandeia conference three years earlier. In terms of the treaty's reception, however, the event meant everything. In the eyes of the Julio-Claudian emperors, Nero's not least, Roman-Parthian relations did not only happen in Armenia or on the Euphrates frontier. They happened in Rome, in view of a domestic audience whose conception of Roman standing in the east in some ways mattered much more than who sat on the Armenian throne. A satisfactory status quo was not merely achieved with armies and diplomacy. It had to be staged—Suetonius uses the theatrical verb *producere*—in the heart of the empire and in public.[117]

If Julio-Claudian mastery of Parthia was a production that required constant reprisal, the Arsacids of Rome were the indispensable supporting cast. The Golden Day may have been especially lavish in the scale of its production, but it followed a script that Nero's predecessors had written. The show required Arsacid bodies to achieve its intended effect, and the numerous submissions of "hostages" from Parthia to Rome supplied the raw material from which the spectacle was fashioned. If Tirdād took a knee in the forum alongside a group of royal children who later remained at the emperor's court, then the affair represents the last major "hostage" transfer of the Julio-Claudian period. Even if none of these Arsacids stayed with Nero, however, the Roman audience would have viewed the ceremony through the lens of hostageship, whose close connections with the triumphal tradition conditioned Romans to see Arsacids in their city as a sign of Parthian subordination.

Collectively, the exhibitions of Augustus, Caligula, and Nero turned the Arsacids of Rome into hostages, trophies, and symbols of control. Encouraged by ingrained imperialism and the triumphal celebration of conquest, the label of "hostage" gave Romans of the early principate confidence in their empire's mastery of the Parthian world beyond the Euphrates. Hence the overwhelming designation of the city's Arsacids as *obsides* or *homēroi* in Greco-Roman literary sources, even by authors who questioned Rome's proclamations of superiority to the Arsacid kingdom or the universality of Roman rule. The Arsacids of Rome were called hostages because the idea flattered Roman self-conception. Public exhibitions, visual representations, and the force of habit made the label stick.

PATRONAL FOSTERAGE

But while hostageship may have been the dominant viewpoint on the Roman side, it was not the *only* viewpoint, because additional evidence suggests that the Arsacids of Rome could also be described as kin of the Julio-Claudian family. One author, Tacitus, directly applies the language of fosterage to the Arsacids

117. See Kierdorf 1992: 177, with comment on the verb *producere*.

of Rome, and several key pieces of evidence from the Augustan period can be reinterpreted against this background. Yet even where kinship offered common ground as a mode of engagement between the Arsacids and the Caesars, the scope for misunderstanding between the two sides was still ample, because their cultures conceived of fosterage in divergent ways. To the limited extent that the Romans regarded their Arsacids as the emperor's foster-children, they had a patronal view of the arrangement that would have been at odds with the Parthian cliental model. The two families may have been kin, in other words, but they had different ideas about the political ramifications of their kinship.

The minimal purchase of fosterage in early imperial sources for the Arsacids of Rome is in one sense attributable to the empire's republican past: as a newcomer to dynasty, Rome had little background with interdynastic kinship. To be sure, Rome saw its share of the "kinship diplomacy" that flourished among the poleis of the Hellenistic world. Literary and epigraphic sources preserve many cases of this diplomatic strategy, which saw poleis appeal to relatedness as a basis for reciprocal obligations in their interaction with foreign communities.[118] But these kinships were attributed to shared descent from mythic ancestors or colonization, and more importantly, they applied to entire political communities, not ruling families. Moreover, Rome may not have taken to kinship diplomacy to the extent that its Greek neighbors did. Even during the republic, in Sue Elwyn's assessment, kinship played "only a small role in Rome's expansion and foreign policy."[119] At any rate, the implication of the Romans in this sort of kinship discourse provided little experience with the kinship politics that had prevailed for so long in the ancient Near East, where interdynastic relations were personal, not communitarian.

Even when Romans of the republic heard kinship appeals from individuals rather than entire political communities, the republic's regime type obstructed the establishment of familial ties. When the Seleucid hostage Demetrius I spoke before the Senate to ask for his release, he called Rome his "fatherland and nurturer," the senators his "fathers," and their sons his "brothers," at least according to Polybius.[120] In a much later account of this speech by the fragmentary historian Granius Licinianus, Demetrius calls the Senate his "parent."[121] The effectiveness of Demetrius's speech is debatable. Polybius says that the senators were touched, but evidently not enough to grant the Seleucid's release. More to the

118. Literary and inscriptional evidence is collected and discussed in Elwyn 1991: 9–138; see more recently the studies of Jones 1999; Patterson 2010a; Patterson 2010b; Gruen 2011: 223–307.

119. Elwyn 1993: 261.

120. Polyb. 31.2.5; discussion in Walbank 1979: 466.

121. Granius Licinianus 28.39.1 = Criniti 1981: 9. Granius lived in the second century C.E. and produced a compendium of Roman history that survives only in fragments. See Criniti 1993; Conte 1994: 551.

point, his appeal to constructed kinship was an awkward fit with the size of his audience. In the world of the Hellenistic courts, fosterers were individual dignitaries. But in the Roman Senate, the title of "father" had to be extended to some three hundred men, or to the institutional body as a whole.[122] This divergence made fosterage, and appeals to the bonds that it formed, a poor way to liaise with the primary institution of Roman foreign affairs.[123] By all indications, then, Rome's republican mode of government limited the scope of interdynastic kinship and elite fosterage as modes of foreign politics, even if the Senate's dealings with Hellenistic dynasts introduced trends that could accelerate once Rome fell under a different type of regime.

The subsumption of Roman imperial governance into the kinship networks of the Julio-Claudian family has been well treated in previous studies, but the Arsacids of Rome show that a part of this story has yet to be properly told: Arsacid fosterage brought dynasts from *outside the empire* into the house of Caesar. Kinship thereby revealed itself not only as a domestic organizing principle, but as a means of interfacing with political entities beyond Rome's borders. The question of "how and why the family of Augustus became a part of the Roman state" has benefited from a number of scholarly treatments, and the role of the dynasty at the center of Rome's transition from republic to empire has been much discussed.[124] Yet the Arsacids of Rome made the Julio-Claudian family not part of the Roman state so much as a political entity that transcended the Roman state, tied together as it was with Parthia's ruling dynasty through the bonds of fosterage. The evidence that the Julio-Claudian family was aware of and perhaps even nurtured these kinships is much slighter than the preponderance of sources that categorize the Arsacids as hostages. There is enough, however, to speak of a "recognized, if limited" Roman espousal of fosterage, if only under discrete circumstances and by a small group of elites.[125]

The main source for Arsacid-Caesarian kinship is Tacitus, who uses the language of fosterage in two passages dealing with the Arsacids of Rome. The first of these shows that the emperor could consider himself their foster-father. The episode in question dates to 35 C.E., when Lucius Vitellius—the future emperor, but at this time governor of Syria—escorted one Tirdād to the banks of the Euphrates. Probably born in Italy, Tirdād was a second generation Arsacid of Rome who had gone east to challenge the kingship of Ardawān II. After partaking in the Zoroastrian tradition of horse sacrifice on the banks of the Euphrates,

---

122. On the size of the Senate in the Middle Republic, see Lintott 1999: 69–70.

123. On the Senate's management of foreign affairs, see Polyb. 6.13.8–9.

124. Quotation: Severy 2003: 3. Other key studies include Kuttner 1995; Bang 2011; Hekster 2015.

125. Quotation: Kuttner 1995: 115.

Tirdād received a few words of advice from Vitellius.[126] Tacitus reports them as follows:[127]

> [Vitellius] monet Tiridaten primoresque, hunc, Phraatis avi et altoris Caesaris quae<que> utrubique pulchra meminerit, illos, obsequium in regem, reverentiam in nos, decus quisque suum et fidem retinerent.

> Vitellius gave advice to Tirdād and the nobility. He advised the former to remember his grandfather Frahād and his foster-father Caesar, and what was good about each of them. He advised the latter to remain obedient to their king and respectful to us, each keeping his own honor and loyalty.

Vitellius imagines that Tirdād has a double lineage, both Parthian and Roman, Arsacid and Caesarian.[128] Most readers take the *altor* of this sentence to simply mean Tiberius, but the use of the dynastic name *Caesar* has a larger significance.[129] The ambiguity of the referent shows that the emperor's foster-fatherhood was, like interdynastic brotherhood in the late Bronze Age, a transferable position in a systemized kinship arrangement, not an individual attribute.[130] The emperor was the fosterer of the Arsacids of Rome no matter who the emperor was. Tacitus's first use of fosterage terminology thus shows the establishment of kinship relations between the dynasties of Rome and Parthia and the acknowledgment of this kinship on the Roman side.

Tacitus's second invocation of such language is less straightforward, however, because this time the terminology of fosterage is applied not to the emperor but to the Roman state as a whole. In 49 C.E., the Senate granted an audience to envoys from the Parthian nobility who requested the release of Mihrdād, yet another Arsacid of Rome.[131] After the Parthians spoke, Claudius delivered an oration that touched on the virtues of Mihrdād, among other topics:[132]

---

126. Tirdād's parentage is not clear. Tac. *Ann.* 6.37.4 says that his grandfather was Frahād, which apparently means Frahād IV; thus Wheeler 2016: 190; Woodman 2017: 229. His father is nowhere specified. Tirdād could have been one of the grandsons of Frahād IV sent to Italy between 19–9 B.C.E. (see table 1). But Tacitus (*Ann.* 6.43.3) writes of his "boyhood," which would not fit a man in his mid-40s. Cass. Dio 58.26 contains no additional information. On balance, it seems best to conclude that Tirdād was born at Rome. Horse sacrifice: Tac. *Ann.* 6.37.2 with Daryaee 2022.

127. Tac. *Ann.* 6.37.4; text from Woodman 2017: 39.

128. Cf. Joseph. *AJ* 18.46 on the double inheritance of Vonones, though without the language of kinship and/or family relations.

129. *Altor* as a reference to Tiberius: Ziegler 1964: 61; Allen 2006: 136.

130. On the transferability of brotherhood in the Amarna system, see chapters 1 and 2 on EA 29.

131. Tac. *Ann.* 11.10.4 says that Mihrdād was "given to us [i.e. the Romans] in hostageship," which might suggest that he was sent to Rome during the kingship of his father Vonones. But it is also possible that he arrived during the transfer of 19–9 B.C.E. (see table 1 for sources), or that he was born in Rome. Vonones died in 19 C.E. (Tac. *Ann.* 2.68), so Mihrdād must have been at least thirty, or just shy of it. Tacitus calls him a *iuvenis* (*Ann.* 12.11.3).

132. Tac. *Ann.* 12.11.3.

Hinc versus ad legatos extollit laudibus alumnum urbis, spectatae ad id modestiae: ac tamen ferenda regum ingenia neque usui crebras mutationes.

Then, having turned to the ambassadors, [Claudius] extolled with praise the foster-child of the city, a man of evident modesty up to that time. All the same, the tempers of kings had to be endured, and numerous revolutions were not useful.

Claudius's description of Mihrdād as an *alumnus* matches Tiberius's role as the *altor* of Tirdād. The etymology of the terms connects the two passages: both words derive from the verb *alere*, "to nourish," figuratively extending the vocabulary of breast-feeding and child-rearing to created kinships.[133] The collocation of the two terms is crucial and not self-explanatory, since *alumnus* is elsewhere paired with different terms like *dominus* ("lord, master") or *erus* ("master of a house/family").[134]

But although the *alumnus* of this speech recalls Vitellius's description of Tiberius as *altor*, the interdynastic aspect of the fosterage arrangement is absent in Claudius's case: Mihrdād is described not as the emperor's foster-son, but as the foster-son *of the city*. What explains the additional qualification? On the one hand, perhaps the phrase was simply idiomatic. There are literary and epigraphic parallels where *alumnus* is paired with a place name in the genitive to indicate where a person was raised.[135] Yet the setting and the audience also help explain the description. Whereas Vitellius addressed only Parthians, Claudius spoke before the Roman Senate. Just as Demetrius the Seleucid applied the concept of fatherhood to the hundreds of senators present at his audience, Claudius's kinship rhetoric made the entire Roman state the *altor* of Mihrdād, and the emperor did not claim this title for himself. Despite the advent of the Julio-Claudian dynasty, the community-based kinship rhetoric of the late republic retained its currency. In this instance, Arsacid fosterage created a kinship that was interstate but not interdynastic.

Indeed, perhaps the most striking feature of *alumnus urbis* is the phrase's ability to simultaneously satisfy the expectations of the emperor's Parthian and Roman audiences. The words capture a basic relationship of fosterage and pro-parentage, but with enough latitude to support variable understandings among the key participants. For those on the Parthian side, including the Arsacids themselves, the *altor*/*alumnus* vocabulary could have seemed like a translation of *dāyagānī*, which (as argued in chapter 1) is likely to have been the operative institution for political

---

133. Dixon 1999: 225; Nielsen 2013: 289; Nielsen 1987: 143, citing Servius *Comm. Aen.* 11.33 and Isid. *Orig.* 10.3. Cf. O'Donnell 2020: 19 on the derivation of Irish foster terminology from *altram*, a verb that "at base, carries connotations of feeding and nurturing."

134. See Stat. *Silv.* 2.1, in which the poet consoles Atedius Melior after the death of Glaucias, his *alumnus* (2.1.1). Melior is called the child's *altor* (2.1.69), but also his *dominus* (2.1.70) and his *erus* (2.1.129). On fosterage in this poem, see further Bernstein 2015: 150–51. Carroll 2006: 204 discusses *CIL* 13.2032, an epitaph set up by a *dominus* for his *alumnus*.

135. See Quint. 8.1.3 with Hölkeskamp 2004: 293; Juv. 1.20 with Larmour 2007: 178 and n.22. For inscriptional evidence, see Hemelrijk 2015: 248–55 and n.68, with references.

elites from the Iranian plateau. Like dāyag, the words *altor* and *alumnus* describe pro-parental relations through the language of nursing and breast-feeding. On the Roman side, the application of kinship terminology to the Roman body politic had precedents in the republican period, and it spoke to the senators in a language they were used to hearing. A phrase like *alumnus urbis* could therefore find anchor points in both Parthian and Roman expectations while leaving ample scope for misunderstanding to persist.

And divergence in understanding there must have been, because the wider evidence for the *altor/alumnus* relationship in the Roman world shows that, as a general rule, foster-children were the social inferiors of their fosterers. Roman fosterage, in other words, was patronal.[136] The epigraphic record is replete with *alumni* from lower status backgrounds. Some, though perhaps not many, may have been foundlings rescued from exposure.[137] Others were apprentices.[138] Still others were *deliciae*, *vernae* (slaves born within the Roman household), or *servi*; sometimes these figures were manumitted before they became *alumni/ae*, but not always.[139] The fosterage of an *alumnus* or *alumna* was also distinct from adoption, a legal process by which elite male Romans acquired an heir to their name and estate—typically another elite male and often a close relative.[140] While *alumni/ae* had rights under Roman law, they were not the legal equivalents of a son or daughter.[141] For a member of the Roman aristocracy, an *alumnus* was no substitute for an adopted son. Adoptees came from social backgrounds closely comparable to those of their adopters, but *alumni/ae* were far more likely to be their inferiors.

The social history of Roman fosterage offers indispensable context for the appearance of *altor* and *alumnus* in Tacitus's descriptions of the Arsacids of Rome. When Vitellius and Claudius describe the Arsacids of Rome as foster-children, they are designating them social inferiors—and asserting, by extension, Roman superiority to the Arsacid dynasty and the empire that it ruled. This is no comment on the emotions that underpinned the personal relationships between Caesarians and Arsacids. Claudius may well have been sincere in his praise of Mihrdād, for instance, though the evidence cannot ultimately resolve that question. Rather, the

---

136. Nielsen 1997: 183, 190. On Tac. *Ann.* 12.11 in this sense, see also Allen 2019: 106–7.

137. Scholars variously assess how frequently *alumni/ae* would have been foundlings; compare e.g. Nielsen 1987: 160; Corbier 2001: 70; Dyson 2011: 37; Edmondson 2011: 358; Grubbs 2013: 95 with Bellemore and Rawson 1990: 5; Nielsen 2013: 289.

138. Carroll 2006: 202–3; Nielsen 2013: 289.

139. Rawson 1986: 173; Nielsen 1987: 144–46, 153; Bradley 1991: 62; Corbier 2001: 70–71; Rawson 2003: 252–54, 262. On *deliciae*, see Laes 2003: 320. See esp. *Dig.* 40.2.14 on the manumission of *alumni*.

140. On adoption and its differences with fosterage, see Corbier 1991: 63–76; Dixon 1992: 112–13 (who mentions that adoption was primarily a custom among the "ruling class"); Rawson 2003: 250; Golden 2009: 47; Lindsay 2011: 354–59; Huebner 2013: 510–11. Roman preference for close relatives as adoptees: Lindsay 2001: 201.

141. On the legal rights of *alumni/ae*, see Nielsen 1987: 148–57.

social dimensions of Roman fosterage—to the extent that this institution applied to the Arsacid case—offered yet another confirmation of Roman supremacy and Arsacid subordination. A Parthian *dāyag* would have looked at his foster-child and seen a social superior; the Roman *altor* saw the opposite.

The kinship and fosterage arrangements attested in Tacitus allow for new perspectives on other key sources for the Arsacids of Rome, and on a crucial passage in the *Res Gestae* not least. Augustus's description of the 19–9 B.C.E. transfer is direct evidence for how the emperor wanted this event to be remembered, and it is the earliest extant testimony for the Arsacids of Rome. Yet the passage's implications for Arsacid-Caesarian kinship have been overlooked. The relevant sentence runs as follows:[142]

> Ad [me re]x Parthorum Phrates, Orod[i]s filius, filios suos nepot[esque omnes] misit in Italiam non bello superatu[s], sed amicitiam nostram per [libe]ror[um] suorum pignora petens.

> To me Urūd's son Frahād, the king of the Parthians, sent all his sons and grandsons into Italy, not because he was conquered in war, but seeking our friendship through the *pignora* of his own children.

What does *pignus* mean here? It is common to translate the word into English as "pledges" in the sense of "guarantees of good behavior."[143] Other scholars take their cues from the literary sources for this Arsacid transfer—all of which call Frahād's children *obsides* or *homēroi*—and conclude that *pignus* basically means "hostage," or was a gentler alternative to it.[144] On this reading, the sentence boasts that the ruler of the Parthian empire has tendered submission.

But the background of Arsacid fosterage suggests a different, though not incompatible, understanding of the phrase: *pignora* means "children." Anthony Birley has broached this possibility, though the idea has not been taken up.[145] *Pignus* can be found with this meaning in Augustan and post-Augustan literature, suggesting a new accretion to the word's valences at the beginning of the Julio-Claudian period.[146] The sense comes from the connection between love and procreation: children are the manifest pledges of love between parents.[147] The usage is more

---

142. *Mon. Anc.* 32.2; text from Cooley 2009: 96.

143. Brunt and Moore 1967: 34–35; Braund 1984: 12; Drijvers 1998: 290 and n.64; Kleiner and Buxton 2008: 59; Cornwell 2017: 149 and n.77; Olbrycht 2018: 391. Cf. "Unterpfand" in German scholarship: Ziegler 1964: 52; Thommen in Hackl et al. 2010: 2.51–52; Wiesehöfer 2010: 187; Strothmann 2012: 85. Nedergaard 1988: 108 translates "tokens"; Allen 2006: 104 opts for "securities."

144. Dąbrowa 1987: 69 n.3.

145. Birley 2007: 539.

146. *TLL* 10.1.2125.35.

147. Ferri 2003: 207; Francese 2007: 18. See esp. Prop. 4.11.12, 73 with Butrica 2006: 32; Heyworth 2007a: 512–13; Heyworth 2007b: 125; Heyworth 2019: 125.

common in poetry, but it is represented in prose as well.[148] There is even a parallel in the *Senatus Consultum de Cn. Pisone Patre* – a public inscription roughly contemporary with the *Res Gestae*—in which reference is made to the "numerous children" (*tot pignora*) of Germanicus and Agrippina.[149] "Children" may not be the only or even the primary meaning of *pignora* in the *Res Gestae*, of course. But there is enough evidence to say that the word had this connotation in Augustan Rome, and that its appearance in the context of a sentence about Arsacid children would have invited readers to consider the familial dimension.

If *pignora* means "children," then the sentence hints at the integration of Arsacid dynasts into Julio-Claudian kinship structures. The phrase in question would then mean that Frahād sought friendship "through the children of his own children." That reading works on a literal level, since the grandchildren (*nepotes*) of Frahād have just been mentioned in the immediately preceding phrase.[150] More generally, though, the point may be that the Parthian king's dispatch of his progeny was not simply a guarantee of good behavior, but rather a confirmation of friendship through joint parentage of sons and daughters. Such a reading recalls Suetonius on Augustus's policy toward client kings, namely that "he brought up many of their children and educated them alongside his own."[151] In this light, the terms of the exchange between Augustus and Frahād diverge from the usual scholarly discussions that revolve around wars, armies, borders, and treaties. The emperor may be speaking of those facets of Roman-Parthian relations, but he is also saying, "to be my friend, Frahād sent me children."

An additional sign of Arsacid-Caesarian unification through kinship may be found in a passage from Ovid's *Ars Amatoria* (The Art of Love) that contains perhaps the sole reference to the Arsacids of Rome in Latin verse.[152] The passage dates to 2 B.C.E., when Augustus's grandson and adopted heir Gaius Caesar prepared to embark for Parthia in a campaign against Frahātak, the son and successor of Frahād IV. Book 1 of Ovid's *Ars Amatoria* dates to the same year and contains a long exhortation to the young commander, including the following lines:[153]

> Cum tibi sint fratres, fratres ulciscere laesos,
> Cumque pater tibi sit, iura tuere patris.
> Induit arma tibi genitor patriaeque tuusque;
> Hostis ab invito regna parente rapit.

---

148. E.g. Tac. *Ann.* 12.2.1.

149. *SCPP* 139 = Potter and Damon 1999: 34–35. On the passage, see also Potter 1999: 76 and n.40; Seager 2013: 52.

150. Cf. Ov. *Met.* 3.134: *tot natos natasque et, pignora cara, nepotes*.

151. Suet. *Aug.* 48.1.

152. I argue in Nabel 2015 that two passages from Horace (*Carm.* 2.2.17–24; *Epist.* 1.12.25–28) may allude to Rome's first Arsacid resident, but the identification is not definitive.

153. Ov. *Ars Am.* 1.195–98; text after Hollis 1977.

Since you have brothers, avenge the brothers who have been wronged. Since you have a father, defend a father's rights. The sire of the fatherland, and of you, girds you with weapons; the enemy snatches rulership from an unwilling parent.

The referents of *fratres* and *pater* have proven difficult to sort out, all the more so because both words are repeated in their respective lines. An earlier commentator thought that both occurrences of the word *fratres* referred to Gaius's biological brothers Lucius Caesar and Agrippa Postumus, while Augustus was the referent of both *paters*.[154] But almost all scholars now accept the reading of A. S. Hollis, whose crucial insight was to understand *fratres laesi* as a reference to the Arsacids of Rome, that is, the four sons of Frahād IV who came to Rome between 19 and 9 B.C.E.[155] On his reading, the "murder" of Frahād IV by Frahātak (the *hostis* of line 198) was an affront to the Roman Arsacids, and Gaius needed to avenge the crime by punishing Frahātak and setting the Arsacid family to rights.[156]

Given the abstruseness of the lines and the fact that "Ovid leaves a fair bit for the reader to do," however, another reading should be entertained: the Arsacids of Rome are Gaius's brothers, and the passage is further evidence for the interconnection of the Caesarian and Arsacid families.[157] A recent suggestion along these lines is made by Nandini Pandey, who speaks of "Gaius' fraternity with [the Arsacids in Rome]" but then calls the latter "Gaius' contemporaries and perhaps even playmates" and stops short of explicit identifications.[158] If the idea of confraternity is taken to its conclusion, the line would mean, in effect, "since you have the Arsacids as brothers, go and avenge the injury to them." But could both occurrences of *fratres* have the same referent? In fact, another line of Ovid uses precisely the same doubling of *frater* to refer to a single individual, and comparable repetitions in Latin poetry refer to brothers from the same family, usually in the context of civil war.[159] The point is not simply that, as a dutiful son, Gaius should help other sons to do their duty. The murder of Frahād IV affects Gaius because the late Parthian king's sons are, in a concrete sense, his own brothers.

This reading of Ovid's text raises the question of whether parental foster-age relationships extended to the fosterer's natal children. Did one become the

<hr>

154. Lenz 1969: 47, 176. For other translations and discussion before Hollis' intervention, see Bornecque 2002 [1924]: 9; Kelk 1975: 112; Williams 1978: 76.

155. Hollis 1977: 77–78, preceded by Hollis 1970; followed by Syme 1978: 9; Pianezzola 1991: 212; Dimundo 2003: 100–1; Casali 2006: 224–26; Luther 2010: 108 and n.22.

156. The assassination of Frahād IV is otherwise attested only in Joseph. *AJ* 18.42–43. Yardley and Heckl 1997: 5 suggest that Just. 42.4.16 may refer to the murder as well, but this reading is not secure: see Bigwood 2004: 42 and n.29.

157. Quotation from Casali 2006: 225.

158. Pandey 2018: 181–82.

159. See Ov. *Met.* 11.410, where two *fraters* on a single line refer to Ceyx's brother, Daedalion; cf. A. Griffin 1997: 185. On other such repetitions of *frater*, see Wills 1996: 205–6.

foster-sibling of their parent's *alumni/ae*? One inscription may suggest so. In a funerary epitaph for one Marcus Vibius Proclus, the dedicator Paenia Daphne calls Vibius her *alumnus*, and she designates her natal son as Vibius's *collact*[*aneus*], which means "foster-brother."[160] The word is not common in literature, though it does appear in legal texts and in a handful of inscriptions.[161] Its literal meaning is "milk-sharer," and it refers to multiple children who were not natal brothers or sisters feeding at the breast of the same woman, most often a wet-nurse.[162] It is unclear, however, whether the term could be used figuratively if the two parties in question had not actually shared breast milk, as Gaius and the sons of Frahād IV certainly did not.[163] Vibius's epitaph is modest testimony that kinship bonds could develop between natal and fostered children, even if it is not conclusive for the meaning of Ovid's verses on Arsacid and Caesarian brotherhood.

A material correlate to the Ovidian passage comes from the south frieze of the Ara Pacis, where a pair of figures may supply evidence for the Arsacids of Rome from the visual arts. The Senate voted to erect the altar in honor of Augustus in 13 B.C.E., and it was dedicated in 9 B.C.E.—a window that corresponds closely to the arrival of Vonones and his brothers.[164] The south frieze shows a procession that some see as a *supplicatio*, but others as a quasi triumph.[165] Among the participants is a young child who is often labeled figure S-30 in discussions of the relief. S-30 wears a decidedly non-Roman getup: he has corkscrew curls, a headband or diadem, a loose tunic, and long-laced shoes (figure 6).[166] He presents a contrast with the three other children on the same face of the monument, all of whom wear the togas and *bullae* that were characteristic of Roman dress. The woman standing behind the young boy is also diademed, and she is the only woman in the entire procession who wears earrings and a scarf.[167] She rests her hand on the boy's head, while the boy himself grabs the toga of the man who precedes him.

160. *CIL* 6.1903. Variant forms of *collactaneus/a* include *conlacteus*, *collacteus*, and *collactius*.

161. Literary references: Hyg. *Fab.* 224.3.3; Maurus Servius Honoratus, *In Vergilii Georgicon Libros* 1.205.5. Legal texts: Gai. *Inst.* 1.38–39; *Dig.* 40.2.13. Inscriptions: see table 1 in Bradley 1979: 60–61.

162. On wet-nursing among Roman elite families, see Joshel 1986; Bradley 1986; Laes 2016: 69–77; Centlivres Challet 2017a: 898; Centlivres Challet 2017b: 377–79. Carroll 2018: 154–55 discusses material evidence and artistic representations. On *collactanei/ae* of dissimilar status, see Bradley 1979: 57–62; Dixon 1992: 128 and n.164.

163. Gaius was born in 20 B.C.E., and at least some of the sons of Frahād IV had children themselves by the time of their arrival in Rome.

164. On the dates of the Ara Pacis's construction, see Weinstock 1960: 48; Rehak 2006: 97.

165. *Supplicatio*: Billows 1993: 89–90; cf. Kleiner and Buxton 2008: 86; Cornwell 2017: 178. Quasi triumph: Settis 1988: 420; Uzzi 2005: 150–55.

166. The child is labeled S-30 in the numbering system of Pollini 1978: 75–173. For other numbering systems, see Kleiner and Buxton 2008: 65 n.28.

167. Pollini 1978: 118–19; Rose 1990: 456–59; Kuttner 1995: 102.

FIGURE 6. The so-called "eastern child" (S-30) from the south frieze of the Ara Pacis. Now in the Museo dell'Ara Pacis, Rome. Photo credit: Miguel Hermoso Cuesta via Wikimedia Commons.

There are various interpretations of the child and his role in the scene, but one view is that he is an Arsacid of Rome. Identification of the figures on the Ara Pacis has always been a contentious subject, and given the idealizing style of Augustan art, it might reasonably be asked whether all its figures are meant to represent specific individuals.[168] But there is reason to believe that certain segments of Roman society, at least, would have had their eyes open to potential identifications, and a few modern scholarly guesses have become deeply entrenched in the literature on the monument.[169] Some scholars have maintained that S-30 represents Gaius

168. Cf. Kleiner 2005: 216–17 and Anderson 1998: 41, who sees the boy and the woman behind him as genre types.

169. In defense of identifying the figures on the Ara Pacis with specific historical figures, see Kleiner and Buxton 2008: 71–72. A more cautionary note is sounded by Rehak 2006: 121–22.

Caesar, clad in eastern garb to celebrate the Trojan games along with his brother Lucius, who supposedly mirrors him on the north frieze (N-34).[170] But others doubt that a Julio-Claudian dynast would appear in non-Roman dress, and prefer to identify the child as a prince of Bosporan, Commagenian, or indeterminate eastern extraction.[171] In more recent studies, however, Brian Rose and Joel Allen argue that the child may represent a son or, rather more likely given his apparent age, a grandson of Frahād IV. Rose additionally suggests that the woman behind the child is his mother and the wife of one of Frahād's sons.[172] This interpretation need not exclude others. Different understandings of the monument would surely have circulated in antiquity and can be reasonably maintained today. But the Arsacid identification is appealing not least because of the close chronological correspondence between the altar's construction and the arrival of Frahād's family members in the city. Moreover, the regular arrival and birth of new Arsacid "hostages" infused the Roman cityscape with young Parthian royalty until at least the end of the Julio-Claudian period. A contemporary could easily have understood S-30 in this sense.

Of course, the lack of consensus among art historians is revealing in its own right of the collapsing distinction between Augustus's Roman sons and his Arsacid fosterlings. Both Gaius Caesar and the Arsacid sons of Frahād IV were, in a way, the children of Augustus, and the ambiguous identity of the figure in eastern dress underlines their interchangeability as youths under Augustan parentage. Some scholars maintain that the Ara Pacis is a monument about dynastic succession, a visual argument that "sustained prosperity depends on the continued rule of the 'male progeny' of the Julian line."[173] If so, however, it is striking that none of the children are accorded visual primacy in the reliefs, and it speaks volumes that Augustus's adopted son Gaius—with all the legal rights that adoption entailed—should be iconographically similar to an Arsacid foster-son. On the Ara Pacis no less than in the *Ars Amatoria*, fosterage had fused Caesarian and Arsacid kinship structures in such a way that, in certain contexts, it was difficult to see where one family ended and the other began.[174]

170. Pollini 1978: 105–6, 157–58 and n.95 (revised in Pollini 1987: 22–27 to "Celtic child"); Zanker 1988: 217–18; Kleiner 1992: 96; Hurlet 1997: 114–15; La Rocca 1983: 24–31; Rossini 2007: 55.

171. Bosporan (child of Dynamis): Rose 1990: 458. Commagenian (son of Iotape I): Kuttner 1995: 103–4. "Prince of an Asiatic dynasty": Kleiner and Buxton 2008: 74. See further Severy 2003: 110.

172. Rose 2005: 40; Allen 2006: 106; followed by Schlude 2020: 98. On Augustus and female hostages, cf. Suet. *Aug.* 21.2.

173. Lamp 2009: 17.

174. For a similar reading, see Schneider 2012: 125–28. For Schneider, however, the ambiguity of S-30 (and his counterpart on the north frieze) is a sign not of Arsacid-Caesarian kinship, but of Rome's selective identification with its own construction of the East—an illustration of "a conceptual overlap between seemingly contradictory categories such as Roman and Oriental, friend and foe" (2012: 127).

FIGURE 7. Aureus of Augustus from Lugdunum, 8 B.C.E. On the reverse side, Augustus receives a child from a bearded Gaul. *RIC* 1 no. 200. Photo credit: Berlin, Münzkabinett der Staatlichen Museen, 18204901.

While the Ara Pacis presents the subsumption of foreign children into Rome's imperial order in a peaceable and benevolent guise, other Roman media underline the power differential between pro-parent and child. To the extent that the emperor served as fosterer, he was a patronal one, and his collection of children had an edge that was imperious and domineering, not innocuously sentimental. In a scene that appears on the Boscoreale Cups, on a glass gem, and on coins minted in 9 B.C.E., Augustus sits atop a platform and receives children from Gallic noblemen.[175] On the coin, he extends his hand to receive a child from a bearded figure who is presumably its natal father (figure 7). Though this child is Gallic, the scene models a pro-parental authority that applied to the empire as a whole, configuring children as symbols of submission and control. Some two centuries later, the paradigm found more violent expression on the triumphal arch of Septimius Severus, which commemorates his campaigns against the Arsacid kingdom. Among the beaten and shackled Parthians who are paraded in subjection at the base of the monument, one prisoner carries a baby (figure 8).[176] The monument parades a captive child's body as an emblem of territorial domination, and it shows the commensurability of imperial pro-parentage with the Roman institution of hostageship. The emperor's paternalism was domination in familial clothing; the children he gathered were so much tribute or war booty. Just as the Roman *paterfamilias*

175. *RIC* 1 no. 200, 201a–b (Sutherland and Carson 1984: 55); Kuttner 1995: 12, 107–11; Cornwell 2017: 181; Gołyźniak 2020: 225–26, 552 with figures 853–54.

176. Brilliant 1967: 151, 155–56, pedestal relief no. 14, plate 53a.

FIGURE 8. On the Arch of Septimius Severus in the Roman forum (203 C.E.), a bearded Parthian in chains carries a baby. Photo credit: Clayton Lose.

wielded uncompromising authority over the members of his household, the head of the Julio-Claudian dynasty expected subjection from his imperial children.

CONCLUSION

For the Romans, then, the Arsacids of their city could be hostages or foster-children—but they were tokens of Parthian inferiority either way. *Hostage* was their primary designation because the label suited the self-conception and public presentation of Rome's rulers. Julio-Claudian regimes repeatedly displayed the Arsacids of Rome in grandiose public spectacles, marshaling the triumphal traditions of the republican past to claim the power of the conqueror over the body of the hostage. When the sons of Frahād IV were led over the sands by Augustus; when Caligula paraded Dārāw across his bridge as human plunder; when Tirdād and his Arsacid retinue bowed before Nero in the forum—all such events pressed Arsacid "hostages" into service to fashion a public image of Roman supremacy and Parthian compliance.

As in Parthia, fosterage too could provide a frame of reference for understanding the Arsacids, but in Rome its degree was limited and its primary valence was patronal. Only one Roman source, Tacitus, is explicit in his application of fosterage terminology to the Arsacids of Rome. His designation of Tiberius as their *altor* is meaningful evidence for interdynastic kinship between the two ruling families, even if the implications of such kinship remain unclear. Claudius's correlative use of *alumnus* shows kinship but not of the interdynastic variety, since the full phrase "foster-child of the city" assigns the role of foster-father to the Roman state rather than to the emperor himself. The foster-childhood of the Arsacids may be alluded to in other Julio-Claudian sources, but not in an obvious or straightforward manner. In the end, fosterage had some purchase in Roman thinking about the Arsacids, but its place was secondary to hostageship, and the notions of kinship that it engendered were faint and subsidiary.

Rome's interpretation of its Arsacid residents therefore set the stage for pragmatic misunderstanding with Parthia over the meaning of their circulation. To the degree that the Romans saw the Arsacids as foster-children, they would have analogized them with the *alumni* of the Roman family who were typically lower in social status than their fosterers. A patronal fosterage view would have led the Romans to conclusions about the Arsacids that were diametrically opposed to those of the Parthians, whose operational model was cliental. But even more dissonance stemmed from the dominant classification of the Arsacids of Rome as hostages, a category of foreigner that Roman triumphalism coded as a type of imperial subject. To the east of the Euphrates, the Arsacids could rejoice that the Roman emperor had accepted Parthian suzerainty by assuming the role of a fosterer. To the west, the Romans could celebrate the surrender of hostages from an eastern imperial neighbor long recalcitrant, but finally, it now appeared, brought to bay. Through fortuitous incomprehension, both sides could claim the upper hand in the transfers that brought Arsacid dynasts to the heart of Roman power.

4

Remission

The Emperor as Parthian Aristocrat

The circulation of Arsacid royalty between the Iranian plateau and the Mediterranean ran in two directions. Members of the dynasty left Parthia for Rome, but some returned, as well. On four occasions, the Arsacids in Italy saw members of their group depart the Julio-Claudian court to contend for their ancestral throne. Powerful factions in the Parthian empire had petitioned the emperor for the release of a new king of kings, and the petition had been granted. In an instant, quiet lives of status and comfort but little actual power were exchanged for the battlefields of dynastic warfare and, in some cases, even the Arsacid kingship itself. The transfer of Arsacids from Parthia to Rome was a function of pragmatic misunderstanding between Arsacid and Julio-Claudian rulers. But why should the trajectory of the Arsacids of Rome have taken them back over the Euphrates in the opposite direction?

The answer routinely offered in the literature adopts a state-centric framework to account for the return of Arsacids to Parthia: the Roman emperors used their Arsacid residents to "interfere" in Parthian domestic politics. Scholars of this persuasion hold that a stable, unified Parthia threatened the Roman east, so the release of Arsacids was a Roman effort to destabilize and divide. State interests and Roman agency are at the center of the story, and the emperor's custody of Arsacid princes facilitates intrusion upon Parthia's internal affairs—a sphere to which the Romans did not belong and where they could act only as interlopers. Parthian motives are left unexplained except as a pretext for Roman action, and Parthia itself is thought to have been left enfeebled or even humiliated by its recourse to the Arsacids of the Julio-Claudian court.

This chapter advances a new interpretation of Arsacid remission that replaces state-centric analysis with a focus on ruling families, royal fosterage, and kinship. Centering Parthia instead of Rome, I advance a reading of Arsacid release that construes the Roman emperor not as a head of state, but as the patriarch of a ruling family performing cliental fosterage for the Arsacid dynasty. This framework opens a new perspective on the relationship between the emperor and the nonroyal Parthian elite, a collection of hereditary clans that supported the Arsacid kingship but also expected privileges and prerogatives from it. From this vantage point, Arsacid remission was not a case of one empire's illicit meddling in the domestic affairs of another, but rather a dialogue among the various parties with a stake in Arsacid fosterage and kinship.

Two bodies of evidence support this reading. First, Near Eastern sources from late antiquity can, with due caution and awareness of their limitations, be used to better understand the Parthian nobility and its interaction with the royal families of Iran and Rome. Few Roman authors offer contemporaneous evidence for the structural role of the Parthian nobility in the first century C.E. Their perspectives, moreover, are external, and their references bare. While sources from Arsacid Armenia and Sasanian Iran postdate the Roman ones, they chronicle a period in which many of the same noble families continued to wield power, and they do so from an internal vantage point. Their testimony sheds new light on the complex negotiations among kings, noblemen, and the royal children who circulated between them. From the standpoint they reveal, the Roman emperor's remission of Arsacids to Parthian custody was not infiltration or subversion, but instead a customary form of resistance among families linked to the Arsacid dynasty through cliental fosterage.

Second, one Roman source, namely Tacitus, attributes detailed argumentation to the envoys of the Parthian elites who petitioned the emperor for Arsacid princes. Scholars discount the historical value of these passages, but they are consistent with the Near Eastern evidence for the Iranian aristocracy and its attitudes toward royal misconduct. Tacitus should not be dismissed out of hand on this topic. Instead, he can be read as a witness to the divergence between Parthian and Roman understandings of Arsacid release. His account shows that the "infiltration" objective so discussed in modern scholarship must be recognized as a particularity of Roman thought, not an objective truth. By the same token, Parthian aspirations to police the Arsacid kingship and to uphold the dynasty's integrity were not Tacitean inventions or empty diplomatic niceties, as is sometimes argued. Rather, these claims illustrate the genuine self-conception of the Parthian aristocracy—a group that now, because of Arsacid fosterage, could reach out to the Roman emperor as a member of its ranks.

INFILTRATION AND FACTIONALISM:
THE STATE OF THE QUESTION

Why, and under what conditions, did Arsacid dynasts leave Rome for Ctesiphon? Most scholars approach this question from a Roman perspective and as an adjunct to the study of Roman hostageship. Their discussions center on Roman agency, interests, and policy. The Romans thought that former hostages made good client-kings, the argument runs, so the release of Arsacids projected their power into Parthia through the installation of a compliant vassal. Over a century ago, Guglielmo Ferrero opined that the emperor's custody of Arsacids gave Rome "an admirable pretext for interference in Parthian policy."[1] The view persists. For Joel Allen, the history of Arsacid release comprises "the efforts of five different emperors to infiltrate the Parthian court with former hostages as vassals."[2] Edward Dąbrowa describes it as "betting on internal conflicts and supporting Parthian pretenders to keep the Arsacids under pressure."[3] Kenneth Harl paints a similar picture: "Augustus and his heirs had a supply of Parthian pretenders, reared at Rome, to produce as rivals to any ambitious Arsacid king who wished to revise the settlement [of 19 B.C.E.]."[4] Many echo this designation of the Arsacids of Rome as "pretenders," as though association with Rome deprived the Arsacid in question of his authenticity.[5] In one assessment, the Roman release of Arsacids is even imagined as an exercise in degradation. Thus Barbara Levick sees Claudius's release of Mihrdād as "another opportunity to inflict a crushing humiliation on the Parthians at no cost by deploying a claimant to their throne."[6] In sum, much of the literature construes Arsacid release as an illicit Roman effort to infiltrate, interfere with, or compromise the sphere of Parthian domestic politics.

Elsewhere, a different perspective is on offer: Arsacid release was not imposed on Parthian domestic politics but rather grew out of them. Here, scholars start from the observation that no Roman emperor ever released an Arsacid without a request from the reigning Arsacid king (in one case) or the Parthian nobility (in four cases). From this vantage point, the motives behind such Parthian initiatives matter and require investigation. Dąbrowa approached this question by positing a division in the Parthian nobility between supporters of a strong monarchy on one side and its antagonists on the other. As he sees it, the opponents of centralized royal power turned to the Arsacids of Rome as a hedge against domineering kings.[7] Another attempt to delimit factions comes from Marek Olbrycht, who connects Arsacid release to divisions within the Arsacid family itself. For Olbrycht, Parthian politics in the early first century C.E. centered on a group he calls the "Sinatrucids" or the "Phraatids." The terms refer to branches of the Arsacid dynasty that were descended from Sanatruq/Sinatruces (r. c. 77–70 B.C.E.) and Frahād/Phraates IV,

---

1. Ferrero 1909: 231.

2. Allen 2020: 256.

3. Dąbrowa 1983: 124 (". . . de miser sur les conflits intérieurs et de soutenir les prétendants parthes comme méthode de pression sur les Arsacides.")

4. Harl 2016: 119; cf. Gregoratti 2020: 82, 86; Hauser 2022: 168.

5. Debevoise 1938: 172; Walker 1980: 163; Bivar 1983: 71, 73–74, 76; Olbrycht 2014: 93; Wiesehöfer 2015: 338; Gregoratti 2017: 110; Dąbrowa 2021: 51; Olbrycht 2021d.

6. Levick 2015: 189.

7. Dąbrowa 1983: 44–45, 90, 121–24.

the latter of whom inaugurated the tradition of sending Arsacids to Rome. Olbrycht holds that the Phraatids and their supporters (among whom he numbers the Sūrēn and Kārin families of the Parthian nobility) represented a distinct party or faction in Parthian domestic politics. The preference of this faction for the descendants of Frahād IV explains its appeals to Rome for the release of that king's children and grandchildren.[8]

I share Dąbrowa's and Olbrycht's interest in the Parthian impetus behind Arsacid remission, but I diverge from their conclusions. Both scholars offer valuable correctives to the Romano-centric "infiltration" view. Yet their arguments can be improved upon, for two reasons. First, Dąbrowa and Olbrycht base their conclusions on Greco-Roman literary texts—a reasonable approach, to be sure, since Roman authors constitute the only direct evidence for Arsacid remission. As both scholars illustrate, however, the relationship between the Arsacid king and the Parthian nobility was a pivotal factor in these exchanges. That relationship can be better understood through non-Roman sources for pre-Islamic Iranian history, especially texts from Sasanian Iran and Arsacid Armenia. Second, even if the evidentiary basis for the question is confined to Roman literature, the reconstructions of Dąbrowa and Olbrycht are too schematic. The existence of organized, coherent, and stable factions within the Parthian domestic sphere is simply not supported by the available sources, and the binaries that these discussions posit— between supporters and opponents of a strong Arsacid monarchy in Dąbrowa's case, and between "Phraatids" and their rivals in Olbrycht's—do not withstand close scrutiny. The topic is better served by a fluid and dynamic model of interaction between the Arsacid dynasty and nonroyal Parthian elites, since a more flexible reconstruction both better fits the Roman texts and can accommodate input from the late antique evidence.

A better accounting of the relationship between Arsacid kings and their Parthian elite interlocutors opens a new perspective on Arsacid remission, one that construes the Roman emperor as a cliental fosterer and, by extension, as a species of Parthian nobleman. For members of the Parthian elite, the emperor's custody of Arsacid children would have made him a peer rather than an alien captor. Consequently, the embassies of the Parthian aristocracy to the Julio-Claudian court can be interpreted not as seditious acts inviting foreign interference, but as a dialogue among stakeholders in Arsacid fosterage. In what follows, then, I investigate the identities of the nonroyal Parthians who petitioned Rome, integrating late antique sources that offer additional insight on the relationship between the Parthian aristocracy and the Arsacid dynasty. I then return to the Arsacids of Rome and reconsider their release from this new vantage point.

---

8. Olbrycht 2013a: 101; Olbrycht 2013b (I rely on the author's English summary, since the work is in Polish, which I do not read); Olbrycht 2014; Olbrycht 2016a: 23–24.

TABLE 2 Arsacids Sent from Rome to Parthia

Name(s)	Date	Sources
Son of Frahād IV	c. 23 B.C.E.	Cass. Dio 51.18.2–3, 53.33.1–2; Just. 42.5.6–9; cf. *Mon. Anc.* 32.1
Vonones	c. 8 C.E.	*Mon. Anc.* 33; *SCPP* 37–45; Joseph. *AJ* 18.46; Tac. *Ann.* 2.2.1
Frahād	35 C.E.	Tac. *Ann.* 6.31.2; Cass. Dio 58.26.2
Tirdād	35/6 C.E.	Tac. *Ann.* 6.32.2–3; Cass. Dio 58.26.2
Mihrdād	49 C.E.	Tac. *Ann.* 11.10.4, 12.10–11

THE CASES

Greek and Latin texts record five cases when an Arsacid departed Rome for Parthian territory. Each time, the release of the dynast came at the request of one or more Parthian dignitaries. Only once, however, was the petitioner the Arsacid king himself. This was during the first case cataloged in table 2, when Frahād IV requested the release of his son—a child, it should be noted, whose submission to Augustus was not his father's wish, but rather a result of his abduction by the rebel king Tirdād.[9] Unfortunately, the Roman sources for this episode leave it mired in obscurity. As far as the remission of the child is concerned, the dispute turns on the contradictory testimony of Dio and Justin: the former seems to regard Augustus's delivery of the Arsacid prince as part of a bargain, while the latter says the child was returned at no cost to his father.[10] Scholars have argued both ways, but a final answer is beyond the reach of the available evidence.[11] The logic of the exchange remains unclear. In any event, the transaction was a one-off, since no subsequent Arsacids would return to Parthia at the reigning king's request.

In every other case, the emperor's remission of an Arsacid dynast came at the request of nonroyal Parthian elites. The sources for these exchanges are entirely Greco-Roman, and their vocabulary for the social status of the petitioners varies. In the *Res Gestae*, Augustus calls the Parthians who requested Vonones the "most distinguished men" of that people.[12] Josephus describes the same group as "the most well-born."[13] In Tacitus, Vonones's adherents were "the first men" of the Parthians, while those who sought Frahād and Tirdād a generation later were "nobles."[14]

9. For background and recent discussion of the "Tiridates episode," see Nabel 2015; Curtis and Magub 2020: 45–47; Schlude 2020: 97–102; Olbrycht 2021b.

10. Cass. Dio 53.33.2, 54.8.1; Just. 42.5.9.

11. For those who detect a contractual arrangement at work, see Timpe 1975: 167–68; Nedergaard 1988: 106; Luther 2010: 104. But others reject the idea; see Ziegler 1964: 46–47 (who prefers to follow Justin); Allen 2006: 85 n.53. Schlude 2020: 98–100, at 98 describes the return of the child as a "trust-building measure."

12. *Mon. Anc.* 33 (*principes*, or *prōtoi* in the Greek).

13. Joseph. *AJ* 18.44–6 (*hoi gennaiotatoi*).

14. Tac. *Ann.* 2.2.1, 6.31.2 (*primores*); 6.31.1 (*nobiles*). The Parthians who sought Mihrdād in 49 C.E. are simply called *legati*, but Tacitus does not specify whose ambassadors, precisely, they were.

In other places, the emperor's petitioners are simply "Parthians" without further specification.[15] On balance, it is clear that the return of Arsacids from Rome to Parthia was initiated by Parthian elites rather than reigning kings, even if the terse references in Roman sources leave their identities unclear.

More information is available on the supporters of the Arsacids of Rome within Parthian territory, however, and the evidence from Tacitus enables their classification into five groups. First, two supporters headed families that belonged to a group conventionally described as the "Parthian nobility." Second, two supporters belonged to a family that may have numbered among these noble clans, but their description is insufficient to say so with confidence. Third, two supporters were Parthian client kings, that is, rulers of regional kingdoms that belonged to the Parthian west. Fourth, two supporters were holders of Parthian administrative offices. Fifth and finally, one supporter's heritage is unknown. His case notwithstanding, the predominant characteristic among these figures is their membership in elite kinship groups. This background matters, for it was precisely such groups that performed cliental fosterage for the ruling dynasty throughout Iranian history. A basic taxonomy of those who sought Arsacid remission provides ample grounds for connecting these exchanges to the matter of fosterage.

The Parthian Nobility

Two figures mentioned by Tacitus belonged to a group that scholars have conventionally labeled the Parthian nobility. The first appears in Tacitus's narrative of Tirdād's campaign in 35/36 C.E. Once the Arsacid of Rome reached Ctesiphon, Tacitus writes, "Surena crowned [him] with the royal insignia according to ancestral custom."[16] The coronation is the only action attributed to Surena, who subsequently disappears from the narrative. The second aristocratic figure is connected to Mihrdād's remission in 49 C.E. As Tacitus tells the story, Mihrdād's wisest and most faithful supporter was one "Carenes." This man admonished the young dynast against the dilatory course his campaign took in its early stages; he contributed a substantial military force that joined the army in northern Mesopotamia; and he was unique among Mihrdād's supporters in his steadfastness during the final battle against the reigning king Gōdarz II, where his contingent achieved initial success before succumbing to a renewed assault by the enemy.[17]

The mention of "Surena" as the figure who crowned Tirdād (at least after his conquest of Mesopotamia) is a clear reference to a relatively well-attested Parthian elite family. Though Roman authors seem to have understood Surena(s) as a personal name, it was in fact the name of a noble family, and its application to individuals is better understood as a hereditary designation connoting patriarchal

---

15. Cass. Dio 58.26.1–2; Tac. *Ann.* 11.10.4, 12.10–11.

16. Tac. *Ann.* 6.42.4. On the right of the Sūrēn to crown the Arsacid king, see also Plut. *Crass.* 21.7.

17. Tac. *Ann.* 12.12.3, 12.13.1, 12.14.2.

authority. The Sūrēn family is first attested as a major political actor in Roman sources for the year 58 B.C.E., when its clan head had amassed enough power to reinstall Urūd II on the Arsacid throne.[18] It is best known for its participation in the Battle of Carrhae, where the same man supplied and commanded the Parthian army.[19] The Sūrēn survived the transition from Arsacid to Sasanian rule, and the family subsequently appears in a diverse range of sources, from Middle Iranian inscriptions to late antique Latin literature to Armenian historiography. The family's base of power during its heyday is thought to have been the eastern Iranian region called Sakastan or Seistan, but this contention is based on a single sentence of questionable relevance in Tabari, and it may be preferable to imagine dispersed territorial possessions on the model of Achaemenid land tenure practices.[20] When the Arabs arrived, the Sūrēn fled east with the Sasanians and remained a potent force even in exile. The final witness to the family's legacy may be a ninth-century C.E. Chinese-Middle Persian epitaph from Tang China that marks the tomb of a Sūrēn princess, though the reading of the family name is contested.[21] Among his supporters, then, the Arsacid of Rome Tirdād could count one of the most powerful and enduring aristocratic families of pre-Islamic Iran.

No meaner in status than the Sūrēn were the Kārin, whose patriarch seems to have numbered among the allies of Mihrdād in 49 C.E. This, at least, is the common understanding of Tacitus's reference to "Carenes," and while there are other entities from Parthian Iran to which the name might be connected, the parallel with the Sūrēn's appearance in the Tirdād narrative makes the identification with the Kārin family a convincing one.[22] While the Kārin are otherwise unattested in Roman sources for the Parthian period, Near Eastern evidence shows the family's elevated status under the Sasanians. Kārin dignitaries are named alongside Sūrēn ones in the royal inscriptions of Shapur I and Narseh, which include the Kārin among the realm's most important aristocrats.[23] Armenian sources confirm

18. Plut. *Crass.* 21.7; cf. Just. 42.4.

19. See Karras-Klapproth 1988: 165–66 for references.

20. The family's supposed heartland in Sakastan/Seistan is firmly entrenched in the literature: see Marquart 1895: 635–37; Herzfeld 1932: 77–78; Lukonin 1983: 705; Shahbazi 1993: 156–57; Tarn 1997 [1922]: 499; Ball 2000: 13; Hauser 2006: 306; Bivar 2007: 28; Pourshariati 2008: 64; Gazerani 2016: 14–17; Ellerbrock 2021: 83. A dissenting voice is Christensen 1993: 327 n.20. Tabari's testimony is at 1.683, trans. Perlmann 1987: 77. On the dispersed land holdings of Persian elites in the Achaemenid period, see Briant 1985: 55–6; Tuplin 2020: 46–61; Basello 2021: 862; Waerzeggers 2021: 999.

21. Baghbidi 2011: 107; but cf. Yoshida 2022: 86–88, discussing alternate readings.

22. The Aramaic legend *krny* appears on the coinage of Aršak I, the founder of the Arsacid dynasty (e.g. Sellwood 1980: 23, type 3.1), and the Achaemenid title *karanos* (a supraregional commander) is found in Greek sources. One might compare these references to Tacitus's Carenes, though on balance the Kārin identification seems more likely. On *krny*, see Sinisi 2012b: 280; Hyland 2013; Rung 2015; Shayegan 2017: 406–21. For the identification of Tacitus's Carenes with the Kārin family, see Herzfeld 1932: 64; Lukonin 1983: 704; Wolski 1989: 226; Hauser 2006: 306; Olbrycht 2016a: 24.

23. ŠKZ 42, 46; NPi 32. On the orthography of the family's name, see Schmitt 1983.

this impression and preserve genealogies that connect the Sūrēn and Kārin to the Arsacid dynasty and to other elite families of the Armenian nobility.[24] Various literary sources from late antiquity demonstrate the immense power the Kārin wielded under the later Sasanians, and several surviving bullae were impressed by a seal whose Middle Persian legend proclaimed the bearer's Kārinid pedigree.[25] As with the Sūrēn, the fortunes of the family seem to have waxed and waned over time, but by all accounts it was a powerful actor in the Iranian world throughout the Arsacid and Sasanian periods.

What structural place did these families occupy in the Arsacid empire? Contemporary evidence is scarce and external, but sources from Arsacid Armenia and Sasanian Iran can provide further basis for reconstruction. Strabo and Justin both claim that the Parthians had a "senate," and Strabo's more detailed report describes this institution as a bicameral body composed of "kinsmen" on one side and "wise people and magi" on the other.[26] If the word "kinsman" denoted an honorific, created kinship rather than a natal one, as is usually assumed, then this advisory body may have comprised Parthian aristocrats, but the absence of evidence for any such formal institution outside of Roman sources makes this testimony suspect.[27] By contrast, for the Sasanian period, Lukonin's scheme of the ruling class's organization identified four groups: the kings, the princes, the great ones, and the free ones.[28] Judging by the Sasanian royal inscriptions where the Sūrēn and Kārin appear, these families belonged to the third tier, though the texts in question do not make a clear distinction between the "great" and the "free" in the lists of dignitaries they rehearse.[29] By any measure, however, the Sūrēn and Kārin were among the most powerful nonroyalty in the empire. In the extant sources, the most observable manifestation of their power is the occupation of Sasanian offices like the post of *hazārbed* and *wuzurg framādār*.[30] It remains unclear, though, whether such posts were hereditary prerogatives or ad hoc appointments; whether noble families were regionally concentrated or geographically dispersed; and whether the collective nobility represented a formal political institution or merely a social

---

24. Genealogy of the Sūrēn and Kārin: MKh 2.27–28, trans. Thomson 1978: 164–66; cf. Garsoïan 1976: 181, 197–98 n.28. Kamsarakan descent from the Kārin: MKh 2.73, 2.87, trans. Thomson 1978: 219, 241; see also the references collected in Toumanoff 1963: 206–7 n.236.

25. For the literary references, see Pourshariati 2020. For the sigillographic evidence, see Gyselen 2007: 67, 308–10; Gyselen 2019: 169.

26. Strab. 11.9.3 (*synedrion*); Just. 42.4.1 (*senatus*). Just. 41.2.1, where the author says "the order of the people (*populorum*) is next to the authority of the [Arsacid] kings" is generally regarded as a textual corruption.

27. For this understanding of "kinsman," see Herzfeld 1932: 53–54.

28. Lukonin 1983: 699; see further chapter 1.

29. ŠKZ 42, 46, trans. Huyse 1999: 54–55, 58–59; NPi 16, 32, trans. Skjærvø 1983: 33–34, 42–43. See Rubin 2021: 245–46 for discussion.

30. Pourshariati 2008: 60–65; Payne 2014: 292; Patterson 2017: 192. On the offices, see Shayegan 2003a.

class.[31] As these issues are debatable even in the Sasanian context where evidence is relatively plentiful, there can be no firm conclusions regarding the Arsacid period.

The longue durée history of the Iranian nobility does make clear, however, that its constituent families could clash both with the king of kings and with each other. Regarding its centrifugal tendency to oppose the monarchy, the sources tell of many episodes when constellations of nobles and other allies deposed a reigning king and replaced him with another member of his dynasty. Deposition was not a constitutional right or formal procedure, but took place on an ad hoc basis when a critical mass of nonroyal elites had both the will and the means to initiate regime change. This pattern is in evidence even before the Arsacid remissions from Rome, and several Sasanian cases are known as well.[32] Such interventions did not signal a complete rejection of the established political order, since the claim of the Arsacid and Sasanian dynasties on the kingship was almost always respected. Rather, they were an exercise of what Zeev Rubin has described as the "noble's right of rebellion" during the Sasanian period: deviant and unsatisfactory kings could be deposed with justice so long as the reigning dynasty's royal prerogative was not challenged.[33] The replacement had to be an Arsacid or Sasanian, but his subsequent reign would be more palatable, or so the aggrieved elites would hope.

Yet aristocratic families feuded not only with the king but also with each other, and it would be a mistake to view the kingship and the nobility as two monolithic and immutable factions. When the king of kings clashed with nonroyal elites, his fight was with specific individuals, not the nobility as a whole. For their part, nobles were as likely to take aim at one another as they were the king.[34] Indeed, the Kārin family features in one such intra-aristocratic conflict from Sasanian late antiquity. Their fight was with the Mihrān, another noble clan that first appears in the inscription of Shapur I in a position that looks inferior to the Sūrēn and Kārin.[35] If the Mihrān began the Sasanian period at a disadvantage, though, they soon made up the ground, and by late antiquity, literary and sigillographic evidence puts its members in charge of key military and administrative posts.[36] The only detailed sources on the rivalry between the Kārin and the Mihrān are postconquest, but the main outlines of the episode are clear enough. In the late fifth century C.E., Kārinid power reached an acme under a patriarch by the name of Sukhra or Zarmihr.[37] The Sasanian king Kavad rankled at the excessive political influence of Sukhra, and he appealed to Shapur, the head of the Mihrān family, for aid. Shapur marched on

31. On the question of hereditary appointments, see Börm 2018: 26–29.

32. For Arsacid cases, see Ellerbrock 2021: 83 n.27. For Sasanian ones, see Börm 2008: 433–35; Pourshariati 2008: 57–58; Mosig-Walburg 2010: 133–34.

33. Rubin 2021: 263, 268–69.

34. Pourshariati 2008: 81; Mosig-Walburg 2010: 155–56; Payne 2014: 291.

35. ŠKZ 50.

36. Shayegan 2022: 222.

37. On the discrepancy of the sources on his name, see Jackson Bonner 2020: 141.

the court, arrested Sukhra, and had the Kārinid leader executed.[38] As the history of the Kārin family itself demonstrates, then, the Iranian nobility was not a unified entity that counterbalanced the kingship as a single bloc. Aristocratic families could fight with one another, whether on behalf of the king of kings, or in conjunction with him, or irrespective of him.

The intra-elite competitive tendencies of the Parthian nobility matter to the cases of Arsacid remission, for they call into question Olbrycht's reconstruction of a "Sinatrucid" or "Phraatid" faction in Parthian domestic politics during the first centuries B.C.E. and C.E. According to Olbrycht, the Sūrēn and Kārin consistently lined up behind the Arsacids of Rome and against the reigning kings Ardawān II and Gōdarz II, since they preferred to have the descendants of Frahād IV on the throne.[39] But there is no possible evidentiary basis for this argument aside from Tacitus, and his text does not support it. Of the four relevant cases of Arsacid remission tabulated above (table 2), the Sūrēn are connected only to one, namely the case of Tirdād. The same is true of the Kārin, who are named only in the context of Mihrdād's campaign. There is no indication whatsoever, in Tacitus or anywhere else, that the Sūrēn supported Mihrdād, or that the Kārin supported Frahād or Tirdād, or for that matter that either family supported Vonones. The notion that these two clans were members of a stable and enduring faction has no basis, then, in any ancient source. In fact, what Tacitus does say about the participation of the Sūrēn and Kārin in these events—namely that one family supported an earlier attempt at regime change, and the other a later one—accords well with the fluid dynamic that is observable in the Near Eastern sources from late antiquity: Iranian families could oppose either the king of kings or their noble peers based not on categorical political commitments, but on shifting and contingent objectives that varied with historical circumstances. Both the Sūrēn and Kārin supported individual Arsacids of Rome, but the idea that they repeatedly supported this group as a matter of principle is unsustainable.

Elite Families of Uncertain Identity

The Sūrēn and Kārin aside, Tacitus's *Annals* mention one other entity involved in Arsacid remission that was clearly a noble family, but one whose name is not known. The prime instigator of the mission to Rome in 35/36 C.E. was one "Sinnaces," or Sēnak in Parthian.[40] The name is known from Parthian documentary evidence, but its other bearers were not political elites, or at least not obviously so. In the Nisa ostraca, one Sēnak is attested as a deliverer of flour, and in the parchments from

---

38. The primary sources are Tabari 1.855, trans. Bosworth 1999: 131–32; Ferdowsi, *Shahnameh* = Khaleghi-Motlagh and Khatibi 2007: 53–60; Dīnawarī, trans. Jackson Bonner 2014: 368. For analysis of the episode and its source tradition, see Pourshariati 2008: 78–81; Rezakhani 2017: 128–34; Jackson Bonner 2020: 141–42; Rubin 2021: 247–48.

39. Olbrycht 2016a: 23–24.

40. Tac. *Ann.* 6.31.2. On the Parthian name, see Schmitt 2016: 203 (no. 474).

Avroman, another is named as a witness on the deed of sale for a vineyard.[41] Both references are devoid of further context, but in neither case does the Sēnak in question seem to occupy a status on par with the nobles from the Sūrēn and Kārin families. Yet Tacitus describes Sēnak as a member of just such a family. The subsequent narrative bears this out, because Sēnak's father Abdagaš (Abdagaeses in Latin) would later join his son as a supporter of Tirdād against Ardawān. Indeed, Sēnak and Abdagaš offered the Arsacid of Rome extensive financial and military support, and Abdagaš fought alongside him until the ultimate failure of his campaign.[42]

The membership of these two figures in an elite family is clear, but less can be said about them than scholars have imagined. One conventional view is that Sēnak and Abdagaš were members of the Sūrēn family, with the latter serving as its clan head or patriarch.[43] The rationale for this identification, however, is a tenuous and arbitrary reading of *Annals* 6.42.4, where adherents of this view understand the name Sūrēn as a roundabout reference to Abdagaš. But Tacitus makes no explicit connection between the two figures, and if he understood them to be the same person, his text as written would be a strange and unparalleled way to express the idea. Evidence external to Tacitus does not support the identification, either. A man named Abdagases is also mentioned by Josephus as the military commander (*stratopedarchēs*) of Ardawān II, Tirdād's Arsacid opponent.[44] It is uncertain whether this official should be identified with the figure of the same name in Tacitus, but in any case, there is no sign of affiliation with the Sūrēn.[45] Josephus mentions an additional Parthian noble of relevance in an episode from the early first century B.C.E. called "Mithridates Sinakes, the *hyparchos* of the Parthians."[46] Pascal Arnaud has connected the name Sēnak with the northern Mesopotamian city of Sinnaca, known from Strabo and Plutarch; he suggests that the Roman authors perhaps mistook the title of a regional office ("governor of Sinnaca" or a comparable designation) for a personal name.[47] At any rate, none of these

41. Diakonoff and Livshits 2001: 168–69 (no. 2599, line 12); Avroman 3, line 6 in Hackl et al. 2010: 2.566–67.

42. Tac. *Ann.* 6.36.2, 6.37.3, 6.43.1, 6.43.3, 6.44.4. On the name Abdagaš, see Schmitt 2016: 33 (no. 1); it need not indicate "Semitic origin" or still less Arab heritage, as claimed by Koestermann 1963–68: 2.316.

43. Cunningham 1890: 119; Marquart 1895: 636–37; Herzfeld 1932: 76–77; Karras-Klapproth 1988: 10, 164; Schottky 2006; Gazerani 2016: 24; Olbrycht 2016a: 25; Woodman 2017: 226. More cautious are Bivar 2007: 32; Brunner 2011.

44. Joseph. *AJ* 18.333–34.

45. On the potential identification between Josephus's and Tacitus's Abdagaš, see Bivar 1983: 73–74; Schottky 2006.

46. Joseph. *AJ* 13.384; cf. Shayegan 2011: 203.

47. Arnaud 1986: 139–41; for the toponym Sinnaca, see Strab. 16.1.23; Plut. *Crass.* 29.4–6. Richardson 2014: 452 n.70 conjectures that Sinnaces might be a "third-hand rendering" of the Assyrian name Sennacherib into Latin/Greek.

references justify an identification with the Sūrēn. The membership of Sēnak and Abdagaš in that family is a figment of scholarly imagination.

More probable, but still unlikely, is an affiliation between Tacitus's Abdagaš and an "Indo-Parthian" king of the same name. The pertinent evidence comes from a series of coins attributed by numismatists to a ruling family that has been called Indo-Parthian, Gondopharid, or Pahlava. These are modern labels of convenience, for the dynasty is unattested in literary sources, and what it called itself is unknown.[48] Two rulers from this line were named Abdagaš. The first reigned in the first century C.E. and minted bilingual coins in Greek and Prakit on which he variously described himself as the "great king," "the king of kings," and the "nephew of Gondophares," the founder of the dynasty.[49] Because this ruler shares a name with Tacitus's Abdagaš, several scholars have posited a family linkage or even a direct identification between the two.[50] The argument rests on their rough chronological correspondence and on the presence of the Indo-Parthians in Sakastan/Seistan, the supposed homeland of the Sūrēn, the family to which Tacitus's Abdagaš supposedly belonged. These are doubtful propositions. Frequently recurring names are common in the onomastic evidence from pre-Islamic Iran. Many other Iranian names are found in the diverse coinages of the Parthian east, including Vonones, Pakōr, and Sasan.[51] The geographic spread of such nomenclature shows the wide remit of Iranian languages and culture, but it cannot be used to establish concrete dynastic relationships among the bearers of these names, especially in view of the obscure political history of the Parthian east. Moreover, it makes little sense to connect Tacitus's Abdagaš, who is clearly at least a notional subordinate of the Arsacid royal house, with an Indo-Parthian ruler who calls himself a "king of kings."[52] That title was an Arsacid prerogative within the Parthian empire, but not in Sakastan or Gandhāra, the regions where Indo-Parthian dynasts ruled. A direct connection between the Abdagaš of the coins and the one from Tacitus is not impossible, but there is no compelling reason to draw one. Nothing can be concluded about the Sēnak and Abdagaš of the *Annals* on this basis.

The information that is on hand in Tacitus's text does, however, constitute sufficient grounds for ascribing Sēnak and Abdagaš to a family that numbered among the ranks of the nobility. The hereditary nature of their power can be inferred from the bare fact of their father-son relationship: these were not two aristocrats

48. For recent overviews of the dynasty and its coinage, see Mac Dowall 2007: 254–55; Coloru 2015: 190–91; Rezakhani 2017: 34–40; Cribb 2021: 658–60; Morris 2020: 68–70.

49. Alram 1986b: 246–50; Senior 2001: 2.159–65.

50. Cunningham 1890: 119; Marquart 1895: 636 n.6; Lohuizen-de Leeuw 1949: 358 (criticized on this point by Basham 1953: 88); Senior 2001: 1.113; Gazerani 2016: 25; Olbrycht 2016a: 25; cf. Bivar 2007: 32–33.

51. See Coloru 2015: 185–91; Cribb 2021: 657–60 for references.

52. Abdagaš was not alone among Indo-Parthian and Indo-Scythian kings in his use of this title; see the list of occurrences tabulated in Theophilos 2019: 543–44, table 1.

who achieved their high statuses independently, but members of a kinship group that transmitted political and financial assets to successive generations along lines of descent.[53] Tacitus is explicit, moreover, that their family was "distinguished," that its wealth was vast, and that its support was essential to Tirdād's efforts to claim the Arsacid throne. There is no explicit evidence that Sēnak and Abdagaš were "Parthian"—an ambiguous term in Iranian history to begin with.[54] The Sūrēn and Kārin families are both called *Pahlaw* ("Parthian") in Sasanian sources, but since the family name of Sēnak and Abdagaš is not recorded, the application of the label is not secure in their case. It can at least be said, however, that the name Sēnak appears already in the Nisa ostraca, the oldest Parthian documentary texts, and that Tacitus is ignorant of their geographical point of origin, as he is for the Sūrēn and Kārin. But even if the Parthian ethnicity of Sēnak and Abdagaš must remain conjectural, the preeminent status of their family in the imperial nobility is not in doubt.

The allocation of Sēnak and Abdagaš to the ranks of the nobility is also justified by their attraction of intra-aristocratic ire for their perceived transgressions against the ruling dynasty—a dynamic that is also attested for Sasanian late antiquity. During Tirdād's brief kingship, Abdagaš made enemies of Frahād/Phraates and Hiero, two dignitaries who "governed the greatest prefectures" of the Parthian empire, according to Tacitus.[55] The names of these administrative districts are not specified, and no further details about their governors are recorded. Frahād/Phraates may be the individual named as an archon of Susa in the epigraphic letter of Ardawān II to that city, but the name is so common in the Arsacid period that this can be no more than a guess.[56] Yet if Tacitus is vague on their identities, he is clear on their reason for rejecting Tirdād's kingship. Frahād and Hiero withheld their support from the Arsacid of Rome because they resented the power of Abdagaš, "who was then in charge of the court and the new king." Hiero bemoans this state of affairs, complaining that "command resided not with an Arsacid, but in the empty name of a man turned unwarlike from foreign softness. True power resided in the house of Abdagaš."[57] In other words, a Parthian aristocrat had achieved de facto rule by reducing the king of kings to a figurehead—a contravention of the proper order between king and nobility.

Late antiquity offers a close parallel: the aristocratic counterreaction to Abdagaš resembles the one against the Kārin family in the late fifth century C.E. as described in postconquest sources. The key figure is once again the Kārinid Sukhra, who is said to have gained undue influence over the Sasanian king Kavad I. As Ferdowsi puts it in his verses, for instance, "Everyone alike said: [Kavad] has

53. On the lineal transmission of status and wealth among the Iranian nobility, cf. Payne 2016: 524.

54. On the variable meanings of "Parthian" in Arsacid history, see de Jong 2013a: 147–48.

55. Tac. *Ann.* 6.42.4.

56. For the suggestion, see Cumont 1932: 250. For text and translation of the letter, see Hackl et al. 2010: 2.486–90.

57. Tac. *Ann.* 6.43.1, 6.43.3.

nothing except for the title of 'king.' Neither the wealth nor the army of Iran is his. Neither his command nor his opinion count for anything. The whole world has become the slave of Sukhra."[58] The words resemble the complaint of Hiero in Tacitus. In both cases, one member of the nobility has reached above his station, enfeebling the king of kings and subverting the empire's traditional distribution of power. The noble peers of the transgressor cannot help but be aggrieved by this state of affairs, which they perceive as a slight. Hiero's accusations against Abdagaš were not unique, then, but a recurring feature of aristocratic competition in post-Hellenistic Iran. Members of noble families could use the king to vault to new heights of power and influence, but if they pressed their advantage too far, those heights could become precipitous, and they risked a fall. Nothing further is known of Sēnak and Abdagaš or their family's fortunes, but they would not be the last Iranian aristocrats to incur the displeasure of their coequals through perceived domination of the king of kings.

Client Kings

Some supporters of the Arsacids of Rome belonged to elite families but were not members of the Parthian nobility as it is usually construed. Instead, they were client kings, local rulers of territories under the suzerainty of the Arsacid dynasty. Client kings are normally treated as distinct entities from the great noble families of Parthia, for two reasons. First, client kings can be located in space, while the Parthian aristocracy cannot, as discussed above. Since the distribution of internal evidence for Parthian history skews west, there is a relative abundance of sources for Parthian clients in Mesene, Adiabene, Armenia, and Hatra. Comparable kingdoms presumably existed in the Parthian east, but the complete absence of textual sources for this region (aside from the ambiguous testimony of numismatics) leaves the matter obscure. Second, client kings were not Parthian in ethnicity. To be sure, it is difficult to understand the boundaries of this ethnonym in the Arsacid period, and one may question its application to families like the Sūrēn and Kārin, since it is not clear that they originated from the territory of Parthia as the empire of the Arsacids did.[59] By the Sasanian period, however, epigraphic sources distinguish between *Pārs ud Pahlaw*—that is, between Persians from southwestern Iran and Parthians from the northeast.[60] Whereas the ethnonym *Pahlaw* is consistently applied to the Sūrēn and Kārin, it is not used for the kings of Hatra, or Adiabene, or Mesene. Client kings belonged to the Parthian empire, but they were not Parthian in this sense.

Two client kings are named in connection with the campaign of Mihrdād in 49 C.E. The first is Acbarus, whom Tacitus calls "king of the Arabs."[61] This figure

---

58. Ferdowsi, *Shahnameh* = Khaleghi-Motlagh and Khatibi 2007: 54, lines 36–37.
59. Hauser 2006: 306.
60. Shayegan 2022: 217–20.
61. Tac. *Ann.* 12.12.2–3, 12.14.1.

can be identified with Abgar V Ukkāmā ("the Black"), king of the northern Mesopotamian region of Osrhoene and its capital Edessa.[62] In this city, Tacitus says, Abgar delayed Mihrdād for many days with sumptuous entertainments, robbing his campaign of energy and momentum and thus dooming the enterprise from the start. Abgar V belonged to a dynasty of the same name that had ruled Edessa for many generations, and though the kingdom would later be annexed by Rome after the campaigns of Lucius Verus, its position on the east side of the Euphrates put it within the Parthian orbit at the time of Mihrdād's remission. Tacitus's identification of Abgar as an Arab can be explained by the Roman geographical conception of this area as "Arabia," and also by local epigraphy from Edessa and nearby Hatra, where titles such as king or governor of ʿrb ("Arab") are attested.[63] Abgar himself is best known from an apocryphal Christian tradition as an epistolary correspondent of Jesus, who supposedly sent a disciple to cure the Edessan king of a terminal illness.[64] Abgar's correspondence with Jesus is also included in the *History* of Movses Khorenatsʿi, who remembers Abgar as an Armenian king.[65] These traditions little pertain to the historical Abgar, but they do give a sense of a consequential ruler who left a distinct mark on the sphere of Roman-Parthian high politics in the first century C.E.

The second client king connected to the campaign of Mihrdād was Izates II of Adiabene, another kingdom in northern Mesopotamia to the east of Osrhoene.[66] As with Abgar, Tacitus's portrayal of this ruler is unflattering. At the approach of Mihrdād's army, Izates feigned support while cherishing a secret preference for the reigning Arsacid Gōdarz II. When the decisive battle loomed, Izates deserted in concert with Abgar.[67] Bereft of auxiliaries, Mihrdād lost the ensuing fight. Whereas Abgar would become an important figure in Christian literature, Izates is best known for his conversion, along with his mother Helena, to Judaism. This event drew the interest of the Jewish historian Josephus, who wrote in detail of the Adiabenian kingdom's transimperial connections with Judaea as well as its political relationship with the Parthian empire.[68] Though Roman influence along its western borders increased over the second and third centuries C.E., Adiabene would remain an integrated Parthian dependency for the rest of the Arsacid period, at least to Roman eyes.[69]

Though Abgar and Izates were not ethnic Parthians, the episode shows that client kings of their ilk could still play kingmaker alongside the great noble families

---

62. Segal 1982; Luther 1999: 451; Ross 2001: 24 (cautiously); Guscin 2009: 165–66.
63. MacDonald et al. 2015: 35–44 with n.75.
64. Ross 2001: 117–38; Mirkovic 2004; Corke-Webster 2017.
65. MKh 2.31–32. See further chapter 1.
66. On the historical geography of Adiabene, see Marciak 2017: 257–62.
67. Tac. *Ann.* 12.13.1, 12.14.1.
68. Joseph. *AJ* 20.17–96; *BJ* 1.6, 2.388, 2.520, 4.567, 5.55, 5.119, 5.147, 5.252, 5.474, 6.355–57.
69. Marciak 2017: 277–78.

like the Sūrēn and Kārin. The support of Abgar and Izates, or more precisely the untimely withdrawal of it, shaped the outcome of Mihrdād's campaign. Tacitus is characteristically acid in his assessment of their desertion, which he attributes to the "fickleness of the people" and sees as an exemplification of the principle that "barbarians like seeking kings from Rome more than keeping them."[70] But these comments, warmed-over clichés in any event, are dismissive of the delicate balancing act that would have been required by Abgar and Izates as they negotiated an Arsacid dynastic war.[71] Neither client king favored Mihrdād's cause, but their temporary participation in his campaign and withdrawal before the decisive battle allowed them to help Gōdarz without incurring the costs of resisting Mihrdād from the outset. Moreover, the evidence from Josephus further supports the portrait of Izates as a kingmaker: the Adiabenian is said to have helped Ardawān II return to power at an earlier date, after the dethroned king fled to him for support.[72] In the complex political processes that selected the Arsacid monarch, it was not only the Arsacid dynasty or the Parthian nobility that determined a candidate's success or failure. As the critical withdrawals of Abgar and Izates from Mihrdād's army show, client kings mattered too.

Parthian Administrators

Whereas Abgar and Izates ruled semi-autonomous kingdoms that were integrated piecemeal into the Arsacid empire, other supporters of the Arsacids of Rome presided over territory as agents of Parthia's central administration. Tacitus attests such a post for Tirdād's ally Ornospades, who "was governor of the fields which have the name Mesopotamia, since they are encompassed by the famous streams of the Euphrates and Tigris."[73] The phrase may correspond to the "general of Mesopotamia" attested for the year 121 C.E. in a Greek papyrus from Arsacid Dura, though the holder of that post ruled Parapotamia as well.[74] In any event, Tacitus's word choice indicates that Ornospades belonged to the formal Arsacid bureaucracy rather than the ranks of client kings.[75] Parthia was not the only administration whose ladder Ornospades had climbed over the course of his career. During a period of exile some thirty years before Tirdād's remission, he had served on the emperor Tiberius's Dalmatian campaign with sufficient distinction to earn Roman citizenship. Many scholars have linked this period of service with the creation of the *ala Parthorum*, a Roman military division composed of "Parthians" both actual and nominal. Ultimately, though, no hard evidence connects Ornospades with the

70. Tac. *Ann.* 12.14.1.

71. On the Roman literary topos of barbarian and Parthian fickleness, see Wheeler 1993: 33 n.100; Barclay 2007: 184; Lerouge 2007: 310–13; Gruen 2011: 142; Bernard 2015: 40, 49 n.55.

72. Joseph. *AJ* 20.54–68.

73. Tac. *Ann.* 6.37.3.

74. *P. Dura* 20, line 5, text and translation in Hackl et al. 2010: 2.448–52.

75. Rostovtzeff and Welles 1931: 48; Olbrycht 2016b: 314.

unit.[76] After reconciling with an unnamed Arsacid king (probably Ardawān II), Ornospades returned to Parthia and assumed his Mesopotamian office. His support of Tirdād was consequential, for he arrived in camp with many thousands of cavalry.

Another supporter of Tirdād is not explicitly said to have held government office, but likely did. This was Abdus, whom Tacitus names as Sēnak's co-petitioner for Tirdād's remission.[77] Tacitus also identifies him as a figure "of removed manhood" (*ademptae virilitatis*)—that is, as a eunuch.[78] The historian's subsequent quip that "among the barbarians, [castration] is not looked down on, but actually confers power" is a typically disdainful remark for a Greco-Roman author writing on eastern eunuchs, and it would be understandable to dismiss the comment as a routine deployment of an orientalist trope with little historical value.[79] But a documentary source from Arsacid Dura-Europos does, in fact, attest a eunuch in a Parthian administrative post. Written in Greek, the document is an antichretic loan contract between a local resident and a certain Phraates (Parthian Frahād), whom the text names as a eunuch and an *arkapatēs*.[80] The latter term is a Greek rendering of Parthian *hargbed*, an administrative title that denoted tax collection or a military command, and perhaps both.[81] The contract records Phraates's disbursal of a considerable four hundred drachms to the loanee, and if the loanee defaulted—a distinct possibility in view of the size of the loan—then the terms consigned him to long-term debt bondage or even permanent enslavement to Phraates.[82] What the document shows, then, is a high-ranking Parthian eunuch leveraging his administrative position and financial resources for personal gain. It is no giant leap from a figure like Phraates to the Abdus of Tacitus's *Annals*: a eunuch with enough institutional and individual power to intervene in Arsacid dynastic politics.

Were Ornospades and Abdus members of nonroyal elite families, or were they of humbler extraction? Tacitus is silent on the issue, and no other evidence permits a conclusive answer. Ornospades may well have come from a kinship group like

76. Wheeler 2016: 193 with n.153 for earlier literature.

77. Tac. *Ann.* 6.31.2, 6.32.2. Ramelli 2006: 91–92 thinks that Tacitus's Sinnaces and Abdus are the same figures mentioned at the court of Abgar V, the Edessan king, in the *Teaching of Addai*, a Syriac text from the fourth or fifth century C.E., under the names "Abdu, son of Abdu" and "Senaq, son of Avida" (trans. Howard 1981: 11, 15, 19, 35, 67, 81). This pair, Ramelli continues, later entered Christian hagiography as the martyrs Abdos and Semnes.

78. Martin 2001: 168; Woodman 2017: 226.

79. On the treatment of eastern eunuchs in Greco-Roman literature, see Hall 1989: 157–59; Bardel 2002; Llewellyn-Jones 2002; Lenfant 2021.

80. *P. Dura* 20, line 4; text and translation in Hackl et al. 2010: 2.448–52. The translation of *arkapatēs* is from Wiesehöfer 2020: 485.

81. More recent discussions favor the translation "tax chief" or similar: Gnoli 2007: 96–113; Herman 2012: 82–92; Wiesehöfer 2020: 485. See also Frye 1962: 353; Chaumont 1986; Shayegan 2003a.

82. Taasob 2022: 151–52.

those of the Sūrēn and Kārin, especially since such families are known to have supplied governmental office holders during the Sasanian period.[83] But he is attested nowhere else, so the idea can be no more than conjecture. Abdus's identification as a eunuch might seem to preclude his belonging to an elite family, but some later evidence leaves the possibility open. Eunuchs were a mainstay of court administration in ancient Near Eastern empires long before the Parthians, and some evidence suggests that they were employed in this capacity precisely because of their inability to propagate family lines of their own.[84] In many cases, moreover, eunuchs came from conquered peoples rather than imperial elites. Literary references, for instance, show Achaemenid and Sasanian Persians receiving eunuchs from provincial populations as tribute or castrating the children of military opponents.[85] It is perhaps no surprise, then, that the name of Phraates in the Dura papyrus is not accompanied by a patronymic, whereas the name of his superior is.[86] And yet there are also indications in late antique evidence that eunuchs could have noble heritage. Of the two eunuchs named in the Shapur inscription from Naqsh-e Rustam, one *is* identified by a patronymic, suggesting a noteworthy lineage.[87] For Arsacid Armenia, historiographical sources attest an Arsacid administrative post called *mardpet* that involved the management of the treasuries. The holder of the office was by rule a eunuch who received the appellation of "Father" along with the post, and according to Movses Khorenats'i, he was always taken from the same "honorable and princely family."[88] Attested also in the Sasanian empire, the title is Iranian in origin, and the institution might be, too.[89] None of this evidence directly bears upon Tacitus's Abdus, of course, but it does allow for the possibility of his membership in a noble family. If an aristocratic origin is probable in Ornospades's case, it is imaginable in his.

Parthians of Uncertain Status

In contrast to the figures allocated above to groups 1–4, one supporter of Mihrdād is a cipher whose station in Parthian society is impossible to discern. After his defeat at the hands of Gōdarz, Mihrdād entrusted himself to a certain Parraces,

83. See above, n.30.

84. See, e.g., SAA 9 no. 7, lines 3–8, trans. Parpola 1997: 38, where a distinction is made between "the sons of the bearded courtiers and the successors of the eunuchs." On eunuchs in the pre-Hellenistic Near East, see further Ambos 2009; Lemos 2011: 49–54; Pirngruber 2011: 287–308.

85. Achaemenid cases: Hdt. 3.92.1 (cf. 3.97), 6.9.4, 6.32 with Scott 2005: 156. A Sasanian case: PB 4.58, trans. Garsoïan 1989: 178.

86. His superior was Manesos, who is inter alia the *strategos* of Mesopotamia in *P. Dura* 20.

87. ŠKZ 50. On Sasanian eunuchs, see further Kolesnikov 2012.

88. MKh 2.7, 3.15, trans. Thomson 1978: 139, 269; PB 3.17–18, 5.7, trans Garsoïan 1989: 92, 198; Agathangelos 795, trans. Thomson 1976: 335; GhP 39, trans. Bedrosian 2021: 1.219.

89. On the word's etymology and its attestation on a Sasanian seal, see Livshits and Xurshudjan 1989. On the "Iranian and probably Parthian origin" of the office, see Chaumont 2020.

who betrayed him to the enemy.[90] The only scrap of information on this Parraces that Tacitus transmits is the phrase *paternus cliens*: he was a "client" of Mihrdād's father, Vonones, the Arsacid of Rome from an earlier generation. What social relationship is this phrase meant to represent, and when and where did it develop? At face value, it might indicate that Vonones met Parraces in Rome, where they entered into a patron-client relationship on the Roman model that they knew from their time in the city. Alternately, Parraces could have journeyed from Parthia to Rome with Vonones when the latter's residence there began, and Tacitus used *cliens* to translate a preexisting dependent status like the Greek *pelatēs* or Parthian *bandag*.[91] Then again, perhaps Parraces became Vonones's "client," however understood, only after the Arsacid of Rome returned to Parthia and began his brief kingship there.[92] Each of these scenarios is possible, but none is provable. Onomastics are no further help. The Parthian name Pārag is attested on an ostracon from Dura-Europos, but the document is a bare receipt, and the relationship of this Parthian name to the Parraces of Tacitus's Latin is debatable.[93] Parraces's place in the Parthian empire, and his reasons for supporting Mihrdād at first and betraying him later, remain obscure.

In sum, from the named accessories of the Arsacids of Rome who were remitted to Parthia, two were from known families of the Parthian nobility (the Sūrēn and the Kārin); two belonged to a powerful family whose name is not recorded (Abdagaš and Sēnak); two were client kings (Abgar and Izates); two held Parthian governmental posts but are of uncertain family background (Ornospades and Abdus); and one is of uncertain background altogether (Parraces).

The feature shared most consistently among these supporters is their membership in elite families. The Sūrēn and Kārin clans are the best-known examples, since they would endure as powerful political units for many centuries, long outlasting the tenure of the Arsacid dynasty in Mesopotamia and Iran. No such longevity is demonstrable in the case of Abdagaš and Sēnak, but the station of their family seems comparable. Abgar and Izates came from groups that were dynasties in their own right, even if their autonomy was limited under Arsacid suzerainty. Nonhereditary elites no doubt figured in these coalitions, as well. No family affiliation can be shown for the Parthian office holders Ornospades or Abdus, and it seems reasonable to assume that at least some such administrators came from nonelite backgrounds. But a critical mass of support for Arsacid remission, from the petitioning of the Roman emperor to the fielding of military forces, came from political groups bound together by kinship.

---

90. Tac. *Ann.* 12.14.3. On "clients" among the Parthians, cf. Tac. *Ann.* 13.37.1.

91. On *cliens* for *pelatēs* see Olbrycht 2003: 85 n.93, though his contention that Parraces was a Parthian noble is without explicit support in Tacitus's text. On *bandag*, see Colditz 2000: 108–65. Cf. Benario 1983: 156: "Parraces was probably a freedman."

92. Suggested by Wheeler 2016: 204 n.237.

93. Harmatta 1958: 111 (no. 2), 122–23; cf. Justi 1895: 242; Bivar 1983: 78 n.2; Schmitt 2016: 148–49.

The familial organization of these groups calls for the contextualization of Arsacid remission within the framework of political fosterage. Each of the groups identified in the breakdown above can be shown to have produced cliental fosterers for the dynasty that supplied Iran's king of kings. For noble families, the most pertinent case is the fosterage of Peroz by Ṙaham, a member of the powerful Mihrān family that was an aristocratic peer (and sometimes rival) of the Sūrēn and Kārin. The Farragān and Kadugān were also noble fosterers, as were the Mamikoneans under the Armenian Arsacids. For the client kings, Abgar and Izates can be paralleled by Monzer, the Arab ruler under Sasanian suzerainty who fostered Bahram Gur. And while Ornospades and Abdus were not demonstrably members of an elite family, their group of governmental officials performed cliental fosterage, as well. Dracontis's foster-father Anagranes is known only as an office holder with the title of *tropheus* and *epitropos*, for example, and the same is true for Abdšalmā, the fosterer of the Hatrene king Sanatruq.[94] In a word, the Parthian supporters of the Arsacids of Rome came from political and social groups that are elsewhere attested as the fosterers of Arsacid and Sasanian kings.

To a Parthian ruling class with a shared experience of cliental fosterage, the Roman emperor's custody of Arsacid children would have presented a challenge, but also an opportunity. Cliental fosterage conferred upon the raisers of royal children both obligation and privileges. Obligation came from the subordinate duty of the role, but the privileges included the honor of the office, networking opportunities with a potential future king, and possession of a dynastic replacement that could be used to effect regime change, should circumstances require. These privileges would have eroded when the emperor became the Arsacid king's chief *dāyag*, since a role ordinarily delegated to Parthians would now be played by a Roman. Deprivation of royal children gave nobles less control over dynastic politics, and it alienated them from the generation of Arsacids that would one day govern the empire. Yet the situation presented an opportunity, as well. Parthian elites could appeal to the emperor as a peer, for he was a ruler who interfaced with the Arsacid dynasty through fosterage, just as they themselves did. The emperor's status as pro-parent could create a community of interest between Rome and the Parthian aristocracy. After all, both sides were now invested in the Arsacid family and the way it managed its dynastic politics. For the Parthian elite, Arsacid submission had been a setback, but contact and collaboration with the emperor held out the possibility of redress. Contact was made, and collaboration pursued.

Against this background, the history of Arsacid remission can be read differently from the accusations of "intervention" or "interference" that are so common in the scholarly literature. From the perspective of a Parthian noble, the Roman emperor would have acted in Parthian domestic politics not as a foreign infiltrator, but as a legitimate participant. His custody of Arsacid children integrated him into

94. On these figures, see chapter 1.

a fosterage system that regulated the relationship between king and aristocracy in Parthian Iran, giving each a stake in the maintenance of the other. The emperor's release of his Arsacid wards was not an imposition on Parthian affairs, but a response to the invitation to take part in them. To be sure, these invitations were never extended by the Parthian elite as a whole: the Iranian aristocracy was not a monolith, and nobles counterbalanced each other no less than they did the king of kings. For disaffected Parthian aristocrats, however, Rome represented a potential ally and remedy against the disorder that prevailed between the royal house and their own. When the emperor acceded to the requests of the Parthian ambassadors who reached his court, he accepted—to Parthian eyes—his role as coadjutant of the nobility. He became a force in Parthian domestic politics, not on them.

TACITUS AND ROMAN-PARTHIAN
MISUNDERSTANDING

This reconstruction of the Parthian interests at play in Arsacid remission opens up fresh perspectives on critical passages in Tacitus, who is the only ancient source to report in detail on the aristocratic missions to Rome (*Annals* 6.31–32 and 12.10–11). Commentary on these audience scenes has been the domain of scholars of Latin literature with primary interests in Tacitean historiography.[95] Their approaches have produced fuller understandings of the passages, but few have investigated how the sentiments that Tacitus attributes to the Parthian aristocracy might actually reflect the values, aspirations, and outreach of that group to a Roman interlocutor. It is productive to note, for example, that "the treacherous subordinates Abdus and Sinnaces must recall Sejanus," the latter of whom betrayed Tiberius as the former did Ardawān.[96] But what about Abdus and Sēnak as agents in their own right? What do their envoys argue, and what do those arguments show about nonroyal Parthian elites? Consideration of these questions can benefit students of Tacitean historiography no less than Parthian historians, since they ask the reader to investigate how Tacitus might have encountered, understood, and represented the rhetoric of the Parthian aristocracy.

Such an approach to the audience scenes allows for Tacitus's text to be read as a reflection of pragmatic misunderstanding between the Roman emperor and the Parthian aristocracy. The statements of the Parthian envoys at *Annals* 6.31–32 and 12.10–11 are in both cases followed by a Roman response that ignores, misconstrues, or talks past the Parthian interlocutor. The Roman reactions are those of the emperors Tiberius and Claudius, who are the immediate targets of the Parthian petitions. But Tacitus, too, was a Roman, and his later overlay is inseparable from

95. Generally, Koestermann 1963–68; Keitel 1978; Gowing 1990; Woodman 2017: 226–28. See further below.

96. Quotation from Ash 1999: 114 n.4, citing parallels drawn by McCulloch 1984: 59–61.

the earlier Julio-Claudian scene. In other words, it is impossible to say whether Tiberius and Claudius really misunderstood their Parthian interlocutors, or Tacitus makes them misunderstand. In either case, though, there is a divergence in his text between the rhetoric of Parthian appeals and the logic of Roman response. That divergence can be interpreted as a consequence of misunderstanding.

Crucial to the evidentiary basis for this reading is the setting of the audience scenes at Rome rather than in the Parthian empire. In the literature, there is a reasonable tendency to speak of Tacitus's "Parthian digressions" as discrete narrative sections of uniform historicity. But a distinction must be made between audiences with Parthians at Rome and the scenes set in Parthia unattended by Roman observers. Tacitus had many potential sources for the former, but virtually none for the latter.[97] In keeping with the conventions of Roman historiography, he does not cite specific authorities for the audience scenes, and it might not be useful even if he did; only in exceptional cases does the survival of documentary material permit an evaluation of Tacitus's fidelity to his sources.[98] But information about these encounters would have been available to a diligent and careful historian, and by the standards of ancient historiography Tacitus was certainly that. The arguments that he attributes to Parthians should therefore be surveyed for sentiments that could plausibly have belonged to the Parthian elite, the political and social class whose interests and commitments have been outlined above.

Such a survey yields three key features of Tacitus's audience scenes that can be better explained and contextualized against the backdrop of political fosterage. The first is the complaint of dynastic assassination that appears in both the audience scenes. During the embassy that led to Tīrdād's remission, Tacitus explains that Sēnak, Abdus, and their affiliates "couldn't find anyone of the Arsacid family to install on the throne, since most had been killed by Ardawān, or had not yet grown up."[99] In the following episode, the Parthian ambassadors speak before Claudius and the Senate about the dynastic assassinations of Gōdarz, lamenting that "already his brothers, kin, and even distant relatives had been executed in his massacres; to these, pregnant women and little children were being added."[100] An element common to both scenes, then, is the Parthian elite's frustration with intra-Arsacid violence: the reigning king is systematically eliminating his family members as insurance against an aristocratic coup.

---

97. On the possible sources for 6.31–32 and 12.10–11, see Koestermann 1963–68: 3.125; Devillers 2003: 17, 60; Dąbrowa 2017: 179; Nabel 2020: 176, 181 (on Ardawān's communication with Tiberius); Olbrycht 2021d. For the Parthian scenes, see the discussion in chapter 5.

98. Exceptional cases: the *SCPP* can be compared to passages from *Ann.* 2 and 3, on which see Barnes 1998; Talbert 1999. The Lyons Tablet (*CIL* 13.1668) can be read against *Ann.* 11.23–25.1, on which see Malloch 2013: 338–41; Malloch 2020: 51–61.

99. Tac. *Ann.* 6.31.2.

100. Tac. *Ann.* 12.10.1.

The historiographers have read these complaints as self-reflexive commentary on Rome's imperial disorders, but they should also be understood as an expression of real dysfunction between the Arsacid dynasty and the Parthian aristocracy. For Elizabeth Keitel, the second passage foreshadows the brutal turns that Julio-Claudian dynastic politics will take under Claudius and Nero with the murders of Lucius Silanus, Domitia Lepida, Claudius himself, Britannicus, Agrippina, Octavia, and the pregnant Poppaea.[101] J. N. Keddie adduces an internal parallel within the *Annals*: the Germanic Cherusci appeal to Claudius for a king with a similar justification, which suggests that "Tacitus had a common approach or technique in treating these fratricidal kingdoms."[102] The repetition of the element may also underline the cyclical pattern of "hostage" remissions in the *Annals*—scenes that follow a predictable trajectory toward unhappy conclusions, as Alan Gowing and Joel Allen have shown.[103] These studies amply demonstrate that Tacitus on Parthia is also Tacitus on Rome. The grim irony of the aristocracy's complaint is that it could apply to the court of Claudius no less than the court of Gōdarz.

But the speakers' statement also tracks as an authentic Parthian attempt to appeal to the Roman emperor as a fellow fosterer. Two phrases in the quotations above enjoin consideration of the aristocracy's values, especially its investment in fosterage. First, the reference of Sēnak and Abdus's messengers to Arsacids who "had not yet grown up" may indicate that some princes were in aristocratic custody at the time of the embassy as part of ongoing fosterage arrangements. Second, the outrage at Gōdarz's assassination of "pregnant women and little children" stems not only from the monstrous nature of the crime in its own right, but from the violent demolition of the fosterage system: the elimination of Arsacid children and even the mothers who birth them has deprived the nobility of fosterage opportunities and corrupted a key mechanism of mediation between their families and the ruling dynasty. In both cases, the Roman emperor is not expected to care about Arsacid familicide simply as a matter of principle. The speakers appeal to him as someone who has a vested interest in the rearing of Arsacid children, because he has done so himself. They expect the commiseration and aid of a colleague in fosterage.

The second section of Tacitus that deserves consideration as authentic Parthian rhetoric comes as the envoys of Sēnak and Abdus conclude their remarks before Tiberius. After they bemoan the purges of Ardawān, the speakers once again appeal to the emperor as a stakeholder in the Arsacid family with the following sentence: "Only a name and an initiator were needed for the family of Arsaces to be seen on the shore of the Euphrates through the will of Caesar."[104] The Latin text

---

101. Keitel 1978: 466.
102. Keddie 1975: 52 n.5.
103. Gowing 1990: 322; Allen 2006: 224–25; cf. Woodman 2017: 224.
104. Tac. *Ann.* 6.31.2

is not entirely secure here, and editors have proposed emendations that construe the phrase "through the will of Caesar" in different ways.[105] But the general thrust of the sentence is clear: if the emperor wants to see regime change in the Parthian empire, he need only release one of his Arsacid wards, and the senders of the envoys will see to his installation on the throne.

Tacitus's authorial hand is once again detectable in this Parthian utterance. The speakers' stated desire for a "name" (*nomen*)—that is, the name of an Arsacid of Rome who will be remitted to Parthian territory—is later echoed in the speech of Hiero, who will complain to Ardawān that Tirdād's kingship is nothing but an "empty name" (*nomen*) devoid of true legitimacy and power.[106] The reappearance of the word is significant, for Hiero's appeal to Ardawān will bring about the downfall of Tirdād and thus the ultimate failure of the Parthian mission to Tiberius. The initial statement of the Parthian envoys during the audience scene, then, is deployed to create internal correspondence within Tacitus's text. The repetition of *nomen* creates a conceptual link between the two passages and prompts the reader to reflect on their relationship. This rhetorical patterning is Tacitus's handiwork. It cannot be attributed to the original utterance of the Parthian characters he uses to craft the parallel.

But the sentence in question also warrants assessment as a real feature of interelite discourse between the Roman emperor and the Parthian nobility. Tacitus could have used any number of words or phrases to link the embassy for Tirdād with the account of his downfall just a few chapters later, and the repetition of *nomen* in itself does not explain the substance of the Parthian appeal. Why should the emperor be swayed by the prospect of installing the Arsacid family across the Euphrates river? Wasn't Ardawān an Arsacid himself, as Tacitus attests in an earlier book?[107] Why is an appeal to Arsacid sovereignty and legitimacy expected to persuade the Roman emperor?

Once again, this feature of the audience scene is best explained as a Parthian aristocratic appeal to a fellow fosterer with a stake in upholding the Arsacid dynasty. The emperor is expected to agree with the speakers' arguments because his custody of Arsacid dynasts gives him a stake in the family's position at the head of the Parthian empire. Moreover, as a foster-father with peers among the Parthian nobility, the emperor is asked to recognize that the reigning Arsacid king has overstepped his bounds and abused his position. In his insolent treatment of Parthian elites and wanton execution of his family members, Ardawān has upset the balance between king and nobility and invited a counterreaction to his injurious reign.

---

105. My translation follows the text and commentary of Woodman 2017: 35 (*nomine tantum et auctore opus, ut sponte Caesaris [ut] genus Arsacis ripam apud Euphratis cerneretur*), 227 (critical remarks on the repetition of *ut*).

106. Tac. *Ann.* 6.43.3; see above.

107. Tac. *Ann.* 2.3.1.

The envoys are thus invoking what Rubin calls the "noble's right of rebellion" in his discussion of Sasanian history: a king who acts in an immoral fashion can neither expect nor compel obedience from the empire's nonroyal elites, who are within their rights to depose him if such behavior persists.[108] Yet there are restrictions on the nobility's behavior, too, because the iniquity of any one ruling king does not invalidate the right of his dynasty to hold the kingship. A coup d'état against one dynast may be justified, but it carries with it the obligation of installing another. When the Parthian ambassadors speak of Ardawān's illegitimacy while calling for Arsacid restoration, then, they are not contradicting themselves or resorting to empty rhetoric. They are initiating the emperor into an Iranian discourse of legitimate rebellion. The emperor's contribution to this discourse is right and proper, because as a fosterer of Arsacids he, too, may participate in the maintenance of the ruling family that is at once the nobility's prerogative and its obligation.

That discourse had many participants, however, and Tacitus's text can only reflect the views of the factions that initiated contact with the emperor. The claims and counterclaims of Arsacid legitimacy that appear in the *Annals* are not definitive pronouncements from *the* Parthian nobility about who was a proper Arsacid and who was not. They are refracted bits of propaganda generated by individual elites who fought in shifting and unstable coalitions to shape dynastic politics as they pleased. The noble appeal to Tiberius to restore the Arsacid family is no objective sign that the dynasty has been disempowered in Parthia; rather, it is one faction's tendentious attempt to delegitimize the reign of a king they disliked. Their rhetoric makes another appearance in Tacitus's narrative when Tirdād, now in Parthian territory, enters Seleucia on the Tigris. According to Tacitus, Tirdād enjoyed a favorable reception by the people of the city, who as a show of support "poured out insults against Ardawān, who was an Arsacid [only] on his mother's side, and otherwise lowborn."[109] That final phrase could be evidence of a categorical Parthian attitude that maternal Arsacid lineage was somehow inferior to paternity, but no external sources corroborate that notion. Instead, it is better to understand the insult as an ad hoc, opportunistic effort to divest the reigning king of Arsacid legitimacy and to bolster the claim of his rival. Such discourse was part of the customary scrum of dynastic politics in Parthian and Sasanian Iran, a setting where royal dynasts and aristocratic clans fought over the kingship in factions of diverse and unstable membership.

Yet if the envoys' speech before Tiberius appealed to the values of a Parthian aristocrat, Tacitus's account reveals a stark disjuncture between the couching of the request and the logic of its acceptance. Tiberius granted what the Parthians asked, but not for the reasons they supplied. When the emperor released his Arsacids, Tacitus writes, he was "keeping to his established aims of managing external affairs

---

108. Rubin 2021: 263, 268–69; see above.
109. Tac. *Ann.* 6.42.3.

with strategy and cunning, and avoiding war."[110] The emperor, it emerges, ascribes the Parthian empire to the realm of "external affairs," and he is remitting Arsacids to manage this realm without resorting to military force. In order to counter Ardawān's invasion of Armenia, he will incite dynastic warfare in the Parthian heartland, undercutting the king's base of power and necessitating his withdrawal from Armenia. So while the Parthian envoys orient their case around the turpitude of Ardawān's purges and the need for Arsacid restoration, the Roman emperor's true motive stems from different concerns, and indeed from an altogether different conception of the Roman-Parthian relationship. The rhetoric of the Parthian envoys initiates and integrates the emperor into Arsacid domestic politics, acknowledging his rightful role there by virtue of his foster-fatherhood. The Roman response conceives of Parthia as a discrete and foreign entity that the emperor can throw into chaos with the Arsacid instruments at his disposal. The dissonance between these two positions and the short, misleadingly simple sentence that connects them—"this was Tiberius's desire"—invites the reader to consider the discrepancy between the Parthian request and the Roman motive for granting it.

It is an open question whether the statist logic of the Roman response belonged to Tiberius or to Tacitus, but both possibilities tend toward the same conclusion: the Roman view diverged from the Parthian one, and the text as written is an exhibition of the misunderstanding between them. There is a case to be made that Tacitus's interpretation of Tiberius dominates the scene. The pragmatic preference of stratagem to war is consistent with the emperor's depiction elsewhere in the *Annals*, and this characterization reappears in other Tacitean works as well.[111] But many historians would agree that circumspection and caution were real features of Tiberius's foreign policy, so his Tacitean portrait may be a faithful one.[112] In either case, Tacitus's text bears witness to Roman incomprehension of the Parthian view. The request of the Parthian envoys is granted, but the arguments they make in its favor are ignored. The Roman justification for remission comes from strategic decisions about "foreign affairs," in which the Parthian empire is treated as distinct and separable from the Roman one. The Parthians appeal to the emperor as a foster-father, but the emperor acts as a head of state. The interlocutors talk, but they do not hear each other.

One piece of sigillographic evidence adds texture to the question of how Tiberius's negotiations with the Parthian aristocracy played out, though it supports no firm conclusions on the topic. Supposedly found in the vicinity of ancient Elam, the object is a gem that depicts a youthful Tiberius crowned with a myrtle wreath (figure 9). His image is consistent with Julio-Claudian portraiture in various media, and the gem was presumably manufactured in the Roman empire.

---

110. Tac. *Ann.* 6.32.1.

111. Koestermann 1963–68: 2.317 and Woodman 2017: 228 adduce the parallels of *Ann.* 2.26.3, 2.43.1, 2.64.1–2; see also *Ann.* 1.11.4 and *Agr.* 13.3 with the discussion in Ober 1982: 311–13.

112. Baar 1990: 177–78; Levick 1999: 111–13; Shotter 2004: 56.

FIGURE 9. Chalcedony intaglio with a portrait of the Roman emperor Tiberius and a later Middle Persian inscription. Photo credit: Bibliothèque nationale de France, Département des Monnaies, Médailles et Antiques, Seyrig.1973.1.516.

But while the object's life began in the Roman empire, it did not end there, for encircling the emperor's portrait is a Middle Persian inscription. The text is datable to the third or fourth centuries C.E. on paleographic grounds. It reads: "Mihrag, son of Frahād [or: member of the Frahād family], behold the radiant paradise."[113] In late antiquity, this portrait of a Julio-Claudian emperor had found new purchase as a seal for a Sasanian dignitary.

There are a thousand stories that could be told about this Roman object and its arrival in Iranian territory, but one intriguing suggestion by M. Rahim Shayegan posits a connection to the Arsacids of Rome. Shayegan notes that Frahād is a common Parthian name and, perhaps not coincidentally, the name of one of the Arsacids whom Tiberius remitted to Parthian territory. He suggests that the gem was a parting gift from the emperor to Frahād or Tirdād, who passed it down to their descendants. The latest of these was Mihrag, who added the inscription in late antiquity.[114] While any number of transmission paths may have brought this object to Iran at various points in time, the situation of the seal in the historical context of Tirdād's remission is compelling. It offers a convincing explanation for an Iranian nobleman's possession of Tiberius's portrait, even if alternate possibilities should also be entertained.

Two additional considerations, however, may be appended to Shayegan's discussion. The first is that the name Frahād is attested not just in the Arsacid family, but among the Parthian nobility as well. The gem could have been gifted to an Arsacid of Rome, but also to one of the Parthian aristocrats whose representatives petitioned Tiberius. Second, the transimperial life of the gem suggests an object whose handlers understood it in different ways. On the Roman side, Tiberius was part of a dynasty well known for deploying the "power of images" in its ruling program.[115] Where the emperor's image went, so too did Julio-Claudian claims to dominance and supremacy. In Iran, however, at least by the Sasanian period, the object is unlikely to have broadcast such a message. Instead, the gem became a seal that represented a Sasanian potentate and exhorted its Middle Persian readers to pursue a Zoroastrian vision of heaven (*wahišt*). In a sense, then, the object is analogous to the Arsacids of Rome themselves: it traversed two empires, but it was understood differently in each one, and it was used to articulate divergent claims to power in its Roman and Iranian iterations. The gem outlived the Arsacids of Rome, but its life shared some features with theirs.

The third section in Tacitus that reflects Parthian aristocratic concerns comes from the speech of the envoys before Claudius and the Senate in their bid to secure Mihrdād's release. After rehearsing the dynastic assassinations and contemptible

---

113. *Mihrag ī Frahādān wēn wahišt ī rōšn*; text and translation after Shayegan 2022: 225; see also Spier et al. 2022: 348 (no. 194).

114. Shayegan 2022: 223–29.

115. Zanker 1988.

misconduct of Gōdarz, the Parthians continue with additional reasons for the Romans to grant their request:[116]

> Veterem sibi ac publice coeptam nobiscum amicitiam, et subveniendum sociis virium aemulis cedentibusque per reverentiam. Ideo regum liberos obsides dari, ut, si domestici imperii taedeat, sit regressus ad principem patresque, quorum moribus adsuefactus rex melior adscisceretur.

> They had an old and publicly initiated friendship with us, and help should be given to allies who were coequals in strength but yielded out of respect. The reason that it was the children of kings who were given as hostages was that, if they tired of their domestic rule, they could resort to the emperor and the senators, from whom a king could be obtained who was better for his habituation to their customs.

The envoys appeal to an old friendship (*amicitia*) between the Parthian aristocrats they represent and the Romans in the audience. Despite their status as peers of the emperor and senators, they showed respect, and deserved reciprocal aid from the Romans on that basis. The emperor's remission of an Arsacid replacement for Gōdarz was justified—required, even—by the logic of the "hostage" system: if the nobility decided to reject a reigning king, they had the right to search for a better Arsacid among the princes in fosterage. Thanks to Gōdarz's purges, the remaining candidates were in Roman custody; hence the appeal.

Scholarly discussions of this section read it as a Tacitean criticism of Roman imperialism through a Parthian mouthpiece. The envoys, on this view, are ventriloquist dummies whose actual voice comes from the historian manipulating them. Genuine Parthian sentiments, whatever they might be, are not on offer. The interpretation has much to commend it, for the signs of Tacitus's authorial hand are all over the passage. The theme of foreign adaptation to Roman mores is especially Tacitean. As the next chapter will discuss, the author's digressions on the return of Rome's "hostages" to their homelands often point to acculturation as an explanation for their failure. The "habituation to [Roman] customs" turns out to be a negative development, since the decadence and chicanery of Roman imperial culture leaves foreign dynastic children ill-equipped to succeed in their countries of origin.[117] Like the audience scene before Tiberius, moreover, this passage shows an internal correspondence with a later section in which the Arsacid of Rome meets his end: Claudius's appeal to "clemency" in his response to the Parthian envoys will there be parodied by Gōdarz, who leaves a mutilated Mihrdād alive

---

116. Tac. *Ann.* 12.10.2. My translation follows the text of Heubner 1994: 240; for discussion of the textual problem with *liberos obsides*, see Koestermann 1963–68: 3.124.

117. For this reading of the passage, see Koestermann 1963–68: 3.124; Keitel 1978: 466; Gowing 1990: 329; Braund 2015: 129. An exception is Matthews 1989a: 38, where the statement is taken as authentic, but without substantive discussion of the Parthian view. On appropriation of barbarian voices in Roman historiography, see Adler 2011, esp. 119–39 on Tacitus. On the supposed acculturation of the Arsacids of Rome, see chapter 5.

"as a sign of his own clemency."[118] The historiographical reading is productive and indispensable, then, illuminating key programmatic features in Tacitus's work.

Yet Tacitus's instrumentalization of the envoys need not mean that their words are divorced from the Parthian viewpoint, and their utterance can also be read as an authentic expression of fosterage values. This interpretation is occasioned by the envoys' representation not of the Arsacid empire as a whole, but of specific Parthian elites, as discussed above. The second phrase in the section—"help should be given to allies who were coequals in strength but yielded out of respect"—is always construed as a statement of equality between the Roman and Parthian *states*.[119] But the "allies" (*socii*) in question can simply refer to the Parthian elites who sought Mihrdād; after all, it was precisely such a group that had sent the envoys. The parity, in other words, is not between Rome and Parthia as empires, but between the emperor and the heads of Parthia's aristocratic families. These nobles are "coequals in strength" (*virium aemulis*) with the emperor because they, too, preside over large armies—the Sūrēn's defeat of the Romans at the Battle of Carrhae had furnished ample evidence of that—and because they, too, foster Arsacid children. In need of a viable contender for the throne, they have deferred to the fosterer in whose custody the eligible princes remained. This is no subordination of the Parthian empire to the Roman one; rather, it is an integration of the emperor into the Parthian aristocracy.

The final sentence from the quotation has always been understood as Tacitean ventriloquism rather than a genuine Parthian statement: "the reason that it was the children of kings who were given as hostages was that, if they [i.e., the Parthian nobles] tired of their domestic rule, they could resort to the emperor and the senators, from whom a king could be obtained who was better for his habituation to their [Roman] customs." The contentious issue of Arsacid acculturation will be addressed in the next chapter. For now, the question is whether any Iranian evidence parallels the sentiment expressed here. Could the Parthian aristocracy have regarded adaptation to the customs and mores of the fosterer as not just a by-product but an objective of fosterage?

The answer is a qualified yes. A comparable scene is presented in Ferdowsi's *Shahnameh* in the section on Bahram Gur, a fifth century C.E. Sasanian king whose life became the subject of an elaborate romantic tradition. As discussed in chapter 1, Bahram's father, Yazdgird I, is remembered in Ferdowsi's epic as a malicious tyrant, disrespectful of political and religious elites alike. When his son Bahram is born, it is precisely those elites who take counsel about how the boy should be raised. They proceed from the premise that "if this new child did not inherit his father's temperament, he would be a just king. But if he did have

---

118. Tac. *Ann.* 12.11.2, 12.14.3; on the repetition of *clementia*, see Koestermann 1963–68: 3.133.

119. Furneaux 1907: 2.73 n.3; Timpe 1962: 128 n.153; Ziegler 1964: 65; Dąbrowa 2017: 178–79; Doležal 2017: 116.

his father's temperament, then all the land would be thrown into upheaval."[120] Since Yazdgird's moral character is deficient, in other words, Bahram must not be allowed to spend his formative years near his father's corrupting influence. A foster-father who is noble, just, and humane is thus a necessity not just for Bahram's sake, but for Iran's, too. The character and customs of the *dāyag*, the scene shows, are crucial for the eventual success of the young dynast and for the prosperity of the realm. In the judgment of the Iranian elite, the idea that the fosterer should mold the disposition and habits of the prince is not empty rhetoric, but rather an essential feature of the arrangement.

The statement of the Parthian envoys before Claudius can be read as an expression of this principle, as well. Gōdarz was not the natal father of Mihrdād, but he was the reigning Arsacid king. He therefore occupied a patriarchal position atop Parthia's ruling family and indeed the empire as a whole. The king's savage behavior and moral transgressions parallel the misconduct attributed to Yazdgird in the postconquest authors, and Tacitus shows that the Parthian envoys rehearsed these crimes in detail at the Senate meeting. The upbringing of Mihrdād in Rome—away from Gōdarz and the toxic environment his reign had created—was accordingly not a deficiency to be excused, but an advantage to be utilized. From the Parthian elite's point of view, fosterage could shield the younger generation from the iniquities of the older one. It is in this spirit that the envoys invoke Mihrdād's acculturation as a moral good.

What the Romans heard in this invocation is another matter, and Tacitus once again gives the reader cause to see misunderstanding at play in the exchange. When the envoys express their wish for an Arsacid who is "better for his habituation to their customs," their point, on the Ferdowsi model, is that the fosterer's ways are superior to those of the reigning king. More specifically, they mean that Claudius is a better Arsacid-raiser than Gōdarz. Claudius's response, however, suggests that he understands the comment as a wholesale affirmation of Rome's superiority to Parthia. In his view, the units under comparison are the empires and their cultures, not the individuals who raise children. As a result, the emperor's "pompous," "ludicrous," or even "silly" oration in response to the embassy is a preening and ceremonious one.[121] Claudius discourses on "Roman supremacy and Parthian compliance (*obsequium*)"—a slap in the face to speakers who just moments ago have spoken of deference among equals from respect, not of state hierarchy and rank. He enjoins Mihrdād to treat his subjects like citizens and not like slaves, as he imagines to be the norm. And he appeals to the lofty abstractions of clemency and justice—two qualities that have been in rather short supply in

120. Ferdowsi, *Shahnameh* = Khaleghi-Motlagh and Omidsalar 2005: 364, lines 48–49.

121. Adjectives from Syme 1958: 2.539; Koestermann 1963–68: 3.125; Keitel 1978: 466; Griffin 1990: 486.

his own reign.[122] Scholars debate the extent to which Tacitus may have played up the irony behind the emperor's words, but in the absence of another Lyons tablet, questions of fidelity to an original text cannot receive a final answer.[123] The situation, in the end, is the same as it was for Tiberius: Tacitus's text, as written, shows a Roman-Parthian dialogue in which the interlocutors are not on the same page. Their interests are aligned and their decisions accord, to be sure—the Parthians want Mihrdād released, and Claudius wants to release him. But each side's logic is opaque to the other. The exchange is made, but both parties misconstrue the other's position.

CONCLUSION

A close look at the Parthian figures who sent to Rome for Arsacid release shows that elite families were the key petitioners. Some of their number belonged to Parthian noble families like the Sūrēn and Kārin, and while little is known about the structural place of these families before the Sasanian period, it seems they furnished some of the political and military office holders that ran the Arsacid empire. Other petitioners came from uncertain backgrounds, but the familial basis of their power is either clear in the sources (as it is for Abdagaš and Sēnak, for instance) or seems likely from context. In the main, it was influential families— whether aristocratic clans, client kings, or a combination of the two—that initiated Arsacid remission from Rome.

That context matters, because it was precisely these types of people who ordinarily served as cliental fosterers in the Parthian and Sasanian periods. The evidence from Sasanian Iran and late antique Armenia shows that the great noble families were routinely involved in these relationships—the Mihrān fostered for the Sasanians, for instance, and the Mamikoneans for the Arshakuni. Non-Iranian client kings could be fosterers too, as Monzer was for Bahram. The Parthian aristocrats who contacted Rome on their own initiative therefore came from the same social groups who supplied the fosterers of Arsacid children in ordinary times, and who had been at least partially supplanted in that role by the Roman emperor.

Against this backdrop, the Parthian embassies that sought Arsacid remission can be understood not as insidious conspiracies enabling Roman intervention in the realm of Parthian domestic affairs, but as a dialogue among cliental fosterers in service to the Arsacid dynasty. Fostering an Arsacid child showed a noble's fealty to the ruling family, and in this sense it was an obligation of a lesser lord to a greater. When the Parthian aristocracy saw the dynasty's princes and princesses relocating to Rome, they assumed that the Roman emperor had been integrated

---

122. Tac. *Ann.* 12.11.

123. See Isaac 2004: 376 n.35 contra Ehrhardt 1998: 302. Koestermann 1963–68: 3.125 thinks Tacitus had access to the original text of the speech.

into this system; he and his realm no longer constituted a discrete and separate state, but rather a part of the Arsacid empire. Yet fosterage came with prerogatives, as well, namely the right to monitor, police, substitute, and resist the Arsacid dynast who reigned as king of kings. This dimension of the practice helps explain why the Parthian envoys who sought Arsacid remission argued in the way Tacitus says they did: through appeals to the moral character of the kingship, the didactic function of the fosterer, and the need to uphold the integrity of the Arsacid family within the Parthian realm.

Such motives were alien to the emperors who remitted the Arsacids of Rome, of course, and Tacitus's accounts of the Parthian audience scenes at Rome are eloquent testimony to the diverging expectations of either side. Appeals to the emperor as a cliental fosterer and thus as a type of Parthian aristocrat fell on deaf ears. Tiberius and Claudius responded to the envoys in keeping with their characters—Tiberius as a cold-blooded realist, Claudius as a preening cosmopolitan—but in both cases as hostage-taking heads of state, not as foster-fathers. The discordance was no obstacle to Arsacid remission, for Roman emperors and Parthian aristocrats were aligned in their wishes to see the Arsacids of Rome enthroned. But their reasons were different, and incomprehensible to the other. Some Arsacids went back, but misunderstanding remained.

5

Return

The Parthian Kingships of the Arsacids of Rome

The embassies of the Parthian nobility to the Roman emperor led to the remission of four Arsacids of Rome. Vonones ruled the longest, taking the Arsacid throne in 8 C.E. and holding it until at least 12, when a rebellion began to erode his grip on power. The subsequent returnees reigned for even shorter durations, if at all. Frahād died in transit through Syria and never reached Parthian territory. Tirdād was crowned in Ctesiphon, but his kingship was over within months. Last and least was Mihrdād, who was crushed in short order by the reigning king, Gōdarz. And yet, despite the abortive and ephemeral nature of these kingships, the attempts of the Arsacids of Rome to rule in Parthia merited lengthy digressions in Tacitus and Josephus, among the most important sources for their lives. How did they assess the Parthian kingships of the Arsacids of Rome, and how did these episodes affect the pragmatic misunderstanding in Roman-Parthian relations?

Tacitus and Josephus suggest that the kingships of the Arsacids of Rome forced Parthians to reckon with the Roman category of hostageship, which, once comprehended, was equated with enslavement to Rome. For the Parthians, moreover, the proof of the humiliating relationship between the Arsacid returnee and the Roman emperor was the acculturation of the former to the customs of the latter. Vonones, Frahād, Tirdād, and Mihrdād had all become Romans thanks to their years of residence in the city, and this alienation from their Parthian heritage made them unacceptable as kings. Taken at face value, then, Tacitus and Josephus enjoin the conclusion that the Parthians gained an understanding of Roman hostageship and its connotation of subordinate political status. If this realization indeed took place, Arsacid return must have forced pragmatic misunderstanding to unravel. This chapter evaluates that proposition.

My reading of Tacitus and Josephus is ambivalent: on this topic, they are at once highly unreliable and possibly right. In their narratives, the Parthian internalization of the "hostage" category is bound up with two discourses: first, the model of enslavement as a Roman paradigm of empire; and second, the fraught issue of barbarian acculturation to Roman habits. The treatment of these themes in Tacitus and Josephus almost certainly does not derive, even indirectly, from authentic Parthian accounts of resistance to the Arsacids of Rome. Instead, the authors take their cues from the rhetorical conventions of Roman historiography and the literary milieu in which they were immersed. Their testimony on Arsacid return therefore warrants major skepticism. However, even if Tacitus and Josephus are underinformed, there are two reasons to entertain the story they tell. The first is comparative history, which shows how cultural anxieties are often projected onto dynastic children who live abroad for extended periods. The second comes from Parthian evidence for a cultural turn in the first century C.E.—precisely when Arsacid returnees are supposed to have forced Parthians to grapple with the effects of acculturation on their would-be kings. So while no Iranian evidence can confirm or disprove the Parthian cognizance of Roman hostageship, Tacitus and Josephus may capture dynamics that really were at play in these episodes. Arsacid return could have triggered a Parthian counterreaction that, over time, led to the breakdown of pragmatic misunderstanding.

In subjecting Tacitus and Josephus to increased scrutiny while rehabilitating certain aspects of their narratives, I seek to improve on scholarly discussions that have been too credulous in their approach to these scenes. Earlier commentators took these passages of Tacitus and Josephus at face value, recycling the ancient accounts or even framing the Arsacid's supposed acculturation in modern terms. In his narrative treatment of Parthian history, Neilson Debevoise spoke of Vonones's "western manners," the "nationalists" who rejected this foreign influence, and the "general dislike of Romanized Parthians" that plagued Mihrdād's bid for the kingship.[1] Rostovtzeff's roughly contemporary view was that Vonones's "hellenizing" tendencies triggered a "national Iranian reaction" against his reign. He also saw Frahād and Tirdād as "romanized Arsacids."[2] More recent studies have shed the anachronistic language of nationalism, but they retain the uncritical use of Tacitus and Josephus as evidence for Arsacid acculturation and the Parthian counterreaction to it.[3] Without due attention to their literary underpinnings, these sources cannot be properly employed, and Roman discourse will be conflated with Parthian reality.

1. Debevoise 1938: 151–52, 172.
2. Rostovtzeff 1936: 107.
3. Ziegler 1964: 57; Moscovich 1974: 425 n.37; Dąbrowa 2012: 174; Ellerbrock 2021: 48–49; Cooley 2023: 8, 174.

Other scholars have highlighted the methodological issues with the use of Tacitus and Josephus as indices of Arsacid acculturation, but without turning to comparative or Parthian cultural history to contextualize their findings. Careful readers of Tacitus and Josephus as literature have shown that these passages mount self-reflexive critiques of Roman imperialism instead of rigorously sourced expositions of Parthian domestic politics. Commentators like Norbert Ehrhardt and Josef Wiesehöfer convincingly read the Arsacid return sections as hopelessly gnarled knots of historical judgment, rhetorical invention, and stock tropes, with *Prinzipatskritik* as perhaps the dominant thread. Yet the disconnection from Parthian realities does not appear to be total: certain ethnographic details seem reliable enough, and the general shape of the narrative is believable.[4] Here comparative case studies can supply vital additional context, as can internal Parthian evidence for the empire's cultural history. Itinerant dynastic children from other premodern settings tended to garner accusations of political and cultural betrayal, and that transhistorical tendency can inform the interpretation of Tacitus and Josephus. Moreover, Parthia's alleged discomfort with the "Romanizing" and/or "Hellenizing" behavior of Arsacid returnees presents intriguing points of contact with the empire's cultural reorientation in the first century C.E. as it emerges from Parthian sources. No pieces of comparative or internal evidence will be dispositive of the Roman texts, but they can offer additional perspective, and support a more balanced treatment, of the vexatious issue of Arsacid return.

THE EVIDENCE

Josephus and Tacitus constitute the traditional evidentiary basis for the Parthian kingships of the Arsacids of Rome. Both authors contain relatively detailed accounts of Vonones, who returned to Parthia in c. 8 C.E. and held the kingship until 12, though his apparent control of the mint at Seleucia on the Tigris as late as 15 suggests that his loss of power was gradual rather than abrupt.[5] Only Tacitus offers extended digressions on Frahād, Tirdād, and Mihrdād, though a cursory reference to the former in Cassius Dio also merits attention. Vonones is the only Arsacid returnee whose issues have been identified. Frahād and Mihrdād never reigned in any meaningful sense, so it is doubtful that they ever minted any coins at all. For a brief moment, Tirdād did control Seleucia on the Tigris and presumably the mint along with it, but no surviving issues have been associated with him.

In the crucial case of Vonones, both Tacitus and Josephus imagine a Parthian counterreaction against a king tainted by foreign influence, but they articulate the

---

4. Ehrhardt 1998: 302–3; Wiesehöfer 2010: 190–92; similar is Matthews 1989a: 39. Heil 2017: 269 also endorses Tacitus on some points of Parthian ethnography.

5. On Vonones's minting of coins at Seleucia in 15 C.E., see Gonnella 2001: 71.

nature of that influence in different ways. Josephus's report is part of a long digression on Parthian affairs, and runs as follows:[6]

ἐδόκει γὰρ χωρεῖν τὴν τύχην, ἣν αὐτῷ δύο μέγισται τῶν ὑπὸ τὸν ἥλιον ἡγεμονίαι προσέφερον, ἰδία καὶ ἀλλοτρία. ταχεῖα δ᾽ ἀνατροπὴ τοὺς βαρβάρους ὕπεισιν ἅτε καὶ φύσει σφαλεροὺς ὄντας πρός τε τὴν ἀναξιοπάθειαν, ἀνδραπόδῳ γὰρ ἀλλοτρίῳ ποιήσειν τὸ προστασσόμενον οὐκ ἠξίουν, τὴν ὁμηρείαν ἀντὶ δουλείας ὀνομάζοντες, καὶ τῆς ἐπικλήσεως τὴν ἀδοξίαν· οὐ γὰρ [ἂν] πολέμου δικαίῳ δεδόσθαι τὸν βασιλεύσοντα Πάρθοις, ἀλλά, ὃ τῷ παντὶ χεῖρον, εἰρήνης ὕβρει.

[Vonones] seemed to encompass a destiny conferred upon him by the two greatest empires under the sun, one his own and the other foreign. But a quick change of heart came over the barbarians [i.e., the Parthians], being fickle by nature, both at the indignity—for they thought it wrong to carry out the commands of a slave of foreigners [or: a foreign slave], considering "hostage" to be synonymous with "slave"—and at the ill-repute of the title, since in their view the man had been given to the Parthians as a king not by the verdict of war but as an insult in a time of peace, which was the worst part of it all.

The first sentence offers the unparalleled suggestion that an Arsacid of Rome could be more than the sum of his parts—that the glory of "the two greatest empires" could be combined in one and the same person. Roman readers may have been reminded of Velleius Paterculus's account of the negotiations between Gaius Caesar and Frahātak on the Euphrates in 1 C.E., a meeting that Velleius called "an exceedingly notable and memorable spectacle" involving "the two most eminent leaders of empires and men."[7] In both passages, the accord between Parthia and Rome inspires awe as the two imperial giants are brought into harmonious alignment. In Vonones's case, however, that harmony proves illusory, and the fallout is swift. His Parthian enemies deride him as an *andrapodon allotrion*, which could be translated "foreign slave" or "slave to foreigners." The point may be either that Vonones has become a servile agent of Roman outsiders, or that he is now, in essence, a foreigner himself. The word *andrapodon*, moreover, is a pointed choice of slave terminology. It can connote enslavement through imprisonment in war, which would imply the military defeat of Parthia by Rome.[8] Against such a background, the practice the Romans call hostageship is tantamount to slavery. It adds insult to injury that Vonones has not been installed through military force, which would at least be comprehensible through the logic of conquest. Instead, Parthia has accepted his degrading kingship in a time of peace, as though it were actively seeking its own enslavement.

6. Joseph. *AJ* 18.46–47.

7. Vell. Pat. 2.101.2.

8. On this connotation of *andrapodon*, see Gaca 2010: 120–21; Vlassopoulos 2011: 119–20; Lewis 2018: 62 n.17.

Tacitus's account of the same episode hits many of the same notes, though the level of rhetorical invention is greater. The Vonones narrative begins the second book of the *Annals* with a lengthy digression on Parthian affairs. The reaction of the Parthians to the kingship of the Arsacid of Rome is described as follows:[9]

> Et accepere barbari laetantes, ut ferme ad nova imperia. Mox subiit pudor degeneravisse Parthos: petitum alio ex orbe regem, hostium artibus infectum; iam inter provincias Romanas solium Arsacidarum haberi darique. Ubi illam gloriam trucidantium Crassum, exturbantium Antonium, si mancipium Caesaris, tot per annos servitutem perpessum, Parthis imperitet? Accendebat dedignantes et ipse diversus a maiorum institutis, raro venatu, segni equorum cura; quotiens per urbes incederet, lecticae gestamine fastuque erga patrias epulas. Inridebantur et Graeci comites ac vilissima utensilium anulo clausa. Sed prompti aditus, obvia comitas, ignotae Parthis virtutes, nova vitia; et quia ipsorum moribus aliena, perinde odium pravis et honestis.

> And the barbarians [i.e., the Parthians] received [Vonones] happily, as is usual with new reigns. But soon shame came over them that the Parthians had degenerated: from another world a king had been sought who was infected by the ways of their enemies. Now the throne of the Arsacids was being held and given away as though it were a Roman province! Where was the glory of those who had butchered Crassus and driven away Antony, if a slave of Caesar, having endured servitude for so many years, was ruling over the Parthians? The man himself incited their disdain all the more in his difference from the customs of their ancestors. He rarely hunted. His interest in horsemanship was slack. Whenever he passed through cities, he was conveyed by litter, and he scorned their ancestral feasts. His Greek companions, too, were the object of ridicule, as was his locking away of even the cheapest materials with a seal ring. But he was approachable and ready with kindness—things unknown as virtues among the Parthians, and thus considered as vices because they were new. And since he differed from them in his habits, they hated both his good ones and his bad ones alike.

Many of Tacitus's phrases parallel those in Josephus, but with further elaborations. One sentence establishes the auspicious beginnings of Vonones's kingship, and the next transitions to the swift (*tacheia / mox*) reversal of sentiment that came upon (*hupeisin / subiit*) the Parthians.[10] Yet another similarity is the couching of hostageship in the language of slavery, the terminology for which is roughly parallel in the two passages. Tacitus's *mancipium* echoes Josephus's *andrapodon* in underlining the mercantile dimension of slavery as an institution where human beings are turned into commodities that are bought and sold.[11] Both authors then proceed to more general, abstract nouns for slavery (*douleia* in Josephus, *servitus* in Tacitus).

9. Tac. *Ann.* 2.2.

10. Parallels noted by Gowing 1990: 318.

11. On the similarity between Greek *andrapodon* and Latin *mancipium*, see Zelnick-Abramovitz 2018.

The two passages are therefore congruent both in their major thematic concerns and in their phrasing.

But there are differences, too. There is no precise counterpart in Josephus to Tacitus's assertions, through his Parthian characters, that the Roman empire is "another world" (*alius orbis*) from the Arsacid empire, or that Parthia had provincialized itself through its acceptance of Vonones as king. Tacitus is also more profuse than Josephus in his representation of Parthian outrage. He has the Parthians reflect on what he imagines to be the high points of their history, namely their defeats of Crassus and Antony, and he assigns them a dramatic rhetorical question about their lost pride. Moreover, he mentions specific cultural practices that Vonones, thanks to his Roman acculturation, now either avoids or cherishes. The Arsacid of Rome neglects hunting, horsemanship, feasting, and court ceremonies, all supposed mainstays of Parthian culture; by contrast, he has adopted the Roman habits of association with Greeks, conveyance by litter, keeping cheap comestibles under seal, and royal affability. It mattered little whether these deviations from Parthian norms were for the better or worse, according to Tacitus. The bare fact of Vonones's difference from his compatriots was the issue. That difference mobilized the Parthians against him and led to his displacement by Ardawān.

Tacitus's subsequent narratives on the other Arsacids of Rome reuse the acculturation paradigm that the case of Vonones has established. In the following episode, Frahād's death in Syria is attributed to the toll of cultural reprogramming. "While he was adopting the ways of the Parthians and desisting from Roman culture, to which he had been accustomed over the course of so many years, he was taken out by an illness, unequal as he was to his native customs," Tacitus writes.[12] Shortly thereafter, the causes of Tirdād's failure are set out in the fiery speech of Hiero, who complains to Ardawān II that "command resided not with an Arsacid, but in the empty name of a man turned unwarlike from foreign softness."[13] Finally, Mihrdād's mutilation by Gōdarz was paired with insults that he was "no kinsman [of Gōdarz] nor a man of the Arsacid family, but rather a foreigner and a Roman."[14] Each passage recycles motifs that first appeared in the section on Vonones. Frahād seems to have learned from his brother's example, but the effort to unlearn Roman customs proves fatal. Parthian culture, it appears, requires a fortitude and vigor that a long-time inhabitant of Rome does not possess. Hiero's slander of Tirdād makes the same point: residence in Rome has alienated the young dynast from his Arsacid heritage and inculcated a characteristic Roman "softness." Gōdarz further underlines the loss of Arsacid status that a Roman upbringing entails. His ascription of "foreign" and "Roman" identity to Mihrdād represents the culmination of

---

12. Tac. *Ann.* 6.32.2. Woodman 2017: 229 observes that the "anagrammatic expression" in these clauses stands in for the process of transformation that Frahād undergoes.

13. Tac. *Ann.* 6.43.3.

14. Tac. *Ann.* 12.14.3.

these invectives. In this final case of return, "Arsacid" and "Roman" have become opposite and mutually exclusive categories.

The only historian to offer additional testimony on these cases is Cassius Dio, who treats the release of Frahād and Tirdād in a fashion that is cursory, yet still consequential for a full assessment of the Roman sources. The entire notice amounts to less than a paragraph on eastern affairs during the reign of Tiberius. Dio writes:[15]

> καὶ αὐτοῖς τότε μὲν Φραάτην τὸν τοῦ Φραάτου, τελευτήσαντος δὲ ἐκείνου κατὰ τὴν ὁδὸν Τιριδάτην, ἐκ τοῦ βασιλικοῦ καὶ αὐτὸν γένους ὄντα, ἔπεμψε ... οὐ μέντοι καὶ ἐπὶ πολὺ ὁ Τιριδάτης ἐβασίλευσεν· ὁ γὰρ Ἀρτάβανος Σκύθας προσλαβὼν οὐ χαλεπῶς αὐτὸν ἐξήλασε.

> To them [i.e., the Parthians who had petitioned Rome], Tiberius sent Frahād son of Frahād, and, after that man died, Tirdād, who was also from the royal family. . . . Tirdād did not rule long, however, for Ardawān secured the help of the Scythians and expelled him without difficulty.

The account is less detailed than the one in Tacitus, but it illustrates an important point: acculturation was not an indispensable explanation for the failure of the Arsacids of Rome. Dio says nothing about the cultural habits of Frahād or Tirdād. The latter did not lose the throne because his character offended key Parthian officials, which is the impression that Tacitus leaves. Instead, Ardawān owed his victory to the enlistment of "Scythian" auxiliaries, which tipped the balance of power in his favor. The conflict turned on military assistance, not cultural affiliation. When Josephus and Tacitus point to enslavement and acculturation as the causes of the Arsacids of Rome's failure, then, they are not adducing a factor that was objectively decisive. They are making a historiographic judgment, and by no means an inevitable one.

Vonones's coins offer additional perspective on the issue of acculturation, though in the final analysis they can neither confirm nor disprove the Roman sources. Vonones minted tetradrachms at Seleucia on the Tigris and drachms at Rhagae and Ecbatana. He could have struck other denominations elsewhere, but no examples are known. The tetradrachms (figure 10) feature a bust on the obverse and Nike on the reverse, and they represent no dramatic departure from established Arsacid numismatic conventions. The Greek legend on the obverse exhibits some novel elements, however. Vonones's name and the title "king of kings" both appear in the nominative case, not the usual genitive (though the genitive is used on the reverse, which features a typical array of epithets).[16] The mere appearance of the king's proper name is a rarity in itself. All Arsacid kings took the throne name of Arsaces/Aršak when they began to rule, and most used this appellation alone

---

15. Cass. Dio 58.26.2–3.
16. Sellwood 1980: 194 (types 60.1–4).

FIGURE 10. Tetradrachm of Vonones I, 10–11 C.E. Sellwood 1980: 194 (type 60.1). Photo credit: American Numismatic Society (ANS 1944.100.82997).

FIGURE 11. Drachm of Vonones I, who wears short hair in his portrait on the obverse. Sellwood 1980: 195 (type 60.5). Photo credit: American Numismatic Society (ANS 0000.999.52971).

on their issues, though exceptions could be made during dynastic wars between two or more royal contenders.[17] Vonones's drachms (figure 11) show additional departures, these ones more dramatic, from Arsacid numismatic precedents. Once again, the king's name and title appear in the nominative on the obverse, but Vonones's portrait here is unconventional. Instead of long locks cascading in serried rows of curls, as would be typical for Arsacid royal portraiture, the king's hair is cropped short. Moreover, the legend that surrounds Nike on the reverse contains a rare reference to a contemporary event. It reads, "King Vonones [who

17. On these exceptions, see Alram 1986a; Errington et al. 2007: 49; Ellerbrock 2021: 52.

has] conquered Ardawān."[18] The rebellion of Ardawān II must have begun at the time of the coin's minting. Josephus and Tacitus mention that Vonones scored an initial victory against his rival before his ultimate expulsion from Parthia, and it could have been just after that battle that these drachms were struck.[19] Vonones's success was fleeting, however, and no coins later than 15 C.E. are known.

Are these the coins of a ruler so indelibly shaped by his years of residence in Rome that he is ignorant of or disinterested in Parthian traditions? Does the portrait on the drachms lend credence to the portrait in Tacitus and Josephus? Different scholars have said yes or no to these questions, but in the end the coins cannot be pressed to validate or repudiate the idea that acculturation fueled the revolt against Vonones. The preeminent Arsacid numismatist David Sellwood saw a close correspondence between Vonones's coins and the narratives of Tacitus and Josephus. From the start, Sellwood writes, "it was clear that a prince brought up to appreciate imperial culture and the hunting of slaves in the arena would have difficulty in adapting to the court of the Arsacids, based as it was on nomad traditions and rising, in its entertainments, no higher than the plays of Euripides." The "occidental aberrations" on the coins are explicable through this lens, from the use of "the nominative customary for Roman issues" to "the adoption of a short westernised hair style."[20] Others avoid the normative cultural judgments found in Sellwood, but they too see signs of acculturation in the coins.[21] Sellwood's description discounts important comparanda, however. A parallel for Vonones's coiffure can be found on the coins of Pakōr, an Arsacid prince of the first century B.C.E. who invaded Judaea and died in battle against the Romans.[22] Was his short hair "westernizing" too? Moreover, the use of the nominative may be unattested in earlier Arsacid issues, but there are parallels with other Indo-Parthian coinages from the first century C.E. Those coins could in turn have been influenced by Vonones's precedent, but in any event it is clear that a ruler need not have resided in Rome to favor the nominative over the genitive.[23] These elements cannot be interpreted as straightforward numismatic corollaries of acculturation.

On the other hand, the changes in coin iconography are significant and should not be downplayed. Joel Allen's otherwise balanced discussion of the iconography

18. Sellwood 1980: 195 (types 60.5–7).

19. Joseph. *AJ* 18.48–49; Tac. *Ann.* 2.2.4. On the probable connection between this initial battle and the legend on the drachms, see Wroth 1903: xlii–xliii; Goodyear 1981: 194; Bivar 1983: 68. The relatively late tetradrachms from Seleucia on the Tigris (Gonnella 2001) accord well with Josephus's assertion that Seleucia was Vonones' final refuge in Parthian territory.

20. Sellwood 1980: 193; Sellwood 1983: 293 ("occidental aberrations").

21. Errington et al. 2007: 49; Keller in Hackl et al. 2010: 2.632; Sinisi 2012b: 286. More cautious about Roman influence is Rezakhani 2013: 770.

22. Sellwood 1980: 157–58 (type 49.1), this time with no explanation for the hairstyle.

23. Cribb 2021: 660, who sees the use of the nominative in both Arsacid and Indo-Parthian coins as "under the influence of Latin coin inscription practices."

ultimately dismisses the departures from numismatic precedent: "In overall aspect, however, [Vonones's] numismatic issues are still unmistakably Parthian, as one would expect."[24] That judgment places too much emphasis on continuity instead of change. Arsacid coin portraiture and iconography were conservative, and elements like throne name, hairstyle, beard length, epithets, headgear, and dress tended to remain consistent over long periods. Where deviations or innovations appear, they matter and should be explained. Primary sources from Parthian territory are far too rare to paint contemporary Arsacid productions with broad brush strokes. The burden of proof belongs on those who deny significance, not those who assert it. Another skeptical reading of Vonones's drachms comes from Everett Wheeler, whose doubts rest on the location of their minting. The acculturation argument, he writes, "would be more convincing if this drachma (like Vonones's tetradrachms) had been minted at Seleucia-on-the-Tigris, a Greek city. But the peculiar drachma was minted at Median Ecbatana, a less likely site for romanized presentation of an Arsacid monarch."[25] But even if one grants the premise that a "romanized presentation" would have been more expedient at Seleucia than at Ecbatana, it could just as well follow that Vonones was *more* acculturated, not less: if he depicted himself in Roman fashion in a place where it would not have been politically advantageous to do so, then perhaps Roman culture was part of his genuine self-conception instead of a costume to be donned where expedient.

In the end, the coins can neither support nor disprove Tacitus and Josephus on Vonones's supposed acculturation, to say nothing of his alleged enslavement to the Roman emperor. There is no denying the novel elements that appear in Vonones's iconography, especially in an otherwise conservative medium where innovations were rare. But the attribution of these novelties to Vonones's cultural preferences is unsupportable without reference to the Roman literary sources. In other words, the coins can only confirm the texts if they are interpreted by means of the texts. The drachms and tetradrachms cannot give testimony as to the reasoning behind their iconographic changes or their reception among Vonones's Parthian subjects—and these are precisely the issues at stake.

ENSLAVEMENT AND ACCULTURATION

If the coins can neither validate nor refute Tacitus and Josephus, then the literary narratives must be evaluated on their own, and the case against their historicity is a strong one. An initial consideration is where the authors got their information, and there is little reason to believe that either was well informed about Parthian domestic politics in the early decades of the first century C.E. The last chapter considered the content of Parthian speeches delivered at Rome by emissaries of

---

24. Allen 2006: 177.
25. Wheeler 2007.

the Parthian nobility. Those appeals took place in the city itself, and plausible paths of transmission can be identified between the original utterances and Tacitus's text: the *Acta Senatus*, the emperor's chancellery, earlier Roman historians, or other sources could all have conveyed the basic thrust of the Parthian arguments to subsequent generations.[26] The downfall of the Arsacids of Rome in Parthia is a different matter. The enemies of Vonones, Tirdād, and Mihrdād raised their armies—and formulated their arguments for resistance—at great remove from Roman territory. No Romans are known to have taken part in these wars, or to have directly observed them. It is difficult to reconstruct how a Roman aristocrat like Tacitus could have learned about the animus behind Parthian resistance to the Arsacids of Rome, not least because Tacitus himself never held a governmental post on the eastern front or personally interacted with Parthia's inhabitants.[27] The outlook might appear more promising in the case of Josephus, whose religion connected him to robust transimperial Jewish networks across the Roman-Parthian frontier.[28] But his narrative of Vonones does not appear to have benefited from his potential access to information. As mentioned above, Josephus and Tacitus resemble each other so closely on this topic that it appears they adapted the same source (perhaps Cluvius Rufus, an earlier Latin historian of consular rank, though this is not certain).[29] Moreover, Josephus's primary concern was with Parthia's Jewish population, not with its succession struggles. Where he does discuss the latter, he favors personality studies and moralizing clichés over substantive analysis of Arsacid dynastic politics.[30] Even if Josephus's sources gave him a deeper understanding of Parthian resistance to the Arsacids of Rome, there is no indication that this knowledge informed his text. Source criticism does not augur well for the reliability of Tacitus or Josephus on the subject of Arsacid return.

A case could be made that Vonones himself served as a source of information on the end of his Parthian reign, but the suggestion is not a satisfying one. Its main shortcoming is that Vonones was treated as spoiled goods when he returned to the Roman empire, never reattaining the status he had held before his kingship. After an abortive attempt to rule in Armenia, Vonones ended up back in Roman Syria. Josephus says that he "handed himself over" to the Roman governor Creticus Silanus, using a verb that often denotes surrender to hostile parties, but also that he was "put under guard out of respect for his Roman education."[31] Tacitus

26. On Tacitus's sources, see Devillers 2003; Potter 2012.

27. On Tacitus's inexperience with Parthia and the Roman east, see Heil 2017: 261.

28. On these networks, and the relations between Jews in Rome and Parthia, see recently Gross 2023.

29. Gowing 1990: 317 with n.8; see also Walser 1951: 72 n.330 contra Täubler 1904: 25. On the career and writings of Cluvius Rufus, see Levick 2013b.

30. Gruen 2017: 232, 234, 239.

31. Joseph. *AJ* 18.51–52. On the verb *paradidōmi* with submission to hostiles, cf. Hdt. 1.45.1, 3.13.3; Thuc. 7.86.4; Andoc. 3.11.

has him "summoned and surrounded with guards" by the same official.[32] Tiberius's biographer Suetonius writes that Vonones fled "to the good faith of the Roman people—or so he thought," only to be immediately despoiled of his financial resources by the emperor.[33] If Josephus was right that Vonones's time at Rome earned him favorable treatment in Syria, the limits of that favor would soon become clear. Tiberius reconciled with Vonones's opponent Ardawān II, at whose request the former Arsacid of Rome was relocated to Pompeiopolis, a city in Cilicia at considerable distance from Parthian territory. Ardawān's discomfort with Vonones's residence in Roman Syria is evident not only in Tacitus but in a contemporary source as well, namely the *Senatus Consultum de Cn. Pisone Patre*, an epigraphic document recording the Senate's verdict in the case of Germanicus's alleged murder.[34] In this text, Vonones is said to have bribed Piso so that he could remain in the east within striking distance of Armenia, despite the emperor's wishes to the contrary. Piso and Vonones are depicted as wicked schemers, warmongers, and violators of the peace that Tiberius, Germanicus, and Ardawān have created, and though the senators are more concerned with passing judgment on Piso than Vonones, they clearly consider the latter to be a malign influence.[35] Thus a preponderance of evidence for Vonones's return to Roman territory reveals an ill-favored and marginalized figure of little account—a dynast who was put out of the way, and ultimately killed, when Rome wished to recognize a different Arsacid as Parthia's ruler. Vonones never returned to the city of Rome itself, nor could he have circulated among the empire's ruling classes as he had before his kingship. He was in no position to inform Romans about the sources of Parthian discontent with his reign, and even if he had been, his testimony might not have counted for much.

Source criticism aside, the problem of historicity is further compounded by the issue of invention, a rhetorical technique that both Tacitus and Josephus employ in keeping with the genre conventions of ancient historiography. Roman historians constructed their narratives around a framework of the facts as they understood them, but within that framework there was ample scope for the elaboration of material, sometimes out of whole cloth. Such inventions were not incompatible with a foundational commitment to accuracy, for they could help the reader access deeper truths in the underlying patterns of history.[36] Certain types of scenes offered greater license for imaginative exposition, especially where the baseline of historical knowledge or memory was low. As Eric Adler has shown, "barbarian" speeches were foremost among these. When Roman historians wrote extensive

---

32. Tac. *Ann.* 2.4.3.

33. Suet. *Tib.* 49.2; on the treasure, cf. Tac. *Ann.* 6.31.1.

34. For background on Piso and the *SCPP*, see Eck et al. 1996: 1–10, 71–77; M. Griffin 1997: 254–55; Lott 2012: 255–58.

35. *SCPP* 37–45, text and trans. Potter and Damon 1999: 18–21; Cooley 2023: 118–19, with commentary at 173–76; cf. Suerbaum 1999: 218.

36. Woodman 1988: 83–94.

rhetorical set pieces and attributed them to non-Romans, they were unlikely to have been guided by textual or oral traditions that preserved the original sentiment of the characters in question.[37] Instead, they had considerable leeway to exhibit their rhetorical skills in a setting largely free of documentary parameters. This is not to say that Tacitus or Josephus was disinterested in Parthian domestic politics, or that they made no effort to understand them. But without any identifiable means of access to authentic Parthian rhetoric, their imaginative reconstructions had to fill in the gap. The elaborated, ornamental, and rhetorical nature of those reconstructions makes them a tenuous basis for understanding the counter-reaction to the Arsacids of Rome in Parthia.

Against this backdrop, it should not be surprising that both Tacitus and Josephus invoke one of the Roman elite's central paradigms for modeling the relationship between the Roman ruling class and its non-Roman subjects: enslavement. Slavery was an omnipresent feature of Roman society, especially for the wealthy, landed, and politically influential members of the aristocracy who owned large numbers of slaves—and who produced and consumed the empire's extant literary sources. As Myles Lavan has shown, the institution could therefore furnish one of the most potent metaphors that guided Roman elite thinking about the nature of their imperial order. The relationship of the metropole to the provincial periphery could be compared to that of master and slave, an analogy that allowed members of the ruling class to "conceptualise empire in terms of the concrete and familiar power structures of daily life."[38] Like Adler, Lavan notes the tendency of Roman historians to write speeches for non-Romans that condemn imperial rule as slavery, and like Adler, he doubts that these compositions had much to do with the original utterances of the peoples in question, stressing that "this notionally hostile rhetoric is itself a Roman construct."[39] Roman writers drew on the language of slavery in such passages because it was a common paradigm for empire among members of their class, not because they knew what the foreign enemies of Rome had actually argued.

Perhaps no Roman author exemplifies this literary tendency more than Tacitus, the main source for the Arsacids of Rome. Whether the foreign people in question are the Parthians or the Britons or the Germans, Tacitus describes the imposition and maintenance of Roman rule with the vocabulary of slavery.[40] The import of the description is open to interpretation and indeed constitutes a central debate in Tacitean studies: is the characterization of Rome as a slave master an indictment and critique of its territorial expansion, or simply an articulation of imperial power relations in the expected idiom? The issue is further complicated

37. Adler 2011: 6–8; cf. Woodman 2009: 1.
38. Lavan 2013: 4.
39. Lavan 2013: 74.
40. Passages in Lavan 2013: 82, 95, 124–55.

by the historian's application of the metaphor to the government of the principate in the postrepublican world, where the emperor has made slaves of the Senate and Rome's citizens.[41] When Tacitus has the Parthians call Vonones a "slave of Caesar," then, he is not only reconciling the Arsacid case with his usual paradigm for Roman imperial control. He is also asking his elite Roman readers to consider their *own* enslavement to the emperor. What purports to be Parthian rejection of slavery is in fact a Tacitean incitement to self-reflection.

It might seem more surprising to find the elite discourse of imperial enslavement in the text of Josephus, who did not belong to the Roman ruling class as Tacitus did, but several scholars have demonstrated the Josephan corpus's dense interconnections with the broader tapestry of Roman historiography. Richard Fowler contends that, by the time Josephus finished the *Antiquities* in 93/94 C.E., he was a "committed and influential member of the Flavian elite."[42] That judgment may go too far, and others have seen Josephus's life in Rome as a marginalized one, at least from the aristocratic sphere of the senators and equestrians.[43] But Steve Mason has shown how, as an *author*, Josephus was a "full participant in his literary environment" at Rome, writing alongside and against other accounts of the Jewish revolt, sharing common historiographical models like Thucydides, and reflecting on the tension between monarchy and aristocracy that so concerned Tacitus.[44] As regards the empire-as-enslavement paradigm, Josephus's exposure to it could have begun as early as the Roman siege of Jerusalem in 70 C.E. During his narrative of that event, Josephus has the future emperor Titus promise to behave "like a gentle master in a household" if the inhabitants surrender.[45] Even if the historian misrepresents Titus's original speech, the sentence nonetheless shows his awareness of, and participation in, the slavery discourse of Roman elites. That discourse is a much better explanation for the appearance of the slavery motif in his Vonones narrative than his potential, but unprovable, knowledge of Parthian political rhetoric from the year 12 C.E.

In addition to enslavement, acculturation is the other major theme that Josephus and Tacitus invoke in their passages on Arsacid return, and here their narratives must be contextualized against the general treatment of boundary-crossing figures in Greco-Roman historiography. Classical authors took a keen interest in characters who negotiated, and thereby defined, the frontier between the civilized and barbarian worlds. An early and paradigmatic example comes from

---

41. On provincial and senatorial enslavement in Tacitus and the interplay between these themes, see recently Andrade 2012; Lavan 2013: 124–55, esp. 129–30; Woodman 2014: 15–25; Damtoft Poulsen 2017: 838.

42. Fowler 2017: 368.

43. Cotton and Eck 2005: 52; Price 2005: 105–7. den Hollander 2014: 217, 279, 285–86 notes consistent patronage from the Flavian emperors, but is also skeptical that Josephus circulated at a high level.

44. Mason 2016: 96 (quotation), 97–102.

45. Joseph. *BJ* 6.350.

Herodotus's account of Anacharsis and Scyles, two royal Scythians who allegedly adopted Greek customs.[46] Anacharsis was exposed to Hellenic practices on his travels, while Scyles learned the Greek language from his mother, who came from Istria. When the Scythians discovered how these two had Hellenized, they put the offenders to death. Herodotus observes, "thus do the Scythians protect their own customs, and these are the sorts of penalties they inflict on those who introduce the customs of foreigners."[47] François Hartog has shown how Herodotus uses his narrative of Anacharsis and Scyles to identify the cultural boundaries between Greece and Scythia, and to illustrate the dangers of crossing them. "To travel and to be bilingual," he writes, "come down to the same thing: both are dangerous, for they lead to forgetting the frontier and thus to transgression."[48] To write such characters was not just to tell their stories, but to inscribe the fault lines between the Greek and non-Greek worlds.

Other ancient authors wrote on Anacharsis as a Greco-Scythian boundary crosser, and their accounts illustrate how literary portrayals of cultural intermediaries drew on stock elements that could be detached from their original context and reused elsewhere. Following Herodotus's lead, many writers crafted scenes in which Anacharsis's outsider wisdom reveals the illogic behind Greek customs like wine consumption, athletics, and commercial trade.[49] But in the third-century C.E. account of Diogenes Laertius, a key detail shifts: here Anacharsis has a Greek mother and is bilingual, whereas Herodotus had said this of Scyles. Diogenes does cite earlier authorities on Anacharsis, so perhaps different historians preserved conflicting traditions about his birth and parentage.[50] But the Scythian's bilingualism seems less like a historical detail and more like a literary marker of his intermediary status. Bilingualism and mixed parentage, in other words, are the sorts of characteristics that an ancient author might assign to a traverser of cultural frontiers. They need not be historically accurate details.[51]

Greco-Roman depictions of Scythian intermediaries matter to the historiography of Roman-Parthian relations, and not just because Mediterranean authors saw a major Scythian component in Parthia's heritage.[52] Historiography on Parthia can draw from the same set of motifs as the various Anacharsis traditions. For

46. Hdt. 4.76–80; cf. 4.46.1.

47. Hdt. 4.80.5.

48. Hartog 1988: 64.

49. For sources and discussion, see Kindstrand 1981; Romm 1992: 74–76; Schubert 2010.

50. Diog. Laert. 1.101; the cited sources are Sosicrates and Hermippus. Tac. *Ann.* 12.44.2 makes the same remark about the Arsacid king Walgaš I.

51. On the historical value of the sources for Anacharsis, see Kindstrand 1981: 6–16. As Kindstrand notes, it is telling that Herodotus, the earliest source for the sage, could not verify his information with Scythian sources (4.76.5).

52. On Parthia's supposed nomadism, see esp. Hauser 2005 *contra* Olbrycht 1998b; see also Lerouge 2007: 174–85.

example, when Dio describes the visit to Rome of the Arsacid dynast Tirdād (not the Arsacid of Rome, but the brother of Walgaš I) in 66 C.E., he has Tirdād watch a *pankration* match and protest when he sees a contestant striking his fallen opponent: "The fight is unfair! It's not fair to hit a man who's down."[53] This is precisely the kind of objection that Anacharsis raises with Solon in Lucian's *Anacharsis*, where the two sages discuss athletics.[54] Jason König suggests that Anacharsis was a popular subject among Second Sophistic authors because "his story could be made to stand for processes of cultural encounter which were central to the experience of many members of the Roman empire elite in this period."[55] Dio's passage shows that Arsacid dynasts could serve the same objective, and that the "outsider" critiques of figures like Anacharsis could be attributed, mutatis mutandis, to Arsacid visitors with equal effect. Parthian boundary-crossers no less than Scythian ones could be literary tools for Roman reflection and self-criticism rather than historical personages to be described only with scrupulously sourced information.

As a prominent type of cultural intermediary, foreign "hostages" were subject to similar literary characterization and treatment. Just as Herodotus's Anacharsis and Scyles turned away from their ancestral way of living and adopted foreign customs, hostages too were supposed to take on the cultural habits of their wardens. In sources from the Roman period, the hostageship at Thebes of Philip II of Macedon is described as an education in military strategy and Pythagorean philosophy.[56] The Seleucid king Antiochus IV is said to have borrowed a diverse set of cultural practices from the Romans as a consequence of his hostageship in their city.[57] The late antique historian Ammianus tells of a German son renamed "Serapio" by his father, who had been initiated into the cult of Serapis as a hostage in Gaul. The same author was a personal acquaintance of Jovinianus, a hostage from Corduene whose education in Syria led him to favor the Roman cause over the Sasanian one.[58] There is even an example of acculturation to Parthian rather than Roman mores: the Seleucid Demetrius II (admittedly a royal prisoner rather than a hostage) supposedly exhibited "Parthian cruelty" after his return to Syria from captivity at the Arsacid court.[59] As the range of these examples shows, the motif of hostage acculturation was an enduring one

53. Cass. Dio 63.7.1a.

54. See esp. Lucian *Anach.* 1, 3. On the place of Scythia in Lucian's writings, see Anderson 1976: 82.

55. König 2005: 94; cf. Remijsen 2015: 253.

56. Diod. 16.2.2–3; Plut. *Pel.* 26.5; Just. 6.9.7, 7.5.3; Dio Chrys. *Or.* 49.5. On the strength of these ancient interpretations, see Worthington 2008: 17–18; Hammond 1997: 356 contra Aymard 1954: 34–35. On the question of whether Philip began his hostageship among the Illyrians, see Borza 1990: 189 n.28.

57. Polyb. 26.1.5–6, 30.25–26; Liv. 41.20.1, 41.20.9–13; Diod. 29.32, 31.16.2–3; Granius Licinianus 28.10; cf. Heliodorus *BNJ* 373 F 8.

58. Amm. 16.12.25 (Serapio), 18.6.20 (Jovinianus). For discussion, see Matthews 1989b: 56–57 with n.18; Lee 1991: 368–69; Kagan 2011: 168–69.

59. Just. 39.1.3; cf. Nabel 2017b: 33.

in Greco-Roman literature. From the republican period through late antiquity, classical authors saw hostages as uniquely positioned between the Roman and non-Roman worlds, and the hostage's acculturation presented rich material for exploring the relationship between those two spaces.

The Arsacid acculturation passages in Tacitus and Josephus are better understood as contributions to this literary tradition rather than as documentations of Parthian reality. In the case of Tacitus, it is crucial to note that his narratives of Arsacid return follow a pattern that is repeated elsewhere in the *Annals*, most prominently during Claudius's dispatch of the Cheruscan prince Italicus in 47 C.E. Like Vonones, Italicus was "enhanced with riches" by the emperor.[60] His initial reception among the Germans was "happy,"[61] but this success soon turned to failure when his opponents argued that he was "infected" by Roman customs and practices.[62] The language of infection also presents an intertext with Livy's narrative of the Antigonid hostage Demetrius, whom his brother Perseus accused of being "infected with Roman enticements."[63] Moreover, Tacitus says that Italicus possessed "affability," a characteristic he also attributes to Vonones.[64] These parallels run deeper than the mere repetition of a type scene; they redeploy the same words and phrases to homogenize the experiences of barbarian dynasts who spent time at Rome and then returned to their home countries. There is reason to believe, then, that these sections derive from Tacitus's dour view of Roman imperial culture rather than from specific knowledge of Parthian or German political discourse.

Josephus's narrative of Vonones also belongs to this historiographic tradition. In place of informed analysis, the reader finds literary commonplaces. For Josephus, the "fickle nature" of "barbarians" explains why the Parthians turned against their recently installed king. The topos of the fickle barbarian appears often in Greco-Roman literature, where it is applied to Parthians and other peoples of the periphery. It also figures in Tacitus's narrative of Mihrdād, where the author speaks of the "fickleness" of Parthian subjects.[65] Faced with the complex task of explaining a dynastic coup in a faraway empire, Josephus instead offers a pat cliché. As an analysis of Parthian behavior in a specific historical moment, in other words, his text has minimal value. Here, too, the narrative of Arsacid return is shaped by editorializing on the relationship between the civilized and noncivilized

60. Koestermann 1963–68: 3.58. Compare 11.16.1 (*auctum [Italicum] pecunia*) with 2.2.1 (*auxitque [Vononen] opibus*).

61. Malloch 2013: 247–48. Compare 11.16.2 (*ac primo laetus Germanis adventus*) with 2.2.1 (*et accepere barbari laetantes*) and 6.42.3 with Woodman 2017: 262.

62. Compare 11.16.3 (*infectum alimonio servitio cultu, omnibus externis*) with 2.2.1 (*hostium artibus infectum*); 6.43.3 (*imbellem externa mollitia*); 12.14.3 (*alienigenam et Romanum increpans*).

63. Liv. 40.11.3: *infecti Romanis delenimentis*.

64. Ash 2007: 207 (Latin *comitas*). For further verbal parallels, see Keddie 1975: 53–54 with n.8, 16.

65. Tac. *Ann.* 12.14.1. On the Roman topos of the fickle barbarian and/or Parthian, see chapter 4.

worlds, and the author employs stock Roman depictions of barbarians to apply texture and detail to the narrative superstructure. Even if Josephus's years in Judaea and his connections to Babylonian Jews gave him deeper insight into Arsacid dynastic politics (a possibility, but nowhere in evidence), the historian does not display the fruits of such knowledge.

In addition to the "fickle barbarian" explanation, two other topoi can be excavated from the Arsacid return narratives of Tacitus. In his account of Vonones, Tacitus writes that the Arsacid of Rome had lost the taste for hunting during his hostageship, and that the Parthians bristled at his refusal to participate in hunts. Wiesehöfer sees a "historical core" underneath this detail, since the importance of hunting in Iranian elite circles was indeed high.[66] But caution is necessary here. To be sure, a preponderance of evidence, internal sources included, amply demonstrates that hunting was central to Iranian elite culture, and there is no reason to doubt the proposition.[67] It is equally the case, however, that Greco-Roman authors viewed the hunt as a characteristically Persian activity, as authors from Herodotus to Ammianus all associate it with the rulers of the Iranian plateau.[68] For Tacitus, then, a distaste for hunting need have been nothing more than a convenient symbol for the alienation of Vonones from his heritage: how profound the Arsacid's corruption by the Julio-Claudians must have been to disengage him from the preferred pastime of his country! The report is no basis for concluding that Vonones had *actually* lost interest in the hunt. The activity has been chosen for its recognizability as a cultural marker, not because Tacitus knew Vonones's feelings towards it. Indeed, Tacitus's own text contradicts the notion that Vonones avoided the sport. Later in the *Annals*, when the Arsacid tries to escape his confinement at Pompeiopolis, he tells his guards that he is departing for a hunt.[69] If his distaste for hunting was indeed common knowledge, why choose it as a pretext? Moreover, the notion that "hostageship" at Rome was incompatible with recreational hunting is refuted by the case of the Seleucid Demetrius I, who frequently hunted during his Roman captivity, as the contemporary eyewitness Polybius attests.[70] Thus the "historical core" to which Wiesehöfer refers cannot be anything more than a general ethnographic point about Parthian society. It has nothing to do with Vonones's acculturation, or the lack thereof.

Yet another conventional topos appears in Tacitus's passage on the short reign of Tirdād. The historian makes the Parthian governor Hiero the spokesman for the opposition, and he has this character condemn the "foreign softness" of the new king in his speech before Ardawān.[71] Softness was a common stereotype for eastern

---

66. Wiesehöfer 2010: 190 ("historischer Kern").

67. Canepa 2018: 354–66; Almagor 2021.

68. See the passages discussed in Shahbazi 2004b, to which add Tac. *Ann.* 2.56.2.

69. Tac. *Ann.* 2.68.1; cf. Goldsworthy 2023: 153–54.

70. Polyb. 31.14.1–3.

71. Tac. *Ann.* 6.43.3 (*mollitia*).

barbarians in late Republican literature, though the Scythian heritage and military success of the Parthians meant that they escaped accusations of effeminacy for the most part.[72] But for the authors who lamented Rome's loss of manliness during the Imperial period—and there were many—the trope could be reversed: exposure to Roman decadence in the metropole could make barbarians effeminate. Rome could out-feminize the feminizers.[73] Juvenal's verses about the Armenian hostage Zalaces offer a roughly contemporary parallel:[74]

> sed quae nunc populi fiunt victoris in urbe
> non faciunt illi quos vicimus. et tamen unus
> Armenius Zalaces cunctis narratur ephebis
> mollior ardenti sese indulsisse tribuno.
> aspice quid faciant commercia: venerat obses,
> hic fiunt homines. nam si mora longior urbem
> induerit pueris, non umquam derit amator.
> mittentur bracae, cultelli, frena, flagellum:
> sic praetextatos referunt Artaxata mores.

The people we conquer don't do what the people in the victor's city now do. And yet one Armenian, Zalaces, softer than all the other young men, is said to have indulged himself with a desirous tribune. Look at what commerce brings: he came as a hostage, but here they become civilized men.[75] If these boys stay any longer in the city, no one will ever lack a lover. Trousers, knives, bridles, and whips will be cast away; thus they take Rome's obscene ways back to Artaxata.

As an Armenian, Zalaces comes from an eastern people predisposed to softness, or so conventional Roman stereotypes would have it. And yet his prior effeminacy pales in comparison to what he encounters during his hostageship at Rome. The city's rampant homosexuality strips Zalaces of his native accoutrements of horsemanship and warfare, rendering him overly refined, unwarlike, and soft—exactly the characterization of Tirdād that Tacitus puts into the mouth of Hiero.[76] The irony would not have been lost on a reader of the poet or the historian. Rome had so degenerated under the Principate that eastern dynasts, far from learning manly virtue during their time in the city, were corrupted there, and bore their corruption back to their native lands. Could the words of Hiero to Ardawān somewhere in Central Asia really have evoked such themes, and could they really have been transmitted, a century later and thousands of miles away, to Tacitus? Maybe, but ventriloquism is far likelier.

72. Isaac 2004: 378; but cf. Luc. 8.365–66.

73. Gowing 1990: 329–30.

74. Juv. 2.163–70.

75. For the translation of *homo* as "civilized man," see Habinek 1997: 33 n.37.

76. The items of dress mentioned in line 169 were part of Armenian and Parthian attire: Courtney 2013: 125.

As for Vonones's alleged "locking away of even the cheapest materials with a seal-ring," here too the charge is mentioned by other literary sources as a malady of Roman imperial culture. The main parallel is in Pliny the Elder, who laments that contemporary aristocrats (unlike the Romans of yesteryear) must keep their foodstuffs under seal to guard against theft from their own slaves: "What a life there was in the old days, what innocence, when nothing was kept under seal! Nowadays even food and drink are guarded by a [signet] ring."[77] Pliny's expression of nostalgia derives from a traditional literary formula: the bygone Republican past was an age of pristine virtue and simple modesty, while the imperial present has been corrupted by power, extravagance, and wealth. For Pliny, then, sealing and ring-wearing practices were a sign of Roman degeneracy from an idealized Republican past.[78] The idea was illusory—literary references from the Republican period already attest pantries under seal at that date—but a potent indicator of decline all the same.[79] That is one note of caution against the historicity of the passage, but another can be found in the Bactrian documents from Afghanistan. In a letter, a subordinate writes to his lord that he cannot recognize the transfer of a local plot of land unless he receives a letter from the lord with two seals of authenticity. He adds, "Your lordship yourself ought to know that they do not give one quart of grain from the lord's house, nor one gallon of wine, to (anyone) who does not bring a sealed document, let alone a (piece of) land!"[80] The complaint here is in essence the same one that Tacitus ascribes to the Parthians aggrieved at Vonones: sealing practices are so restrictive that even trivial food items are kept under guard of seal. Far from being a unique vice of the Roman empire, then, excessive seal use was bemoaned in the Iranianate world as well. All told, there is little reason to credit Tacitus on Vonones's stingy accounting practices or the supposed Parthian counterreaction to them.

In sum, Tacitus and Josephus are problematic sources for Arsacid acculturation. Dio's account reveals that Romanization was not an unavoidable explanation for Arsacid failure, and that Tacitus and Josephus made a choice to highlight it. No sources can be identified that might have informed the Roman world about the animus behind Parthian resistance to Arsacid returnees. The passages in question belong to an established literary tradition of meditating on the civilized world's frontiers through description of the intermediaries who crossed them. In some places, Tacitus and Josephus substitute literary commonplaces and xenophobic caricatures for informed analysis, and in others, they use their Parthian characters as mouthpieces for Roman self-criticism. Supposed signs of Romanization like

77. Plin. *HN* 33.26.

78. In a similar vein, cf. Macrobius, *Saturnalia* 7.13.11–16 with Hawley 2007: 107.

79. See Plautus, *Casina* 144 and Cicero, *Ad Fam.* 351 (16.26). From the imperial period, Goodyear 1981: 193 also notes Horace, *Epistles* 2.2.133–34 and Martial 9.87.7, to which add Juvenal 14.132.

80. BD 2, Document ci, lines 8–11 = Sims-Williams 2007: 84–85; cf. Rezakhani 2010: 196.

disinterest in hunting, effeminacy, or overzealousness in sealing can be shown to derive from the ideas of Romans about their culture's own excesses or from Roman stereotypes (even if well founded) about Parthian culture. None of this can disprove Tacitus or Josephus on Arsacid acculturation—no surviving evidence can do that. But it is sufficient grounds to regard their narratives on this topic with considerable skepticism, and perhaps even to dismiss them as unreliable.

ACCULTURATION: COMPARATIVE PERSPECTIVES

And yet, although Tacitus and Josephus cannot be trusted on this topic, they may have hit on the truth, or something close to it, by accident. Two considerations point in this direction. The first is the comparative history of dynastic intermediaries, which suggests that anxieties about cultural transfer tend to attach themselves to such figures across a range of temporal and regional contexts. The second is Parthia's so-called Iranian revival in the early and middle first century c.e.—precisely the period when the Arsacids of Rome were circulating between Parthian and Roman territory. Neither of these histories amounts to conclusive proof of Arsacid acculturation or a definitive explanation for the end of pragmatic misunderstanding. Taken together, however, they are reason to entertain Tacitus's and Josephus's core assertions on this topic, even if the authors arrived at the right idea for the wrong reasons.

In pre- and early modern historical contexts around the globe, young dynasts went abroad to foreign courts to fill a variety of institutional roles, and their mobility could trigger cultural anxieties in both the host and home societies. Fosterage and hostageship were two vital mechanisms of dynastic exchange, but princes and princesses also served as brides and grooms, pages, students, captives, prisoners, exiles, and in other capacities as well. Moreover, the definitional lines around these statuses were often blurry, and dynasts could hold several in combination. Regardless of their formal role, the itinerant children of ruling families were often the focus of discomfort with acculturation. As prominent figures who personally encapsulated the relationship between two societies, the assimilation of young dynasts to the mores of their hosts—whether real or perceived—could give rise to fear or anger on both sides of the divide they bridged. Royal children were closely watched, and they were freighted with the apprehensions of disparate communities in contact.

The secondary literature on pre-modern hostageship has abundant discussion of royal children whose acculturation could be viewed as a threat to hostage-givers and receivers alike. Maribel Fierro discusses two cases from Ummayad Corduba that illustrate how "cultural transfer was evaluated as dangerous" by agents on opposite sides.[81] One case concerns a Christian youth named Pelagius

---

81. Fierro 2012: 74.

(d. 925/926 C.E.), a hostage at the court of ʿAbd ar-Raḥmān III, emir and later caliph of Ummayad Corduba. Christian sources tell a lurid tale of ʿAbd ar-Raḥmān's lust for his young hostage, whom he attempted to seduce and convert to Islam. Pelagius resisted on both counts and was martyred. The available texts, which were composed within 50 years of Pelagius's death, are unreliable on the facts of the case, but useful for Christian anxieties over Muslim hostage-taking.[82] They exhibit a distinct unease with hostageship's potential to compromise, corrupt, and alienate the hostage from the mores of his upbringing—in this case, his Christian faith and refusal to yield to homosexual desires. Fierro's other example shows acculturation fears among the Muslim takers of hostages, as well. In his history of the Muslim conquest of Andalusia, the author Ibn al-Qūṭiyya (d. 977 C.E.) tells the story of an Ummayad administrator inspecting the education of young hostages from a Spanish tribe.[83] To the administrator's dismay, the hostages are reciting heroic odes, which he fears will inculcate a warrior spirit and incite them to rebellion. "You have gone to demons who have sorely grieved the emirs and taught them poetry, which will give them an insight into real courage," he exclaims.[84] He suggests that the hostages learn only drinking songs and other trifling compositions, since this material is more suitable for the manufacture of docile underlings. Fierro notes that "the process of acculturation—unavoidable and desirable as it was—had to take place in a controlled way so as to avoid any backfiring."[85] On both sides of the Muslim-Christian divide, the transformative dimension of hostageship could elicit real alarm.

A similar dynamic can be found at the other end of Eurasia, where royal youths were a vital conduit of relations between the states of pre-modern China and the peoples of the central Asian steppe. Foreign children at the court of the Han emperor, for example, could be called either "hostage sons" or "attending princes" in Chinese sources, though there was considerable overlap between these two categories.[86] Many foreign peoples sent princes to the Han, Sui, and Tang dynasties to serve in these capacities. In some cases, they did so voluntarily or even enthusiastically, since a well-positioned prince with facility in Chinese law, letters, and customs could be a major asset.[87] The cultural transfer that could attend hostage submission was not always welcome, however. Jonathan Skaff describes one such occasion that involved Wendi, the Sui emperor of China, and the Turkic ruler Ishbara Qaghan in 585 C.E.[88]

<hr>

82. Jordan 1999: 23.
83. The tribe is the Banū Qasī, on which see Coope 2016: 144–54.
84. Translation from James 2009: 121.
85. Fierro 2012: 78.
86. Yang 1952: 509.
87. Yang 1952: 510; Skaff 2012: 130–31, 198–200.
88. Skaff 2012: 199.

> Ishbara offered to guard the frontiers, send a hostage-page to the Sui court, and proffer annual tribute of fine horses. On the other hand, he requested retaining traditional Turkic dress, hairstyle, language, law, and customs. Wendi's verdict accepted these terms . . . The patron, Wendi, would not interfere with Ishbara's domestic affairs (law, customs, etc.), but the two would cooperate militarily. A hostage and annual tribute would symbolize Ishbara's inferior position.

The Turkic ruler Ishbara was at pains to ensure that his dispatch of a hostage to the Sui court would not be accompanied by the wholesale imposition of Chinese law and culture. Behind his request is an implicit admission that hostage submission leaves the giver vulnerable to cultural encroachment. The political advantages of the practice had to be balanced against cultural considerations, and the situation had to be carefully managed lest the surrendering party be deprived of their native customs.

Cultural tensions could also attend the travels of princes and princesses who married across state lines, for dynasts whose marital relations took them to foreign countries could be accused of neglecting their own. Bethany Aram sees this dynamic at play in the union of Juana of Castile with the Habsburg dynast Philip I (1478–1506 C.E.), the ruler of the Burgundian Netherlands.[89] On his wife's account, Philip was twice obliged to travel to Spain on lengthy trips that kept him away from the Low Countries for years at a time. To commemorate his return from the first of these journeys, a panegyric was composed in Philip's honor by no less a figure than Desiderius Erasmus. In the work, Erasmus dwells at length on the fear and displeasure of Philip's Dutch subjects at the departure of their ruler for Spain, since, as Erasmus says, "the ideas sometimes passed through their minds (for why should I not venture to admit it?) that perhaps other realms might captivate you and make you less mindful of your own." In one of the more elaborate rhetorical passages in the speech, Erasmus gives voice to the country of the Netherlands itself, which complains in anguished tones over Philip's absence: "If you do not tear yourself away before Spain has had her fill of you, before you quench the thirst of your father- and mother-in-law . . . I doubt if I shall ever see you again."[90] Despite its adulatory tone, the piece betrays concern over Philip's commitment to the speaker's homeland, furnishing ample demonstration of the rift that interstate marriage could open between a ruler and their local subjects.

Just as kinship created through marriage could threaten to override the primacy of local ties, so too could kinship created through fosterage. Pertinent examples can be found in Norse-Irish relations during the medieval period. Both Gaelic and Scandinavian cultures had robust traditions of fosterage, and the interaction of these peoples during the Viking age led to the exchange of children between them. But the Irish were Christians and the Norse were not, and as Irish sources saw it, this religious difference had a malign effect on Irish foster-children. A medieval

---

89. Aram 2016: 98.
90. Erasmus, *Panegyricus ad Philippum Austriae ducem*, trans. Radice in Levi 1986: 14, 17.

Irish source gives voice to the problem in its discussion of the Gall Gaedil, a tribe of mixed Gaelic and Norse heritage: "they were men who had forsaken their baptism, and they used to be called Norsemen, for they had the customs of the Norse, and had been fostered by them, and though the original Norsemen were evil to the churches, these were much worse, these people, wherever in Ireland they were."[91] Another example of fosterage across ethnic and cultural demarcations comes from late medieval Ireland in the early years of English colonization. In the fourteenth century C.E., English marcher lords interfaced with the Irish through fosterage, making use of the long-standing tradition for aristocratic networking. But these arrangements broke down when English children returned as Irish-speakers and, according to some sources, with political allegiances to the Irish rather than to their natal kin. As an English treatise of 1515 put it:[92]

> the Englyshe noble folke useith to delyver therre children to the Kynges Irysshe enymyes to foster, and therwyth, as well as wyth maryage, makeyth bandes, and in consyderations with the Kynges enymyes, wherof groweth manye inconveniences and grete domage [damage] to the Kynges subgettes.

Displeased with these developments, the English colonial administration issued numerous prohibitions of English-Irish fosterage in the thirteenth and fourteenth centuries C.E. Similar bans were sometimes passed on fosterage among the Welsh, where the institution had comparable purchase.[93] The advantages of fosterage as a mode of engagement between noble families were considerable, but when the practice took place across political, ethnic, cultural, and religious borders, its transformative impact on fostered children could cause one side to recoil.

It should be stressed that the comparative cases demonstrate anxieties surrounding the acculturation of royal children, and there are two other issues that must be treated separately: first, the dynast's actual cultural orientation; and second, the sincerity with which accusations of acculturation were made against them. The charge that a prince or princess has adopted the culture of a foreign host cannot be taken at face value in any historical setting, especially when ruling families are involved. To be sure, some degree of acculturation would have been likely or even inevitable. No one spends years abroad without adapting to the foreign environment, least of all children at an impressionable age. All of the Arsacid returnees spent many years or their entire childhoods in Rome before departing for the east, and those years must have shaped who they were. The epitaph of Seraspadanes and Rhodaspes is not in Parthian or even Greek but in Latin, which suggests that they (and/or the members of the group who survived

---

91. *Fragmentary Annals of Ireland* 260, ed. and trans. Radner 1978: 104–5; quoted in O'Donnell 2016: 37. On the dating of this passage, see Ní Mhaonaigh 2007: 87–88.

92. "The State of Ireland and Plan for Its Reformation," quoted in Booker 2018: 171.

93. Smith 1992: 26–27; Booker 2018: 171.

them) learned the language in Rome and adopted it for the purpose of funerary commemoration.[94] In itself, this linguistic choice is a significant type of acculturation, and there may well have been others, too. But it is impossible to say much more on the basis of the sources that the Arsacids of Rome themselves produced; as discussed above, Vonones's coins are not independent testimony of acculturation, and the other evidence adds little to the epitaph. Political discourse about the cultural preferences of elite, prominent, and contentious dynastic figures cannot be taken as straightforward proof of how they changed while abroad.

By the same token, it is best to reserve judgment on the sincerity, or the lack thereof, with which charges of acculturation were levied against dynastic intermediaries. Because of their membership in ruling families, royal children were big political game, and their enemies may have found success by imputing cultural treachery to them whether they meant it or not. "You are a traitor to your homeland" is a potent accusation, and it can be effective even if the accuser makes it in bad faith or the guilt of the accused is questionable. But where charges of acculturation find purchase, they play on real anxieties and require ready ears to heed them. Different cases would have mixed cynical political rhetoric and genuine fear of cultural Others in varying proportions. It is both methodologically difficult and, for present purposes, unnecessary to separate these factors out, since in the end they point in the same direction.

The comparative examples reviewed above are not dispositive of the Arsacid case, but they do establish the inherent plausibility of Tacitus's and Josephus's acculturation narratives. Whether the Arsacids of Rome are best described as foster-children, hostages, or some other status, they were the scions of a ruling family who lived in a different political unit—and a different cultural setting—for years, decades, or even their entire lives. For those that returned to Parthia and sought the kingship, their bearing and disposition would have been the subject of close scrutiny, and in comparative perspective, it is plausible that any real or perceived divergences from Parthian convention could have triggered a hostile reaction. Plausible does not mean provable, and the existence of comparable cases from other historical contexts does not mean that Tacitus and Josephus were well informed about the episodes of Arsacid return that they narrate. But the basic story is observable elsewhere, and it may well have taken place along the lines that Tacitus and Josephus imagined.

THE IRANIAN TURN

In addition to the background from comparative history, there is evidence from the Parthian empire itself that bears on the question of Arsacid acculturation, though here, too, the relevant sources can only offer further context, not ultimate

94. See the balanced discussion of Álvarez-Pedrosa 2022: 114–15. On this inscription, see further chapter 3.

verification. The cases of Arsacid return all took place in the early and mid-first century C.E. It was during this period that Parthia experienced what some historians have called an "Iranian revival" or a wave of "neo-Iranism" that changed the trajectory of the empire. These terms should be regarded with caution, and some aspects of this narrative are based on tenuous assumptions. Even if the historiography of the period rests on slim evidence, however, significant changes are apparent and, since some of them concern the Arsacid kingship, they can be woven into a narrative that includes the Arsacids of Rome. Taken together, Arsacid return and "Iranian revival" may have been mutually reinforcing historical developments: Parthian counterreactions to Arsacid returnees may have been prompted by, and may have fed into, the broader transformation of the empire in the first century C.E.

If Parthian history has a lynchpin, many scholars would put it in this period. "Iranian renaissance" was Georgina Herrmann's term and "neo-Iranism" Józef Wolski's, and though adoption of these labels has not been universal, the view of the period as a cultural turning point has many endorsements.[95] Several historians ascribe special importance to the reigns of Ardawān II (c. 10–38 C.E.) and Walgaš I (c. 51–79 C.E.), epochal rulers who are said to have reoriented the Arsacid dynasty and the Parthian empire in key respects.[96] To be sure, there are reasons to object to the vocabulary of *revival* and *restoration* that is often used to describe this era, and it may be preferable to say that the Arsacids were articulating a new identity that combined novel innovations with a strategic reuse of the past.[97] *Iranian* has its problems, too, since it is not until the Sasanian period that this word is attested in reference to a territorial empire and its ruling class.[98] Still, the trail of evidence, breadcrumbs though it may be, is suggestive. As the Arsacids of Rome returned to Parthia, they did so against a backdrop of change. What was the nature of this shift, and what, if anything, did they have to do with it?

As ever, Arsacid coins offer indispensable testimony that directly reflects the priorities of the kings themselves, and the issues of Ardawān II and Walgaš I both display features of considerable significance. Ardawān did not follow his predecessor Vonones in the adoption of a short hairstyle on his drachms, though Sellwood's view that this choice "proclaimed his rejection of western fashions implicitly" can be challenged, as discussed above.[99] But an iconographic rejoinder to Vonones's kingship may appear in the form of a kneeling man positioned between the king and the goddess Tyche, offering up what could be a diadem in a gesture of

---

95. Renaissance: Herrmann 1977: 53; see also Curtis 2007: 15–16, who applies the term to Parthian history more generally. Neo-Iranism: Wolski 1993: 151; Dąbrowa 2012: 174. First century as transition period: Debevoise 1938: 196; Neusner 1963: 47–48; Wiesehöfer 2015: 339; Gnoli 2022: 328.

96. Ardawān II: Kahrstedt 1950: 11; Dąbrowa 1983: 73–92; Frye 1984: 237. Walgaš I: Bivar 1983: 85–86; Olbrycht 1998a: 125–38; Wiesehöfer 2005: 133.

97. Canepa 2018: 68, 93; Nabel 2022: 161.

98. Gnoli 1989: 113–15.

99. Sellwood 1980: 196.

FIGURE 12. Tetradrachm of Ardawān II, 23 C.E. The reverse shows three figures. At left, the goddess Tyche offers a palm to an enthroned Ardawān, who is seated on the right. In the center, a kneeling figure, perhaps Vonones, offers a diadem to the king. Sellwood 1980: 200 (type 62.3). Photo credit: American Numismatic Society (ANS 1944.100.83011).

humble submission (figure 12). The kneeler may represent Vonones.[100] Moreover, on this coin and on others as well, Ardawān chose to depart from the standard set of epithets traditionally attached to the king's name. On some tetradrachms, amid the usual appellations like the Just and the Illustrious, the epithet "Greek-lover" (*philhellēn*) is conspicuously omitted. Sellwood called this decision "an important initial step in the emancipation of Iran from Greek influence."[101] However, Wiesehöfer sees it more narrowly as an expression of the king's displeasure with Seleucia on the Tigris, the most powerful Greek polis in the empire.[102] Ardawān was often in conflict with this city. Seleucia had served as Vonones's final refuge in Parthia; it had been quick to support the Arsacid of Rome Tirdād; and it rebelled against Ardawān after his return from central Asia. The omission of "Greek-lover" was not a salvo in a culture war, then, but an *ad hoc* response to Seleucia's intransigence. Whether it was Greek political actors or Greek culture in the crosshairs, though, Ardawān's measure presaged Hellenism's decline in the self-representation of the Arsacids.

The trend continued in the coinage of Walgaš I, the last Arsacid ruler to send his family members to Rome. In one set of drachms, a striking new element emerges (figure 13). To the right of the conventional royal bust on the obverse, two Aramaic letters appear. They read *wl*, an abbreviation of Walgaš, the king's Parthian name.[103] With the single exception of an Aramaic title on the coins of Aršak I some three

100. Sellwood 1980: 200; Sinisi 2012b: 286.
101. Sellwood 1980: 196.
102. Wiesehöfer 2015: 338.
103. Sinisi 2012a: type IVc; on the onomastic evidence, see further Schmitt 2016: 224–25.

FIGURE 13. Drachm of Walgaš I. Sellwood 1980: 231 (type 71.1); Sinisi 2012a: type IVc/4a.α(1c.α). Photo credit: American Numismatic Society (ANS 1992.45.60).

centuries prior, this is the first appearance of any language but Greek on a Parthian coin.[104] Greek ostensibly appears on Walgaš's drachm, too, but closer inspection of the reverse suggests otherwise. The usual legend that surrounds the king in a square is here blundered and illegible, its letters malformed or misplaced. The die engravers have treated it as pictorial element, not a textual one.[105] To be sure, both of these features—the use of Parthian, and the disuse of Greek—heralded changes that were gradual, not abrupt; some of Walgaš's successors minted coins with legible Greek, and many of them forwent the use of Parthian. Over time, however, these trends would strengthen.[106] In this most vital medium of Arsacid political communication, an Iranian language had begun to displace Greek.

That trend is also observable in documentary texts from Arsacid territory. In the set of three parchments from Avroman (modern Kurdistan in northwest Iran), the two earliest documents are in Greek, but the last one, which dates to the reign of Walgaš I, is in Parthian.[107] Three texts is a slim dataset, but royal inscriptions demonstrate the same transition: the letter of Ardawān II to Susa (21 C.E.) is in Greek, but the inscriptions of Walgaš IV on the Bronze Heracles of Mesene (151 C.E.) are in Greek and Parthian, and thereafter, the inscriptions of (perhaps)

104. For the Aramaic *krny* on the coins of Aršak I, see chapter 4.

105. Sinisi 2012a: 139.

106. For the Parthian legends on the coins of the later Arsacids, see Weber in Hackl et al. 2010: 633–39.

107. This is true whether Avroman 1 and 2 should be dated by the Seleucid era (which would yield dates of 88/87 B.C.E. and 22/21 B.C.E., respectively) or the Arsacid era (which yields 24 B.C.E. and 43/44 C.E.). The usual assumption is the former, but Luther 2018 has recently argued for the latter. Avroman 3 dates to 52/53 C.E. For texts and translations of the Avroman documents, see Minns 1915; Hackl et al. 2010: 2.467–76, 2.566–67.

Walgaš V and Ardawān IV (215 C.E.) are both in Parthian.[108] To be sure, there are non-Greek documentary texts before the first century C.E., especially from the Nisa ostraca, and there are Greek documentary texts after it, especially from the city of Dura-Europos.[109] But the Avroman documents and the royal inscriptions reinforce the impression that, in legal and governmental contexts that concerned the Arsacid dynasty, the Greek language was losing ground to Parthian.[110]

Another Iranian reorientation may have been underway in the realm of religion and pertains to the history of Zoroastrianism. Here the relevant evidence is in Middle Persian rather than Parthian, and it comes from Zoroastrian texts that are difficult to date. The pertinent compositions were not committed to writing until the late Sasanian period and the extant manuscripts postdate the Arab conquest, but the texts are based on much older oral compositions that go back to the Parthian period, and in some cases even earlier. In at least one passage, and perhaps in two, Zoroastrian literature preserves a memory of an epochal Arsacid king named Walgaš (Walaxš in Middle Persian). The first passage comes from the *Dēnkard*, an account of the transmission of the religion's central compositions, the Avesta and the Zand. One pivotal figure in this history was Walgaš:[111]

> Walaxš ī Aškānān Abestāg ud Zand čiyōn abēzagīhā andar āmad ēstād hammōg-iz ī aziš harw čē az wizend ud ašuftkārīh ī Aleksandar ud ēwār ud rōb ī Hrōmāyān andar Ērānšahr pargandagīhā abar nibištag tā čē uzwān abespārišnīg pad dastwar mānd ēstād andar šahr čiyōn frāz āmad ēstād nigāh dāštan ō šahrīhā ayādgār kerdan framūd.

> Walgaš the Arsacid ordered a memorandum sent to the provinces, [which contained the directive] to preserve the Avesta and the Zand, as they had come down in pristine transmission, and also the teachings derived from them which, scattered throughout Iran by the harm and disruption of Alexander and the pillaging and looting of the Romans, remained among the priests, whether they had been committed to writing or oral tradition, just as they had been transmitted in each province.

The text inserts the Arsacid Walgaš into a series of Iranian rulers—Dārā the Kayanian comes before him, and the Sasanians Ardashir and Shapur after—who made essential contributions to the preservation of Zoroastrian works. This history is an invented one in many respects: the Kayanian dynasty is mythical, and there was almost certainly no authoritative written copy of the Avesta at these early dates. Moreover, most of the *Dēnkard* is based on late Sasanian material, and the extant redaction dates

---

108. Hackl et al. 2010: 2.486–90 (Letter of Ardawān II), 2.461–2, 2.569–71 (Bronze Heracles of Walgaš IV), 2.571–72 (inscription of Ardawān IV). For the Parthian inscription of a Walgaš (perhaps V), see Gropp and Nadjmabadi 1970; Fowler 2005: 140.

109. On the language of the Nisa ostraca, which could be Aramaic or Parthian, see Haruta 1992: 29–30.

110. Cf. Wiesehöfer 2015: 339.

111. *Dēnkard* 4.16, transcription after Shayegan 2011: 297.

to the ninth or tenth century C.E.[112] But these considerations make the appearance of Walgaš more remarkable, not less. In a Sasanian historiography that otherwise denigrated or outright erased the Arsacid contribution to the Iranian past, the persistence of an Arsacid king in this tradition must mean that his place in Zoroastrian history was considered unimpeachable.[113] That impression would be reinforced if it were correct to see the name of "Walgaš the Arsacid" in a passage of the *Zand ī Wahman Yasn*, a Zoroastrian apocalyptic text, but the reading is not secure and editors are divided on the issue.[114] Even if the *Dēnkard* is the only secure reference to an Arsacid king in Zoroastrian literature, however, the passage is compelling evidence that Walgaš's reign was a watershed moment in the history of the religion.

It is not certain that the figure mentioned in the *Dēnkard* should be identified with Walgaš I rather than one of his homonymous Arsacid successors, but this is the usual assumption, and there are sound reasons to make it.[115] The simple fact that Walgaš I was the first Arsacid king of several to bear this name suggests a ruler whose legacy was especially impactful and enduring. The king's commitment to Zoroastrianism may also be reflected in Greco-Roman sources. Roman authors refer to Walgaš's brother Tirdād as a *magus*, or Zoroastrian priest, and they attribute religious scruples to the pair that prevented them from traveling to Rome over water.[116] That excuse may have been a convenient pretext, at least in part, but the sentiment does have an authentic basis in Zoroastrian purity codes.[117] To be sure, Zoroastrianism of one variety or another had adherents in the Parthian empire long before the first century C.E., as early sources like the Nisa ostraca reveal.[118] It is not until Walgaš I, however, that the Roman literary sources directly connect the religion with the behavior of Arsacid dynasts. From what is known of the Arsacids who went by the name of Walgaš, then, its first bearer is the most likely figure to have entered Zoroastrian tradition as an epochal king.

What, if anything, does this reorientation toward Iranian language and religion, perhaps at Hellenism's expense, have to do with the Arsacids of Rome? To some extent, these are discrete histories, each with its own trajectory. The Arsacids of Rome belonged to the sphere of high politics, and their lives were subject to the

112. On these issues, see Boyce 1979: 94; Secunda 2011: 358–61; Mokhtarian 2015: 84–87; Zeini 2018: 156–57.

113. Cf. Zakeri 2022: 65.

114. *Zand ī Wahman Yasn* 3.26. Compare the editions of Anklesaria 1957: 14 (who restores the name Walgaš) and Cereti 1995: 87, 135 (who does not).

115. Darmesteter 1895: xxxix–xl; Wolski 1993: 174; Rose 2011: 71; Sinisi 2012a: 20; cf. Boyce 1975: 103. Zakeri 2022: 88 suggests an identification with Walgaš IV, but does not argue the point.

116. Plin. *HN* 30.16; Tac. *Ann.* 15.2.1, 15.24.2; Cass. Dio 63.7.2.

117. See de Jong 1997: 416–17; but cf. Cass. Dio 63.7.1 (where Tirdād returns to Parthia by sailing) with Heil 1997: 130 n.63; Nabel 2019c: 228–29.

118. On Zoroastrianism's long history in the Parthian empire, see Boyce 1979: 81–100; de Jong 2008; de Jong 2013b: 31–35; Rose 2011: 65–97.

ephemeral, shifting forces of the competition for power. By contrast, the Iranian turn was a moment in Parthia's social and cultural history. The ascendance of the Parthian language and Zoroastrianism were gradual trends that would have developed over the course of generations, and the same goes for the eclipse of Greek and the setting of Hellenism's star. Political elites played a part, but so too did broad societal changes that can hardly be tracked in the meager internal sources. Demographics, settlement patterns, environmental history, migration, scribal practices, marital customs—all these factors and more would have shaped Parthian cultural history in the long term, and the extant evidence provides little basis for examining them in detail. In this respect, the Iranian turn cannot be reduced to a top-down program with a direct connection to the Arsacids of Rome.

Yet it is possible to locate a nexus between these two histories, to see them as interrelated developments that went hand in hand, though certainly not in lockstep. Every Arsacid of Rome who returned to Parthia had enemies whom they fought to gain or keep the throne, and even the kings who did not clash with the Arsacids of Rome had to live under the shadow of their prospective return. Tacitus and Josephus give the impression that the Parthian enemies of Arsacid returnees used their residence abroad as a rhetorical cudgel against them, and while the provenance of this argument deserves scrutiny, the idea is plausible in comparative perspective. In such an environment, kings like Ardawān II, Gōdarz II, or Walgaš I may have looked for ways to distinguish their brand of Arsacid kingship from the one they imputed to the Arsacids of Rome. Those efforts at self-distinction, in turn, may have led them away from the Hellenistic aspects of their heritage and toward the Iranian features which, though they had always been present in Parthian history, were now invested with fresh significance and increased visibility. Such an evolution in royal representation need not have been the only or even the primary impetus behind the Iranian turn, but it could have fed into, and been fueled by, the larger social, cultural, and demographic changes that transformed Parthia in the first century C.E.

CONCLUSION

The Roman literary sources on Arsacid return are best read with ambivalence. Tacitus and Josephus both suggest that Arsacid returnees forced Parthians to confront the Roman classification of their princes as hostages. They also give the impression that the Parthians equated such classification with enslavement and political humiliation, and that the Parthian counterreaction to these developments expressed itself as anger at the (real or perceived) romanization of the Arsacid returnee. On balance, it is misguided to accept any of these propositions as authentic Parthian rhetoric. They are far more likely to derive from the genre conventions, thematic concerns, and rhetorical inventions of Roman literature than from actual knowledge of Arsacid dynastic politics.

Yet comparative history suggests that Tacitus and Josephus may be telling the right story for the wrong reasons. Children from ruling families were commonly raised, or spent parts of their young adulthood, in locations far from their natal parents. When they returned, their prolonged absence could trigger questions about their cultural preferences and political loyalties, especially if their fosterage, hostageship, marriage, or pagehood had taken them across hostile territorial lines, as it often did. Anxieties over dynastic acculturation are evident in diverse kinds of primary sources across a range of geographic and temporal contexts from the pre- and early modern world. These comparative cases cannot prove Tacitus or Josephus right. But they can and do suggest that the story of the Arsacids of Rome may have played out along the lines that Tacitus and Josephus imagined—whether or not the Roman historians were well informed about the topic.

If there is something to the idea that Arsacid returnees triggered a counter-reaction to their apparent romanization, then their ephemeral kingships might have contributed to the Iranian turn of the Parthian empire in the first century C.E. Indigenous sources from Arsacid territory are meager, but the extant evidence points to a shift from Hellenistic to Iranian cultural forms during these years, especially in the areas of law, language, and royal self-representation. As the enemies of the Arsacids of Rome sought to distinguish themselves from their "romanized" foes, they may have leaned into this shift, aligning themselves most closely with the facets of Arsacid heritage from which the Arsacids of Rome would have been most alienated—and, by the same token, turning away from the Greek aspects of Parthian history that furnished middle ground with Rome. Such political maneuvering cannot explain the entire Iranian turn, which involved a complex constellation of social and cultural changes over the course of many generations. But it could have been implicated in those changes as both a cause and an effect. Over time, the Parthian body politic developed a resistance to Arsacid return, and culture may have strengthened its immune response.

Conclusion

Why did the exchange of Arsacid children end?

One way to answer is to attack the question: did it? There is some evidence for the continued circulation of Arsacids even after the transfers under Walgaš and Nero. Trajan captured a daughter of Husraw I during his Parthian expedition, and the Arsacid princess spent some time in Roman custody before Hadrian released her.[1] This woman was taken prisoner in a military campaign, though, which differentiates her case from the Arsacids of Rome. In a poem published c. 116/117 C.E., the satirist Juvenal refers to an Armenian hostage named Zalaces. If this young man existed and is not a generic, type-figure eastern "barbarian," then he might have been royalty from the cadet branch of the Arsacids in Armenia. But this is conjecture, since he is unattested elsewhere.[2] By contrast, strong evidence for the residence of Armenian Arsacids in Rome comes from a Greek funerary epitaph composed by one Aurelius Pacorus, "king of Great Armenia," for his brother Aurelius Merithates.[3] According to most scholars, however, this Pacorus/Pakōr was the Armenian Arsacid deposed in 164 C.E. as part of Lucius Verus's Parthian campaign.[4] His residence at Rome was presumably the result of forced exile or political imprisonment (though probably in comfort, since his names suggest the receipt of citizenship from Marcus Aurelius). Finally, an unnamed brother

---

1. SHA *Had.* 13.8; Aurel. Vict. *Lib. Caes.* 13.3 with Chaumont 1987.

2. Juv. 2.164. Allen 2006: 199: "probably fictional"; contrast Wheeler 2002: 290; Courtney 2013: 124. On the passage, see also chapter 5.

3. *CIG* 3.6559 = *IG* 14.1472 = *OGIS* 382.

4. Key to this identification is Fronto, *ad Verum imp.* 2.16 = van den Hout 1988: 126; but the succession of Armenian Arsacids during these years is unclear. For discussion, see Vinogradov 1992: 19–21; Ricci 1996: 581–83; van den Hout 1999: 302; Gnoli 2007: 71–74; Schottky 2010: 210.

of the reigning Arsacid king Walgaš V joined the army of Septimius Severus during the emperor's second Parthian expedition.[5] Yet nothing is known of how he came to Rome in the first place, and if another coordinated exchange of Arsacid children had taken place, the Roman sources preserve no mention of it.

So while the cumulative weight of this evidence is enough to show that Arsacid residence in Rome continued after Nero's death, it would appear that the submission of Arsacid children did not. The Arsacids in Roman custody during the second and third centuries C.E. were not of a piece with the Arsacids of Rome. These later dynasts did not arrive in Italy as part of intentional, uncoerced transfers on the Arsacid king's initiative, but through the direct application of Roman force, or for reasons that are totally unclear. It is conceivable that the relative paucity of Roman literary sources for this period hides additional exchanges like those of the Julio-Claudian period. This possibility does not have much to commend it, however. The arrival of Arsacid "hostages" in Italy attracted considerable attention from contemporaries in the first century C.E. and from later authors who wrote about the period. There would have been every reason to document and comment upon subsequent cases. Instead, none are recorded. By all indications, the circulation of Arsacid children ceased, and pragmatic misunderstanding broke down.

Why? In the absence of express ancient testimony on the end of the arrangement, several explanations can be posited, even if none can be proven. The first was set out in chapter 5. According to Tacitus and Josephus, the Parthian enemies of Arsacid returnees from Rome reviled them as debased slaves of the Roman emperor and acculturated traitors of their heritage. These accounts must be approached with caution, but if their representation of Parthian political rhetoric is accurate, then the homegrown kings who emerged triumphant over the Arsacids of Rome had to confront a novel dilemma: how could one justify sending Arsacid children to Rome when they returned in such a degraded state? What kind of Arsacid father would condemn his child to a condition of Roman slavery? The frame of cliental fosterage could have been overpowered by the xenophobic rhetoric that the enemies of the Arsacids of Rome had adopted. In this sense, pragmatic misunderstanding might have collapsed because it ceased to be pragmatic. That is, it was no longer useful for Arsacid kings to send their children to Rome, since new political considerations had rendered cliental fosterage unviable.

On the other hand, pragmatic misunderstanding might have ended because mutual comprehension took over. Perhaps the Parthians learned enough about the Roman view to rethink the exchange of Arsacid children, and vice versa. On the Parthian side, the key testimony of Movses Khorenats'i on Abgar and Arshavir might suggest such an outcome.[6] When Germanicus exhibited the children of these kings in his triumph, Abgar heard about it, grew angry, and prepared

5. Cass. Dio 75.9.3; discussion in Hartmann 2009: 255–61.
6. MKh 2.27; see chapter 1.

for war. News of the triumphal exhibition of the Arsacids had reached the east, where it clashed with local expectations of how the princes would be treated. Movses's text too has major shortcomings as evidence for the first century C.E., but it at least broaches the possibility that Rome's position became legible to the Parthians, who perceived its discordance with their own. On the Roman side, the same point might emerge from Strabo and Tacitus. Both authors adumbrate a Roman realization that the Parthians saw "hostage" submission differently and thus maintained a divergent view of the practice's underlying power dynamics.[7] Of course, such an idea may have been a purely Roman concoction, and it need not reflect Roman cognizance of an authentic Parthian viewpoint. But it might, and if it does, there would be some evidentiary basis for a cross-pollination of perspectives. As Roman-Parthian dialogue increased, the two sides may have understood each other better, and that mutual knowledge may have eroded the basis for the pragmatic misunderstanding behind Arsacid child transfer.

Alternately, the arrangement could have collapsed not because of its inherent features, but because of independent developments unrelated to the Arsacids of Rome. One potential reason for its discontinuation could have come from Rome's internal politics: in 68 C.E., the Julio-Claudian dynasty came to an end with the coup that unseated Nero. The Romans equated Nero's death with the extinction of the Julian line, and thus as an inflection point that marked the transfer of the principate from one ruling family to another.[8] If the Arsacids shared this view, then the events of 69 C.E. could have prompted them to reassess their mode of engagement with their western imperial neighbor. What was the point of forging kinship bonds with Rome's ruling dynasty when its scions could be ousted and replaced? Why dialogue today with a family that could be gone tomorrow? In Parthia, the Arsacids had reigned since their empire's inception. In Rome, it must now have appeared, the situation would be otherwise. Dealing with Rome as an empire was still necessary, of course, but dealing with its rulers as a dynasty was not. The destruction of the Julio-Claudians could have forced the Arsacids to renounce their foundational assumptions about Roman-Parthian relations in the era of the principate, and to abandon kinship networking as a method of interface. When Nero died, so too did Arsacid fosterage in Rome.

Yet another explanation could come from the structuralist analysis favored by Eckstein and Overtoom: in the second and third centuries C.E., Parthia weakened and Rome strengthened, precluding Arsacid claims to supremacy over the emperors. As many historians of the Roman-Parthian relationship have noted, the scope of Roman campaigns against Parthia in the second century was much greater than in the first.[9] Emperors in the later period led Roman armies deep

---

7. Strab. 16.1.28; Tac. *Ann.* 2.1.2, 13.9.1; cf. chapter 1.

8. Suet. *Galba* 1; Cass. Dio 62.18.4.

9. Ziegler 1964: 117; Campbell 1993: 215; Harl 2016: 122–27; Schlude 2020: 156; Gnoli 2022: 335–36.

into Mesopotamia and even sacked Ctesiphon, a key Arsacid royal city. The Parthians led no comparable expeditions into Roman Syria, Egypt, or Anatolia, and still less into Greece or Italy. Rome's aggression was not an existential threat, but it did put Parthia on the back foot. In this context, the Arsacid kings could have found it harder to maintain the impression of Parthian superiority and Roman subordination. Sending Arsacid children under these conditions would have been irreconcilable with the cliental fosterage paradigm, inviting unflattering interpretations of the exchange from Parthian audiences. Once cliental fosterage lost its viability as a frame of reference, in other words, the Arsacid kings stopped sending their children. It is a telling indictment of the Roman paradigm that the cases of Arsacid "hostageship" date to the first century c.e. and not the second, despite the inferior status of Parthia in the later period. If Arsacids in Rome were tokens of Parthian submission, one would expect more of them at times of Parthian weakness, not fewer. But such a distribution is not what the evidence shows.

So much for why Arsacid dynasts stopped going to Rome; but why did they stop coming back? On any reading of the sources, several children at least were still resident in Rome at the end of the Julio-Claudian period. There is no evidence of their return to Parthia, and they presumably lived out the remainder of their lives in Italy like Seraspadanes and Rhodaspes in an earlier generation. The disappearance of the last Arsacids of Rome from the historical record might be attributable to gaps in the source material or the vicissitudes of preservation. But just as the initial submission of Arsacids elicited frequent comment from the Roman literary sources, their departures, too, were ceremonious occasions deemed worthy of commemoration by emperors and senatorial elites alike. It would be surprising for subsequent Arsacid remissions to have entirely escaped discussion. But if none took place, why not?

Two factors from chapters 4 and 5 supply potential answers. First, as discussed in chapter 4, one can read Tacitus as evidence for a failure of communication between the Parthian nobility and the Roman emperor (alone or in tandem with the Senate). The two sides wanted the same thing, but for different reasons, and they spoke past one another in their dialogues. Eventually, it may have dawned on Parthian elites that the emperor did not regard himself as a cliental *dāyag* as others of their class did. He was not releasing his wards to aid the Parthian nobility in its righteous management of the Arsacid dynasty, but to inflict harm and to advertise his supremacy over the Parthian empire as a whole. Triumphalist speeches like the one Claudius delivered when he released Mihrdād may, over time, have exposed the discordance between the Roman emperor and the Parthian aristocracy. Second, as discussed in chapter 5, the Arsacids of Rome who returned to Parthia were unsuccessful, failing either to gain the throne or keep it. Over the course of the first century c.e., the Parthian coalitions that sought to replace the ruling king must have noticed this underwhelming record and turned elsewhere for Arsacid rivals. That decision would have been all the more prudent if the Arsacids of Rome failed in Parthia because of their association with the emperor, as Tacitus and Josephus say. By the mid-first century C.E., the Parthian enemies of Rome's Arsacid children might have had a robust tradition of xenophobic invective at their disposal. With every victory those enemies scored, such rhetoric would have gained power and acceptance until its logic became axiomatic: an Arsacid of Rome was a Roman, not an Arsacid. Once the brand was tainted, the invitations to return dried up.

Whether individually or collectively, these factors must have eroded the foundations of pragmatic misunderstanding as a mediating force in Roman-Parthian relations. Conditions had changed at every stage of Arsacid circulation, from submission and reception to remission and return. To some degree, the changes came from Roman-Parthian contact itself. As interaction between the two sides became more regular and frequent, there were more opportunities for viewpoints to proliferate. Over time, mutual association could have produced an environment where it was harder for misunderstanding to thrive. But independent or unrelated developments played a role, too. The Arsacids of Rome were not purely a feature of Roman-Parthian interaction; in both empires, internal political factors animated their exchange as well. When domestic circumstances shifted, so too did the impetus for sending, receiving, and recalling royal children. Rome and Parthia moved on, and they left the Arsacids of Rome behind.

Interdynastic kinship was not abandoned, however, and while subsequent Roman emperors and Iranian kings made no formal fosterage arrangements, several cases of pro-parentage during the Sasanian period recall the precedent of the Arsacids of Rome. First, in 408 C.E., the moribund emperor Arcadius supposedly made the Sasanian king Yazdgird the "guardian" (*epitropos*) of his young son Theodosius (II) in an effort to ensure the child's succession.[10] The sources say that Yazdgird happily accepted the role—a surprising reaction if, as this study has argued, cliental fosterage provided the dominant framework for such exchanges among the Parthians and Sasanians. But just as Greek *epitropos* differs from *tropheus*, there was a distinction in Middle Persian between a *dāyag* and a *parwartār* (Parthian *parwarāg*, "guardian"), even if a figure like Anagranes could occupy both offices.[11] More importantly, it appears that Yazdgird delegated the office to a Persian subordinate at the Roman court, though the extant sources are a muddle on

---

10. The main Roman sources are Procopius, *Wars* 1.2.1–10; Theophanes the Confessor, *Chronicle* AM 5900, trans. Mango and Scott 1997: 123–24. A Persian tradition also survives in the Arabic *Annals* of Hamzah al-Isfahani, trans. Daudpota 1932: 71–72. For additional sources and discussion, see Greatrex and Bardill 1996; Börm 2007: 308–11; Luther 2016: 648 n.6–11, 652 n.24–25; Greatrex 2022: 45–46.

11. On the meaning of *epitropos* in Procopius, see Börm 2007: 309 n.2; and Andres 2022: 242–46, who also judiciously treats Yazdgird's point of view. *Parwartār/āg*: Perikhanian 1997: 94–95, 252–53, 378; Durkin-Meisterernst 2004: 281. For Anagranes as both *tropheus* and *epitropos*, see chapter 1. If Sundermann's restoration is correct, *dāyag* and *parwarāg* are both applied to the god (or goddess) of water in the Manichaean Parthian hymn *The Sermon of the Soul*: Sundermann 1997: 64 (line 60), 121; cf. Sundermann 1991: 14.

the issue, so much so that some scholars doubt the episode's historicity.[12] In any event, it is clear that Theodosius never left Roman territory and thus was never fostered by Yazdgird.

A second such case came a century later (c. 520 C.E.), when the Sasanian king Kavad tried to have his son Husraw (I) adopted by the emperor Justin.[13] Justin was agreeable until, in Procopius's telling, he was informed that such an adoption would make Husraw heir to the Roman empire—a puzzling legal argument that modern scholars reject.[14] As a compromise, the Romans suggested Husraw's adoption "in arms," a legally nonbinding form of the practice more suitable for Roman-"barbarian" relations.[15] But Kavad and Husraw found the idea insulting, according to Procopius, and the negotiations came to nothing. From the Sasanian point of view, the overture might have looked like an effort to secure Justin as a cliental *dāyag* for Husraw, though if that were the case, the pejorative connotations of adoption in arms must have outweighed the benefits of such an arrangement. As with the Arcadius/Yazdgird affair, the dubious representation of events in Procopius raises many questions, and some scholars doubt the historicity of the episode and/or its associated details.[16]

A final set of pro-parental arrangements is observable in literary representations of epistolary correspondence between Sasanian kings and Roman emperors in the generations preceding the Arab conquest. In several such passages, "father" and "son" feature as forms of address. When Husraw II fled to Roman territory as a refugee from the rebellion of Bahram Čubin in 590 C.E., he presented himself as the son of the emperor Maurice as part of his plea for aid. Maurice supposedly reciprocated by self-identifying as Husraw's father. What actually transpired during Husraw's stay in Roman territory is obscured by spurious accounts of his conversion to Christianity, but the use of father/son salutations is well attested in a broad range of Greek, Armenian, and Arabic sources.[17] Later, the Senate would ask Husraw II to accept the royal aspirant Heraclius as his son.[18] Once enthroned, Heraclius wrote a letter of his own in which he called Husraw's successor Kavad II his (Heraclius's) son.[19] Since these communications are attested only secondhand in literary sources rather than in documentary originals, it is difficult to establish

12. Varying assessments of the episode's historicity are cited in Greatrex 2022: 44–45.

13. Procopius, *Wars* 1.11.1–30; Evagrius Scholasticus, *Ecclesiastical History* 4.12, trans. Whitby 2000: 212; Theophanes the Confessor, *Chronicle* AM 6013; Zonaras 14.5.

14. Börm 2007: 315; Heather 2013: 124–25.

15. On *adoptio in/per arma*, see Kiss 2015.

16. References in Pazdernik 2015: 243 n.43; more recent discussion in Andres 2022: 254–62.

17. Schilling 2008: 235–98, esp. 248–51 for sources and discussion; see also Payne 2015: 164–65.

18. *Chronicon Pascale* 615, Dindorf 1832: 709, trans. Whitby and Whitby 1989: 161; discussion in Howard-Johnston 2021: 107–9.

19. Nikephoros, *Breviarium* 15, trans. Mango 1990: 63.

their historical value, and some of the passages in question are pseudepigraphic.[20] The implications for hierarchy are also unclear. The usual view is that son status entailed subordination to a dominant father.[21] This need not have been the case on the Iranian side, however. For a Sasanian king like Husraw, the construal of the Roman emperor as a parental figure might have been empowering rather than concessive, coming as Husraw did from a society where the fosterer, a pro-parental figure, could be a cliental dependent.

While questions of historicity attend all these cases, the collective impression is that pro-parentage continued to connect Iranian and Roman rulers in late antiquity, building on the precedent of the Arsacids of Rome and forging an interdynastic ruling family along the lines of the late Bronze Age. This development found additional expression in the reemergence of the "brother" salutation in correspondence between Roman emperors and Sasanian kings, and while this form of address too is attested only in literary sources, it appears with such frequency that it may reflect actual epistolary practice.[22] Created siblinghood and pro-parentage together heralded a new "family of kings" in which an assemblage of kinship practices offered rulers a mode of interface with their distant counterparts. The scope and interconnectedness of this family is up for debate, to be sure, and scholars variously assess its impact on high politics.[23] On any reading, though, Roman-Sasanian relations went further than their Roman-Parthian precursors in forging an interdynastic family that transcended state boundaries.

But even the Roman-Sasanian relationship never achieved the interconnectedness of the Bronze Age eastern Mediterranean or, to take another example, early modern Europe. In those historical settings, one can speak of a highly integrated, cosmopolitan, and interstate ruling family linked by strong bonds of kinship. Hans Morgenthau's description of Europe in the seventeenth century C.E. is apt: "The prince and the aristocratic rulers of a particular nation were in constant, intimate contact with the princes and aristocratic rulers of other nations. They were joined together by family ties, a common language (French), common cultural values, a common style of life, and common moral convictions. . . . The princes competing for power considered themselves to be competitors in a game whose rules were

20. Thus, e.g., Schilling 2008: 248, on Agapius of Manbij.

21. For this view, see Whitby and Whitby 1989: 188–89 n.491; Schilling 2008: 249; Maksymiuk 2018: 598; Greatrex 2022: 151.

22. Eusebius, *Life of Constantine* 4.11; Ammianus 17.5.3, 17.5.10; Malalas 17.10, 18.44, 18.76 (trans. Jeffreys et al. 2017); Procopius, *Wars* 1.16.1; Menander Protector frg. 6.1; Theophylact Simocatta 4.11.11, 5.3.11; *Chronicon Paschale* 628 (Dindorf 1832: 735, trans. Whitby and Whitby 1989: 188); Theophanes the Confessor, *Chronicle* AM 6013. For kinship salutations in the correspondence between Maurice and Husraw II, see Schilling 2008: 235–98. Other Sasanian usages appear in MKh 3.17; PB 4.20.

23. Shahbazi 1990; Dignas and Winter 2007: 232–34; Canepa 2009: 124–27; Nechaeva 2014: 70; Maksymiuk 2018. On the Roman-Sasanian impact on subsequent medieval and esp. Byzantine history, see Brandes 2013 contra Dölger 1953.

accepted by all the other competitors."[24] A realist himself, Morgenthau did not argue that a cosmopolitan overclass of this kind guaranteed untrammeled peace and harmony (though he did contrast it with the democratizing nationalism that ushered in the total wars of the twentieth century). His point, rather, was that even armed conflict was pursued within a set of parameters. Wars could be brutal, violent, and traumatic. But they were part of a game, and games have rules that structure competition. The close interconnectedness of the dynastic elites that presided over the European interstate system at this time helped establish the rules of the game and promoted their acceptance by the players.

The Arsacids of Rome gesture toward such a system, but the pragmatic misunderstanding behind them represented an order of a different kind. On the basis of non-Roman sources from the ancient Near East, especially Iran and Armenia, this study has concluded that Roman and Parthian conceptions of the Arsacids of Rome were divergent. Since the Parthian view was framed by fosterage rather than Roman hostageship, each side understood the transfer of Arsacid children in different ways. The Arsacids thus created an interdynastic ruling family, but not a cosmopolitan or highly integrated one. Its Roman and Parthian constituents had different views of their membership; they were separated by a substantial cultural gulf; and the traffic between them was minimal. As discussed above, moreover, it is possible that increased contact between the two sides narrowed the scope for accommodation instead of widening it. The more they associated, the greater the gap between them grew.

And yet, despite the lack of agreement between their givers and receivers, the Arsacids of Rome were at the center of an order that prevailed in Roman-Parthian relations for nearly a century. That order rested not on intimacy, shared values, or law, but on misunderstanding. When the Parthians and Romans slotted Arsacid children into the paradigms of fosterage and hostageship, respectively, each side could maintain the pretension of its superiority to the other. In Morgenthau's terms, the Arsacids and Julio-Claudians were playing two different games, but since the players defined winning in perfectly opposite ways, neither had to reckon with his loss in the other's estimation. In this mutual incomprehension, there was equipoise, symmetry, harmony. This was a structure with no architect, a balance with no fulcrum, an arrangement with no arranger. The legacy of the Arsacids of Rome was an order fashioned from the chaos of misunderstanding.

24. Morgenthau 1948: 184.

ACKNOWLEDGMENTS

Many pages in this book were awful to write. These few, by contrast, are a pleasure. I owe the merits of *The Arsacids of Rome*, such as they may be, to the generosity of scholars the world over who helped me learn a historian's craft. No words can express my gratitude for their support, but it is a joy to make the attempt all the same.

This study began as a PhD dissertation at Cornell University, where faculty and fellow graduate students in several departments helped me in its formative stages. For inspiration and advice I am grateful to Fred Ahl, Annetta Alexandridis, Caitlín Barrett, Dave Blome, Charles Brittain, Michael Esposito, Michael Fontaine, Perri Gerard-Little, Katie Jarriel, Peter Katzenstein, Katie Kearns, Athena Kirk, Jonathan Kirshner, Sam Kurland, Jeff Leon, Max McComb, Nathan Pilkington, Pietro Pucci, Hunter Rawlings, Courtney Roby, Jeffrey Rusten, Samantha Sanft, Matt Sears, Tim Sorg, Benjamin Sullivan, Robert Travers, Michael Weiss, and Conner Wiktorowicz. Special thanks are due to my committee members Lori Khatchadourian, Sturt Manning, and Éric Rebillard, and most of all to my advisor Barry Strauss, to whom my debt is immeasurable.

For a latecomer to the world of ancient Iran, it has been my good fortune to meet and work alongside the luminaries of the field, especially at Christian-Albrechts-Universität in Kiel and at the Getty Museum and UCLA in Los Angeles. A formative influence was Josef Wiesehöfer, a man whose magisterial scholarship is matched only by the depth of his generosity. From my days in Kiel, I am also grateful to Andreas Luther, Rüdiger Schmitt, Sabine Müller, Milinda Hoo, Raphaël Weyland, Eltje Böttcher, and Marie Oellig. Thank you as well to Gunnar Dumke and Stefan Pfeiffer, my generous hosts for a talk at Martin-Luther-Universität in Halle.

In Los Angeles, it was a stroke of luck beyond all reckoning to write my first chapters alongside the scholars who assembled at the Getty Museum for a research year on "The Classical World in Context: Persia." In those days I had the benefit, and the joy, of conversation with Judith Barr, Maria Brosius, Nicole Budrovich, Roselyn Campbell, Henry Colburn, Sara E. Cole, Albert de Jong, Kenneth Lapatin, Vito Messina, Margaret Miller, Kathryn Morgan, Alessandro Poggio, Alexa Sekyra, Jeffrey Spier, Rolf Strootman, Branko van Oppen, and Miguel John Versluys.

At the Pourdavoud Institute for the Study of the Iranian World at UCLA, my luck continued. No academic home could have been better, no colleagues more supportive, of a wayward Classics PhD whose education in Iranian studies had yet so far to go. I owe so much to the insights afforded me by the UCLA community, and the Iranian community of Los Angeles more generally. From that happy year I especially thank Nastaran Akhavan, Sarah Beckmann, Catherine Bonesho, Aaron Burke, Elizabeth Carter, Kara Cooney, Negin Fadaee, Christelle Fischer-Bovet, Latifeh Hagigi, Domenico Ingenito, Deirdre Klokow, Sarah Morris, Ali Mousavi, David Potter, Lydia Spielberg, Marissa Stevens, Adriana Vazquez, and Jonathan Winnerman.

Other valued partners in conversation are almost too numerous to name, but they are too dear to omit. Endless gratitude to Jesse Arlen, Supratik Baralay, Matthew Canepa, Timothy Clark, Touraj Daryaee, Dick Davis, Carolyn Dewald, Lucinda Dirven, Lara Fabian, Leonardo Gregoratti, Simcha Gross, Stefan Hauser, Yanxiao He, John Hyland, Ted Kaizer, Hilmar Klinkott, Alireza Khounani, John Lee, Jeffrey Lerner, Kyle Mahoney, Krzysztof Nawotka, Marek Olbrycht, Josiah Osgood, Nikolaus Overtoom, Manana Odisheli and Michael Vickers, Matt Pihokker, Daniel Potts, Khodadad Rezakhani, Robert Rollinger, James Romm, Benjamin Rubin, Jason Schlude, Fabrizio Sinisi, and Yvona Trnka-Amrhein. They all taught me so much.

My colleagues in the Department of Classics and Ancient Mediterranean Studies at Pennsylvania State University have given me the most supportive home imaginable for a historian concerned with the Roman Mediterranean and the ancient Near East in equal measure. Here I have benefited from the brilliant scholarship and wide expertise of Kristen Baxter, Michael Beshay, Jonathan Brockopp, Pamela Cole, Daniel Falk, Jacob Glenister, Taylor Gray, Mathias Hanses, Erin Hanses, Tawny Holm, Charles Jones, Robert Jones, Ann Killebrew, Laura Marshall, Christopher Moore, Mark Munn, Thaddeus Olson, Anna Peterson, Gonzalo Rubio, Jennifer Singletary, Hannah Smagh, Michael Stahl, Rebecca Wang, and Stephen Wheeler. I learned much from my students, too, especially Carlyle James Engel and Larry Corridoni, who were not only superb research assistants but also genuine collaborators.

Early drafts were workshopped at the Mediterranean Seminar at Brown University in Spring 2019, where Ali Atabey, Mohamad Ballan, John Bodel, Jonathan Conant, and Sergio La Porta offered especially perceptive comments; and at Penn State, where Nathanael Andrade, Anne Hunnell Chen, Richard Payne, and Gonzalo Rubio generously commented on a full draft. Their insights greatly improved the final manuscript.

I reserve a special place of thanks for M. Rahim Shayegan—director of the Pourdavoud Institute, series editor of *Iran and the Ancient World*, scholar extraordinaire of Parthia and many other subjects besides, and a treasured collaborator and friend. The most I could ever wish for any early career researcher is to find the kind of supporter that I found in Rahim. On my gratitude to him much more could be said, though it would never be enough.

For institutional support I am indebted to the Loeb Classical Library Foundation; the Center for Hellenic Studies; the Tombros Early Career Professorship at Penn State; the

Bard College Memorial Fund for William Mullen, my dear instructor whom I sorely miss; the Open Access Monograph Funding program at the Penn State University Libraries; the Pourdavoud Institute at UCLA; and the Dumbarton Oaks / Hill Museum and Manuscript Library Armenian Summer School Fellowship. At the University of California Press, Eric Schmidt, Jyoti Arvey, and Andrew Frisardi were generous in their editorial guidance, as were three anonymous readers during the review process.

This study of kinship would never have been written without my own kin: the Nabels, the Neubergers, the Carringtons, the Lakes, and above all my sister, Hannah, and my father, William. I would be nowhere without their encouragement, care, and support. To Jenny, my wife and partner in everything: not in a thousand volumes could I begin to express what your love has meant to me. I hope only to return it in kind.

The Arsacids of Rome is dedicated to my mother, Susan Nabel, who died of cancer late in its composition. I remember too well the ashen look on her face, and can only imagine the one on mine, when I explained the book's long timeline to her. We both knew, though neither of us would say it, that she would not live to see it published. I'd rip up every page to talk with her another five minutes. It's done now, Mom, and it's for you.

Adams, Tracy. 2008. "Fostering Girls in Early Modern France." In *Emotions in the Household, 1200–1900*, edited by Susan Broomhall, 103–18. Palgrave Macmillan.

Adler, Emanuel. 1997. "Seizing the Middle Ground: Constructivism in World Politics." *European Journal of International Relations* 3: 259–392.

Adler, Eric. 2011. *Valorizing the Barbarians: Enemy Speeches in Roman Historiography.* University of Texas Press.

Ager, Sheila L. 2017. "Symbol and Ceremony: Royal Weddings in the Hellenistic Age." In *The Hellenistic Court: Monarchic Power and Elite Society from Alexander to Cleopatra*, edited by Andrew Erskine, Lloyd Llewellyn-Jones, and Shane Wallace, 165–88. Classical Press of Wales.

Ahlström, Gösta W. 1993. *The History of Ancient Palestine.* Fortress.

Alföldi, A. 1935. "Insignien und Tracht der römischen Kaiser." *Mitteilungen des Deutschen Archäologischen Instituts, Römische Abteilung* 50: 1–171.

Alidoust, Fuad. 2020. *Natio molestissima: Römerzeitliche Perserbilder von Cicero bis Ammianus Marcellinus.* Computus Druck Satz & Verlag.

Allen, Joel. 2006. *Hostages and Hostage-Taking in the Roman Empire.* Cambridge University Press.

———. 2019. "C. Asinius Pollio and the Politics of Cosmopolitanism." In *The Alternative Augustan Age*, edited by Kit Morrell, Josiah Osgood, and Kathryn Welch, 96–112. Oxford University Press.

———. 2020. *The Roman Republic and the Hellenistic Mediterranean: From Alexander to Caesar.* Blackwell.

Almagor, Eran. 2021. "Hunting and Leisure Activities." In *A Companion to the Achaemenid Persian Empire*, edited by Bruno Jacobs and Robert Rollinger, 1107–20. Wiley Blackwell.

Alram, Michael. 1986a. S.v. "Arsacids iii: Arsacid Coinage." In *Encyclopedia Iranica*, www.iranicaonline.org/articles/arsacids-iii (accessed August 19, 2024).

———. 1986b. *Iranisches Personennamenbuch*. Vol. 4, *Nomina Propria Iranica in Nummis*. Verlag der Österreichischen Akademie der Wissenschaften.

Altorki, Soraya. 1980. "Milk-Kinship in Arab Society: An Unexplored Problem in the Ethnography of Marriage." *Ethnology* 19 (2): 233–44.

Álvarez Pérez-Sostoa, Denis. 2010. "Opsides abdoucit: la toma de rehenes en la latina." *Epigraphica* 72: 169–89.

Álvarez-Pedrosa, Juan Antonio. 2022. "La epigrafía como símbolo de identidad religiosa: El caso de los príncipes orientales en Roma en el siglo I D.C." *Bandue: Revista de la Sociedad Española de Ciencias de las Religiones* 14: 107–16.

Ambos, Claus. 2009. "Eunuchen als Thronprätendenten und Herrscher im Alten Orient." In *Of God(s), Trees, Kings, and Scholars: Neo-Assyrian and Related Studies in Honour of Simo Parpola*, edited by Mikko Luukko, Saana Svärd, and Raija Mattila, 2–7. Finnish Oriental Society.

Anderson, Graham. 1976. *Lucian: Theme and Variation in the Second Sophistic*. Brill.

Anderson, J. C. 1998. "The Ara Pacis Augustae: Legends, Facts and Flights of Fancy." In *The Shapes of City Life in Rome and Pompeii: Essays in Honor of Lawrence Richardson, Jr., on the Occasion of His Retirement*, edited by Mary T. Boatwright and Harry B. Evans, 27–51. Caratzas.

Anderson, Katharine. 2004. "*Urth Noe e Tat*: The Question of Fosterage in High Medieval Wales." *North American Journal of Welsh Studies* 4 (1): 1–11.

Ando, Clifford, and Seth Richardson, eds. 2017. *Ancient States and Infrastructural Power: Europe, Asia, and America*. University of Pennsylvania Press.

Andrade, Nathanael. 2012. "Seducing Autocracy: Tacitus and the Dynasts of the Near East." *American Journal of Philology* 133 (3): 441–75.

———. 2018. *The Journey of Christianity to India in Late Antiquity: Networks and the Movement of Culture*. Cambridge University Press.

Andres, Hansjoachim. 2022. *Bruderzwist: Strukturen und Methoden der Diplomatie zwischen Rom und Iran von der Teilung Armeniens bis zum Fünfzigjährigen Frieden*. Franz Steiner.

Andrewes, A. 1978. "Spartan Imperialism?" In *Imperialism in the Ancient World*, edited by P. D. A. Garnsey and C. R. Whittaker, 91–102. Cambridge University Press.

Anklesaria, Behramgore Tehmurasp. 1957. *Zand-ī Vohūman Yasn and Two Pahlavi Fragments: With Text, Transliteration and Translation in English*. K. L. Bhargava.

Aram, Bethany. 2016. "Voyages from Burgundy to Castile: Cultural Conflict and Dynastic Transitions, 1502–06." In *Early Modern Dynastic Marriages and Cultural Transfer*, edited by Joan-Lluís Palos and Magdalena Sanchez, 91–114. Routledge.

Archi, Alfonso. 2015. *Ebla and Its Archives: Texts, History, and Society*. De Gruyter.

Archi, Alfonso, and Maria Giovanna Biga. 2003. "A Victory over Mari and the Fall of Ebla." *Journal of Cuneiform Studies* 55: 1–44.

Arnaud, Pascal. 1986. "Doura-Europos, microcosme grec ou rouage de l'administration arsacide? Modes de maîtrise du territoire et intégration des notables locaux dans la pratique administrative des rois arsacides." *Syria* 63 (1–2): 135–55.

Ash, Rhiannon. 1999. "An Exemplary Conflict: Tacitus' Parthian Battle Narrative (*Annals* 6.34–35)." *Phoenix* 53 (1–2): 114–35.

———. 2007. *Tacitus: Histories, Book II*. Cambridge University Press.

Askari, Nasrin. 2016. *The Medieval Reception of the Shāhnāma As a Mirror for Princes*. Brill.

Aucher, Joannes Baptista, ed. 1818. *Eusebii Pamphili Caesariensis episcopi Chronicon bipartitum*. Vol. 2. Typis Coenobii.

Aymard, André. 1954. "Philippe de Macédoine otage à Thèbes." *Revue des Études Anciennes* 56 (1): 15–36.

Baar, Manfred. 1990. *Das Bild des Kaisers Tiberius bei Tacitus, Sueton und Cassius Dio*. Teubner.

Babnis, Tomasz. 2022. *The Image of the Iranian World in the Roman Poetry of the Republican and Augustan Ages*. Księgarnia Akademicka.

Badian, E. 1967. *Foreign Clientelae, 264–70 B.C.* Clarendon.

Baghbidi, Hassan Rezai. 2011. "New Light on the Middle Persian-Chinese Bilingual Inscription from Xī'ān." In *The Persian Language in History*, edited by Mauro Maggi and Paola Orsatti, 105–15. Reichert.

Baldwin, Barry. 1995. "The Composition of Pliny's *Natural History*." *Symbolae Osloenses* 70: 72–81.

Ball, Warwick. 2000. *Rome in the East: The Transformation of an Empire*. Routledge.

Balsdon, J. P. V. D. 1934. *The Emperor Gaius (Caligula)*. Clarendon.

Bang, Peter F., and Dariusz Kołodziejczyk, eds. 2012. *Universal Empire: A Comparative Approach to Imperial Culture and Representation in Eurasian History*. Cambridge University Press.

Bang, Peter Fibiger. 2011. "Court and State in the Roman Empire: Domestication and Tradition in Comparative Perspective." In *Royal Courts in Dynastic States and Empires: A Global Perspective*, edited by Jeroen Duindam, Tülay Artan, and Metin Kunt, 103–28. Brill.

Barclay, John M. G. 2007. *Flavius Josephus: Translation and Commentary*. Vol. 10, *Against Apion*. Edited by Steve Mason. Brill.

Bardel, Ruth. 2002. "Eunuchizing Agamemnon: Clytemnestra, Agamemnon, and *Maschalismos*." In *Eunuchs in Antiquity and Beyond*, edited by Shaun Tougher, 51–70. Classical Press of Wales.

Barnes, T. D. 1998. "Tacitus and the *Senatus Consultum de Cn. Pisone Patre*." *Phoenix* 52 (1–2): 125–48.

Barrett, Anthony. 1989. *Caligula: The Corruption of Power*. Yale University Press.

Barton, George A. 1931. "A New Inscription of Entemena." *Journal of the American Oriental Society* 51 (3): 262–65.

Basello, Gian Pietro. 2021. "Hierarchy and *Ethno-classe Dominante*." In *A Companion to the Achaemenid Persian Empire*, edited by Bruno Jacobs and Robert Rollinger, 859–70. Wiley Blackwell.

Basham, A. L. 1953. "A New Study of the Śaka-Kuṣāṇa Period." *Bulletin of the School of Oriental and African Studies* 15 (1): 80–97.

Bastet, F. L. 1966. "Feldherr mit Hund auf der Augustusstatue von Prima Porta." *Bulletin Antieke Beschaving* 41: 77–90.

Beagon, Mary. 2005. *The Elder Pliny on the Human Animal: Natural History Book 7*. Oxford University Press.

Beard, Mary. 2007. *The Roman Triumph*. Belknap Press of Harvard University Press.

Bedjan, Paul. 1891. *Acta Martyrum et Sanctorum II*. Harrassowitz.

Bedrosian, Robert. 1984. "*Dayeakut'iwn* in Ancient Armenia." *Armenian Review* 37 (2): 23–47.

———. 1985. *Ghazar P'arpec'i's History of the Armenians.* Sources of the Armenian Tradition.

———. 1994. S.v. "Dayeakut'iwn." In *Encyclopedia Iranica,* https://iranicaonline.org/articles/dayeakutiwn (accessed August 19, 2024).

———. 2021. *Ghazar P'arpec'i: History of the Armenians.* 2 vols. Sophene.

Beeston, A. F. L., and Irfan Shahîd. 2012. S.v. "Al-Ḥira." In *Encyclopaedia of Islam,* edited by P. Bearman et al. 2nd ed. Brill Online, https://doi.org/10.1163/1573-3912_islam_SIM_2891 (accessed August 19, 2024).

Bellemore, Jane, and Beryl Rawson. 1990. "*Alumni:* The Italian Evidence." *Zeitschrift für Papyrologie und Epigraphik* 83: 1–19.

Benario, Herbert W., ed. 1983. *Tacitus Annals 11 and 12.* University Press of America.

Benveniste, E. 1966. *Titres et noms propres en iranien ancien.* C. Klincksieck.

Bernard, Jacques-Emmanuel. 2015. "Portraits of Peoples." In *A Companion to Livy,* edited by Bernard Mineo, 39–51. Wiley Blackwell.

Bernstein, Neil W. 2015. "Family and Kinship in the Works of Statius." In *Brill's Companion to Statius,* edited by William J Dominik, Carole Elizabeth Newlands, and Kyle Gervais, 139–54. Brill.

Betzig, Laura L. 1986. *Despotism and Differential Reproduction: A Darwinian View of History.* Routledge.

Beyer, Klaus. 1998. *Die aramäischen Inschriften aus Assur, Hatra und dem übrigen Ostmesopotamien.* Vandenhoeck & Ruprecht.

Biga, Maria Giovanna. 2003. "The Reconstruction of a Relative Chronology for the Ebla Texts." *Orientalia* 72 (4): 345–67.

Bigwood, J. M. 2004. "Queen Mousa, Mother and Wife (?) of King Phraatakes of Parthia: A Re-Evaluation of the Evidence." *Mouseion* 4: 35–70.

Billows, Richard. 1993. "The Religious Procession of the Ara Pacis Augustae: Augustus' *Supplicatio* in 13 B.C." *Journal of Roman Archaeology* 6: 80–92.

Birley, Anthony R. 2007. Review of Joel Allen, *Hostages and Hostage-Taking in the Roman Empire. L'Antiquité Classique* 76: 538–40.

Bisht, Medha. 2020. *Kautilya's* Arthashastra: *Philosophy of Strategy.* Routledge.

Bivar, A. D. H. 1983. "The Political History of Iran under the Arsacids." In *The Cambridge History of Iran,* edited by E. Yarshater, vol. 3.1, 21–99. Cambridge University Press.

———. 2007. "Gondophares and the Indo-Parthians." In *The Age of the Parthians,* edited by Vesta Sarkhosh Curtis and Sarah Stewart, 26–36. Tauris.

Blamire, Alec. 1970. "Pausanias and Persia." *Greek, Roman, and Byzantine Studies* 11: 295–305.

Blockley, R. C. 1984. "Roman-Barbarian Marriages in the Late Empire." *Florilegium* 4: 63–79.

Boatwright, Mary T. 2021. *Imperial Women of Rome: Power, Gender, Context.* Oxford University Press.

Böck, Barbara. 2010. "Keilschriftliche Texte." In *Quellen zur Geschichte des Partherreiches: Textsammlung mit Übersetzungen und Kommentaren,* edited by Ursula Hackl, Bruno Jacobs, and Dieter Weber, vol. 3, 1–174. Vandenhoeck & Ruprecht.

Bonechi, Marco. 2016. "Chi scrisse cosa a chi: Struttura e prosopografia di 75.2342 = ARET XIII 3, la 'Lettera da Ḥamazi' eblaita." In *Libiamo ne' lieti calici: Ancient Near Eastern Studies Presented to Lucio Milano on the Occasion of his 65th Birthday by Pupils, Colleagues and Friends,* edited by Paola Corò et al., 3–27. Ugarit.

Booker, Sparky. 2018. *Cultural Exchange and Identity in Late Medieval Ireland: The English and Irish of the Four Obedient Shires.* Cambridge University Press.

Börm, Henning. 2007. *Prokop und die Perser: Untersuchungen zu den römisch-sasanidischen Kontakten in der ausgehenden Spätantike.* Franz Steiner.

———. 2008. "Das Königtum der Sasaniden—Strukturen und Probleme: Bemerkungen aus althistorischer Sicht." *Klio* 90 (2): 423–43.

———. 2018. "König und Gefolgschaft im Sasanidenreich: Zum Verhältnis zwischen Monarch und imperialer Elite im spätantiken Persien." In *Die Interaktion von Herrschern und Eliten in imperialen Ordnungen des Mittelalters,* edited by Wolfram Drews, 23–42. De Gruyter.

Bornecque, Henri. 2002 [1924]. *Ovide: L'art d'aimer.* 8th ed. Société d'édition "Les Belles Lettres."

Borza, Eugene N. 1990. *In the Shadow of Olympus: The Emergence of Macedon.* Princeton University Press.

Bosworth, C. E. 1999. *The History of Al-Ṭabarī.* Vol. 5, *The Sāsānids, the Byzantines, the Lakhmids, and Yemen.* State University of New York Press.

Bowersock, G. W. 1983. *Roman Arabia.* Harvard University Press.

———. 1984. "Augustus and the East: The Problem of Succession." In *Caesar Augustus: Seven Aspects,* edited by Fergus Millar and Erich Segal, 169–88. Clarendon.

Boyce, Mary. 1957. "The Parthian Gōsān and Iranian Minstrel Tradition." *Journal of the Royal Asiatic Society* 89 (1–2): 10–45.

———. 1975. "Iconoclasm among the Zoroastrians." In *Christianity, Judaism, and Other Greco-Roman Cults: Studies for Morton Smith at Sixty,* edited by Jacob Neusner, 93–111. Brill.

———. 1979. *Zoroastrians: Their Religious Beliefs and Practices.* Routledge & Kegan Paul.

———. 1983. "Parthian Writings and Literature." In *The Cambridge History of Iran,* edited by E. Yarshater, vol. 3.2, 1149–65. Cambridge University Press.

———. 2002. S.v. "Gōsān." In *Encyclopedia Iranica,* https://iranicaonline.org/articles/gosan (accessed August 19, 2024).

Bradley, Guy, and Joshua Hall. 2018. "The Roman Conquest of Italy." In *The Peoples of Ancient Italy,* edited by Gary D. Farney and Guy Bradley, 191–214. De Gruyter.

Bradley, Keith. 1979. "Dislocation in the Roman Family." *Historical Reflections / Réflexions Historiques* 14 (1): 33–62.

———. 1986. "Wet-Nursing at Rome: A Study in Social Relations." In *The Family in Ancient Rome,* edited by Beryl Rawson, 201–29. Oxford University Press.

———. 1991. *Discovering the Roman Family: Studies in Roman Social History.* Oxford University Press.

Brandes, Wolfram. 2013. "Die 'Familie der Könige' im Mittelalter: Ein Diskussionsbeitrag zur Kritik eines vermeintlichen Erkenntnismodells." *Rechtsgeschichte* 21: 262–84.

Braund, David. 1984. *Rome and the Friendly King: The Character of the Client Kingship.* St. Martin's Press.

———. 1994. *Georgia in Antiquity: A History of Colchis and Transcaucasian Iberia.* Clarendon.

———. 2002. "Anagranes the ΤΡΟΦΕΥΣ: The Court of Caucasian Iberia in the Second-Third Centuries AD." In *Autour de la mer Noire. Hommage de Otar Lordkipanidzé,* edited by Daredjan Kacharava, Murielle Faudot, and Evelyne Geny, 23–34. Institut des Sciences et Techniques de l'Antiquité.

———. 2015. "Kings beyond the *Claustra*: Nero's Nubian Nile, India and the *Rubrum Mare* (Tacitus, *Annals* 2.61)." In *Amici—Socii—Clientes? Abhängige Herrschaft im Imperium Romanum*, edited by Ernst Baltrusch and Julia Wilker, 123–59. Edition Topoi.

Bremmer, Jan. 1976. "Avunculate and Fosterage." *Journal of Indo-European Studies* 4: 65–78.

Briant, Pierre. 1985. "Dons de terres et de villes: L'Asie mineure dans le contexte Achéménide." *Revue des Études Anciennes* 87 (1): 53–72.

———. 2002. *From Cyrus to Alexander: A History of the Persian Empire*. Eisenbrauns.

Bridges, Emma. 2015. *Imagining Xerxes: Ancient Perspectives on a Persian King*. Bloomsbury.

Brijder, Herman A. G. 2014. *Nemrud Daği: Recent Archaeological Research and Conservation Activities in the Tomb Sanctuary on Mount Nemrud*. De Gruyter.

Brilliant, Richard. 1967. *The Arch of Septimius Severus in the Roman Forum*. American Academy in Rome.

Brisson, Pierre-Luc. 2023. *Le moment unipolaire: Rome et la Méditerranée hellénistique (188–146 a.C.)*. Les Presses de l'Université Laval.

Brosius, Maria. 1996. *Women in Ancient Persia, 559–331 BC*. Clarendon.

———. 2021. "Achaemenid Women." In *The Routledge Companion to Women and Monarchy in the Ancient Mediterranean World*, edited by Elizabeth Carney and Sabine Müller, 149–60. Routledge.

Brunner, Christopher. 2011. S.v. "Abdagases." In *Encyclopedia Iranica*, www.iranicaonline.org/articles/abdagases-great-king-of-the-pahlava-dynasty-in-drangiana-arachosia-gandhara (accessed August 19, 2024).

Brunt, P. A. 1990. *Roman Imperial Themes*. Clarendon.

Brunt, P. A., and J. M. Moore, eds. 1967. *Res Gestae Divi Augusti: The Achievements of the Divine Augustus*. Oxford University Press.

Bruun, Christer. 1995. "Private Munificence in Italy and the Evidence from Lead Pipe Stamps." In *Acta colloquii epigraphici Latini Helsingiae 3.-6. Sept. 1991 habiti*, edited by Heikki Solin, Olli Salomies, and Uta-Maria Liertz, 41–58. Societas Scientiarum Fennica.

Bryce, Trevor. 1990. "The Death of Niphururiya and Its Aftermath." *Journal of Egyptian Archaeology* 76: 97–105.

———. 2003. *Letters of the Great Kings of the Ancient Near East: The Royal Correspondence of the Late Bronze Age*. Routledge.

———. 2005. *The Kingdom of the Hittites*. Oxford University Press.

Buccellati, Giorgio, and Marilyn Kelly-Buccellati. 2002. "Tar'am-Agade, Daughter of Naram-Sin, at Urkesh." In *Of Pots and Plans: Papers on the Archaeology and History of Mesopotamia and Syria Presented to David Dates in Honour of His 75th Birthday*, edited by L. Al-Ghailani et al., 11–31. Nabu.

Bühler, Theodor. 1964. "Fosterage." *Schweizerisches Archiv für Volkskunde* 60 (1–2): 1–17.

Burbank, Jane, and Frederick Cooper. 2010. *Empires in World History: Power and the Politics of Difference*. Princeton University Press.

Burling, Robbins. 1974. *The Passage of Power: Studies in Political Succession*. Academic Press.

Burton, Paul J. 2011. *Friendship and Empire: Roman Diplomacy and Imperialism in the Middle Republic (353–146 BC)*. Cambridge University Press.

Busby, Cecilia. 1997. "Of Marriage and Marriageability: Gender and Dravidian Kinship." *Journal of the Royal Anthropological Institute* 3 (1): 21–42.

Butrica, James. 2006. "The Transmission of the Text of Propertius." In *Brill's Companion to Propertius*, edited by Hans-Christian Günther, 25–43. Brill.

Cameron, Hamish. 2019. *Making Mesopotamia: Geography and Empire in a Romano-Iranian Borderland.* Brill.

Campbell, Brian. 1993. "War and Diplomacy: Rome and Parthia, 31 BC–AD 235." In *War and Society in the Roman World*, edited by John Rich and Graham Shipley, 213–40. Routledge.

———. 2001. "Diplomacy in the Roman World (c. 500 BC–AD 235)." *Diplomacy and Statecraft* 12 (1): 1–22.

Candelora, Danielle. 2019. "The Eastern Delta as a Middle Ground for Hyksos Identity Negotiation." *Mitteilungen des Deutschen Archäologischen Instituts, Abteilung Kairo* 75: 77–94.

Canepa, Matthew P. 2009. *The Two Eyes of the Earth: Art and Ritual of Kingship between Rome and Sasanian Iran.* University of California Press.

———. 2018. *The Iranian Expanse: Transforming Royal Identity through Architecture, Landscape, and the Built Environment, 550 BCE–642 CE.* University of California Press.

———. 2020. "The Parthian and Sasanian Empires." In *The Oxford World History of Empire.* Vol. 2, *The History of Empires*, edited by C. A. Bayly, Peter F. Bang, and Walter Scheidel, 290–324. Oxford University Press.

Caquot, André. 1964. "Nouvelles inscriptions araméennes de Hatra (VI)." *Syria* 41 (3–4): 251–72.

Carney, Elizabeth. 2000. *Women and Monarchy in Macedonia.* University of Oklahoma Press.

———. 2015. *King and Court in Ancient Macedonia: Rivalry, Treason, and Conspiracy.* Classical Press of Wales.

Carroll, Kevin K. 1982. *The Parthenon Inscription.* Duke University Press.

Carroll, Maureen. 2006. *Spirits of the Dead: Roman Funerary Commemoration in Western Europe.* Oxford University Press.

———. 2018. "Archaeological and Epigraphic Evidence for Infancy in the Roman World." In *The Oxford Handbook of the Archaeology of Childhood*, edited by Sally Crawford, Dawn M. Hadley, and Gillian Shepherd, 148–64. Oxford University Press.

Carsten, Janet. 1991. "Children in Between: Fostering and the Process of Kinship on Pulau Langkawi, Malaysia." *Man* 26 (3): 425–43.

———. 2000. "Introduction: Cultures of Relatedness." In *Cultures of Relatedness: New Approaches to the Study of Kinship*, edited by Janet Carsten, 1–36. Cambridge University Press.

———. 2004. *After Kinship.* Cambridge University Press.

———. 2011. "Substance and Relationality: Blood in Contexts." *Annual Review of Anthropology* 40: 19–35.

Carter, Elizabeth, and Matthew Stolper. 1984. *Elam: Surveys of Political History and Archaeology.* University of California Press.

Casali, Sergio. 2006. "The Art of Making Oneself Hated: Rethinking (Anti-) Augustanism in Ovid's *Ars Amatoria*." In *The Art of Love: Bimillennial Essays on Ovid's Ars Amatoria and Remedia Amoris*, edited by Roy Gibson, Steven Green, and Alison Sharrock, 216–34. Oxford University Press.

Catagnoti, Amalia. 2003. "Anatolia and the Levant: Ebla." In *A History of Ancient Near Eastern Law*, edited by Raymond Westbrook, 227–39. Brill.

Cathcart, Alison. 2006. *Kinship and Clientage: Highland Clanship, 1451–1609.* Brill.

Centlivres Challet, Claude-Emmanuelle. 2017a. "Feeding the Roman Nursling: Maternal Milk, Its Substitutes, and Their Limitations." *Latomus* 76 (4): 895–909.

———. 2017b. "Roman Breastfeeding: Control and Affect." *Arethusa* 50 (3): 369–84.

Cereti, Carlo G. 1995. *The Zand ī Wahman Yasn: A Zoroastrian Apocalypse.* Istituto Italiano per il Medio ed Estremo Oriente.

———. 2001. *La letteratura pahlavi: Introduzione ai testi con riferimenti alla storia degli studi e alla tradizione manoscritta.* Mimesis.

———. 2011. S.v. "Kār-Nāmag ī Ardašīr ī Pābagān." In *Encyclopedia Iranica,* www.iranicaonline .org/articles/karnamag-i-ardasir (accessed August 19, 2024).

Cereti, Carlo G., and Gianfilippo Terribili. 2014. "The Middle Persian and Parthian Inscriptions on the Paikuli Tower. New Blocks and Preliminary Studies." *Iranica Antiqua* 49: 347–82.

Chabot, Jean-Baptiste, ed. 2010. *Synodicon Orientale: Recueil de Synodes Nestoriens.* Gorgias Press.

Champion, Craige B. 2017. *The Peace of the Gods: Elite Religious Practices in the Middle Roman Republic.* Princeton University Press.

Champlin, Edward. 2003. *Nero.* Belknap Press of Harvard University Press.

Chapman, Cynthia R. 2012. "'Oh That You Were like a Brother to Me, One Who Had Nursed at My Mother's Breasts.' Breast Milk as a Kinship-Forging Substance." *Journal of Hebrew Scriptures* 12: 1–41.

Charles-Edwards, T. M. 2013. *Wales and the Britons, 350–1064.* Oxford University Press.

Charpin, D., and J.-M. Durand. 1991. "La suzeraineté de l'empereur (sukkalmah) d'Elam sur la Mésopotamie et le 'nationalisme' Amorrite." In *Mesopotamie et Elam: Actes de la XXXVIème Rencontre Assyriologique Internationale, Gand, 10–14 juillet 1989,* edited by L. De Meyer and H. Gasche, vol. 1, 59–66. Mesopotamian History and Environment, Occasional Publications.

Chaumont, Marie-Louise. 1976. "L'Arménie entre Rome et l'Iran. I: De l'avènement d'Auguste à l'avènement de Dioclétien." *Aufstieg und Niedergang der römischen Welt* part 2, vol. 9.1: 71–194.

———. 1986. S.v. "Argbed." In *Encyclopedia Iranica,* https://iranicaonline.org/articles/argbed (accessed August 19, 2024).

———. 1987. S.v. "Aurelius Victor." In *Encyclopedia Iranica,* www.iranicaonline.org/articles /aurelius-victor-sextus-born-in-africa-ca (accessed August 19, 2024).

———. 1991. S.v. "Cinnamus." In *Encyclopedia Iranica,* https://iranicaonline.org/articles /cinnamus-gk (accessed August 19, 2024).

———. 1992. "Remarques sur la dédicace d'un monument (ex-voto) élevé à Cybèle par la fille d'un roi Tigrane à Falerii Veteres (Città Castellana)." *Ancient Society* 23: 43–60.

———. 2002. S.v. "Axse." In *Encyclopedia Iranica,* www.iranicaonline.org/articles/axse (accessed August 19, 2024).

———. 2020. S.v. "Armenia and Iran ii: The Pre-Islamic Period." In *Encyclopedia Iranica,* www.iranicaonline.org/articles/armenia-ii.

Chen, Anne Hunnell. 2021. "Late Antiquity between Sasanian East and Roman West: Third-Century Imperial Women as Pawns in Propaganda Warfare." In *Late Antique Studies in Memory of Alan Cameron,* edited by William V. Harris, 168–97. Brill.

Cherry, David. 1990. "The Minician Law: Marriage and the Roman Citizenship." *Phoenix* 44 (3): 244–66.

Cheung, Johnny. 2007. *Etymological Dictionary of the Iranian Verb.* Brill.

Christensen, Peter. 1993. *The Decline of Iranshahr: Irrigation and Environments in the History of the Middle East, 500 B.C. to A.D. 1500.* Museum Tusculanum Press.

Clark, Timothy. 2021. "Processing into Dominance: Nero, the Crowning of Tiridates I, and a New Narrative of Rome's Supremacy in the East." *Journal of Ancient History* 9 (2): 269–96.

Cline, Diane H., and Eric H. Cline. 2015. "Text Messages, Tablets, and Social Networks in the Late Bronze Age Eastern Mediterranean: The 'Small World' of the Amarna Letters." In *There and Back Again—the Crossroads II. Proceedings of an International Conference Held in Prague, September 15–18, 2014*, edited by Jana Mynářová, Pavel Onderka, and Peter Pavúk, 17–44. Charles University in Prague, Faculty of Arts.

Cline, Eric H. 1995. "'My Brother, My Son': Rulership and Trade between the LBA Aegean, Egypt and the Near East." In *The Role of the Ruler in the Prehistoric Aegean*, edited by P. Rehak, 143–50. Université de Liège.

———. 2014. *1177 B.C: The Year Civilization Collapsed*. Princeton University Press.

Coarelli, Filippo. 1987. *I santuari del Lazio in età repubblicana*. La Nuova Italia Scientifica.

Cohen, G. M. 1974. "The Diadochoi and the New Monarchies." *Athenaeum* 52: 177–79.

Cohen, Raymond. 1996. "All in the Family: Ancient Near Eastern Diplomacy." *International Negotiation* 1 (1): 11–28.

Colditz, Iris. 2000. *Zur Sozialterminologie der iranischen Manichäer: Eine semantische Analyse im Vergleich zu den nichtmanichäischen iranischen Quellen*. Harrassowitz.

———. 2018. *Iranisches Personennamenbuch*. Vol. 2.1, *Iranische Personnamen in manichäischer Überlieferung*. Verlag der Österreichischen Akademie der Wissenschaften.

Coleman, K. M. 1990. "Fatal Charades: Roman Executions Staged as Mythological Enactments." *Journal of Roman Studies* 80: 44–73.

———. 1993. "Launching into History: Aquatic Displays in the Early Empire." *Journal of Roman Studies* 83: 48–74.

Coloru, Omar. 2012. "The Language of the *Oikos* and the Language of Power in the Seleucid Kingdom." In *Families in the Greco-Roman World*, edited by Ray Laurence and Agneta Strömberg, 84–94. Continuum.

———. 2015. "I Am Your Father! Dynasties and Dynastic Legitimacy on Pre-Islamic Coinage between Iran and Northwest India." *Electrum* 22: 173–99.

Conlan, Thomas D. 2005. "Thicker than Blood: The Social and Political Significance of Wet Nurses in Japan, 950–1330." *Harvard Journal of Asiatic Studies* 65 (1): 159–205.

Conte, Gian Biagio. 1994. *Latin Literature: A History*. Translated by Joseph B. Solodow. Johns Hopkins University Press.

Cooley, Alison, ed. 2009. *Res Gestae Divi Augusti: Text, Translation, and Commentary*. Cambridge University Press.

———, ed. 2023. *The* Senatus Consultum de Cn. Pisone Patre: *Text, Translation, and Commentary*. Cambridge University Press.

Coope, Jessica A. 2016. *The Most Noble of People: Religious, Ethnic, and Gender Identity in Muslim Spain*. University of Michigan Press.

Cooper, Jerrold. 1986. *Sumerian and Akkadian Royal Inscriptions*. Vol. 1, *Presargonic Inscriptions*. American Oriental Society.

———. 2003. "International Law: International Law in the Third Millennium." In *A History of Ancient Near Eastern Law*, edited by Raymond Westbrook, 241–51. Brill.

Corbier, Mireille. 1991. "Divorce and Adoption as Roman Familial Strategies." In *Marriage, Divorce, and Children in Ancient Rome*, edited by Beryl Rawson, 47–78. Humanities Research Centre and Clarendon.

———. 2001. "Child Exposure and Abandonment." In *Childhood, Class, and Kin in the Roman World*, edited by Suzanne Dixon, 52–73. Routledge.

Corke-Webster, James. 2017. "A Man for the Times: Jesus and the Abgar Correspondence in Eusebius of Caesarea's Ecclesiastical History." *Harvard Theological Review* 110 (4): 563–87.

Cornell, Tim. 1993. "The End of Roman Imperial Expansion." In *War and Society in the Roman World*, edited by John Rich and Graham Shipley, 139–70. Routledge.

———, ed. 2013. *The Fragments of the Roman Historians.* 3 vols. Oxford University Press.

Cornwell, Hannah. 2017. Pax *and the Politics of Peace: Republic to Principate.* Oxford University Press.

Cotton, Hannah M., and Werner Eck. 2005. "Josephus' Roman Audience: Josephus and the Roman Elites." In *Flavius Josephus and Flavian Rome*, edited by Jonathan Edmondson, Steve Mason, and James Rives, 37–52. Oxford University Press.

Courtney, Edward. 2013. *A Commentary on the Satires of Juvenal.* 2nd ed. California Classical Studies.

Cribb, Joe. 2021. "Greekness after the End of the Greco-Bactrian and Indo-Greek Kingdoms." In *The Graeco-Bactrian and Indo-Greek World*, edited by Rachel Mairs, 653–81. Routledge.

Criniti, Nicola, ed. 1981. *Grani Liciniani Reliquiae.* Teubner.

———, ed. 1993. "Granio Liciniano." *Aufstieg und Niedergang der römischen Welt* part 2, vol. 34.1: 119–205.

Cross, Cameron. 2015. "The Poetics of Romantic Love in *Vis & Rāmin*." PhD diss., University of Chicago.

———. 2018. "A Tree Atop the Mountain: Mobad Manikan and the Elusive Promises of Masculinity." *Iran Namag* 3 (1): xxvi–lxiii.

———. 2023. *Love at a Crux: The New Persian Romance in a Global Middle Ages.* University of Toronto Press.

Cumont, Franz. 1932. "Une lettre du roi Artaban III à la ville de Suse." *Comptes Rendus des Séances de l'Académie des Inscriptions et Belles-Lettres* 76 (3): 238–60.

Cunningham, A. 1890. "Coins of the Sakas." *Numismatic Chronicle and Journal of the Numismatic Society* 10: 103–72.

Curtis, Vesta Sarkhosh. 2007. "The Iranian Revival in the Parthian Period." In *The Age of the Parthians*, edited by Vesta Sarkhosh Curtis and Sarah Stewart, 7–25. I. B. Tauris.

Curtis, Vesta Sarkhosh, and Alexandra Magub. 2020. *Rivalling Rome: Parthian Coins and Culture.* Spink.

Cussini, Eleonora. 2016. "Reconstructing Palmyrene Legal Language." In *The World of Palmyra*, edited by Andreas Kropp and Rubina Raja, 44–54. Det Kongelige Danske Videnskabernes Selska.

Dąbrowa, Edward. 1983. *La politique de l'État parthe à l'égard de Rome–d'Artaban II à Vologèse I (ca 11–ca 79 de n.e.) et les facteurs qui la conditionnaient.* Nakł. Uniwersytetu Jagiellońskiego.

———. 1987. "Les premiers 'otages' parthes à Rome." *Folia Orientalia* 24: 63–71.

———. 1992. "Könige Syriens in der Gefangenschaft der Parther: Zwei Episoden aus der Geschichte der Beziehungen zwischen Seleukiden und Arsakiden." *Tyche* 7: 45–54.

———. 2012. "The Arsacid Empire." In *The Oxford Handbook of Iranian History*, edited by Touraj Daryaee, 164–86. Oxford University Press.

———. 2017. "Tacitus on the Parthians." *Electrum* 24: 171–89.

———. 2018. "Arsacid Dynastic Marriages." *Electrum* 25: 73–83.

———. 2021. "Parthian-Armenian Relations from the 2nd Century BCE to the Second Half of the 1st Century CE." *Electrum* 28: 41–57.

D'Agostini, Monica. 2021. "Seleukid Marriage Alliances." In *The Routledge Companion to Women and Monarchy in the Ancient Mediterranean World*, edited by Elizabeth Carney and Sabine Müller, 198–209. Routledge.

Damtoft Poulsen, Aske. 2017. "The Language of Freedom and Slavery in Tacitus' *Agricola*." *Mnemosyne* 70 (5): 834–58.

Darke, Hubert. 2002. *The Book of Government or Rules for Kings: The Siyar Al-Muluk or Siyasat-Nama of Nizam Al-Mulk*. Routledge.

Darling Young, Robin. 2018. "Armenian." In *A Companion to Late Antique Literature*, edited by Scott McGill and Edward J. Watts, 75–85. Wiley Blackwell.

Darmesteter, James. 1895. *The Zend Avesta, Part 1: The Vendîdâd*. Clarendon.

Darnell, John Coleman, and Colleen Manassa. 2007. *Tutankhamun's Armies: Battle and Conquest during Ancient Egypt's Late Eighteenth Dynasty*. John Wiley & Sons.

Daryaee, Touraj. 2009. *Sasanian Persia: The Rise and Fall of an Empire*. I. B. Tauris.

———. 2016. "Refashioning the Zoroastrian Past: From Alexander to Islam." In *The Zoroastrian Flame: Exploring Religion, History, and Tradition*, edited by A. Williams, S. Stewart, and A. Hintzc, 135–46. I. B. Tauris.

———. 2018. "Pahlavi Literature." In *A Companion to Late Antique Literature*, edited by Scott McGill and Edward Watts, 103–21. Wiley Blackwell.

———. 2022. "Alexander at Pasargadae and the Frawaši of Cyrus." In *The World of Alexander in Perspective: Contextualizing Arrian*, edited by Robert Rollinger and Julian Degen, 357–67. Harrassowitz.

Daudpota, U. M. 1932. "The Annals of Hamzah Al-Isfahānī." *Journal of the K. R. Cama Oriental Institute* 22: 58–120.

David, Steven. 2000. "Realism, Constructivism, and the Amarna Letters." In *Amarna Diplomacy: The Beginnings of International Relations*, edited by Raymond Cohen and Raymond Westbrook, 55–63. Johns Hopkins University Press.

Davies, Penelope. 2000. *Death and the Emperor: Roman Imperial Funerary Monuments from Augustus to Marcus Aurelius*. Cambridge University Press.

———. 2010. "Living to Living, Living to Dead: Communication and Political Rivalry in Roman Tomb Design." In *Deathscapes: Spaces for Death, Dying, Mourning, and Remembrance*, edited by Avril Maddrell and James Sidaway, 225–41. Ashgate.

Davis, Dick. 2005. S.v. "Vis o Rāmin." In *Encyclopedia Iranica*, https://iranicaonline.org /articles/vis-o-ramin (August 19, 2024).

———. 2006. *Abolqasem Ferdowsi: Shahnameh; The Persian Book of Kings*. Penguin.

———. 2008. *Fakhraddin Gorgani: Vis and Ramin*. Penguin.

de Jong, Albert. 1997. *Traditions of the Magi: Zoroastrianism in Greek and Latin Literature*. Brill.

———. 2008. "Regional Variation in Zoroastrianism: The Case of the Parthians." *Bulletin of the Asia Institute* 22: 17–27.

———. 2013a. "Hatra and the Parthian Commonwealth." In *Hatra: Politics, Culture, and Religion between Parthia and Rome*, edited by Lucinda Dirven, 143–60. Franz Steiner.

———. 2013b. "Religion in Iran: The Parthian and Sasanian Periods (247 BCE–654 CE)." In *The Cambridge History of Religions in the Ancient World*. Vol. 2, *From the Hellenistic Age to Late Antiquity*, edited by Michele Renee Salzman and William Adler, 23–53. Cambridge University Press.

———. 2015. "Religion and Politics in Pre-Islamic Iran." In *The Wiley Blackwell Companion to Zoroastrianism*, edited by Michael Stausberg and Yuhan Sohrab-Dinshaw Vevaina, 85–101. Wiley Blackwell.

———. 2017a. "Being Iranian in Antiquity (at Home and Abroad)." In *Persianism in Antiquity*, edited by Rolf Strootman and Miguel John Versluys, 35–47. Franz Steiner.

———. 2017b. "The Women Who Witnessed Zoroaster's Birth." In *Studia Philologica Iranica: Gherardo Gnoli Memorial Volume*, edited by Enrico Morano, Elio Provasi, and Adriano Valerio Rossi, 85–91. Scienze e Lettere.

———. 2022. "Religion in the Parthian Empire." In *Persia: Ancient Iran and the Classical World*, edited by Jeffrey Spier, Timothy Potts, and Sara E. Cole, 185–91. J. Paul Getty Museum.

de la Vaissière, Étienne. 2005. *Sogdian Traders: A History*. Translated by James Ward. Brill.

Debevoise, Neilson Carel. 1938. *A Political History of Parthia*. University of Chicago Press.

Dehkhoda, Ali Akbar, and Muhammad Mu'in. 1947. *Luġatnāma [Lexicon]*. University of Tehran.

Demandt, Alexander. 1997. *Das Privatleben der römischen Kaiser*. Beck.

den Hollander, William. 2014. *Josephus, the Emperors, and the City of Rome: From Hostage to Historian*. Brill.

Devillers, Olivier. 2003. *Tacite et les sources des annales: Enquêtes sur la méthode historique*. Peeters.

Diakonoff, I. M., and V. A. Livshits. 2001. *Parthian Economic Documents from Nisa: Texts I*. School of Oriental and African Studies.

Dignas, Beate, and Engelbert Winter. 2007. *Rome and Persia in Late Antiquity: Neighbours and Rivals*. Cambridge University Press.

Dimundo, Rosalba. 2003. *Ovidio, Lezioni d'amore, saggio di commento al I Libro dell'Ars amatoria*. Edipuglia.

Dindorf, Ludwig August, ed. 1832. *Chronicon Paschale ad exemplar Vaticanum*. Weber.

Dixon, Suzanne. 1985. "The Marriage Alliance in the Roman Elite." *Journal of Family History* 10 (4): 353–78.

———. 1992. *The Roman Family*. Johns Hopkins University Press.

———. 1999. "The Circulation of Children in Roman Society." In *Adoption et Fosterage*, edited by Mireille Corbier, 217–30. De Boccard.

Doležal, Stanislav. 2017. "Did Hadrian Ever Meet a Parthian King?" *Acta Universitatis Carolinae Philologica* 2: 111–25.

Dölger, Franz. 1953. "Die 'Familie der Könige' im Mittelalter." In *Byzanz und die europäische Staatenwelt: Ausgewählte Vorträge und Aufsätze*, 34–69. Buch-Kunstverlag.

Dowling, Melissa Barden. 2006. *Clemency and Cruelty in the Roman World*. University of Michigan Press.

Drijvers, Jan Willem. 1998. "Strabo on Parthia and the Parthians." In *Das Partherreich und seine Zeugnisse = The Arsacid Empire—Sources and Documentation: Beiträge des internationalen Colloquiums, Eutin (27.-30. Juni 1996)*, edited by Josef Wiesehöfer, 279–93. Franz Steiner.

Drijvers, Jan Willem, and John F. Healey, eds. 1999. *The Old Syriac Inscriptions of Edessa and Osrhoene*. Brill.

Drinkwater, John. 2019. *Nero: Emperor and Court*. Cambridge University Press.

Duindam, Jeroen. 2016. *Dynasties: A Global History of Power, 1300–1800*. Cambridge University Press.

———. 2021. "Gender, Succession, and Dynastic Rule." *History and Anthropology* 32 (2): 151–70.

Dunn, Daisy. 2019. *The Shadow of Vesuvius: A Life of Pliny*. Liveright.

Durkin-Meisterernst, Desmond. 2004. *Dictionary of Manichaean Middle Persian and Parthian*. Brepols.

Dyson, Stephen L. 2011. "The Family and the Roman Countryside." In *A Companion to Families in the Greek and Roman Worlds*, edited by Beryl Rawson, 431–44. Wiley-Blackwell.

Eck, Werner, Antonio Caballos, and Fernando Fernández Gómez. 1996. *Das Senatus Consultum de Cn. Pisone Patre*. Beck.

Eckstein, Arthur M. 2006. *Mediterranean Anarchy, Interstate War, and the Rise of Rome*. University of California Press.

———. 2008. *Rome Enters the Greek East: From Anarchy to Hierarchy in the Hellenistic Mediterranean, 230–170 BC*. Blackwell.

Edel, Elmar. 1994. *Die ägyptisch-hethitische Korrespondenz aus Boghazköi in babylonischer und hethitischer Sprache*. 2 vols. Westdeutscher.

Edmondson, Jonathan. 1992. *Dio, the Julio-Claudians: Selections from Books 58–63 of the Roman History of Cassius Dio*. London Association of Classical Teachers.

———. 2011. "Slavery and the Roman Family." In *The Cambridge World History of Slavery*. Vol. 1, *The Ancient Mediterranean World*, edited by Keith Bradley and Paul Cartledge, 337–61. Cambridge University Press.

———. 2014. "Roman Family History." In *The Oxford Handbook of Roman Epigraphy*, edited by Christer Bruun and Jonathan Edmondson, 559–81. Oxford University Press.

Edwell, Peter. 2021. *Rome and Persia at War: Imperial Competition and Contact, 193–363 CE*. Routledge.

Ehrhardt, Norbert. 1998. "Parther und parthische Geschichte bei Tacitus." In *Das Partherreich und seine Zeugnisse = The Arsacid Empire—Sources and Documentation: Beiträge des internationalen Colloquiums, Eutin (27.-30. Juni 1996)*, edited by Josef Wiesehöfer, 295–307. Franz Steiner.

Eidem, J., and Jørgen Læssøe. 2001. *The Shemshara Archives*. Vol. 1, *The Letters*. Royal Danish Academy of Sciences and Letters.

Elbern, Stephan. 1990. "Geiseln in Rom." *Athenaeum* 68: 97–140.

Ellerbrock, Uwe. 2021. *The Parthians: The Forgotten Empire*. Routledge.

Elwyn, Sue. 1991. "The Use of Kinship Terminology in Hellenistic Diplomatic Documents: An Epigraphical Study." PhD diss., University of Pennsylvania.

———. 1993. "Interstate Kinship and Roman Foreign Policy." *Transactions of the American Philological Association* 123: 261–86.

Eph'al, I. 1982. *The Ancient Arabs: Nomads on the Borders of the Fertile Crescent, 9th–5th Centuries B.C.* Magnes Press.

Errington, Elizabeth, Vesta Sarkhosh Curtis, and Joe Cribb. 2007. *From Persepolis to the Punjab: Exploring Ancient Iran, Afghanistan, and Pakistan*. British Museum Press.

Evans, Rhiannon. 2008. *Utopia Antiqua: Readings of the Golden Age and Decline at Rome*. Routledge.

Fabian, Lara. 2020. "The Arsakid Empire." In *Handbook of Ancient Afro-Eurasian Economies*. Vol. 1, *Contexts*, edited by Sitta von Reden, 205–39. De Gruyter.

———. 2021. "Bridging the Divide: Marriage Politics across the Caucasus." *Electrum* 28: 221–44.

Fales, Frederick Mario. 2017. "Assyrian Legal Traditions." In *A Companion to Assyria*, edited by Eckart Frahm, 398–422. Wiley Blackwell.

Faruqui, Munis D. 2012. *The Princes of the Mughal Empire, 1504–1719*. Cambridge University Press.

Ferrero, Guglielmo. 1909. *The Greatness and Decline of Rome*. Vol. 5, *The Republic of Augustus*. Translated by H. J. Chaytor. Putnam.

Ferri, Rolando, ed. 2003. *Octavia: A Play Attributed to Seneca*. Cambridge University Press.

Fierro, Maribel. 2012. "Hostages and the Dangers of Cultural Contact: Two Cases from Umayyad al-Andalus." In *Acteurs des transferts culturels en Méditerranée médiévale*, edited by R. Abdellatif et al., 73–83. Oldenbourg.

Finnemore, Martha. 1996. *National Interests in International Society*. Cornell University Press.

Fisher, Greg. 2020. *Rome, Persia, and Arabia: Shaping the Middle East from Pompey to Muhammad*. Routledge.

Flower, Michael, and John Marincola, eds. 2002. *Herodotus, Histories Book IX*. Cambridge University Press.

Fornara, Charles W. 1966. "Some Aspects of the Career of Pausanias of Sparta." *Historia: Zeitschrift für Alte Geschichte* 15 (3): 257–71.

Forte, Antonino. 1995. *The Hostage An Shigao and His Offspring: An Iranian Family in China*. Istituto italiano di cultura, Scuola di studi sull'Asia orientale.

Fortes, Meyer. 1949. *The Web of Kinship among the Tallensi*. Oxford University Press.

Fowler, Richard. 2005. "'Most Fortunate Roots': Tradition and Legitimacy in Parthian Royal Ideology." In *Imaginary Kings: Royal Images in the Ancient Near East, Greece, and Rome*, edited by Olivier Hekster and Richard Fowler, 125–55. Franz Steiner.

———. 2017. "Cyrus to Arsakes, Ezra to Izates: Parthia and Persianism in Josephus." In *Persianism in Antiquity*, edited by Rolf Strootman and Miguel John Versluys, 355–79. Franz Steiner.

Francese, Christopher. 2007. *Ancient Rome in So Many Words*. Hippocrene.

Frank, Richard I. 1975. "Augustus' Legislation on Marriage and Children." *California Studies in Classical Antiquity* 8: 41–52.

Frayne, Douglas R. 2008. *Presargonic Period (2700–2350 BC)*. University of Toronto Press.

Frézouls, Edmond. 1995. "Les relations romano-parthes avant l'époque flavienne." In *Les relations internationales: Actes du Colloque de Strasbourg, 15–17 juin 1993*, edited by Edmond Frézouls and A. Jacquemin, 479–98. Université des sciences humaines de Strasbourg.

Fronda, Michael P. 2010. *Between Rome and Carthage: Southern Italy during the Second Punic War*. Cambridge University Press.

Frye, Richard N. 1962. "Some Early Iranian Titles." *Oriens* 15: 352–59.

———. 1984. *The History of Ancient Iran*. Beck.

Fuchs, Andreas. 2017. "Assyria and the East: Western Iran and Elam." In *A Companion to Assyria*, edited by Eckart Frahm, 259–67. Wiley Blackwell.

Furneaux, Henry, ed. 1907. *P. Cornelii Taciti Annalium ab excessu divi Augusti libri = The Annals of Tacitus.* 2nd ed. 2 vols. Clarendon.

Gaca, Kathy L. 2010. "The Andrapodizing of War Captives in Greek Historical Memory." *Transactions of the American Philological Association* 140: 117–61.

Gadjiev, M. S. 2020. "The Chronology of the Arsacid Albanians." In *From Albania to Arrān: The East Caucasus between the Ancient and Islamic Worlds (ca. 330 BCE–1000 CE),* edited by Robert Hoyland, 29–35. Gorgias.

Gagé, J. 1959. "L'empereur romain et les rois: Politique et protocole." *Revue Historique* 221 (2): 221–60.

Gardner, Jane F., and Thomas E. J. Wiedemann. 1991. *The Roman Household: A Sourcebook.* Routledge.

Garsoïan, Nina G. 1969. "Quidam Narseus? A Note on the Mission of St. Nerses the Great." In *Armeniaca: Mélanges d'études Arméniennes,* 147–64. Saint Lazare.

———. 1976. "Prolegomena to a Study of the Iranian Aspects in Arsacid Armenia." *Handes Amsorya* 90: 177–234.

———. 1989. *The Epic Histories Attributed to P'awstos Buzand* (Buzandaran Patmut'iwnk'). Harvard University Press.

Gazerani, Saghi. 2016. *The Sistani Cycle of Epics and Iran's National History: On the Margins of Historiography.* Brill.

Geller, Mark, and Giusto Traina. 2013. "Tigranu, the Crown Prince of Armenia: Evidence from the Babylonian Astronomical Diaries." *Klio* 95 (2): 447–54.

Gera, Dov. 1998. *Judaea and Mediterranean Politics, 219 to 161 B.C.E.* Brill.

Gershevitch, Ilya. 1962. "The Sogdian Word for 'Advice,' and Some Mugh Documents." *Central Asiatic Journal* 7 (2): 77–95.

Gignoux, Philippe. 1972. *Glossaire des inscriptions pehlevies et parthes.* Lund Humphries.

Giladi, Avner. 1999. *Infants, Parents, and Wet Nurses: Medieval Islamic Views on Breastfeeding and Their Social Implications.* Brill.

Giorgieri, Mauro, and Clelia Mora. 2010. "Kingship in Ḫatti during the 13th Century: Forms of Rule and Struggles for Power before the Fall of the Empire." In *Pax Hethitica: Studies on the Hittites and Their Neighbours in Honour of Itamar Singer,* edited by Yoram Cohen, Amir Gilan, and Jared L. Miller, 136–57. Harrassowitz.

Gleick, James. 1987. *Chaos: Making a New Science.* Viking.

Gnoli, Gherardo. 1989. *The Idea of Iran: An Essay on Its Origin.* Istituto Italiano per il Medio ed Estremo Oriente.

Gnoli, Tommaso. 2007. *The Interplay of Roman and Iranian Titles in the Roman East.* Verlag der Österreichischen Akademie der Wissenschaften.

———. 2022. "The Parthian and Sasanian Near East (Including Hatra, Edessa, and the Characene)." In *A Companion to the Hellenistic and Roman Near East,* edited by Ted Kaizer, 327–37. Wiley Blackwell.

Goldbeck, Fabian. 2016. "Die Triumphe der julisch-claudischen Zeit." In *Der römische Triumph in Prinzipat und Spätantike,* edited by Fabian Goldbeck and Johannes Wienand, 103–22. De Gruyter.

Goldbeck, Fabian, and Johannes Wienand, eds. 2016. *Der römische Triumph in Prinzipat und Spätantike.* De Gruyter.

Golden, Mark. 2009. "Oedipal Complexities." In *Growing Up Fatherless in Antiquity*, edited by Sabine R. Hübner and David M. Ratzan, 41–60. Cambridge University Press.

Goldin, Paul R. 2013. "Introduction: Han Fei and the *Han Feizi*." In *Dao Companion to the Philosophy of Han Fei*, edited by Paul R. Goldin, 1–21. Springer.

Goldsworthy, Adrian. 2023. *Rome and Persia: The Seven Hundred Year Rivalry*. Basic.

Gołyźniak, Paweł. 2020. *Engraved Gems and Propaganda in the Roman Republic and under Augustus*. Archaeopress.

Gonnella, R. 2001. "New Evidence for the Dating of the Reign of Vonones I." *Numismatic Chronicle* 161: 67–73.

Goody, Esther N. 1982. *Parenthood and Social Reproduction: Fostering and Occupational Roles in West Africa*. Cambridge University Press.

Goody, Jack. 1969. "Adoption in Cross-Cultural Perspective." *Comparative Studies in Society and History* 11 (1): 55–78.

Goodyear, F. R. D., ed. 1981. *The Annals of Tacitus, Books 1–6*. Vol. 2, Annals *1.55–81 and* Annals 2. Cambridge University Press.

Gowing, Alain M. 1990. "Tacitus and the Client Kings." *Transactions of the American Philological Association* 120: 315–31.

Grainger, John D. 1990. *Seleukos Nikator: Constructing a Hellenistic Kingdom*. Routledge.

Grayson, Albert Kirk, and Jamie Novotny. 2012. *The Royal Inscriptions of the Neo-Assyrian Period*. Vol. 3.1. Eisenbrauns.

Greatrex, Geoffrey. 2022. *Procopius of Caesarea: The Persian Wars: A Historical Commentary*. Cambridge University Press.

Greatrex, Geoffrey, and Jonathan Bardill. 1996. "Antiochus the *Praepositus*: A Persian Eunuch at the Court of Theodosius II." *Dumbarton Oaks Papers* 50: 171–97.

Green, C. M. C. 2007. *Roman Religion and the Cult of Diana at Aricia*. Cambridge University Press.

Gregoratti, Leonardo. 2013. "Parthian Women in Flavius Josephus." In *Jüdisch-hellenistische Literatur in ihrem interkulturellen Kontext*, edited by M. Hirschberger, 183–91. Peter Lang.

———. 2015. "In the Land West of the Euphrates: The Parthians in the Roman Empire." In *Soma 2011: Proceedings of the 15th Symposium on Mediterranean Archaeology, Held at the University of Catania, March 3–5th, 2011*, edited by P. Militello and H. Oniz, vol. 2, 731–35. Archaeopress.

———. 2017. "Corbulo versus Vologases: A Game of Chess for Armenia." *Electrum* 24: 107–21.

———. 2018. "Tacitus and the Great Kings." In *Iran and the West: Cultural Perceptions from the Sasanian Empire to the Islamic Republic*, edited by David Bagot and Margaux Whiskin, 21–34. I. B. Tauris.

———. 2020. "Augustus and the Parthians." In *Augustan Papers: New Approaches to the Age of Augustus on the Bimillennium of His Death*, edited by Maria Cristina Pimentel et al., vol. 1, 79–93. Georg Olms.

———. 2023. "'Parthian' Women in Vīs and Rāmīn." In *The Reality of Women in the Universe of the Ancient Novel*, edited by María Paz López Martínez, Carlos Sánchez-Moreno Ellart, and Ana Zaera García, 396–406. John Benjamins.

Grenet, Frantz. 2003. *Le geste d'Ardashir fils de Pâbag = Kārnāmag ī Ardaxšēr ī Pābagān*. Éditions A Die.

Griffin, A. H. F. 1997. "A Commentary on Ovid 'Metamorphoses' Book XI." *Hermathena*, nos. 162–63: 1–290.

Griffin, Miriam. 1984. *Nero: The End of a Dynasty*. Routledge.

———. 1990. "Claudius in Tacitus." *Classical Quarterly* 40 (2): 482–501.

———. 1992. *Seneca: A Philosopher in Politics*. Clarendon.

———. 1997. "The Senate's Story (Review of Das Senatus Consultum de Cn. Pisone Patre by Werner Eck, Antonio Caballos, Fernando Fernández)." *Journal of Roman Studies* 87: 249–63.

Griffith, R. Drew. 2010. "ΤΡΕΦΕΙΝ ΓΑΛΑ (Odyssey 9.246)." *Classical Philology* 105 (3): 301–8.

Gropp, Gerd, and Saifeddin Nadjmabadi. 1970. "Bericht über eine Reise in West- und Südiran." *Archaeologische Mitteilungen aus Iran* 3: 173–230.

Gross, Simcha. 2023. "Hopeful Rebels and Anxious Romans: Jewish Interconnectivity in the Great Revolt and Beyond." *Historia: Zeitschrift für Alte Geschichte* 72 (4): 479–513.

———. 2024. *Babylonian Jews and Sasanian Imperialism in Late Antiquity*. Cambridge University Press.

Grubbs, Judith Evans, ed. 2002. *Women and the Law in the Roman Empire: A Sourcebook on Marriage, Divorce, and Widowhood*. Routledge.

———. 2013. "Infant Exposure and Infanticide." In *The Oxford Handbook of Childhood and Education in the Classical World*, edited by Judith Evans Grubbs and Tim Parkin, 83–107. Oxford University Press.

Gruen, Erich S. 1996. "The Expansion of the Empire under Augustus." In *The Cambridge Ancient History*, edited by Alan K. Bowman et al., 2nd ed., 147–97. Cambridge University Press.

———. 2011. *Rethinking the Other in Antiquity*. Princeton University Press.

———. 2017. "Josephus' Image of the Parthians." In *Parthika: Greek and Roman Authors' Views of the Arsacid Empire*, edited by Josef Wiesehöfer and Sabine Müller, 223–40. Harrassowitz.

Guscin, Mark. 2009. *The Image of Edessa*. Brill.

Güterbock, Hans Gustav. 1956. "The Deeds of Suppiluliuma as Told by His Son, Mursili II." *Journal of Cuneiform Studies* 10 (2–4): 41–68, 75–98, 107–30.

Gyselen, Rika. 2007. *Sasanian Seals and Sealings in the A. Saeedi Collection*. Peeters.

———. 2016. "The Parthian Language in Early Sasanian Times." In *The Parthian and Early Sasanian Empires: Adaptation and Expansion*, edited by Vesta Sarkhosh Curtis et al., 61–68. Oxbow.

———. 2019. *La géographie administrative de l'Empire sassanide: Les témoignages épigraphiques en moyen-perse*. Groupe pour l'étude de la civilisation du Moyen-Orient.

Gzella, Holger. 2008. "Aramaic in the Parthian Period: The Arsacid Inscriptions." In *Aramaic in Its Historical and Linguistic Setting*, edited by Holger Gzella and Margaretha L. Folmer, 107–30. Harrassowitz.

Habinek, Thomas. 1997. "The Invention of Sexuality in the World-City of Rome." In *The Roman Cultural Revolution*, edited by Thomas Habinek and Alessandro Schiesaro, 23–43. Cambridge University Press.

Hackl, Ursula, Bruno Jacobs, and Dieter Weber, eds. 2010. *Quellen zur Geschichte des Partherreiches: Textsammlung mit Übersetzungen und Kommentaren.* 3 vols. Vandenhoeck & Ruprecht.

Hackl, Ursula, Hanna Jenni, and Christoph Schneider, eds. 2003. *Quellen zur Geschichte der Nabatäer: Textsammlung mit Übersetzung und Kommentar.* Vandenhoeck & Ruprecht.

Hall, Edith. 1989. *Inventing the Barbarian: Greek Self-Definition through Tragedy.* Clarendon.

Hall, Joshua R. 2021. "The State of the State: Why It Matters for the Ancient World." *Ancient World Magazine,* www.ancientworldmagazine.com/articles/state-ancient-world (accessed August 19, 2024).

Hallo, William W., and K. Lawson Younger, eds. 2003. *The Context of Scripture.* 3 vols. Brill.

Hammond, N. G. L. 1989. *The Macedonian State: Origins, Institutions, and History.* Clarendon.

———. 1990. "Royal Pages, Personal Pages, and Boys Trained in the Macedonian Manner during the Period of the Temenid Monarchy." *Historia: Zeitschrift für Alte Geschichte* 39 (3): 261–90.

———. 1997. "What May Philip Have Learnt as a Hostage in Thebes?" *Greek, Roman, and Byzantine Studies* 38: 355–72.

Hanaway, Jr., W. L. 1988. S.v. "Bahrām V Gōr in Persian Legend and Literature." In *Encyclopedia Iranica,* www.iranicaonline.org/articles/bahram-05-lit (accessed August 19, 2024).

Hansen, Anna. 2008. "Bonds of Affection between Children and Their Foster-Parents in Early Icelandic Society." In *Emotions in the Household, 1200–1900,* edited by Susan Broomhall, 38–52. Palgrave Macmillan.

Hansen, Valerie. 2003. "New Work on the Sogdians, the Most Important Traders on the Silk Road, A.D. 500–1000." *T'oung Pao* 89 (1–3): 149–61.

Hardie, Philip. 2007. "Images of the Persian Wars in Rome." In *Cultural Responses to the Persian Wars: Antiquity to the Third Millennium,* edited by Emma Bridges, Edith Hall, and P. J. Rhodes, 127–43. Oxford University Press.

Harl, Kenneth W. 2016. "Rome's Greatest Foe: Rome versus Parthia and Sassanid Persia." In *Great Strategic Rivalries: From the Classical World to the Cold War,* edited by James Lacey, 103–53. Oxford University Press.

Harmatta, J. 1958. "Die parthischen Ostraka aus Dura-Europos." *Acta Antiqua Academiae Scientarum Hungaricae* 6: 87–175.

Hartmann, Udo. 2009. "Ein Arsakide im Heer des Septimius Severus: Überlegungen zu den Hintergründen des zweiten Partherkrieges." *Electrum* 15: 249–66.

Hartog, François. 1988. *The Mirror of Herodotus: The Representation of the Other in the Writing of History.* University of California Press.

Haruta, Seiro. 1992. "Formation of Verbal Logograms (Aramaeograms) in Parthian." *Orient* 28: 17–36.

Hauser, Stefan. 2005. "Die ewigen Nomaden: Bemerkungen zu Herkunft, Militär, Staatsaufbau und nomadischen Traditionen der Arsakiden." In *Krieg-Gesellschaft-Institutionen: Beiträge zu einer vergleichenden Kriegsgeschichte,* edited by Burkhard Meißner, Oliver Schmitt, and Michael Sommer, 163–208. Akademie.

———. 2006. "Was There No Paid Standing Army? A Fresh Look on Military and Political Institutions in the Arsacid Empire." In *Arms and Armour as Indicators of Cultural Transfer: The Steppes and the Ancient World from Hellenistic Times to the Early Middle Ages,* edited by M. Mode and J. Tubach, 295–319. Reichert.

———. 2016. "Münzen, Medien und der Aufbau des Arsakidenreiches." In *Diwan: Untersuchungen zu Geschichte und Kultur des Nahen Ostens und des östlichen Mittelmeerraumes im Altertum: Festschrift für Josef Wiesehöfer zum 65. Geburtstag*, edited by Carsten Binder, Henning Börm, and Andreas Luther, 433–92. Wellem.

———. 2022. "Parthia and the Geography of Empire." In *Persia: Ancient Iran and the Classical World*, edited by Jeffrey Spier, Timothy Potts, and Sara E. Cole, 165–73. J. Paul Getty Museum.

Hawley, Richard. 2007. "Lords of the Rings: Ring-Wearing, Status, and Identity in the Age of Pliny the Elder." In *Vita Vigilia Est: Essays in Honour of Barbara Levick*, edited by Edward Bispham and Greg Rowe, 103–11. Institute of Classical Studies.

Healey, John F. 2018. "The Pre-Christian Religions of the Syriac-Speaking Regions." In *The Syriac World*, edited by Daniel King, 47–67. Routledge.

Heather, Peter. 2013. *The Restoration of Rome: Barbarian Popes and Imperial Pretenders*. Oxford University Press.

Heffron, Yağmur. 2017. "Testing the Middle Ground in Assyro-Anatolian Marriages of the *Kārum* Period." *Iraq* 79: 71–83.

Heil, Matthäus. 1997. *Die orientalische Außenpolitik des Kaisers Nero*. Tuduv-Verlagsgesellschaft.

———. 2017. "Die Parther bei Tacitus." In *Parthika: Greek and Roman Authors' Views of the Arsacid Empire*, edited by Josef Wiesehöfer and Sabine Müller, 259–78. Harrassowitz.

Hekster, Olivier. 2015. *Emperors and Ancestors: Roman Rulers and the Constraints of Tradition*. Oxford University Press.

Helms, Mary W. 1988. *Ulysses' Sail: An Ethnographic Odyssey of Power, Knowledge, and Geographical Distance*. Princeton University Press.

Hemelrijk, Emily A. 2015. *Hidden Lives, Public Personae: Women and Civic Life in the Roman West*. Oxford University Press.

Henning, W. B. 1965. "A Sogdian God." *Bulletin of the School of Oriental and African Studies* 28 (2): 242–54.

Herman, Geoffrey. 2012. *A Prince without a Kingdom: The Exilarch in the Sasanian Era*. Mohr Siebeck.

Herrmann, Georgina. 1977. *The Iranian Revival*. Elsevier-Phaidon.

Herzfeld, Ernst. 1932. "Sakastan: Geschichtliche Untersuchungen zu den Ausgrabungen am Kūh ī Khwādja." *Archaeologische Mitteilungen aus Iran* 4: 1–116.

Heubner, Henricus, ed. 1994. *P. Cornelius Tacitus: Libri Qui Supersunt*. Vol. 1, *Annales*. Teubner.

Hey, David. 1996. *The Oxford Companion to Local and Family History*. Oxford University Press.

Heyworth, S. J. 2007a. *Cynthia: A Companion to the Text of Propertius*. Oxford University Press.

———. 2007b. "Propertius, Patronage and Politics." *Bulletin of the Institute of Classical Studies* 50: 93–128.

———, ed. 2019. *Ovid, Fasti Book III*. Cambridge University Press.

Hillers, Delbert R., and Eleonora Cussini. 1996. *Palmyrene Aramaic Texts*. Johns Hopkins University Press.

Hoftijzer, J., and K. Jongeling. 1995. *Dictionary of the North-West Semitic Inscriptions*. 2 vols. Brill.

Hölkeskamp, Karl-Joachim. 2004. *Senatus populusque romanus: Die politische Kultur der Republik—Dimensionen und Deutungen*. Franz Steiner.

Hollander, Lee M. 1964. *Snorri Sturluson: Heimskringla; History of the Kings of Norway*. University of Texas Press.

Hollis, A. S. 1970. "Ovid, A.A. i. 197–8: The Wrong Phraates?" *Classical Review* 20 (2): 141–42.

———, ed. 1977. *Ovid: Ars Amatoria, Book I*. Clarendon.

Hölscher, Tonio. 1988. "Beobachtungen zu römischen historischen Denkmälern III." *Archäologischer Anzeiger* 3: 523–41.

Hopkins, Keith. 1983. *Death and Renewal*. Cambridge University Press.

Hornblower, Simon. 1991. *A Commentary on Thucydides*. Vol. 1. Clarendon.

Howard, George. 1981. *The Teaching of Addai*. Scholars Press.

Howard-Johnston, James. 2021. *The Last Great War of Antiquity*. Oxford University Press.

Howell, Signe. 2009. "Adoption of the Unrelated Child: Some Challenges to the Anthropological Study of Kinship." *Annual Review of Anthropology* 38: 149–66.

Huang, Debby Chih-Yen, and Paul R. Goldin. 2018. "Polygyny and Its Discontents: A Key to Understanding Traditional Chinese Society." In *Sexuality in China: Histories of Power and Pleasure*, edited by Howard Chiang, 16–33. University of Washington Press.

Huber, Irene, and Udo Hartmann. 2006. "'Denn ihrem Diktat vermochte der König nicht zu widersprechen . . . ' Die Position der Frauen am Hof der Arsakiden." In *Proceedings of the 5th Conference of the Societas Iranologica Europæa, Ravenna, 6–11 Oct 2003*, edited by Antonio Panaino and Andrea Piras, vol. 1, 485–517. Mimesis.

Huebner, Sabine R. 2013. "Adoption and Fosterage in the Ancient Eastern Mediterranean." In *The Oxford Handbook of Childhood and Education in the Classical World*, edited by Judith Evans Grubbs and Tim G. Parkin, 510–31. Oxford University Press.

Huff, Dietrich. 2008. "Formation and Ideology of the Sasanian State in the Context of Archaeological Evidence." In *The Sasanian Era*, edited by Vesta Sarkhosh Curtis and Sarah Stewart, 31–59. I. B. Tauris.

Hurlet, Frédéric. 1997. *Les collègues du prince sous Auguste et Tibère: De la légalité républicaine à la légitimité dynastique*. École Française de Rome.

Hurley, Donna W. 1993. *An Historical and Historiographical Commentary on Suetonius' Life of C. Caligula*. Scholars Press.

Huyse, Philip. 1999. *Die dreisprachige Inschrift Šābuhrs I. an der Kaʿba-i Zarduŝt (ŠKZ)*. 2 vols. School of Oriental and African Studies.

Hyland, John. 2013. "Vishtaspa *Krny*: An Achaemenid Military Official in 4th-Century Bactria." *ARTA: Achaemenid Research on Texts and Archaeology* 2: 1–7.

———. 2018. "Hystaspes, Gobryas, and Elite Marriage Politics in Teispid Persia." *Dabir* 5: 30–35.

Icks, Martijn. 2016. "Turning Victory into Defeat: Negative Assessments of Imperial Triumphs in Greco-Roman Literature." In *Der römische Triumph in Prinzipat und Spätantike*, edited by Fabian Goldbeck and Johannes Wienand, 317–33. De Gruyter.

Imber, Colin. 2002. *The Ottoman Empire, 1300–1650: The Structure of Power*. Palgrave Macmillan.

Isaac, Benjamin. 1992. *The Limits of Empire: The Roman Army in the East*. Rev. ed. Clarendon.

———. 2004. *The Invention of Racism in Classical Antiquity*. Princeton University Press.

Itgenshorst, Tanja. 2005. *Tota illa pompa: Der Triumph in der römischen Republik*. Vandenhoeck & Ruprecht.

————. 2008. "Der Princeps triumphiert nicht: Vom Verschwinden des Siegesrituals in augusteischer Zeit." In *Triplici invectus triumpho: Der römische Triumph in augusteischer Zeit*, edited by Helmut Krasser, Dennis Pausch, and Ivana Petrovic, 27–54. Franz Steiner.

————. 2016. "Die Transformation des Triumphes in augusteischer Zeit." In *Der römische Triumph in Prinzipat und Spätantike*, edited by Fabian Goldbeck and Johannes Wienand, 59–81. De Gruyter.

Jackson Bonner, Michael R. 2014. "An Historiographical Study of Abū Ḥanīfa Aḥmad ibn Dāwūd ibn Wanand al-Dīnawarī's *Kitāb al-Aḥbār al-Ṭiwāl* (Especially of That Part Dealing with the Sasanian Kings)." PhD diss., Oxford University.

————. 2020. *The Last Empire of Iran*. Gorgias Press.

Jacobs, Bruno, and Robert Rollinger, eds. 2021. *A Companion to the Achaemenid Persian Empire*. 2 vols. Wiley Blackwell.

Jakob, Stefan. 2017. "The Middle Assyrian Period (14th to 11th Century BCE)." In *A Companion to Assyria*, edited by Eckart Frahm, 117–42. Wiley Blackwell.

James, David, ed. 2009. *Early Islamic Spain: The History of Ibn al-Qūṭiya; A Study of the Unique Arabic Manuscript in the Bibliothèque Nationale de France, Paris, with a Translation, Notes, and Comments*. Routledge.

Jeffreys, Elizabeth, Michael Jeffreys, and Roger Scott. 2017. *The Chronicle of John Malalas*. Brill.

Johnson, Kent M., and Kathleen S. Paul. 2016. "Bioarchaeology and Kinship: Integrating Theory, Social Relatedness, and Biology in Ancient Family Research." *Journal of Archaeological Research* 24 (1): 75–123.

Jones, C. P. 1999. *Kinship Diplomacy in the Ancient World*. Harvard University Press.

Jordan, Mark. 1999. "Saint Pelagius, Ephebe and Martyr." In *Queer Iberia: Sexualities, Cultures, and Crossings from the Middle Ages to the Renaissance*, edited by Josiah Blackmore and Gregory S. Hutcheson, 23–47. Duke University Press.

Joshel, Sandra R. 1986. "Nurturing the Master's Child: Slavery and the Roman Child-Nurse." *Signs* 12 (1): 3–22.

Jucker, Hans. 1977. "Dokumentationen zur Augustusstatue von Primaporta." *Hefte des archäologischen Seminars der Universität Bern* 3: 16–37.

Jussen, Dennis. 2022. "Foreign Royals at the Imperial Court." In *The Roman Emperor and His Court, c. 30 BC–c. AD 300*. Vol. 1, *Historical Essays*, edited by Benjamin Kelly and Angela Hug, 146–67. Cambridge University Press.

Justi, Ferdinand. 1895. *Iranisches Namenbuch*. Elwert.

Kagan, Kim. 2011. "Spies Like Us: Treason and Identity in the Late Roman Empire." In *Romans, Barbarians, and the Transformation of the Roman World: Cultural Interaction and the Creation of Identity in Late Antiquity*, edited by Ralph W. Mathisen and Danuta Shanzer, 161–73. Ashgate.

Kähler, Heinz. 1959. *Die Augustusstatue von Primaporta*. M. DuMont Schauberg.

Kahrstedt, Ulrich. 1950. *Artabanos III. und seine Erben*. A. Francke.

Kaim, Barbara. 2016. "Women, Dance, and the Hunt: Splendour and Pleasures of Court Life in Arsacid and Early Sasanian Art." In *The Parthian and Early Sasanian Empires: Adaptation and Expansion; Proceedings of a Conference Held in Vienna, 14–16 June 2012*, edited by Vesta Sarkhosh Curtis et al., 90–105. Oxbow.

Karras-Klapproth, Margarete. 1988. *Prosopographische Studien zur Geschichte des Parther-reiches auf der Grundlage antiker literarischer Überlieferung*. In Kommission bei R. Habelt.

Katzenstein, Peter J., ed. 1996. *The Culture of National Security: Norms and Identity in World Politics*. Columbia University Press.

Keaveney, Arthur. 1981. "Roman Treaties with Parthia circa 95–circa 64 B.C." *American Journal of Philology* 102 (2): 195–212.

———. 1982. "The King and the War-Lords: Romano-Parthian Relations Circa 64–53 B.C." *American Journal of Philology* 103 (4): 412–28.

Keddie, J. N. 1975. "Italicus and Claudius: Tacitus, *Annales* Xi 16–17." *Antichthon* 9: 52–60.

Keitel, Elizabeth. 1978. "The Role of Parthia and Armenia in Tacitus *Annals* 11 and 12." *American Journal of Philology* 99 (4): 462–73.

Kelk, Donald Christopher. 1975. "A Commentary on Ovid's *Ars Amatoria* 1.1–504." PhD diss., McMaster University.

Kellens, Jean. 2021. "The Achaemenids and the Avesta." In *A Companion to the Achaemenid Persian Empire*, edited by Bruno Jacobs and Robert Rollinger, 1211–20. Wiley Blackwell.

Kellert, Stephen H. 1993. *In the Wake of Chaos: Unpredictable Order in Dynamical Systems*. University of Chicago Press.

Khaleghi-Motlagh, Djalal, ed. 1990. *Abu'l-Qasem Ferdowsi: The Shahnameh (The Book of Kings)*. Vol. 2. Mazda.

———. 2012. *Women in the Shāhnāmeh: Their History and Social Status within the Framework of Ancient and Medieval Sources*. Mazda.

Khaleghi-Motlagh, Djalal, and Abolfazl Khatibi, eds. 2007. *Abu'l-Qasem Ferdowsi: The Shahnameh (The Book of Kings)*. Vol. 7. Mazda.

Khaleghi-Motlagh, Djalal, and M. Omidsalar, eds. 2005. *Abu'l-Qasem Ferdowsi: The Shahnameh (The Book of Kings)*. Vol. 6. Mazda.

Khatchadourian, Lori. 2016. *Imperial Matter: Ancient Persia and the Archaeology of Empires*. University of California Press.

Kienast, Dietmar. 1973. *Philipp II. von Makedonien und das Reich der Achaimeniden*. W. Fink.

Kierdorf, Wilhelm, ed. 1992. *Sueton: Leben des Claudius und Nero*. F. Schöningh.

Kindstrand, Jan Fredrik. 1981. *Anacharsis: The Legend and the Apophthegmata*. Almqvist & Wiksell.

King, Carol J. 2018. *Ancient Macedonia*. Routledge.

King, Rhyne. 2020. "Local Powerbrokers in Iranian and Post-Iranian Bactria (ca. 300–800 CE): Aristocrats, Dependents, and Imperial Regimes." In *The Limits of Empire in Ancient Afghanistan: Rule and Resistance in the Hindu Kush, circa 600 BCE–600 CE*, edited by Richard Payne and Rhyne King, 245–70. Harrassowitz.

Kirshner, Jonathan. 2022. *An Unwritten Future: Realism and Uncertainty in World Politics*. Princeton University Press.

Kiss, Attila. 2015. "Per arma adoptio: Eine gotische Sitte in den frühmittelalterlichen schriftlichen Quellen." In *Romania Gothica II: The Frontier World: Romans, Barbarians and Military Culture*, edited by Tivadar Vida, 95–105. Eötvös Loránd Univ. / Martin Optiz Kiadó.

Kissane, Dylan. 2014. *Beyond Anarchy: The Complex and Chaotic Dynamics of International Politics*. Ibidem.

Kitchen, Kenneth A. 1998. "Amenhotep III and Mesopotamia." In *Amenhotep III: Perspectives on His Reign*, edited by David O'Connor and Eric H. Cline, 250–61. University of Michigan Press.

Kleijwegt, Marc. 1994. "Caligula's 'Triumph' at Baiae." *Mnemosyne* 47 (5): 652–71.

Kleiner, Diana E. E. 1992. *Roman Sculpture*. Yale University Press.

———. 2005. "Semblance and Storytelling in Augustan Rome." In *The Cambridge Companion to the Age of Augustus*, edited by Karl Galinsky, 197–233. Cambridge University Press.

Kleiner, Diana E. E., and Bridget Buxton. 2008. "Pledges of Empire: The Ara Pacis and the Donations of Rome." *American Journal of Archaeology* 112 (1): 57–89.

Kleiner, Fred S. 1985. *The Arch of Nero in Rome: A Study of the Roman Honorary Arch before and under Nero*. L'Erma di Bretschneider.

Klinkott, Hilmar. 2005. *Der Satrap: Ein achaimenidischer Amtsräger und seine Handlungsspielräume*. Antike.

Koestermann, Erich. 1963–68. *Cornelius Tacitus, Annalen*. 4 vols. C. Winter.

Kolesnikov, A. 2012. S.v. "Eunuchs, II: The Sasanian Period." In *Encyclopedia Iranica*, https:// iranicaonline.org/articles/eunuchs#ii (accessed August 19, 2024).

König, Jason. 2005. *Athletics and Literature in the Roman Empire*. Cambridge University Press.

Kotwal, Firoze M. P. 1969. *The Supplementary Texts to the* Šāyest Nē Šāyest. Royal Danish Academy of Sciences and Letters.

Kotyk, Jeffrey. 2024. *Sino-Iranian and Sino-Arabian Relations in Late Antiquity: China and the Parthians, Sasanians, and Arabs in the First Millennium*. Brill.

Krasser, Helmut, Dennis Pausch, and Ivana Petrovic, eds. 2008. *Triplici invectus triumpho: Der römische Triumph in augusteischer Zeit*. Franz Steiner.

Kühne, Cord. 1973. *Die Chronologie der internationalen Korrespondenz von El-Amarna*. Butzon & Bercker.

Kuttner, Ann L. 1995. *Dynasty and Empire in the Age of Augustus: The Case of the Boscoreale Cups*. University of California Press.

———. 1999. "Hellenistic Images of Spectacle, from Alexander to Augustus." In *The Art of Ancient Spectacle*, edited by Bettina Ann Bergmann and Christine Kondoleon, 96–123. National Gallery of Art.

La Rocca, Eugenio. 1983. *Ara Pacis Augustae*. L'Erma di Bretschneider.

———. 1992. "'Disiecta membra Neroniana'. L'arco partico di Nerone sul Campidoglio." In *Kotinos: Festschrift für Erika Simon*, edited by Heide Froning, Tonio Hölscher, and Harald Mielsch, 400–14. Philipp von Zabern.

Labas, Kamila. 2014. "Studien zur Geschichte der georgischen Länder vom 4. bis zum früheren 7. Jh." PhD diss., Universität Wien.

Laes, Christian. 2003. "Desperately Different? *Delicia* Children in the Roman Household." In *Early Christian Families in Context: An Interdisciplinary Dialogue*, edited by David L. Balch and Carolyn Osiek, 298–326. Eerdmans.

———. 2016. *Children in the Roman Empire: Outsiders Within*. Cambridge University Press.

Lafont, B. 1987. "Les filles du roi de Mari." In *La Femme dans le Proche-Orient antique*, edited by J.-M. Durand, 113–21. Editions Recherche sur les Civilisations.

———. 2001. "The Women of the Palace at Mari." In *Everyday Life in Ancient Mesopotamia*, edited by Jean Bottéro and André Finet, 127–40. Edinburgh University Press.

Lallemand, Suzanne. 1988. "Adoption, fosterage et alliance." *Anthropologie et Sociétés* 12 (2): 25–40.

Lamp, Kathleen. 2009. "The *Ara Pacis Augustae*: Visual Rhetoric in Augustus' Principate." *Rhetoric Society Quarterly* 39 (1): 1–24.

Lane Fox, Robin. 2011. "399–369 BC." In *Brill's Companion to Ancient Macedon: Studies in the Archaeology and History of Macedon, 650 BC–300 AD*, edited by Robin Lane Fox, 209–34. Brill.

Lang, Mabel L. 1967. "Scapegoat Pausanias." *Classical Journal* 63 (2): 79–85.

Lange, Carsten Hjort. 2009. *Res Publica Constituta: Actium, Apollo, and the Accomplishment of the Triumviral Assignment*. Brill.

———. 2016a. "Mock the Triumph: Cassius Dio, Triumph and Triumph-Like Celebrations." In *Cassius Dio: Greek Intellectual and Roman Politician*, edited by Jesper Majbom Madsen and Carsten Hjort Lange, 92–114. Brill.

———. 2016b. *Triumphs in the Age of Civil War: The Late Republic and the Adaptability of Triumphal Tradition*. Bloomsbury.

Larmour, David H. J. 2007. "Holes in the Body: Sites of Abjection in Juvenal's Rome." In *The Sites of Rome: Time, Space, Memory*, edited by David H. J. Larmour and Diana Spencer, 168–210. Oxford University Press.

Lavan, Myles. 2013. *Slaves to Rome: Paradigms of Empire in Roman Culture*. Cambridge University Press.

———. 2016. "The Spread of Roman Citizenship, 14–212 CE: Quantification in the Face of High Uncertainty." *Past and Present* 230 (1): 3–46.

———. 2019. "Epistemic Uncertainty, Subjective Probability, and Ancient History." *Journal of Interdisciplinary History* 50 (1): 91–111.

Lee, A. D. 1991. "The Role of Hostages in Roman Diplomacy with Sasanian Persia." *Historia: Zeitschrift für Alte Geschichte* 40 (3): 366–74.

Leichty, Erle, ed. 2011. *The Royal Inscriptions of Esarhaddon, King of Assyria (680–669 BC)*. The Royal Inscriptions of the Neo-Assyrian Period 4. Eisenbrauns.

Leinaweaver, Jessaca B. 2008. *The Circulation of Children: Kinship, Adoption, and Morality in Andean Peru*. Duke University Press.

———. 2014. "Informal Kinship-Based Fostering around the World: Anthropological Findings." *Child Development Perspectives* 8 (3): 131–36.

———. 2018. "Adoption." In *The Open Cambridge Encyclopedia of Anthropology*, edited by F. Stein et al. Available at http://doi.org/10.29164/18adopt (accessed August 19, 2024).

Lemos, T. M. 2011. "'Like the Eunuch Who Does Not Beget': Gender, Mutilation, and Negotiated Status in the Ancient Near East." In *Disability Studies and Biblical Literature*, edited by Candida R. Moss and Jeremy Schipper, 47–66. Palgrave Macmillan.

Lendon, J. E. 2002. "Primitivism and Ancient Foreign Relations." *Classical Journal* 97 (4): 375–84.

———. 2010. *Song of Wrath: The Peloponnesian War Begins*. Basic.

Lenfant, Dominique. 2021. "Eunuchs as Guardians of Women in Achaemenid Persia: Orientalism and Back Projection in Modern Scholarship." *Greek, Roman, and Byzantine Studies* 61: 456–74.

Lenski, Noel Emmanuel. 2002. *Failure of Empire: Valens and the Roman State in the Fourth Century A.D.* University of California Press.

Lenz, Friedrich Walter. 1969. *Ovid: Die Liebeskunst*. Akademie.

Leone, Anna. 2000. "Darius Rex a Nemi." In *Nemi—Status Quo: Recent Research at Nemi and the Sanctuary of Diana*, edited by J. Rasmus Brandt et al., 29–34. L'Erma di Bretschneider.

Lerouge, Charlotte. 2007. *L'image des Parthes dans le monde gréco-romain*. Franz Steiner.

Lerouge-Cohen, Charlotte. 2010. "Entre légende monétaire et légende noire: De nouveau sur Q. Labienus Parthicus Imp(erator)." *Historia: Zeitschrift für Alte Geschichte* 59: 176–88.

Levi, A. H. T., ed. 1986. *Collected Works of Erasmus: Literary and Educational Writings 5–6*. University of Toronto Press.

Levick, Barbara. 1999. *Tiberius the Politician*. Routledge.

———. 2013a. "C. Plinius Secundus." In *The Fragments of the Roman Historians*, edited by Tim Cornell, vol. 1, 525–34. Oxford University Press.

———. 2013b. "Cluvius Rufus." In *The Fragments of the Roman Historians*, edited by Tim Cornell, vol. 1, 549–60. Oxford University Press.

———. 2015. *Claudius*. 2nd ed. Routledge.

Lévi-Strauss, Claude. 1969. *The Elementary Structures of Kinship*. Edited by Rodney Needham. Translated by James Harle Bell and John Richard von Sturmer. Beacon Press.

Lewis, David M. 2018. *Greek Slave Systems in Their Eastern Mediterranean Context, c. 800–146 BC*. Oxford University Press.

Lindsay, Hugh. 2001. "Adoption and Its Function in Cross-Cultural Contexts." In *Childhood, Class, and Kin in the Roman World*, edited by Suzanne Dixon, 190–204. Routledge.

———. 2011. "Adoption and Heirship in Greece and Rome." In *A Companion to Families in the Greek and Roman Worlds*, edited by Beryl Rawson, 346–60. Blackwell.

Lintott, Andrew. 1999. *The Constitution of the Roman Republic*. Oxford University Press.

Lippold, Adolf. 1965. "Pausanias von Sparta und die Perser." *Rheinisches Museum für Philologie* 108 (4): 320–41.

Liverani, Mario. 2000. "The Great Powers' Club." In *Amarna Diplomacy: The Beginnings of International Relations*, edited by Raymond Cohen and Raymond Westbrook, 15–27. Johns Hopkins University Press.

———. 2001. *International Relations in the Ancient Near East, 1600–1100 BC*. Palgrave.

Livshits, V. A., and A. B. Nikitin. 1995. "Parthian and Middle-Persian Documents From South Turkmenistan: A Survey." *Ancient Civilizations from Scythia to Siberia* 1 (3): 312–23.

Livshits, V. A., and E. S. Xurshudjan. 1989. "Le titre *mrtpty* sur un seau [sic] parthe et l'arménien *mardpet*." *Studia Iranica* 18 (2): 169–91.

Llewellyn-Jones, Lloyd. 2002. "Eunuchs and the Royal Harem in Achaemenid Persia (559–331 BC)." In *Eunuchs in Antiquity and Beyond*, edited by Shaun Tougher, 19–49. Classical Press of Wales.

———. 2020. "Violence and the Mutilated Body in Achaemenid Iran." In *The Cambridge World History of Violence*. Vol. 1, *The Prehistoric and Ancient Worlds*, edited by Garrett G. Fagan et al., 360–79. Cambridge University Press.

Llewellyn-Jones, Lloyd, and Alex McAuley. 2023. *Sister-Queens in the High Hellenistic Period: Kleopatra Thea and Kleopatra III*. Routledge.

Lohuizen-de Leeuw, J. E. van. 1949. *The "Scythian" Period: An Approach to the History, Art, Epigraphy, and Palaeography of North India from the 1st Century B.C. to the 3rd Century A.D.* Brill.

Lott, J. Bert. 2012. *Death and Dynasty in Early Imperial Rome: Key Sources with Text, Translation, and Commentary.* Cambridge University Press.

Louis, Nathalie. 2010. *Commentaire historique et traduction du Diuus Augustus de Suétone.* Latomus.

Low, Polly. 2007. *Interstate Relations in Classical Greece: Morality and Power.* Cambridge University Press.

Lukonin, V. G. 1983. "Political, Social, and Administrative Institutions, Taxes and Trade." In *The Cambridge History of Iran*, edited by E. Yarshater, vol. 3.1, 681–746. Cambridge University Press.

Luther, Andreas. 1999. "Die ersten Könige von Osrhoene." *Klio* 81 (2): 437–54.

———. 2010. "Zum Orientfeldzug des Gaius Caesar." *Gymnasium* 117: 103–27.

———. 2016. "Arcadius und die Perser." In *Diwan: Untersuchungen zu Geschichte und Kultur des Nahen Ostens und des östlichen Mittelmeerraumes im Altertum: Festschrift für Josef Wiesehöfer zum 65. Geburtstag*, edited by Carsten Binder, Henning Börm, and Andreas Luther, 647–63. Wellem.

———. 2018. "Zu den Dokumenten aus Avroman." *Gymnasium* 125 (2): 155–77.

Luukko, Mikko, and Greta van Buylaere, eds. 2002. *The Political Correspondence of Esarhaddon.* Helsinki University Press.

Ma, John. 2013. "Hellenistic Empires." In *The Oxford Handbook of the State in the Ancient Near East and Mediterranean*, edited by Peter Fibiger Bang and Walter Scheidel, 324–57. Oxford University Press.

Mac Dowall, David W. 2007. "Coinage from Iran to Gandhāra." In *On the Cusp of an Era: Art in the Pre-Kuṣāṇa World*, edited by Doris Srinivasan, 233–65. Brill.

Macdonald, Michael C. A., et al. 2015. "Arabs and Empires before the Sixth Century." In *Arabs and Empires before Islam*, edited by Greg Fisher, 11–89. Oxford University Press.

Mack, Beverly. 1991. "Royal Wives in Kano." In *Hausa Women in the Twentieth Century*, edited by Catherine Coles and Beverly Mack, 109–29. University of Wisconsin Press.

MacKenzie, D. N. 1971. *A Concise Pahlavi Dictionary.* Oxford University Press.

Macuch, Maria. 2009. "Pahlavi Literature." In *The Literature of Pre-Islamic Iran*, edited by Ronald E. Emmerick and Maria Macuch, 116–96. I. B. Tauris.

———. 2013. "Iranische Literaturen in vorislamischer Zeit." In *Handbuch Iranistik*, edited by Ludwig Paul, 281–311. Reichert.

———. 2014. "Ardashir's Genealogy Revisited." *Iran Nameh* 29 (2): 80–94.

Macurdy, Grace Harriet. 1932. *Hellenistic Queens: A Study of Woman-Power in Macedonia, Seleucid Syria, and Ptolemaic Egypt.* Johns Hopkins Press.

Maderna-Lauter, Caterina. 1988. "Glyptik." In *Kaiser Augustus und die verlorene Republik: Eine Ausstellung im Martin-Gropius-Bau, Berlin 7. Juni–14. August 1988*, edited by Wolfgang D. Heilmeyer, Eugenio La Rocca, and Hans G. Martin, 441–73. Philipp von Zabern.

Madreiter, Irene, and Udo Hartmann. 2021. "Women at the Arsakid Court." In *The Routledge Companion to Women and Monarchy in the Ancient Mediterranean World*, edited by Elizabeth Carney and Sabine Müller, 234–45. Routledge.

Maguinness, W. S. 1932. "Some Methods of the Latin Panegyrists." *Hermathena* 22 (47): 42–61.

Maksymiuk, Katarzyna. 2015. "The Pahlav-Mehrān Family: Faithful Allies of Xusrō I Anōšīrvān." *Metamorfozy Istorii* 6: 163–79.

———. 2018. "The Two Eyes of the Earth: The Problem of Respect in Sasanid-Roman Relations." *Greek, Roman, and Byzantine Studies* 58: 591–606.

Mallan, Christopher Thomas. 2013. "The Style, Method, and Programme of Xiphilinus' *Epitome* of Cassius Dio's *Roman History*." *Greek, Roman, and Byzantine Studies* 53 (3): 610–44.

Malloch, S. J. V. 2001. "Gaius' Bridge at Baiae and Alexander-*Imitatio*." *Classical Quarterly* 51 (1): 206–17.

———, ed. 2013. *The Annals of Tacitus: Book 11*. Cambridge University Press.

———, ed. 2020. *The* Tabula Lugdunensis: *A Critical Edition with Translation and Commentary*. Cambridge University Press.

Mango, Cyril. 1990. *Nikephoros, Patriarch of Constantinople. Short History*. Dumbarton Oaks.

Mango, Cyril, and Roger Scott. 1997. *The Chronicle of Theophanes Confessor: Byzantine and Near Eastern History, AD 284–813*. Clarendon.

Marcato, Enrico. 2018. *Personal Names in the Aramaic Inscriptions of Hatra*. Edizioni Ca' Foscari.

Marciak, Michał. 2014. *Izates, Helena, and Monobazos of Adiabene: A Study on Literary Traditions and History*. Harrassowitz.

———. 2017. *Sophene, Gordyene, and Adiabene: Three Regna Minora of Northern Mesopotamia between East and West*. Brill.

Marquart, J. 1895. "Beiträge zur Geschichte und Sage von Erān." *Zeitschrift der Deutschen Morgenländischen Gesellschaft* 49 (4): 628–72.

Martin, Ronald, ed. 2001. *Tacitus: Annals V & VI*. Aris & Phillips.

Martirosyan, Hrach K. 2010. *Etymological Dictionary of the Armenian Inherited Lexicon*. Brill.

Mascitelli, Daniele. 2006. "Il *rb* di Ǧadīma: Considerazioni sull'iscrizione bilingue greco-nabatea di Umm al-Ǧimāl (CIS A 192)." *Egitto e Vicino Oriente* 29: 231–37.

Mason, Steve. 2014. "Why Did Judaeans Go to War with Rome in 66–67 CE? Realist-Regional Perspectives." In *Jews and Christians in the First and Second Centuries: How to Write Their History*, edited by Peter J. Tomson and Joshua Schwartz, 126–206. Brill.

———. 2016. "Josephus as a Roman Historian." In *A Companion to Josephus*, edited by Honora Howell Chapman and Zuleika Rodgers, 89–107. Wiley Blackwell.

Master, Jonathan. 2016. *Provincial Soldiers and Imperial Instability in the* Histories *of Tacitus*. University of Michigan Press.

Mathisen, Ralph. 2009. "Provinciales, Gentiles, and Marriages between Romans and Barbarians in the Late Roman Empire." *Journal of Roman Studies* 99: 140–55.

Matthews, John F. 1989a. "Hostages, Philosophers, Pilgrims, and the Diffusion of Ideas in the Late Roman Mediterranean and Near East." In *Tradition and Innovation in Late Antiquity*, edited by F. M. Clover and R. S. Humphreys, 29–50. University of Wisconsin Press.

———. 1989b. *The Roman Empire of Ammianus*. Duckworth.

Maurer, Joseph A. 1949. "A Commentary on C. Suetonii Tranquilli Vita C. Caligulae Caesaris, Chapters I–XXI." PhD diss., University of Pennsylvania.

Mayes, Andrew D. H. 2016. "International Diplomacy in the Amarna Age." In *The Land of Canaan in the Late Bronze Age*, edited by Lester L. Grabbe, 147–58. Bloomsbury.

McCulloch, Harold Y. 1984. *Narrative Cause in the Annals of Tacitus*. Anton Hain.

McEvedy, Colin, and Richard Jones. 1978. *Atlas of World Population History*. Facts on File.

McGinn, Thomas A.J. 2002. "The Augustan Marriage Legislation and Social Practice: Elite Endogamy versus Male 'Marrying Down.'" In *Speculum Iuris: Roman Law as a Reflection of Social and Economic Life in Antiquity*, edited by Jean-Jacques Aubert and Adriaan Johan Boudewijn Sirks, 46–93. University of Michigan Press.

McMahon, Keith. 2013. "The Institution of Polygamy in the Chinese Imperial Palace." *Journal of Asian Studies* 72 (4): 917–36.

Mearsheimer, John J. 2001. *The Tragedy of Great Power Politics*. Norton.

Meier, Samuel A. 2000. "Diplomacy and International Marriages." In *Amarna Diplomacy: The Beginnings of International Relations*, edited by Raymond Cohen and Raymond Westbrook, 165–73. Johns Hopkins University Press.

Meisami, Julie Scott. 1987. *Medieval Persian Court Poetry*. Princeton University Press.

Meister, Jan B. 2016. "Tracht, Insignien und Performanz des Triumphators zwischen später Republik und früher Kaiserzeit." In *Der römische Triumph in Prinzipat und Spätantike*, edited by Fabian Goldbeck and Johannes Wienand, 83–102. De Gruyter.

Melville, Sarah C. 2004. "Neo-Assyrian Royal Women and Male Identity: Status as a Social Tool." *Journal of the American Oriental Society* 124 (1): 37–57.

———. 2005. "Royal Women and the Exercise of Power in the Ancient Near East." In *A Companion to the Ancient Near East*, edited by Daniel Snell, 219–28. Blackwell.

Meyer, Robin. 2017. "Iranian-Armenian Language Contact in and before the 5th Century CE: An Investigation into Pattern Replication and Societal Multilingualism." PhD diss., University of Oxford.

Michalowski, Piotr. 1993. *Letters from Early Mesopotamia*. Scholars Press.

Michel, Cécile. 2017. "Economy, Society, and Daily Life in the Old Assyrian Period." In *A Companion to Assyria*, edited by Eckart Frahm, 80–107. Wiley Blackwell.

Millar, Fergus. 1964. *A Study of Cassius Dio*. Clarendon.

Miller, Jared L. 2007. "Amarna Age Chronology and the Identity of Nibḫururiya in the Light of a Newly Reconstructed Hittite Text." *Altorientalische Forschungen* 34 (1): 256–97.

———. 2017. "Political Interactions between Kassite Babylonia and Assyria, Egypt, and Ḫatti during the Amarna Age." In *Karduniaš: Babylonia under the Kassites*, edited by Alexa Bartelmus and Katja Sternitzke, vol. 1, 93–111. De Gruyter.

Minns, Ellis H. 1915. "Parchments of the Parthian Period from Avroman in Kurdistan." *Journal of Hellenic Studies* 35: 22–65.

Minorsky, Vladimir. 1964. *Iranica: Twenty Articles*. University of Tehran Press.

Mirkovic, Alexander. 2004. *Prelude to Constantine: The Abgar Tradition in Early Christianity*. Peter Lang.

Miron, Dolores. 2000. "Transmitters and Representatives of Power: Royal Women in Ancient Macedonia." *Ancient Society* 30: 35–52.

Mitra, Rajendralala, ed. 1982. *The Nītisāra, or The Elements of Polity by Kāmandaki*. Translated by Sisir Kumar Mitra. Asiatic Society.

Mohler, S. L. 1940. "Slave Education in the Roman Empire." *Transactions and Proceedings of the American Philological Association* 71: 262–80.

Mokhtarian, Jason Sion. 2015. *Rabbis, Sorcerers, Kings, and Priests: The Culture of the Talmud in Ancient Iran*. University of California Press.

Moran, William L., ed. 1992. *The Amarna Letters*. Johns Hopkins University Press.

Morgenthau, Hans J. 1948. *Politics among Nations: The Struggle for Power and Peace*. Knopf.

Morkot, Robert. 2013. "From Conquered to Conqueror: The Organization of Nubia in the New Kingdom and the Kushite Administration of Egypt." In *Ancient Egyptian Administration*, edited by Juan Carlos Moreno García, 911–63. Brill.

Morley, Craig. 2015. "Rome and the Sasanian Empire in the Fifth Century A.D.: A Necessary Peace." PhD diss., University of Liverpool.

———. 2017. "The Arabian Frontier: A Keystone of the Sasanian Empire." In *Sasanian Persia: Between Rome and the Steppes of Eurasia*, edited by Eberhard W. Sauer, 268–83. Edinburgh University Press.

Morpurgo, L. 1931. "Nemi—Teatro ed altri edifici romani in contrada 'La Valle.'" *Notizie degli Scavi di Antichità* 7: 237–305.

Morris, Lauren. 2020. "Central Asian Empires." In *Handbook of Ancient Afro-Eurasian Economies*. Vol. 1, *Contexts*, edited by Sitta von Reden, 53–93. De Gruyter.

Morrison, George. 1972. *Vis and Ramin (Translated from the Persian of Fakhr ud-Dīn Gurgānī)*. Columbia University Press.

Moscovich, M. James. 1974. "Hostage Regulations in the Treaty of Zama." *Historia: Zeitschrift für Alte Geschichte* 23 (4): 417–27.

Mosig-Walburg, Karin. 2010. "Königtum und Adel in der Regierungszeit Ardashirs II., Shapurs III. und Wahrams IV." In *Commutatio et Contentio: Studies in the Late Roman, Sasanian, and Early Islamic Near East*, edited by Josef Wiesehöfer and Henning Börm, 133–58. Wellem.

Mratschek, Sigrid. 2013. "Nero the Imperial Misfit: Philhellenism in a Rich Man's World." In *A Companion to the Neronian Age*, edited by Emma Buckley and Martin T. Dinter, 45–62. Wiley-Blackwell.

Müller, Sabine. 2021. "Argead Women." In *The Routledge Companion to Women and Monarchy in the Ancient Mediterranean World*, edited by Elizabeth Carney and Sabine Müller, 294–306. Routledge.

Munt, Harry, et al. 2015. "Arabic and Persian Sources for Pre-Islamic Arabia." In *Arabs and Empires before Islam*, edited by Greg Fisher, 434–500. Oxford University Press.

Murphy, Trevor Morgan. 2004. *Pliny the Elder's Natural History: The Empire in the Encyclopedia*. Oxford University Press.

Murray, William M., and Photios M. Petsas. 1989. "Octavian's Campsite Memorial for the Actian War." *Transactions of the American Philosophical Society* 79 (4): i–172.

Nabel, Jake. 2015. "Horace and the Tiridates Episode." *Rheinisches Museum für Philologie* 158 (3–4): 304–25.

———. 2017a. "The Arsacids of Rome: Royal Hostages and Roman-Parthian Relations in the First Century CE." PhD diss., Cornell University.

———. 2017b. "The Seleucids Imprisoned: Arsacid-Roman Hostage Submission and Its Hellenistic Precedents." In *Arsacids, Romans, and Local Elites: Cross-Cultural Interactions of the Parthian Empire*, edited by Jason M. Schlude and Benjamin B. Rubin, 25–50. Oxbow.

———. 2018. "Alexander between Rome and Persia: Politics, Ideology, and History." In *Brill's Companion to the Reception of Alexander the Great*, edited by K. R. Moore, 197–232. Brill.

———. 2019a. "Lucan's Parthians in Nero's Rome." *Classical Philology* 114 (4): 604–25.

———. 2019b. "Remembering Intervention: Parthia in Rome's Civil Wars." *Historia: Zeitschrift für Alte Geschichte* 68 (3): 327–52.

———. 2019c. "Tiridates in the Forum, Peroz on His Knees: Religion and Reputation in Ancient Iranian Diplomacy." *Anabasis* 10: 214–36.

———. 2020. "Exemplary History and Arsacid Genealogy in Tacitus, *Annals* 6.31." *Dabir* 7: 175–91.

———. 2022. "The Parthian Empire." In *Persia: Ancient Iran and the Classical World*, edited by Jeffrey Spier, Timothy Potts, and Sara E. Cole, 157–63. J. Paul Getty Museum.

Nechaeva, Ekaterina. 2014. *Embassies—Negotiations—Gifts: Systems of East Roman Diplomacy in Late Antiquity*. Franz Steiner.

Nedergaard, Elisabeth. 1988. "The Four Sons of Phraates IV in Rome." In *East and West: Cultural Relations in the Ancient World*, edited by Tobias Fischer-Hansen, 102–15. Museum Tusculanum Press.

Needham, Rodney. 1971. "Remarks on the Analysis of Kinship and Marriage." In *Rethinking Kinship and Marriage*, edited by Rodney Needham, 1–34. Tavistock.

Neusner, Jacob. 1963. "Parthian Political Ideology." *Iranica Antiqua* 3: 40–59.

———. 1964. "The Conversion of Adiabene to Judaism: A New Perspective." *Journal of Biblical Literature* 83 (1): 60–66.

———. 1966. *A History of the Jews in Babylonia*. Vol. 2, *The Early Sasanian Period*. Brill.

Nexon, Daniel H. 2009. *The Struggle for Power in Early Modern Europe: Religious Conflict, Dynastic Empires, and International Change*. Princeton University Press.

Ní Mhaonaigh, Máire. 2007. *Brian Boru: Ireland's Greatest King?* Tempus.

Nielsen, Hanne Sigismund. 1987. "*Alumnus*: A Term of Relation Denoting Quasi-Adoption." *Classica et Mediaevalia* 38: 141–88.

———. 1997. "Interpreting Epithets in Roman Epitaphs." In *The Roman Family in Italy: Status, Sentiment, Space*, edited by Beryl Rawson and Paul Weaver, 169–204. Humanities Research Centre and Clarendon.

———. 2013. "Slave and Lower-Class Roman Children." In *The Oxford Handbook of Childhood and Education in the Classical World*, edited by Judith Evans Grubbs and Tim Parkin, 286–301. Oxford University Press.

Nikitin, A. B. 1992. "Middle Persian Ostraca from South Turkmenistan." *East and West* 42 (1): 103–29.

Nikolaishvili, Vakhtang. 2015. "Historical Topography of Greater *Mtskheta*." *Iberia-Colchis: Researches on the Archaeology and History of Georgia in the Classical and Early Medieval Period* 11: 174–81.

Ober, Josiah. 1982. "Tiberius and the Political Testament of Augustus." *Historia: Zeitschrift für Alte Geschichte* 31: 306–28.

O'Donnell, Tom C. 2016. "The Affect of Fosterage in Medieval Ireland." PhD diss., University College London.

———. 2020. *Fosterage in Medieval Ireland: An Emotional History*. Amsterdam University Press.

Ogden, Daniel. 1999. *Polygamy, Prostitutes, and Death: The Hellenistic Dynasties*. Duckworth.

Olbrycht, Marek. 1998a. "Das Arsakidenreich zwischen der Mediterranean Welt und Innerasien: Bemerkungen zur politischen Strategie der Arsakiden von Vologases I. bis zum Herrschaftsantritt des Vologases III. (50–147 n. Chr.)." In *Ancient Iran and the*

Mediterranean World: Proceedings of an International Conference in Honour of Professor Józef Wolski, Held at the Jagiellonian University, Cracow, in September 1996, edited by Edward Dąbrowa, 123–59. Jagiellonian University Press.

———. 1998b. "Die Kultur der Steppengebiete und die Beziehungen zwischen Nomaden und der Sesshaften Bevölkerung (Der Arsakidische Iran und die Nomadenvölker)." In *Das Partherreich und seine Zeugnisse / The Arsacid Empire: Sources and Documentation. Beiträge des internationalen Colloquiums, Eutin (27.-30. Juni 1996)*, edited by Josef Wiesehöfer, 11–43. Franz Steiner.

———. 1998c. *Parthia et Ulteriores Gentes: Die politischen Beziehungen zwischen dem arsakidischen Iran und den Nomaden der eurasischen Steppen.* tuduv-Verlagsgesellschaft.

———. 2003. "Parthia and Nomads of Central Asia: Elements of Steppe Origin in the Social and Military Developments of Arsacid Iran." In *Militar und Staatlichkeit: Beitrage des Kolloquiums vom 29.-30.4.2002*, edited by I. Schneider, 69–109. Orientwissenschaftliches Zentrum.

———. 2013a. "From Babylonia to the Fields of Bactria: Parthia after the Death of Artabanos II." *Przegląd Humanistyczny* 2: 101–7.

———. 2013b. *Imperium Parthicum: Kryzys i odbudowa państwa Arsakidów w pierwszej połowie pierwszego wieku po Chrystusie.* Towarzystwo Wydawnicze "Historia Iagellonica."

———. 2014. "The Genealogy of Artabanos II (AD 8/9–39/40), King of Parthia." *Miscellanea Anthropologica et Sociologica* 15 (3): 92–97.

———. 2016a. "Dynastic Connections in the Arsacid Empire and the Origins of the House of Sāsān." In *The Parthian and Early Sasanian Empires: Adaptation and Expansion*, edited by Vesta Sarkhosh Curtis et al., 23–35. Oxbow.

———. 2016b. "Manpower Resources and Army Organization in the Arsakid Empire." *Ancient Society* 46: 291–338.

———. 2018. "Augustus versus Phraates IV: Some Remarks on the Parthian-Roman Relations." In *Emas non quod opus est, sed quod necesse est. Beiträge zur Wirtschafts-, Sozial-, Rezeptions- und Wissenschaftsgeschichte der Antike: Festschrift für Hans-Joachim Drexhage zum 70. Geburtstag*, edited by Kai Ruffing and Kerstin Droß-Krüpe, 389–97. Harrassowitz.

———. 2021a. *Early Arsakid Parthia (ca. 250–165 B.C.).* Brill.

———. 2021b. S.v. "Phraates IV." In *Encyclopedia Iranica*, https://referenceworks.brill.com/display/entries/EIRO/COM-336464.xml (accessed August 19, 2024).

———. 2021c. S.v. "Phraates V." In *Encyclopedia Iranica*, https://referenceworks.brill.com/display/entries/EIRO/COM-336465.xml (accessed August 19, 2024).

———. 2021d. S.v. "Tacitus." In *Encyclopedia Iranica*, https://referenceworks.brill.com/display/entries/EIRO/COM-362447.xml (accessed August 19, 2024).

Olivelle, Patrick. 2013. *King, Governance, and Law in Ancient India: Kauṭilya's Arthaśāstra.* Oxford University Press.

Olsen, Birgit Anette. 1999. *The Noun in Biblical Armenian: Origin and Word-Formation with Special Emphasis on the Indo-European Heritage.* De Gruyter.

Omidsalar, Mahmoud, and Theresa Omidsalar. 1996. S.v. "Dāya." In *Encyclopedia Iranica*, www.iranicaonline.org/articles/daya (accessed August 19, 2024).

Osgood, Josiah. 2018. *Rome and the Making of a World State, 150 BCE–20 CE.* Cambridge University Press.

Östenberg, Ida. 2009. *Staging the World: Spoils, Captives, and Representations in the Roman Triumphal Procession*. Oxford University Press.

———. 2014. "Animals and Triumphs." In *The Oxford Handbook of Animals in Classical Thought and Life*, edited by Gordon Lindsay Campbell, 491–506. Oxford University Press.

Overtoom, Nikolaus Leo. 2016. "The Power-Transition Crisis of the 240s BCE and the Creation of the Parthian State." *International History Review* 38 (5): 984–1013.

———. 2019. "The Power-Transition Crisis of the 160s–130s BCE and the Formation of the Parthian Empire." *Journal of Ancient History* 7 (1): 111–55.

———. 2020. *Reign of Arrows: The Rise of the Parthian Empire in the Hellenistic Middle East*. Oxford University Press.

Padilla Peralta, Dan-el. 2020. "Epistemicide: The Roman Case." *Classica: Revista Brasileira de Estudos Clássicos* 33 (2): 151–86.

Palermo, Rocco. 2019. *On the Edge of Empires: North Mesopotamia during the Roman Period (2nd–4th c. CE)*. Routledge.

Pandey, Nandini B. 2018. *The Poetics of Power in Augustan Rome: Latin Poetic Responses to Early Imperial Iconography*. Cambridge University Press.

Parker, Victor. 2002. "Zur Chronologie des Šuppiluliumaš I." *Altorientalische Forschungen* 29 (2): 31–62.

Parkes, Peter. 2001. "Alternative Social Structures and Foster Relations in the Hindu Kush: Milk Kinship Allegiance in Former Mountain Kingdoms of Northern Pakistan." *Comparative Studies in Society and History* 43 (1): 4–36.

———. 2003. "Fostering Fealty: A Comparative Analysis of Tributary Allegiances of Adoptive Kinship." *Comparative Studies in Society and History* 45 (4): 741–82.

———. 2004a. "Fosterage, Kinship, and Legend: When Milk Was Thicker than Blood?" *Comparative Studies in Society and History* 46: 587–615.

———. 2004b. "Milk Kinship in Southeast Europe: Alternative Social Structures and Foster Relations in the Caucasus and the Balkans." *Social Anthropology* 12 (3): 341–58.

———. 2005. "Milk Kinship in Islam: Substance, Structure, History." *Social Anthropology* 13 (3): 307–29.

———. 2006. "Celtic Fosterage: Adoptive Kinship and Clientage in Northwest Europe." *Comparative Studies in Society and History* 48 (2): 359–95.

Parpola, Simo. 1997. *Assyrian Prophecies*. Helsinki University Press.

Patterson, Lee E. 2010a. *Kinship Myth in Ancient Greece*. University of Texas Press.

———. 2010b. "Strabo, Local Myth, and Kinship Diplomacy." *Hermes* 138 (1): 109–18.

———. 2017. "Minority Religions in the Sasanian Empire: Suppression, Integration, and Relations with Rome." In *Sasanian Persia: Between Rome and the Steppes of Eurasia*, edited by Eberhard W. Sauer, 181–98. Edinburgh University Press.

———. 2020. "Mithridates II's Invasion of Armenia." *Revue des Études Arméniennes* 39: 187–98.

Payne, Richard. 2013. "Cosmology and the Expansion of the Iranian Empire, 502–628 CE." *Past and Present* 220 (1): 3–33.

———. 2014. "The Reinvention of Iran: The Sasanian Empire and the Huns." In *The Cambridge Companion to the Age of Attila*, edited by Michael Maas, 282–99. Cambridge University Press.

———. 2015. *A State of Mixture: Christians, Zoroastrians, and Iranian Political Culture in Late Antiquity*. University of California Press.

———. 2016. "Sex, Death, and Aristocratic Empire: Iranian Jurisprudence in Late Antiquity." *Comparative Studies in Society and History* 58 (2): 519–49.

———. 2017. "Territorializing Iran in Late Antiquity: Autocracy, Aristocracy, and the Infrastructure of Empire." In *Ancient States and Infrastructural Power: Europe, Asia, and America*, edited by Clifford Ando and Seth Richardson, 179–217. University of Pennsylvania Press.

Pazdernik, Charles F. 2015. "The Quaestor Proclus." *Greek, Roman, and Byzantine Studies* 55: 221–49.

Peirce, Leslie P. 1993. *The Imperial Harem: Women and Sovereignty in the Ottoman Empire*. Oxford University Press.

Penrose, Walter Duvall. 2018. "Queens and Their Children: Dynastic Dis/Loyalty in the Hellenistic Period." In *Royal Women and Dynastic Loyalty*, edited by Caroline Dunn and Elizabeth Carney, 49–65. Palgrave Macmillan.

Perikhanian, Anahit. 1997. *The Book of a Thousand Judgements: A Sasanian Law-Book*. Mazda.

Perlmann, Moshe. 1987. *The History of Al-Ṭabarī*. Vol. 4, *The Ancient Kingdoms*. State University of New York Press.

Petrantoni, Giuseppe. 2021. *Corpus of Nabataean Aramaic-Greek Inscriptions*. Edizioni Ca' Foscari.

Petrosian, H. Matatʻeay V. 1879. *Nor Baṙagirkʻ Hay-Angliarēn [New Dictionary Armenian-English]*. S. Lazarus Armenian Academy.

Phiphia, Natia, and Ekaterine Kobakhidze. 2021. "To the Question of the Identifying King Amazasp of Iberia, Queen Dracontis and a Royal Official Anagranes Mentioned in Three Greek Inscriptions Found at Mtskheta." *МАИАСП* 13: 925–33.

Pianezzola, Emilio, ed. 1991. *Ovidio, L'arte di amare*. Fondazione Lorenzo Valla.

Pirngruber, Reinhard. 2011. "Eunuchen am Königshof: Ktesias und die altorientalishe Evidenz." In *Ktesias' Welt / Ctesias' World*, edited by Josef Wiesehöfer, Robert Rollinger, and Giovanni B. Lanfranchi, 279–312. Harrassowitz.

Pittenger, Miriam R. Pelikan. 2009. *Contested Triumphs: Politics, Pageantry, and Performance in Livy's Republican Rome*. University of California Press.

Podany, Amanda H. 2010. *Brotherhood of Kings: How International Relations Shaped the Ancient Near East*. Oxford University Press.

Pollini, John. 1978. "Studies in Augustan 'Historical' Reliefs." PhD diss., University of California, Berkeley.

———. 1987. *The Portraiture of Gaius and Lucius Caesar*. Fordham University Press.

———. 2012. *From Republic to Empire: Rhetoric, Religion, and Power in the Visual Culture of Ancient Rome*. University of Oklahoma Press.

Potter, D. S. 1999. "Political Theory in the *Senatus Consultum Pisonianum*." *American Journal of Philology* 120 (1): 65–88.

———. 2006. "The Transformation of the Empire: 235–337 CE." In *A Companion to the Roman Empire*, edited by D. S. Potter, 153–73. Blackwell.

———. 2012. "Tacitus' Sources." In *A Companion to Tacitus*, edited by Victoria Emma Pagán, 125–40. Wiley-Blackwell.

Potter, D. S., and Cynthia Damon. 1999. "The *Senatus Consultum de Cn. Pisone Patre.*" *American Journal of Philology* 120 (1): 13–42.

Potts, D. T. 1999. *The Archaeology of Elam: Formation and Transformation of an Ancient Iranian State.* Cambridge University Press.

———. 2014. "Iranian Nomads in the Achaemenid, Seleucid, and Arsacid Periods." In *Nomadism in Iran: From Antiquity to the Modern Era,* edited by D. T. Potts, 88–119. Oxford University Press.

———. 2023. *Aspects of Kinship in Ancient Iran.* University of California Press.

Pourshariati, Parvaneh. 2008. *Decline and Fall of the Sasanian Empire: The Sasanian-Parthian Confederacy and the Arab Conquest of Iran.* I. B. Tauris.

———. 2010. "The Parthians and the Production of the Canonical Shāhnāmas: Of Pahlavī, Pahlavānī and the Pahlav." In *Commutatio et Contentio: Studies in the Late Roman, Sasanian, and Early Islamic Near East,* edited by Josef Wiesehöfer and Henning Börm, 347–92. Wellem.

———. 2020. S.v. "Kārin." In *Encyclopedia Iranica,* https://iranicaonline.org/articles/karin (accessed August 19, 2024).

Powers, David. 2011. "Demonizing Zenobia: The Legend of al-Zabbā' In Islamic Sources." In *Histories of the Middle East: Studies in Middle Eastern Society, Economy, and Law in Honor of A. L. Udovitch,* edited by Roxani Eleni Margariti et al., 127–82. Brill.

Preston-Matto, Lahney. 2011. "Saints and Fosterage in Medieval Ireland: A Sanctified Social Practice." *Eolas: The Journal of the American Society of Irish Medieval Studies* 5: 62–78.

———. 2018. "Are You My Brother? Medieval Irish Ecclesiastical Fosterage." In *Church and Settlement in Ireland,* edited by James Lyttleton and Matthew Stout, 86–100. Four Courts Press.

Preud'homme, Nicolas. 2019. "Rois et royauté en Ibérie du Caucase. Entre monde romain et monde iranien. De l'époque hellénistique au début du Ve siècle de notre ère." PhD diss., Sorbonne Université.

Price, Jonathan J. 2005. "The Provincial Historian in Rome." In *Josephus and Jewish History in Flavian Rome and Beyond,* edited by Joseph Sievers and Gaia Lembi, 101–18. Brill.

Priuli, Stefano. 1977. "Appendice epigrafica." *Notizie degli Scavi di Antichità* 31: 326–41.

Qaukhchishvili, T. 1996. "Akhali berdznuli tsartserebi armazistsikhe-baginetidan (New Greek Inscriptions from Armazistsikhe-Bagineti)." *Mtskheta* 11: 81–92.

———. 2009. *Korpus der griechischen Inschriften in Georgien.* Edited by Levan Gordesiani. 3rd ed. Logos.

Radcliffe-Brown, A. R. 1952. *Structure and Function in Primitive Society: Essays and Addresses.* Free Press.

Radner, Joan Newlon. 1978. *Fragmentary Annals of Ireland.* Dublin Institute for Advanced Studies.

Radner, Karen. 2012. "After Eltekeh: Royal Hostages from Egypt at the Assyrian Court." In *Stories of Long Ago: Festschrift für Michael D. Roaf,* edited by H. D. Baker, K. Kaniuth, and A. Otto, 471–79. Ugarit.

———. 2013. "Royal Marriage Alliances and Noble Hostages." Assyrian Empire Builders, www.ucl.ac.uk/sargon/essentials/diplomats/royalmarriage (accessed August 19, 2024).

Rahbari, Ladan. 2020. "Milk Kinship and the Maternal Body in Shi'a Islam." *Open Theology* 6 (1): 43–53.

Rainey, Anson F. 2015. *The El-Amarna Correspondence: A New Edition of the Cuneiform Letters from the Site of El-Amarna Based on Collations of All Extant Tablets*. Edited by William Schniedewind and Zipora Cochavi-Rainey. Brill.

Ramelli, Ilaria L. E. 2006. "Possible Historical Traces in the *Doctrina Addai*." *Hugoye: Journal of Syriac Studies* 9 (1): 51–127.

Rangarajan, L. N. 1992. *Kautilya: The Arthashastra*. Penguin Books India.

Rapp, Stephen H. 2003. *Studies in Medieval Georgian Historiography: Early Texts and Eurasian Contexts*. Peeters.

———. 2009. "The Iranian Heritage of Georgia: Breathing New Life into the Pre-Bagratid Historiographical Tradition." *Iranica Antiqua* 44: 645–92.

Rawski, Evelyn S. 2012. "Sons of Heaven: The Qing Appropriation of the Chinese Model of Universal Empire." In *Universal Empire: A Comparative Approach to Imperial Culture and Representation in Eurasian History*, edited by Dariusz Kołodziejczyk and Peter Fibiger Bang, 233–49. Cambridge University Press.

Rawson, Beryl. 1986. "Children in the Roman *Familia*." In *The Family in Ancient Rome: New Perspectives*, edited by Beryl Rawson, 170–200. Cornell University Press.

———. 2003. *Children and Childhood in Roman Italy*. Oxford University Press.

Ray, Himanshu Prabha. 2021. "The Mauryan Empire." In *The Oxford World History of Empire*. Vol. 2: *The History of Empires*, edited by Peter Fibiger Bang, C. A. Bayly, and Walter Scheidel, 198–217. Oxford University Press.

Read, Lewis. 2023. "Fostering in Early Medieval Armenian Sources from the Fifth to the Seventh Century." *Journal of Late Antique, Islamic and Byzantine Studies*, 1–32. Edinburgh University Press Journals, https://doi.org/10.3366/jlaibs.2023.0026 (accessed August 19, 2024).

Rehak, Paul. 2006. *Imperium and Cosmos: Augustus and the Northern Campus Martius*. University of Wisconsin Press.

Remijsen, Sofie. 2015. *The End of Greek Athletics in Late Antiquity*. Cambridge University Press.

Retsö, Jan. 2003. *The Arabs in Antiquity: Their History from the Assyrians to the Umayyads*. Routledge.

Rezakhani, Khodadad. 2010. "Balkh and the Sasanians: The Economy and Society of Northern Afghanistan as Reflected in the Bactrian Economic Documents." In *Ancient and Middle Iranian Studies: Proceedings of the 6th European Conference of Iranian Studies, Held in Vienna, 18–22 September 2007*, edited by Maria Macuch, Dieter Weber, and Desmond Durkin-Meisterernst, 191–204. Harrassowitz.

———. 2013. "Arsacid, Elymaean, and Persid Coinage." In *The Oxford Handbook of Ancient Iran*, edited by D. T. Potts, 766–77. Oxford University Press.

———. 2017. *ReOrienting the Sasanians: East Iran in Late Antiquity*. Edinburgh University Press.

Ricci, Cecilia. 1996. "Principes et reges externi (e loro schiavi e liberti) a Roma e in Italia: Testimonianze epigrafiche di età imperiale." *Atti della Accademia Nazionale dei Lincei. Rendiconti: Classe di Scienze Morali*, series 9, 7 (3): 561–92.

Rich, J. W. 1998. "Augustus's Parthian Honours, the Temple of Mars Ultor, and the Arch in the Forum Romanum." *Papers of the British School at Rome* 66: 71–128.

Richardson, Seth. 2010. *Rebellions and Peripheries in the Cuneiform World*. American Oriental Society.

———. 2014. "The First 'World Event': Sennacherib at Jerusalem." In *Sennacherib at the Gates of Jerusalem: Story, History, and Historiography*, edited by Isaac Kalimi and Seth Richardson, 433–505. Brill.

———. 2016. "Getting Confident: The Assyrian Development of Elite Recognition Ethics." In *Cosmopolitanism and Empire: Universal Rulers, Local Elites, and Cultural Integration in the Ancient Near East and Mediterranean*, edited by Myles Lavan, Richard Payne, and John Weisweiler, 29–64. Oxford University Press.

Ristvet, Lauren. 2017. "'Assyria' in the Third Millennium BCE." In *A Companion to Assyria*, edited by Eckart Frahm, 36–56. Wiley Blackwell.

Roaf, Michael. 2017. "Kassite and Elamite Kings." In *Karduniaš: Babylonia under the Kassites*, edited by Alexa Bartelmus and Katja Sternitzke, vol. 1, 166–95. De Gruyter.

Röllig, Wolfgang. 1974. "Politische Heiraten im Alten Orient." *Saeculum* 25: 11–23.

Rollinger, Robert. 2023. "The Persian Empire and the Outside World." In *The Oxford History of the Ancient Near East*. Vol. 5, *The Age of Persia*, edited by Karen Radner, Nadine Moeller, and D. T. Potts, 887–948. Oxford University Press.

Romm, James. 1992. *The Edges of the Earth in Ancient Thought*. Princeton University Press.

Rose, Charles Brian. 1990. "'Princes' and Barbarians on the Ara Pacis." *American Journal of Archaeology* 94 (3): 453–67.

———. 2005. "The Parthians in Augustan Rome." *American Journal of Archaeology* 109 (1): 21–75.

Rose, Jenny. 2011. *Zoroastrianism: An Introduction*. I. B. Tauris.

Roselaar, Saskia T. 2014. "The Concept of *Conubium* in the Roman Republic." In *New Frontiers: Law and Society in the Roman World*, edited by Paul J. du Plessis, 102–22. Edinburgh University Press.

Ross, Steven K. 2001. *Roman Edessa: Politics and Culture on the Eastern Fringes of the Roman Empire, 114–242 C.E.* Routledge.

Rossini, Orietta. 2007. *Ara Pacis*. Electa.

Rostovtzeff, Michael I. 1936. "The Sarmatae and Parthians." In *The Cambridge Ancient History*, edited by S. A. Cook, F. E. Adcock, and M. P. Charlesworth, vol. 11, 91–130. Cambridge University Press.

Rostovtzeff, Michael I., and C. Bradford Welles. 1931. "A Parchment Contract of Loan from Dura-Europus on the Euphrates." *Yale Classical Studies* 2: 3–78.

Roy, Kaushik. 2014. "Hinduism." In *Religion, War, and Ethics: A Sourcebook of Textual Traditions*, edited by Gregory M Reichberg, 471–543. Cambridge University Press.

Rubin, Zeev. 2002. "*Res Gestae Divi Saporis*: Greek and Middle Iranian in a Document of Sasanian Anti-Roman Propaganda." In *Bilingualism in Ancient Society: Language Contact and the Written Text*, edited by J. N. Adams, Mark Janse, and Simon Swain, 267–97. Oxford University Press.

———. 2021. "Nobility, Monarchy, and Legitimation under the Later Sasanians." In *The Byzantine and Early Islamic Near East*. Vol. 4, *Elites Old and New*, edited by John Haldon and Lawrence I. Conrad, 235–74. Gerlach Press.

Rubio-Campillo, Xavier, et al. 2017. "Bayesian Analysis and Free Market Trade within the Roman Empire." *Antiquity* 91 (359): 1241–52.

Rung, Eduard. 2015. "Some Notes on Karanos in the Achaemenid Empire." *Iranica Antiqua* 50: 333–56.

Russell, J. R. 1986. "Some Iranian Images of Kingship in the Armenian Artaxiad Epic." *Revue des Études Arméniennes* 20: 253–70.

———. 2004. S.v. "Hymn of the Pearl." In *Encyclopedia Iranica*, www.iranicaonline.org /articles/hymn-of-the-pearl (accessed August 19, 2024).

Sachs, A. J., and H. Hunger. 1996. *Astronomical Diaries and Related Texts from Babylonia*. Vol. 3, *Diaries from 164 B.C. to 61 B.C.* Verlag der Österreichischen Akademie der Wissenschaften.

Sadeghi, Fatemeh. 2018. *The Sin of the Women: Interrelations of Religious Judgments in Zoroastrianism and Islam*. Klaus Schwarz.

Sahlins, Marshall. 2013. *What Kinship Is–and Is Not*. University of Chicago Press.

Sallaberger, W., and A. Westenholz. 1999. *Ur III-Zeit*. Universitätsverlag and Vandenhoeck and Ruprecht.

Sasson, Jack M. 1973. "Biographical Notices on Some Royal Ladies from Mari." *Journal of Cuneiform Studies* 25 (2): 59–78.

Savalli-Lestrade, Ivana. 1998. *Les* philoi *royaux dans L'Asie hellénistique*. Droz.

———. 2017. "ΒΙΟΣ ΑΥΛΙΚΟΣ: The Multiple Ways of Life of Courtiers in the Hellenistic Age." In *The Hellenistic Court: Monarchic Power and Elite Society from Alexander to Cleopatra*, edited by Andrew Erskine, Lloyd Llewellyn-Jones, and Shane Wallace, 101–20. Classical Press of Wales.

Schäfer, Thomas. 1998. *Spolia et signa: Baupolitik und Reichskultur nach dem Parthererfolg des Augustus*. Vandenhoeck & Ruprecht.

Scheidel, Walter. 1996. "Brother-Sister and Parent-Child Marriage Outside Royal Families in Ancient Egypt and Iran: A Challenge to the Sociobiological View of Incest Avoidance?" *Ethology and Sociobiology* 17 (5): 319–40.

———. 2009a. "A Peculiar Institution? Greco–Roman Monogamy in Global Context." *History of the Family* 14 (3): 280–91.

———. 2009b. "Sex and Empire: A Darwinian Perspective." In *The Dynamics of Ancient Empires: State Power from Assyria to Byzantium*, edited by Ian Morris and Walter Scheidel, 255–324. Oxford University Press.

———. 2011. "Monogamy and Polygyny." In *A Companion to Families in the Greek and Roman Worlds*, edited by Beryl Rawson, 108–15. Blackwell.

———, ed. 2015. *State Power in Ancient Rome and China*. Oxford University Press.

———. 2019. *Escape from Rome: The Failure of Empire and the Road to Prosperity*. Princeton University Press.

Schilling, Alexander. 2008. *Die Anbetung der Magier und die Taufe der Sāsāniden: Zur Geistesgeschichte des iranischen Christentums in der Spätantike*. Peeters.

Schine, Rachel. 2019. "Nourishing the Noble: Breastfeeding and Hero-Making in Medieval Arabic Popular Literature." *Al-ʿUsūr al-Wustā: Journal of Middle East Medievalists* 27: 165–200.

Schlude, Jason M. 2020. *Rome, Parthia, and the Politics of Peace: The Origins of War in the Ancient Middle East*. Routledge.

Schlude, Jason M., and Benjamin B. Rubin. 2017. "Finding Common Ground: Roman-Parthian Embassies in the Julio-Claudian Period." In *Arsacids, Romans, and Local Elites: Cross-Cultural Interactions of the Parthian Empire*, edited by Jason M. Schlude and Benjamin B. Rubin, 65–92. Oxbow.

Schmitt, Rüdiger. 1983. "Sūrēn, aber Kārin: Zu den Namen zweier Parthergeschlechter." *Münchner Studien zur Sprachwissenschaft* 42: 197–205.

———. 2005. S.v. "Personal Names, Iranian VI: Armenian Names of Iranian Origin." In *Encyclopedia Iranica*, https://iranicaonline.org/articles/personal-names-iranian-vi -armenian-names (accessed August 19, 2024).

———. 2016. *Iranisches Personennamenbuch*. Vol. 2.5, *Personennamen in Parthischen Epigraphischen Quellen*. Verlag der Österreichischen Akademie der Wissenschaften.

Schneider, David M. 1984. *A Critique of the Study of Kinship*. University of Michigan Press.

Schneider, Rolf Michael. 1986. *Bunte Barbaren: Orientalenstatuen aus farbigem Marmor in der römischen Repräsentationskunst*. Wernersche Verlagsgesellschaft.

———. 1998. "Die Faszination des Feindes: Bilder der Parther und des Orients in Rom." In *Das Partherreich und seine Zeugnisse/The Arsacid Empire: Sources and Documentation. Beiträge des internationalen Colloquiums, Eutin (27.-30. Juni 1996)*, edited by Josef Wiesehöfer, 95–146. Franz Steiner.

———. 2007. "Friend and Foe: The Orient in Rome." In *The Age of the Parthians*, edited by Vesta Sarkhosh Curtis and Sarah Stewart, 50–86. I. B. Tauris.

———. 2012. "The Making of Oriental Rome: Shaping the Trojan Legend." In *Universal Empire: A Comparative Approach to Imperial Culture and Representation in Eurasian History*, edited by Peter F. Bang and Dariusz Kołodziejczyk, 76–129. Cambridge University Press.

Schneider, Thomas. 2010. "Contributions to the Chronology of the New Kingdom and the Third Intermediate Period." *Ägypten und Levante/Egypt and the Levant* 20: 373–403.

Schottky, Martin. 1991. "Parther, Meder, und Hyrkanier: Eine Untersuchung der dynastischen und geographischen Verflechtungen im Iran des I. Jhs. n. Chr." *Archaeologische Mitteilungen aus Iran* 24: 61–134.

———. 2006. "Abdagaeses." In *Der Neue Pauly*, edited by Hubert Cancik, Helmuth Schneider, and Manfred Landfester. Brill.

———. 2010. "Armenische Arsakiden zur Zeit der Antonine: Ein Beitrag zur Korrektur der armenischen Königsliste." *Anabasis* 1: 208–24.

Schubert, Charlotte. 2010. *Anacharsis der Weise: Nomade, Skythe, Grieche*. Narr.

Schulman, Alan R. 1979. "Diplomatic Marriage in the Egyptian New Kingdom." *Journal of Near Eastern Studies* 38 (3): 177–93.

Schuol, Monika. 2000. *Die Charakene: Ein mesopotamisches Königreich in hellenistisch-parthischer Zeit*. Franz Steiner.

Schwartz, Martin. 1967. "Studies in the Texts of the Sogdian Christians." PhD diss., University of California, Berkeley.

Scopacasa, Rafael. 2019. "Old Habits Die Hard: Samnites, Rome, and the Perception of International Relations in Republican Italy, c. 350–200 BC." *Historia: Zeitschrift für Alte Geschichte* 68 (1): 50–75.

Scott, Lionel. 2005. *Historical Commentary on Herodotus Book 6*. Brill.

Seager, Robin. 2013. "Perceptions of the *Domus Augusta*, AD 4–24." In *The Julio-Claudian Succession: Reality and Perception of the "Augustan Model,"* edited by Alisdair Gibson, 41–57. Brill.

Sears, Matthew A. 2013. *Athens, Thrace, and the Shaping of Athenian Leadership*. Cambridge University Press.

Secunda, Shai. 2011. "The Talmudic *Bei Abedan* and the Sasanian Attempt to 'Recover' the Lost Avesta." *Jewish Studies Quarterly* 18: 343–66.

Segal, J. B. 1982. S.v. "Abgar." In *Encyclopedia Iranica*, www.iranicaonline.org/articles/abgar -dynasty-of-edessa-2nd-century-bc-to-3rd-century-ad (accessed August 19, 2024).

Seibert, Jakob. 1967. *Historische Beiträge zu den Dynastischen Verbindungen in Hellenistischer Zeit.* Franz Steiner.

Sellwood, David. 1980. *An Introduction to the Coinage of Parthia.* 2nd ed. Spink.

———. 1983. "Parthian Coins." In *The Cambridge History of Iran*, edited by E. Yarshater, vol. 3.2, 277–98. Cambridge University Press.

Senior, R. C. 2001. *Indo-Scythian Coins and History.* 2 vols. Classical Numismatic Group.

Settis, Salvatore. 1988. "Die Ara Pacis." In *Kaiser Augustus und die verlorene Republik: Eine Ausstellung im Martin-Gropius-Bau, Berlin 7. Juni–14. August 1988*, edited by Wolfgang D. Heilmeyer, Eugenio La Rocca, and Hans G. Martin, 400–26. Philipp von Zabern.

Severy, Beth. 2003. *Augustus and the Family at the Birth of the Roman Empire.* Routledge.

Shackleton Bailey, D. R. 1960. "The Roman Nobility in the Second Civil War." *Classical Quarterly* 10 (2): 253–67.

Shahbazi, A. Shahpur. 1990. S.v. "Byzantine-Iranian Relations." In *Encyclopedia Iranica*, www.iranicaonline.org/articles/byzantine-iranian-relations (accessed August 19, 2024).

———. 1993. "The Parthian Origins of the House of Rustam." *Bulletin of the Asia Institute* 7: 155–63.

———. 2004a. "Hormozd III." In *Encyclopedia Iranica*, www.iranicaonline.org/articles /hormozd-iii (accessed August 19, 2024).

———. 2004b. S.v. "Hunting in Iran." In *Encyclopedia Iranica*, www.iranicaonline.org /articles/hunting-in-iran (accessed August 19, 2024).

Shahîd, Irfan. 2012. S.v. "Tanūkh." In *Encyclopaedia of Islam*, edited by P. Bearman et al. 2nd ed. Brill.

Shayegan, M. Rahim. 2003a. S.v. "Hazārbed." In *Encyclopedia Iranica*, www.iranicaonline .org/articles/hazarbed (accessed August 19, 2024).

———. 2003b. "On Demetrius II Nicator's Arsacid Captivity and Second Rule." *Bulletin of the Asia Institute* 17: 83–103.

———. 2011. *Arsacids and Sasanians: Political Ideology in Post-Hellenistic and Late Antique Persia.* Cambridge University Press.

———. 2016. "Old Iranian Motifs in *Vīs o Rāmīn*." In *Essays in Islamic Philology, History, and Philosophy*, edited by Alireza Korangy et al., 29–50. De Gruyter.

———. 2017. "Persianism: Or Achaemenid Reminiscences in the Iranian and Iranicate World(s) of Antiquity." In *Persianism in Antiquity*, edited by Rolf Strootman and Miguel John Versluys, 401–55. Franz Steiner.

———. 2022. "The End of the Parthian Arsacid Empire." In *The End of Empires*, edited by Michael Gehler, Robert Rollinger, and Philipp Strobl, 213–47. Springer.

Sheikh, Hossein. 2023. *Studies of Bactrian Legal Documents.* Brill.

Shotter, David. 2004. *Tiberius Caesar.* 2nd ed. Routledge.

Sidebottom, Harry. 2007. "International Relations." In *The Cambridge History of Greek and Roman Warfare.* Vol. 2, *Rome from the Late Republic to the Late Empire*, edited by Philip Sabin, Hans van Wees, and Michael Whitby, 3–29. Cambridge University Press.

Silk, Jonathan A. 2008. "Putative Persian Perversities: Indian Buddhist Condemnations of Zoroastrian Close-Kin Marriage in Context." *Bulletin of the School of Oriental and African Studies, University of London* 71 (3): 433–64.

Silverstein, Adam J. 2018. *Veiling Esther, Unveiling Her Story: The Reception of a Biblical Book in Islamic Lands*. Oxford University Press.

Simon, Erika. 1991. "Altes und Neues zur Statue des Augustus von Primaporta." In *Saeculum Augustum III*, edited by G. Binder, 204–33. Wissenschaftliche Buchgesellschaft.

Sims-Williams, Nicholas. 1985. *The Christian Sogdian Manuscript C2*. Akademie.

———. 1992. *Sogdian and Other Iranian Inscriptions of the Upper Indus II*. School of Oriental and African Studies.

———. 2000. *Bactrian Documents from Northern Afghanistan*. Vol. 1, *Legal and Economic Documents*. Nour Foundation.

———. 2007. *Bactrian Documents from Northern Afghanistan*. Vol. 2, *Letters and Texts*. Nour Foundation.

———. 2008. "The Sasanians in the East: A Bactrian Archive from Northern Afghanistan." In *The Idea of Iran*. Vol. 3, *The Sasanian Era*, edited by Vesta Sarkhosh Curtis and Sarah Stewart, 88–102. I. B. Tauris.

———. 2020. "The Bactrian Documents as a Historical Source." In *The Limits of Empire in Ancient Afghanistan: Rule and Resistance in the Hindu Kush, circa 600 BCE–600 CE*, edited by Richard Payne and Rhyne King, 231–44. Harrassowitz.

Sinclair, Upton. 1994 [1935]. *I, Candidate for Governor: And How I Got Licked*. University of California Press.

Singer, Itamar. 2002. *Hittite Prayers*. Society of Biblical Literature.

Singh, Upinder. 2017. *Political Violence in Ancient India*. Harvard University Press.

———. 2021. "The State and Violence: Perspectives from Ancient India." In *Historians of Asia on Political Violence*, edited by Anne Cheng and Sanchit Kumar, 11–18. Collège de France.

Sinisi, Fabrizio A. 2012a. *Sylloge Nummorum Parthicorum*. Vol. 7, *Vologaeses I—Pacorus II*. Edited by Vesta Sarkhosh Curtis, Dāriyūsh Akbarzādah, and Michael Alram. Verlag der Österreichischen Akademie der Wissenschaften.

———. 2012b. "The Coinage of the Parthians." In *The Oxford Handbook of Greek and Roman Coinage*, edited by W. E. Metcalf, 275–94. Oxford University Press.

Skaff, Jonathan Karam. 2012. *Sui-Tang China and Its Turko-Mongol Neighbors: Culture, Power, and Connections, 580–800*. Oxford University Press.

Skjærvø, Prods O. 1983. *The Sassanian Inscription of Paikuli*. Part 3.1, Restored Text and Translation; Part 3.2, Commentary. Reichert.

———. 2013. S.v. "Marriage ii: Next-of-Kin Marriage in Zoroastrianism." In *Encyclopedia Iranica*, www.iranicaonline.org/articles/marriage-next-of-kin (accessed August 19, 2024).

Smith, Kyle. 2016. *Constantine and the Captive Christians of Persia: Martyrdom and Religious Identity in Late Antiquity*. University of California Press.

Smith, Llinos Beverley. 1992. "Fosterage, Adoption, and God-Parenthood: Ritual and Fictive Kinship in Medieval Wales." *Welsh History Review* 16 (1): 1–35.

Sonnabend, Holger. 1986. *Fremdenbild und Politik: Vorstellungen der Römer von Ägypten und dem Partherreich in der späten Republik und frühen Kaiserzeit*. Peter Lang.

Soraci, Rosario. 1974. *Ricerche sui conubia tra Romani e Germani nei secoli IV–VI.* 2nd ed. Muglia.

Southgate, Minoo S. 1985. "Conflict between Islamic Mores and the Courtly Romance of *Vīs and Rāmin.*" *Muslim World* 75 (1): 17–28.

Spawforth, Antony. 1994. "Symbol of Unity? The Persian-Wars Tradition in the Roman Empire." In *Greek Historiography*, edited by Simon Hornblower, 233–47. Clarendon.

Spier, Jeffrey, Timothy Potts, and Sara E. Cole, eds. 2022. *Persia: Ancient Iran and the Classical World.* J. Paul Getty Museum.

Stausberg, Michael, and Yuhan Sohrab-Dinshaw Vevaina, eds. 2015. *The Wiley Blackwell Companion to Zoroastrianism.* Wiley Blackwell.

Stavi, Boaz. 2015. *The Reign of Tudhaliya II and Šuppiluliuma I: The Contribution of the Hittite Documentation to a Reconstruction of the Amarna Age.* Winter.

Stawoska-Jundziłł, Bożena. 2002. "*Mamma, tata* i *papas* w łacińskich inskrypcjach chrześcijańskich z Rzymu III-VI wieku [*Mamma, tata* and *papas* in Christian Latin Inscriptions from Rome of III-VI Centuries]." *Vox Patrum* 42: 487–500.

Stevens, Anna. 2016. "Tell El-Amarna." *UCLA Encyclopedia of Egyptology* 1 (1). UCLA Near Eastern Languages and Cultures, https://escholarship.org/uc/item/1k66566f (accessed August 19, 2024).

Stoneman, Richard. 2012. "Persian Aspects of the Romance Tradition." In *The Alexander Romance in Persia and the East*, edited by Richard Stoneman, Kyle Erickson, and Ian Richard Netton, 3–18. Barkhuis.

Strathern, Marilyn. 1992. *After Nature: English Kinship in the Late Twentieth Century.* Cambridge University Press.

Strogatz, Steven. 2003. *Sync: How Order Emerges from Chaos in the Universe, Nature, and Daily Life.* Theia.

Stronach, David. 2019. "Cyrus, Anshan, and Assyria." In *Cyrus the Great: Life and Lore*, edited by M. Rahim Shayegan, 46–66. Harvard University Press.

Strootman, Rolf. 2014. *Courts and Elites in the Hellenistic Empires.* Edinburgh University Press.

———. 2021. "Women and Dynasty at the Hellenistic Imperial Courts." In *The Routledge Companion to Women and Monarchy in the Ancient Mediterranean World*, edited by Elizabeth Carney and Sabine Müller, 333–45. Routledge.

———. 2023. "How Iranian Was the Seleucid Empire?" In *Iran and the Transformation of Ancient Near Eastern History: The Seleucids (ca. 312–150 BCE): Proceedings of the Third Payravi Conference on Ancient Iranian History, UC Irvine, February 24th–25th, 2020*, edited by Touraj Daryaee, Robert Rollinger, and Matthew P. Canepa, 11–35. Harrassowitz.

Strothmann, Meret. 2012. "Feindeskinder an Sohnes statt: Parthische Königssöhne im Haus des Augustus." In *The Parthian Empire and Its Religions: Studies in the Dynamics of Religious Diversity = Das Partherreich und seine Religionen: Studien zu Dynamiken religiöser Pluralität*, edited by Peter Wick and Markus Philipp Zehnder, 83–102. Computus Druck Satz & Verlag.

Strugnell, Emma. 2008. "Thea Musa, Roman Queen of Parthia." *Iranica Antiqua* 43: 275–98.

Suerbaum, Werner. 1999. "Schwierigkeiten bei der Lektüre des SC de Cn. Pisone patre: Durch die Zeitgenossen um 20 n. Chr., durch Tacitus und durch heutige Leser." *Zeitschrift für Papyrologie und Epigraphik* 128: 213–34.

Sumi, Geoffrey S. 2005. *Ceremony and Power: Performing Politics in Rome between Republic and Empire*. University of Michigan Press.

Sundermann, Werner. 1973. *Mittelpersische und parthische kosmogonische und Parabeltexte der Manichäer*. Akademie.

———. 1981. *Mitteliranische manichäische Texte kirchengeschichtlichen Inhalts*. Akademie.

———. 1991. *Der Sermon von der Seele: Ein Literaturwerk des östlichen Manichäismus*. Westdeutscher.

———. 1992. *Der Sermon vom Licht-Nous: Eine Lehrschrift des östlichen Manichäismus; Edition der parthischen und soghdischen Version*. Akademie.

———. 1997. *Der Sermon von der Seele: Eine Lehrschrift des östlichen Manichäismus*. Brepols.

Sutherland, C. H. V., and R. A. G. Carson, eds. 1984. *The Roman Imperial Coinage*. Rev. ed. Spink.

Swan, Peter Michael. 2004. *The Augustan Succession: An Historical Commentary on Cassius Dio's Roman History, Books 55–56 (9 B.C.–A.D. 14)*. Oxford University Press.

Syme, Ronald. 1958. *Tacitus*. Clarendon.

———. 1978. *History in Ovid*. Clarendon.

———. 1984. *Roman Papers*. Edited by A. R. Birley. Vol. 3. Clarendon.

———. 1989. "Janus and Parthia in Horace." In *Studies in Latin Literature and Its Tradition: In Honour of C.O. Brink*, edited by James Diggle, John Barrie Hall, and H. D. Jocelyn, 113–24. Cambridge Philological Society.

Taasob, Razieh. 2022. "Economic Actors in the Arsakid Empire." In *Handbook of Ancient Afro-Eurasian Economies*. Vol. 2, *Local, Regional, and Imperial Economies*, edited by Sitta von Reden, 147–58. De Gruyter.

Talbert, Richard. 1999. "Tacitus and the *Senatus Consultum de Cn. Pisone Patre*." *American Journal of Philology* 120 (1): 89–97.

Tarn, W. W. 1997 [1922]. *The Greeks in Bactria and India*. 3rd ed. Ares.

Täubler, Eugen. 1904. "Die Parthernachrichten bei Josephus." PhD diss., Friedrich-Wilhelms-Universität zu Berlin.

Ter-Minasyan, E., ed. 1957. *Eghishē: Vasn Vardanay ew Hayotsʿ Paterazmin*. Haykakan SSṚ Gitutʿyunneri Akademiayi Hratarakchʿutʿyun.

Thapar, Romila. 2002. *The Penguin History of Early India: From the Origins to AD 1300*. Penguin.

Theis, Christoffer. 2011. "Der Brief der Königin Daḫamunzu an den hethitischen König Šuppiluliuma I. im Lichte von Reisegeschwindigkeiten und Zeitabläufen." In *Identities and Societies in the Ancient East-Mediterranean Regions: Comparative Approaches; Henning Graf Reventlow Memorial Volume*, edited by Thomas R. Kämmerer, 301–31. Ugarit.

Theophilos, Michael P. 2019. "ΒΑΣΙΛΕΥΣ ΒΑΣΙΛΕΩΝ (Rev 17.14; 19.16) in Light of the Numismatic Record." *New Testament Studies* 65 (4): 526–51.

Thijs, Simon. 2019. *Obsidibus imperatis: Formen der Geiselstellung und ihre Anwendung in der Römischen Republik*. Harrassowitz.

Thomson, Robert W. 1976. *Agathangelos: History of the Armenians*. State University of New York Press.

———. 1978. *Moses Khorenatsʿi: History of the Armenians*. Harvard University Press.

———. 1982. *Eḷishē: History of Vardan and the Armenian War*. Harvard University Press.

———. 1991. *The History of Łazar Pʿarpecʿi*. Scholars Press.

Thomson, Robert W., and James Howard-Johnston. 1999. *The Armenian History Attributed to Sebeos*. Liverpool University Press.

Thornbury, Emily V. 2014. *Becoming a Poet in Anglo-Saxon England*. Cambridge University Press.

Timpe, Dieter. 1962. "Die Bedeutung der Schlacht von Carrhae." *Museum Helveticum* 19: 104–29.

———. 1967. "Ein Heiratsplan Kaiser Caracallas." *Hermes* 95 (4): 470–95.

———. 1975. "Zur augusteischen Partherpolitik zwischen 30 und 20 v. Chr." *Würzburger Jahrbücher für die Altertumswissenschaft* 1: 155–69.

Todua, Magali A., and Alexander A. Gwakharia, eds. 1970. *Vīs va Rāmīn of Fakhr alDīn Gorgānī: Persian Critical Text Composed from the Persian and Georgian Oldest Manuscripts*. Entešārāte Bonyāde Farhange Īrān.

Toral-Niehoff, Isabel. 2013. "Late Antique Iran and the Arabs: The Case of al-Hira." *Journal of Persianate Studies* 6: 115–26.

———. 2014. *Al-Ḥīra: Eine arabische Kulturmetropole im spätantiken Kontext*. Brill.

Toumanoff, Cyril. 1963. *Studies in Christian Caucasian History*. Georgetown University Press.

———. 1986. S.v. "Arsacids vii: The Arsacid Dynasty of Armenia." In *Encyclopedia Iranica*, www.iranicaonline.org/articles/arsacids-vii (accessed August 19, 2024).

Townend, G. B. 1980. "Tacitus, Suetonius, and the Temple of Janus." *Hermes* 108 (2): 233–42.

Traina, Giusto. 2004. "Un *dayeak* armeno nell'Iberia precristiana." In *Bnagirkʿ Yišatakacʿ. Documenta Memoriae: Dall'Italia e dall'Armenia; Studi in onore di Gabriella Uluhogian*, edited by Valentina Calzolari, Anna Sirinian, and Boghos Levon Zekiyan, 255–62. University of Bologna.

———. 2007. "Moïse de Khorène et l'empire sassanide." *Res Orientales* 17: 157–79.

Tremblay, Xavier. 2007. "The Spread of Buddhism in Serindia: Buddhism among Iranians, Tocharians and Turks before the 13th Century." In *The Spread of Buddhism*, edited by Ann Heirman and Stephan Peter Bumbacher, 75–129. Brill.

Tuplin, Christopher. 2020. "Aršāma: Prince and Satrap." In *Aršāma and His World: The Bodleian Letters in Context*, edited by Christopher Tuplin and John Ma, vol. 3, 3–72. Oxford University Press.

Utz, David A. 2012. "Aršak, Parthian Buddhists, and 'Iranian' Buddhism." In *Buddhism across Boundaries: The Interplay of Indian, Chinese, and Central Asian Source Materials*, edited by John R. McRae and Jan Nattier, 179–91. Sino-Platonic Papers.

Uzzi, Jeannine D. 2005. *Children in the Visual Arts of Imperial Rome*. Cambridge University Press.

Van De Mieroop, Marc. 2005. *King Hammurabi of Babylon: A Biography*. Blackwell.

———. 2007. *The Eastern Mediterranean in the Age of Ramesses II*. Blackwell.

van den Hout, Michael Petrus Josephus, ed. 1988. *M. Cornelii Frontonis Epistulae*. Teubner.

———. 1999. *A Commentary on the Letters of M. Cornelius Fronto*. Brill.

van den Hout, Theo. 2021. *A History of Hittite Literacy: Writing and Reading in Late Bronze-Age Anatolia (1650–1200 BC)*. Cambridge University Press.

van der Steen, Jasper. 2022. "Dynastic Scenario Thinking in the Holy Roman Empire." *Past and Present* 256 (1): 87–128.

Van der Vin, J. P. A. 1981. "The Return of Roman Ensigns from Parthia." *Bulletin Antieke Beschaving* 56: 117–39.

van Dijk, Jan. 1986. "Die dynastischen Heiraten zwischen Kassiten und Elamern: Eine verhängnisvolle Politik." *Orientalia* 55 (2): 159–70.

van Kooten, George. 2015. "Matthew, the Parthians, and the Magi: A Contextualization of Matthew's Gospel in Roman-Parthian Relations of the First Centuries BCE and CE." In *The Star of Bethlehem and the Magi: Interdisciplinary Perspectives from Experts on the Ancient Near East, the Greco-Roman World, and Modern Astronomy*, edited by George van Kooten and Peter Barthel, 496–646. Brill.

Van't Dack, E. 1989. "Apollodôros et Helenos: Deux ΤΡΟΦΕΙΣ de Ptolémée X Alexandre I." *Sacris Erudiri* 31: 429–41.

Vermeule, Cornelius C. 1968. *Roman Imperial Art in Greece and Asia Minor*. Belknap Press of Harvard University Press.

Versnel, H. S. 1970. *Triumphus: An Inquiry into the Origin, Development, and Meaning of the Roman Triumph*. Brill.

Vervaet, Frederik Juliaan. 2002. "Domitius Corbulo and the Senatorial Opposition to the Reign of Nero." *Ancient Society* 32: 135–93.

Vevaina, Yuhan Sohrab-Dinshaw. 2018. "A Father, a Daughter and a Son-in-Law in Zoroastrian Hermeneutics." In *The Bahari Lecture Series at the Oxford University: Sasanian Iran in the Context of Late Antiquity*, edited by Touraj Daryaee, 119–45. Jordan Center for Persian Studies.

Vinogradov, Jurij G. 1992. "The Goddess *Ge Meter Olybris:* A New Epigraphic Evidence from Armenia." *East and West* 42 (1): 13–26.

Vlassopoulos, Kostas. 2011. "Greek Slavery: From Domination to Property and Back Again." *Journal of Hellenic Studies* 131: 115–30.

Vogt, Joseph. 1969. "Zu Pausanias und Caracalla." *Historia: Zeitschrift für Alte Geschichte* 18 (3): 299–308.

Waerzeggers, Caroline. 2021. "Babylonian Entrepreneurs." In *A Companion to the Achaemenid Persian Empire*, edited by Bruno Jacobs and Robert Rollinger, 993–1004. Wiley Blackwell.

Walbank, F. W. 1979. *A Historical Commentary on Polybius*. Vol. 3, *Commentary on Books XIX–XL*. Oxford University Press.

Walker, Cheryl. 1980. "Hostages in Republican Rome." PhD diss., University of North Carolina.

Wallace-Hadrill, Andrew. 2014. "Family and Inheritance in the Augustan Marriage Laws." In *Augustus*, edited by Jonathan Edmondson, 250–74. Edinburgh University Press.

Walser, Gerold. 1951. *Rom, das Reich und die fremden Völker in der Geschichtsschreibung der frühen Kaiserzeit: Studien zur Glaubwürdigkeit des Tacitus*. Verlag für Kunst und Wissenschaft.

Waltz, Kenneth N. 1979. *Theory of International Politics*. McGraw-Hill.

Wang, Ziting. 2023. "Intercultural Communication and Miscommunication: Egyptian Diplomacy in the New Kingdom Period." PhD diss., University of Chicago.

Wardle, David. 1994. *Suetonius' Life of Caligula: A Commentary*. Latomus.

———. 2007. "Caligula's Bridge of Boats—AD 39 or 40?" *Historia: Zeitschrift für Alte Geschichte* 56 (1): 118–20.

———. 2014. *Suetonius: Life of Augustus.* Oxford University Press.

Wardrop, Oliver. 1914. *Visramiani: The Story of the Loves of Vis and Ramin; A Romance of Ancient Persia Translated from the Georgian Version.* Royal Asiatic Society.

Waters, Matt. 2000. *A Survey of Neo-Elamite History.* Neo-Assyrian Text Corpus Project.

———. 2011. "Parsumaš, Anšan, and Cyrus." In *Elam and Persia*, edited by Javier Álvarez-Mon and Mark B. Garrison, 285–96. Eisenbrauns.

———. 2014. *Ancient Persia: A Concise History of the Achaemenid Empire, 550–330 BCE.* Cambridge University Press.

Watson, Burton. 1964. *Han Fei Tzu: Basic Writings.* Columbia University Press.

Weber, Ursula. 2012. "Narseh, König der Könige von Ērān und Anērān." *Iranica Antiqua* 47: 153–302.

Weber, Ursula, and Josef Wiesehöfer. 2010. "König Narsehs Herrschaftsverständnis." In *Commutatio et Contentio: Studies in the Late Roman, Sasanian, and Early Islamic Near East in Memory of Zeev Rubin*, edited by Henning Börm and Josef Wiesehöfer, 89–132. Wellem.

Weinstock, Stefan. 1960. "Pax and the 'Ara Pacis.'" *Journal of Roman Studies* 50: 44–58.

Weismantel, Mary. 1995. "Making Kin: Kinship Theory and Zumbagua Adoptions." *American Ethnologist* 22 (4): 685–704.

Wendt, Alexander. 1992. "Anarchy Is What States Make of It: The Social Construction of Power Politics." *International Organization* 46 (2): 391–425.

Westbrook, Raymond. 2000. "Babylonian Diplomacy in the Amarna Letters." *Journal of the American Oriental Society* 120 (3): 377–82.

———. 2003. Introduction to *A History of Ancient Near Eastern Law*, edited by Raymond Westbrook, 1–90. Brill.

Westlake, H. D. 1977. "Thucydides on Pausanias and Themistocles—A Written Source?" *Classical Quarterly* 27 (1): 95–110.

Wheeler, Everett L. 1993. "Methodological Limits and the Mirage of Roman Strategy: Part I." *Journal of Military History* 57 (1): 7–41.

———. 2002. "Roman Treaties with Parthia: Völkerrecht or Power Politics?" In *Limes XVIII: Proceedings of the XVIIIth International Congress of Roman Frontier Studies, Held in Amman, Jordan (September 2000)*, edited by Philip Freeman et al., vol. 1, 287–92. Archaeopress.

———. 2007. Review of *Hostages and Hostage-Taking in the Roman Empire*, by Joel Allen. *Bryn Mawr Classical Review*, https://bmcr.brynmawr.edu/2007/2007.02.04 (accessed August 19, 2024).

———. 2016. "Parthian *Auxilia* in the Roman Army, Part I: From the Late Republic to c. 70 A.D." In *Les auxiliaires de l'armée romaine: Des alliés aux fédérés: Actes du sixième congrès de Lyon (23–25 Octobre 2014)*, edited by Catherine Wolff and Patrice Faure, 171–222. De Boccard.

Whitby, Michael. 2000. *The Ecclesiastical History of Evagrius Scholasticus.* Liverpool University Press.

Whitby, Michael, and Mary Whitby. 1989. *Chronicon Paschale, 284–628 AD.* Liverpool University Press.

White, Richard. 2011 [1991]. *The Middle Ground: Indians, Empires, and Republics in the Great Lakes Region, 1650–1815.* Twentieth Anniversary ed. Cambridge University Press.

Widengren, Geo. 1969. *Der Feudalismus im alten Iran: Männerbund, Gefolgswesen, Feudal-ismus in der iranischen Gesellschaft im Hinblick auf die indogermanischen Verhältnisse.* Westdeutscher.

———. 1976. "Iran, der grosse Gegner Roms." *Aufstieg und Niedergang der römischen Welt* part 2, vol. 9.1: 219–306.

Wiesehöfer, Josef. 1993. *Das antike Persien: von 550 v. Chr. bis 650 n. Chr.* Artemis & Winkler.

———. 2005. *Iraniens, Grecs et Romains.* Association pour l'Avancement des Etudes Iraniennes.

———. 2010. "Augustus und die Parther." In *Imperium–Varus und seine Zeit: Beiträge zum internationalen Kolloquium des LWL-Römermuseums am 28. und 29. April 2008 in Mün-ster,* edited by Rudolf Aßkamp and Tobias Esch, 187–95. Aschendorff.

———. 2015. "Greek Poleis in the Near East and Their Parthian Overlords." In *Urban Dreams and Realities in Antiquity,* edited by Adam Kemezis, 328–46. Brill.

———. 2020. "Evidence for Arsakid Economic History." In *Handbook of Ancient Afro-Eurasian Economies.* Vol. 1, *Contexts,* edited by Sitta von Reden, 477–96. De Gruyter.

Wiesehöfer, Josef, and Sabine Müller, eds. 2017. *Parthika: Greek and Roman Authors' Views of the Arsacid Empire.* Harrassowitz.

Wilhite, David E. 2007. *Tertullian the African: An Anthropological Reading of Tertullian's Context and Identities.* De Gruyter.

Williams, A. V. 1990. *The Pahlavi Rivāyat Accompanying the Dādestān ī Dēnig: Part 1, Trans-literation, Transcription and Glossary.* Royal Danish Academy of Sciences and Letters.

Williams, Gordon. 1978. *Change and Decline: Roman Literature in the Early Empire.* Univer-sity of California Press.

Wills, Jeffrey. 1996. *Repetition in Latin Poetry: Figures of Allusion.* Clarendon.

Wilson, John A. 1956. *The Culture of Ancient Egypt.* University of Chicago Press.

Winterling, Aloys. 2009. *Politics and Society in Imperial Rome.* Translated by Katrin Lüd-decke. Wiley-Blackwell.

———. 2011. *Caligula: A Biography.* Translated by Paul Psoinos. University of California Press.

Wiseman, Timothy Peter. 1971. *New Men in the Roman Senate 139 B.C.—14 A.D.* Oxford University Press.

Wolff, Fritz. 1933. *Glossar zu Firdosis Schahname.* Notgemeinschaft der Deutschen Wissenschaft.

Wolski, Józef. 1954. "Pausanias et le problème de la politique spartiate." *Eos* 47: 75–94.

———. 1989. "Die gesellschaftliche und politische Stellung der großen parthischen Familien." *Tyche* 4: 221–27.

———. 1993. *L'Empire des Arsacides.* In Aedibus Peeters.

Woodman, A. J., ed. 1977. *Velleius Paterculus: The Tiberian Narrative (2.94–131).* Cambridge University Press.

———. 1988. *Rhetoric in Classical Historiography: Four Studies.* Routledge.

———. 2009. Introduction to *The Cambridge Companion to Tacitus,* edited by A. J. Woodman, 1–14. Cambridge University Press.

———, with C.S. Kraus, eds. 2014. *Tacitus: Agricola.* Cambridge University Press.

———, ed. 2017. *The Annals of Tacitus: Books 5 and 6.* Cambridge University Press.

Worthington, Ian. 2008. *Philip II of Macedonia.* Yale University Press.

Wroth, Warwick William. 1903. *Catalogue of the Coins of Parthia.* British Museum.

Yakubovich, Ilya. 2006. "Marriage Sogdian Style." In *Iranistik in Europa: Gestern, Heute, Morgen*, edited by Heiner Eichner et al., 307–44. Verlag der Österreichischen Akademie der Wissenschaften.

Yang, Lien-sheng. 1952. "Hostages in Chinese History." *Harvard Journal of Asiatic Studies* 15 (3–4): 507–21.

Yardley, John, and Waldemar Heckel. 1997. *Epitome of the Philippic History of Pompeius Trogus*. Clarendon.

Yarshater, E. 1983. "Iranian National History." In *The Cambridge History of Iran*, edited by E. Yarshater, vol. 3.1, 359–478. Cambridge University Press.

Yon, Jean-Baptiste. 2013. "Hatra and Palmyra: The Monumentalization of Public Space." In *Hatra: Politics, Culture, and Religion between Parthia and Rome*, edited by Lucinda Dirven, 161–70. Franz Steiner.

Yoshida, Yutaka. 2022. "Three Scenarios for the Historical Background of the Xi'an Sino-Pahlavi Inscription." In *The History and Culture of Iran and Central Asia: From the Pre-Islamic to the Islamic Period*, edited by D. G. Tor and Minoru Inaba, 73–92. University of Notre Dame Press.

Young, T. C. 1988. "The Early History of the Medes and the Persians and the Achaemenid Empire to the Death of Cambyses." In *Cambridge Ancient History*, edited by John Boardman et al., vol. 4, 1–52. Cambridge University Press.

Zacchetti, Stefano. 2019. S.v. "An Shigao." In *Brill's Encyclopedia of Buddhism Online*, edited by Jonathan Silk, Richard Bowring, and Vincent Eltschinger. Brill, https://referenceworks.brill.com/display/entries/ENBO/COM-2088.xml?rskey=LFi7uG&result=1 (accessed August 19, 2024).

Zakeri, Mohsen. 2022. "Translations from Greek into Middle Persian as Repatriated Knowledge." In *Why Translate Science? Documents from Antiquity to the 16th Century in the Historical West (Bactria to the Atlantic)*, edited by Dimitri Gutas, 52–169. Brill.

Zanker, Paul. 1988. *The Power of Images in the Age of Augustus*. Translated by Alan Shapiro. University of Michigan Press.

Zawadski, Stefan. 1995. "Hostages in Assyrian Royal Inscriptions." In *Immigration and Emigration within the Ancient Near East: Festschrift E. Lipinski*, edited by K. Van Lerberghe and A. Schoors, 449–58. Uitgeverij Peeters.

Zehnder, Markus. 2010. "Aramäische Texte." In *Quellen zur Geschichte des Partherreiches: Textsammlung mit Übersetzungen und Kommentaren*, edited by Ursula Hackl, Bruno Jacobs, and Dieter Weber, vol. 3, 175–401. Vandenhoeck & Ruprecht.

Zeini, Arash. 2018. "The King in the Mirror of the Zand: Secrecy in Sasanian Iran." In *Sasanian Iran in the Context of Late Antiquity*, edited by Touraj Daryaee, 149–62. Jordan Center for Persian Studies.

Zelnick-Abramovitz, Rachel. 2018. "Greek and Roman Terminologies of Slavery." In *The Oxford Handbook of Greek and Roman Slaveries*, edited by Stephen Hodkinson, Marc Kleijwegt, and Kostas Vlassopoulos. Oxford University Press. Oxford Academic, https://doi.org/10.1093/oxfordhb/9780199575251.001.0001 (accessed August 19, 2024).

Ziegler, Karl-Heinz. 1964. *Die Beziehungen zwischen Rom und dem Partherreich: Ein Beitrag zur Geschichte des Völkerrechts*. Franz Steiner.

Zimmermann, Martin. 1999. *Kaiser und Ereignis: Studien zum Geschichtswerk Herodians*. Beck.

www.ingramcontent.com/pod-product-compliance
Ingram Content Group UK Ltd.
Pitfield, Milton Keynes, MK11 3LW, UK
UKHW050746260525
458907UK00004BA/104